PROJECT APPRAISAL AND VALUATION
OF THE ENVIRONMENT

Also by Peter Abelson

COST-BENEFIT ANALYSIS AND ENVIRONMENTAL PROBLEMS

PRIVATISATION: An Australian Perspective (*editor*)

THE ECONOMIC EVALUATION OF ROADS IN AUSTRALIA

Project Appraisal and Valuation of the Environment

General Principles and Six Case-Studies in Developing Countries

Peter Abelson
Associate Professor of Economics
Macquarie University
Sydney, Australia

First published in Great Britain 1996 by
MACMILLAN PRESS LTD
Houndmills, Basingstoke, Hampshire RG21 6XS
and London
Companies and representatives
throughout the world

A catalogue record for this book is available
from the British Library.

ISBN 0–333–63916–2

First published in the United States of America 1996 by
ST. MARTIN'S PRESS, INC.,
Scholarly and Reference Division,
175 Fifth Avenue,
New York, N.Y. 10010

ISBN 0–312–12984–X

Library of Congress Cataloging-in-Publication Data
Abelson, P. W.
Project appraisal and valuation of the environment : general principles and six case-studies in developing countries / Peter Abelson.
p. cm.
Includes bibliographical references and index.
ISBN 0–312–12984–X (cloth)
1. Economic development projects—Developing countries–
–Evaluation. 2. Economic development projects—Developing countries—Cost effectiveness. 3. Economic development projects–
–Environmental aspects—Developing countries. I. Title.
HC59.72.E44.A24 1996
333.7'09172'4—dc20 95–42137
CIP

---

10 9 8 7 6 5 4 3
05 04 03 02 01 00 99 98

Printed and bound in Great Britain by
Antony Rowe Ltd, Chippenham, Wiltshi

To Jeanne, David, Julian and Antonia

Contents

List of Tables

List of Figures

Preface

In 1992 the Overseas Development Institute (London) commissioned the writer to prepare a guide to valuing environmental costs and benefits based on six international case-studies. The case-studies were chosen to reflect a representative set of environmental issues and a range of developing countries. The case-studies and the funding for the study were provided by the Overseas Development Administration (UK). This book is the result.

The main purpose of the book is to present a number of in-depth studies that illustrate the application of economic concepts and techniques to environmental problems. It is hoped that this will clarify the ways in which economic analysis can be applied to environmental issues and show the relevance of economic analysis to policy making.

The book consists of two main parts. The first deals with the general issues of project appraisal and valuation methods for the environment. The second part describes the six case-studies and draws conclusions. Nearly all the general discussion in the first part applies to developed as well as to developing countries. Likewise most of the conclusions have general application.

The approach in the book is to treat environmental issues within a consistent and unified cost–benefit framework rather than as a separate set of issues. It examines how people value environmental services compared with other goods and services and how this should affect policy making. Within this framework, both market and non-market methods of valuing the environment are discussed.

It is intended that the book should be of use to all those interested (as policy makers, professionals, academics or students) in the application of economic analysis to the use and improvement of the environment. I have tried to present the economic analysis with a rigour acceptable to professional economists and in language accessible to students and non-economists.

It has been a privilege and a pleasure to be entrusted the task of producing this book by the Overseas Development Institute. I hope that I have repaid this trust with a volume that is interesting and useful to the reader.

Macquarie University, Sydney, and
Overseas Development Institute, London

PETER ABELSON

Acknowledgements

Many people have contributed in one or other way to the production of this book. First and foremost I acknowledge the roles of the Overseas Development Administration (ODA) and the Overseas Development Institute (ODI). The ODA both funded the work and organised the six case-studies in the book. The organisation was no small task as anyone familiar with the logistics of international work will appreciate. Special thanks are due to the key administrators of the project, Dr Nick Highton and Peter Landymore (who also commented on several chapters), and the head of the Evaluation Department, John Morris, for organising and facilitating the project.

Professor John Howell, director of the ODI, developed the project as a successor to the work by Jim Winpenny (of the ODI), which was published in 1991 under the title *Values for the Environment*. My thanks are due especially to Jim Winpenny for his assistance in developing the case-studies for this book and for commenting on most of the draft chapters. The ODI provided excellent library and office support. Clare Johnson and the ODI staff were most helpful throughout the project and it was always a pleasure to return to the ODI, if not to British Rail, after a period of overseas research.

Turning to the case-studies, for the study of water quality in Wuxi, China, I received considerable help from the Wuxi Science and Technology Commission, other members of the Wuxi municipal authorities, and Watson Hawksley Engineering Consultants. Special thanks are due to Sun Xiaobing, who arranged many meetings for me in Wuxi and interpreted for me, and to David Angus of Watson Hawksley, who organised my trip to Wuxi and commented on an early draft of the chapter. I am also grateful to Peter Faircloth for several discussions about valuation issues in water quality in Wuxi.

I owe much of my knowledge of the electricity sector in Bangladesh to discussions with other members of the ODA Evaluation Mission of which I was a member, namely Andrew Barnett, David Watson, John Woodhouse, John Tyson and Simon Henderson, as well as to discussions with officers of the Bangladesh Power Development Board and the Dhaka Electricity Supply Authority. The chapter also benefited from comments on an earlier draft by Andrew Barnett.

I am particularly grateful to David Crapper (ODA) for organising my field trip to Visakhapatnam, India, for briefing me on the slum improvement programme in Visakhapatnam, and for commenting in detail on a draft paper on this programme. In preparing this chapter I was also assisted greatly by Mr Patrudu and Mr Kumar from the Visakhapatnam Urban Community Development Program and Michael Slingsby (ODA).

The case-study on mass transit in Lagos would not have been possible without invaluable assistance from Peter Speight, who guided me around Lagos and introduced me to computer chess. I am also most grateful to Dar al-Handassah Consultants for their professional cooperation and hospitality in Lagos and London. The chapter has benefited from comments on an earlier draft by two reviewers from the journal *Transport Reviews*, which is publishing a slightly shorter version of the chapter. I am grateful to Taylor and Francis, publishers of *Transport Reviews*, for agreeing to the publication of this chapter.

Much of the work reported in the case-study on Kenyan forests was developed initially by Lucy Emerton (economist with Kenya Indigenous Forestry Conservation project) and refined by Michael Flint (economist with the ODA Kenyan forestry review missions). This chapter has also benefited from in-house ODA comments.

The case-study on soil conservation in Bolivia was developed and written jointly with Penny Davies, who worked for several years with the British Tropical Agricultural Mission (BTAM) in Santa Cruz. This chapter draws heavily on Penny's accumulated research and experience of local conditions. I am most grateful to John Wilkins (then director of BTAM) for organising my visit to Santa Cruz. Both Penny and I are grateful to Jim Johnston and Graham Thiele for comments on an early draft of the chapter.

Needless to say, this project was made possible by the generous leave granted to me by Macquarie University. When I returned to Macquarie, I received skilled and unstinted support from Jane Oldroyd in manuscript preparation.

Last, but certainly not least, I am most grateful to my family, Jeanne, David, Julian and Antonia, who put up with my frequent absences overseas and arrived at Heathrow and Gatwick airports at forsaken hours in the early morning and London mist to greet me on my return.

It should be stressed that, notwithstanding these many and varied contributions to the production of the book, the work published below is entirely my responsibility. In particular, the discussions of the case-studies represent my views and not necessarily those of the ODA or ODI. The case-studies are employed to illustrate technical approaches to valuation questions and not to evaluate the overall merits or otherwise of the projects discussed.

PETER ABELSON

1 Environmental Issues: An Overview

> Overall, global environmental trends are not reassuring. The health of the planet has deteriorated dangerously during the 20 years since Stockholm [the UN meeting on Environment and Development in Stockholm in 1972]..... Muddling through will not work. Either we turn things around quickly or the self-reinforcing internal dynamic of the deterioration-and-decline scenario will take over. The policy decisions we make in the years immediately ahead will determine whether our children live in a world of development or decline. There is no precedent for the change in prospect. Building an environmentally sustainable future depends on restructuring the global economy, major shifts in human reproductive behaviour, and dramatic changes in values and lifestyles. Doing all this quickly adds up to a revolution, one defined by the need to restore and preserve the earth's environment. If this Environmental Revolution succeeds, it will rank with the Agricultural and Industrial Revolutions as one of the great economic and social transformations in human history (Brown, 1992, p. 174).

1.1 INTRODUCTION

There is widespread concern that the voracious demands of modern society exceed the carrying capacity of the environment, that resources are being exhausted, and that pollution and congestion pose grave threats to our health and well-being. It is feared that, if the carrying capacity of the environment is exceeded, widespread ecological breakdown could occur with disastrous consequences for mankind. As Tietenberg (1992, p. 2) notes: 'The focus is no longer on individual societies but on the survival of the planet'.

On the other hand, hundreds of millions of people on our planet live in conditions of unacceptable poverty. These poor communities naturally aspire to substantial improvements in their income and consumption. At the same time people in developed countries also seek ever more material goods.

The economic activity required to alleviate poverty almost always involves rearranging the environment in some way. To achieve significant gains in living standards, substantial rearrangements may be needed.

Communities must decide what energy sources to exploit and how to do so, what land to develop and how, what transport and communications systems to develop, what resources to allocate to cleaning up pollution, and must regularly make a myriad of other decisions about the use and protection of the environment.

Addressing environmental problems requires that the value of the environment be factored into these decisions. As the World Bank (1992, pp. 34–5) noted:

> Values that are difficult to measure are often implicit in decision making, but the tradeoffs are not well thought through. There is a clear need to make such costs and benefits as explicit as possible so as to better inform policy makers and citizens. This does not imply that it is possible or even desirable to put monetary values on all types of environmental resources. But it is desirable to know how much environmental quality is being given up in the name of development, and how much development is being given up in the name of environmental protection.

This book takes up these issues. It discusses the general principles that should govern decisions about development and the environment and illustrates these principles with six case-studies. Although all the case-studies are placed in developing countries, the principles of project appraisal and environmental valuation apply generally in developed as well as in developing countries.

But first, to set the scene, we look in this chapter at the nature and scale of environmental issues and introduce the main valuation issues. The chapter draws heavily on the surveys of environmental conditions by the OECD (1991) and the World Bank (1992) and to a lesser extent on the annual *State of the World* series published by the Worldwatch Institute.

1.2 MAIN ENVIRONMENTAL ISSUES

Environmental Uses and Impacts

The natural environment has three main uses to mankind. It provides essential life-support services (air, water and basic food supplies), the energy and raw materials that make possible our living standards, and natural amenities that are so important to our quality of life. This quality of life depends not only on the recreational opportunities provided by the environment, but also on the aesthetic pleasures and spiritual feelings that many people experience in a natural environment. In addition, many people hold strongly that the natural environment has an inherent (or existence) value that is independent of its particular uses to man and that we have a special responsibility to preserve the environment both for its own sake and for the benefit of other species.

Conversely, when the environment is exploited non-sustainably or degraded, there is a loss of one or more of these environmental services (health, productivity or amenity). And when a rare species or feature of the environment disappears, there is not only a loss to man, but also an irreversible loss of existence value.

However, it is not always possible or desirable to distinguish between the natural and the man-made environment. Although popular concern has focused on damage to the natural environment, it is often in the social environment, in industry and in urban areas especially, that people work and live in the most degraded and dangerous conditions. The Three Gorges hydroelectric project on the Yangtze River in China will result in the displacement and resettlement of over one million people. Accordingly this book adopts the World Bank's broad definition of the environment as 'the natural and social conditions surrounding all mankind, and including future generations' (World Bank, 1992, p. 2).

The Context: Population Growth

Population growth is a critical issue. Population growth increases the pressure on depletable and renewable resources, reduces the amount of capital per worker and productivity per worker, increases the inequality of income, and directly increases crowding and congestion (US National Research Council, 1986; Lindert, 1978).

The Earth's population has increased at unprecedented rates over the last two decades from 3.8 billion in 1970 to 5.5 billion in 1993. Three quarters of the population now live in developing countries and the proportion is rising. Currently the global population is increasing annually by 95 million. Even allowing for significant recent declines in fertility rates, the World Bank (1992) forecast that global population will nearly double to 10.5 billion by the year 2050 and increase to 12.5 billion by 2150, when it may stabilise. At present more people live in rural than in urban areas. The Bank also forecast that urban populations will be twice the size of rural populations by 2030.

Thus population growth alone will double the demand for goods and services in about 60 years. When rising incomes are allowed for, the demand for food is expected to increase threefold and the demand for energy, water and manufactured goods by four to sixfold. Pressures on natural resources and habitats and on space in cities will be intense. Also, the increase in wastes will tax the assimilative capacity of the planet.

Water Pollution and Scarcity

The World Bank (1992) argues that water pollution and scarcity are the most severe environmental problems confronting mankind. According to the Bank, one billion people in developing countries lack access to clean water and 1.7 billion lack access to sanitation. Unsafe water contributes to an estimated 900 million cases of diarrhoeal diseases annually, causing the death of five million children. At any time an estimated 500 million people suffer from trachoma, 200 million from schistosomiasis or bilharzia and 900 million from hookworm. Cholera, typhoid and paratyphoid remain major diseases. Substantially to reduce water-related mortality and diseases will require billions of dollars of capital investment in sanitation services and the collection and treatment of waste water.

In many parts of the world, including much of the Middle East and Africa and parts of India, China and Australia, the demand for water resources greatly exceeds the supply. In these areas some aquifers are being depleted and the scope for expansion of irrigation and hydroelectric schemes is limited. In some major cities, such as Bangkok, Mexico City, Jakarta and Venice, excessive pumping of groundwater has led to subsidence, structural damage and flooding. In some rural areas people take over two hours each day to fetch water.

In OECD countries contamination of drinking water supplies has been nearly eliminated and the management of wastewater has greatly improved (OECD, 1991). Nevertheless 330 million people, mainly in southern Europe and Japan, are not connected to sewer systems. Groundwaters have been contaminated by fertilisers, pesticides and seepages from industrial sites; waterways have been polluted by nitrates; and lakes suffer from eutrophication. Deteriorating infrastructures are increasing the risks of water pollution and the costs of avoiding it.

Air Pollution

The impact on health of air pollution in cities is also a major problem. The World Bank (1992) reports that over one billion people live in urban areas, mainly but not only in developing countries that do not meet WHO standards for suspended particulate matter and risk serious respiratory disorders and cancers; nearly one billion live in cities that exceed WHO standards for sulphur dioxide; and high levels of lead substantially reduce IQ levels in millions of children and increase hypertension disorders – including heart attacks and strokes – in adults.

Indoor air pollution in the home and workplace is a special concern because of the relatively high concentrations of pollutants and long exposure times. Studies in Chinese cities have shown excessively high levels of particulates, sulphur dioxide, carbon monoxide and benzopyrenes in houses using coal stoves for heating or cooking (Krupnick and Sebastian, 1990). Highly excessive particulate concentrations and benzopyrene levels have also been found in poorly ventilated Indian houses using wood or dung as cooking fuel (Shin *et al.*, 1992). According to the World Bank (1992), hundreds of millions in developing countries suffer respiratory ailments from indoor use of biomass fuel. Air pollutants in workplaces include toxic chemicals such as asbestos, and heavy concentrations of dust. Shin *et al.* (1992) noted that between 1978 and 1987 Thailand experienced a tenfold increase in occupational diseases attributable to toxic substance exposure. In addition, many cases of ill-health, disability and death due to workplace pollution are unreported.

In OECD countries, emissions of sulphur dioxide, particulate matter and lead have declined significantly over the last two decades (OECD, 1991). On the other hand emissions of nitrogen oxides and volatile organic compounds have increased as motor vehicle usage has outstripped implementation of emission controls. Also, more toxic pollutants (for instance cadmium, benzene, radon, asbestos) are being released into the atmosphere both outdoors and indoors. Many of these are carcinogenic or have other deleterious health effects, possibly on a large scale though estimates of risk vary widely. Air pollution may also cause extensive damage to crops and buildings (Pearce and Markandya, 1989).

There is also greatly increased anxiety about regional air pollution. Some air pollutants, notably sulphur and nitrogen, can travel long distances. Acid rain, which originates in sulphur and nitrogen oxides from power stations, motor vehicles and natural sources such as volcanoes, is carried in clouds before being deposited as sulphuric and nitric acid in rain and snow. Acid rain is charged with causing substantial damage to lakes, forests and crops in continental Europe and to fish populations in remote parts of Scandinavia.

Global Atmospheric Changes

There are two main sources of concern about global atmospheric change: ozone depletion and global warming. Changes in the ozone concentration are difficult to measure because of large natural spatial and temporal variations. However it appears that annual average total column ozone has fallen by about 3 per cent over large parts of the globe in the last 20 years and, more dramatically, that a hole in the ozone layer has occurred above Antarctica, due in large part to the breakdown of chlorofluorocarbons (CFCs) in the stratosphere. The reduced ozone will lead to increased ultraviolet radiation reaching the earth, with potentially very harmful effects on human health (skin cancer, eye damage and suppression of the immune response system). Reductions in CFC production under the Montreal and London Protocols, signed in 1987 and 1990 respectively, were designed to stabilise ozone concentration. However Brown (1992) estimates that ozone depletion could cause 200 000 skin cancer fatalities in the next 50 years in the US alone.

Emissions of carbon dioxide (CO_2 is the major greenhouse gas) have risen from about 6.0 to 7.5 billion tonnes per annum over the last 20 years. Three quarters of these emissions are caused by the burning of fossil fuels and most of the rest by deforestation and land use changes. Increasing emissions of CO_2 and other greenhouse gases are forecast to raise average world temperatures by between 1.5 and 4.5 degrees Celsius in 60 to 80 years. Some of the uncertainty depends on the extent to which policies reduce CO_2 emissions. Global warming would damage low-lying areas (unless they are protected), cause major changes in agricultural productivity (not all negative changes) and affect many other aspects of economic life such as electricity requirements and water supply. Nordhaus (1991a) estimates that the net costs of global warming will be less than 1 per cent of GDP in the middle of the next century, which would be comparatively small. Cline (1992) forecasts that the damages are more likely to be around 6 per cent of GDP by 2050, and even higher in the long run.

Solid and Hazardous Wastes

The worldwide solid waste disposal task is huge and increasing. Depending on the level of consumption, between 0.5 and 2.0 kg of waste per capita is generated daily. In 1990 OECD countries alone generated nine billion tonnes of domestic and industrial waste to be managed, including over 300 million tonnes of hazardous waste.

In OECD countries most businesses and households receive a waste disposal service. Disposal methods include landfills, composting and recycling plants, and incinerators. This collection comes at a high cost (an average of \$50 to \$60 per tonne for hazardous waste). Lack of suitable land in or close to urban areas is also a major problem. Methane gas at landfills is an explosion risk. On the other hand incinerators create air pollution and ash disposal problems.

The situation is far worse in many developing countries, where there are often few or no official waste disposal services. Dumpsites, especially informal ones, are major health risks due to the breeding of rats, flies and mosquitoes. They cause air pollution from fires, are associated with the leaching of chemicals into surface and groundwater, and have unpleasant appearance and odour. Much solid waste is dumped into waterways, polluting the water, blocking drains and causing flooding.

Hazardous waste includes reactive, toxic, ignitable, infectious and corrosive wastes. Contact with such wastes is a major health risk. The largest volumes of waste comes from mining, petroleum, pulp and paper and metallurgical industries. Small-scale businesses, including tanneries and car battery recycling, can cause local problems. On the other hand nuclear waste has a potentially huge geographical impact. In 1972 there were just over 100 nuclear reactors generating electricity in 15 countries; in 1992 there were 428 reactors in 31 countries. Although technical solutions are available for handling most sorts of hazardous waste, inadequate management is a chronic risk. Routine disposal of hazardous waste may cause water or air pollution. Also, major industrial accidents occur quite frequently. Major oil spills have occurred off Alaska, France and Spain; there have been major chemical plant accidents in India and Italy; and large-scale nuclear radiation accidents have taken place in the US and the Ukraine.

Urban Areas: Congestion, Noise and Poverty

Urban areas suffer not only from water and air pollution and waste disposal problems, but also from congested living conditions and poverty. The worst problems occur in the largest cities. In 1972 there were three megacities with over 10 million inhabitants, including one in a developing country, and 250 million motor vehicles in all countries. By 1992 there were 13 megacities, including nine in developing countries, and 650 million motor vehicles. In addition slum conditions exist in hundreds of smaller cities in developing countries.

Crowded living conditions, especially slums, are fertile ground for infectious diseases, including AIDS. Slums breed informal local power structures based on physical enforcement outside the reach of legitimate authorities. Traffic congestion causes accidents, major losses of productivity and low amenity. On the other hand, solutions involving major civil engineering projects in cities usually require substantial population resettlement.

Noise is a general feature of crowded conditions. The OECD (1991) estimates that 130 million people in OECD countries are exposed to unacceptable noise levels in their homes and that 400 million people have an unsatisfactory acoustic environment. Moreover the noise environment has worsened in many countries over the last 20 years due to the increase in road and air traffic. Excessive noise can disturb sleep, impair hearing and cause stress and is a widespread cause of annoyance. However in developing countries noise is generally perceived to be a minor environmental problem.

Rural Areas: Soils and Forests

Soil productivity is threatened in various ways: by nutrient loss, soil erosion, desertification, water pollution, salinisation and waterlogging, and air pollutants.

In many natural systems the rate of soil production equals or exceeds the rate of removal, so that soil depth and fertility tend to increase. However natural soil erosion combined with farming activities is causing a net loss of soil on 35 per cent of the world's cropland (OECD, 1991). Many developed countries have compensated successfully, in the short run at least, with increased fertilisation. But soil loss in many developing countries has reduced agricultural productivity. Studies have estimated that soil loss is reducing annual GDP in Mali, Costa Rica, Mexico and Malawi by between 0.5 and 1.5 per cent annually (World Bank, 1992).

Desertification occurs when productive semi-arid regions are converted into deserts. The main causes are natural droughts and overgrazing as well as soil erosion. Desertification is a major problem in China (World Resources Institute, 1994) and has also damaged some local communities in the Sahel region in sub-Saharan Africa.

Salt-affected soils are a natural problem exacerbated by salt deposited from irrigation water. Globally, 950 million hectares (nearly one third of arable land) are affected by excessive salt concentration (World Bank, 1992). About 60 million hectares suffer from salination and reduced productivity from bad irrigation practices. Also, poor drainage causes waterlogging and reduces plant growth as water seeps from unlined canals and groundwater rises. To counter these various problems and to maximise output from scarce farming land, farmers often adopt intensive farming practices, multicropping, extensive machinery and heavy use of agrochemicals. Multicropping tends to exhaust soil nutrients and heavy machinery compacts soil excessively. Fertilisers and pesticides, when used excessively, pollute waterways.

Deforestation is another response to the shortage of productive agricultural land. The world has lost one fifth of its tropical forests in this century, including one tenth in the last decade. Currently, 17 million hectares of tropical forests are destroyed each year. These losses reduce forest products (the annual world trade in timber products is US$40 billion) and the real income of many subsistence households. Deforestation also increases erosion and reduces watershed protection, especially in hilly areas, endangers biodiversity because tropical forests are the habitats for the majority of the world's species, and may have profound ecological effects, including impacts on regional and global climates. However, to produce a balanced picture it should be noted that, as a result of deliberate forest management practices, the forest resources of OECD countries have increased over the last 20 years and are expected to continue to grow (OECD, 1991).

Ecosystems, Other Natural Areas and Biodiversity

In concentrating on particular environmental media (water, air and land) and the main geographical areas, there is a danger that we may overlook interactions between the media, impacts in less accessible regions and changes to complex ecosystems. Other elements at risk are the oceans, wetlands, coral reefs, natural habitats, and remote wilderness areas, including the polar regions. The degradation of these areas reduces productivity, recreational opportunities and wildlife.

Productive benefits of natural habitats are various. For example, the OECD (1991) reports that the value of prescription drugs with plant-derived ingredients was about US$40 billion for all OECD countries in 1980. US trade in food and industrial products from wild sources exceeded $200 million annually. Moreover the genetic resources in wild species are important for crop productivity and resistance to disease and pests.

The natural environment is also the basis of a huge amount of tourism and informal recreation. In 1980 Americans spent US$30 billion on fishing, hunting and non-consumptive wildlife activities (OECD, 1991). Increased income and population have created a rapidly rising demand for natural recreation in nearly all parts of the globe. This demand greatly exceeds the capacity of many countries to manage the natural environment. Vast areas are not protected. Perhaps worse, many of the world's protected areas exist only on paper. As Ryan (1992) notes, most parks in the tropics have little or no staff or budget, and are controlled by politically weak or corrupt departments. A survey by the Organisation of American States (1988) showed that only 16 out of 100 Caribbean marine parks had adequate management plans and staff. Edmund Hillary has described the top of Mount Everest as one of the world's worst rubbish dumps. Pollution is also severely degrading recreational amenities, such as the Mediterranean, in more developed parts of the world.

Estimates of total species and species at risk vary greatly. But most authorities agree that many species are threatened with extinction. Known species number about 1.7 million. Total species could exceed 30 million (OECD, 1991). Based on the sources of the Worldwatch Institute, Ryan (1992) reports that three quarters of the world's bird species are declining in population or are threatened with extinction; one third of North America's freshwater fish species are rare, threatened or endangered; virtually all species of wild cats and most bears are declining seriously in numbers; more than two thirds of the world's primates are threatened with extinction; and in the order of 100 species of invertebrates are lost to deforestation each day. The OECD (1991) reports that in some large OECD countries 40 per cent of mammal species and 30 per cent of the bird species are threatened with extinction. The World Bank (1992) estimates more conservatively that habitat destruction (including forest loss) has endangered about 5 per cent of the world's species of mammals, birds and fish.

Resource Depletion

In the early 1970s the Club of Rome Report (Meadows *et al.*, 1972) typified the then common view that the world would face severe resource shortages as it depleted energy, metal, mineral and food resources. However, both before then and since, the supply of resources has outstripped demand and the real price of most commodities has fallen. As noted by the World Bank (1992), metal prices were lower in the early 1990s than at any previous time in the twentieth century. The energy intensity of output has reduced sharply in the industrialised countries since the early 1970s and the current consumption of energy supplies, as a share of commercially viable reserves, has declined for all energy resources. Over the past 30 years food production has outpaced population growth by 50 per cent and food prices have halved in real terms. Also, although global annual fishery harvests have increased from 60 million tonnes to 90 million tonnes in the last 20 years, this is still 10 million tonnes below the Food and Agriculture Organisation's estimated maximum global sustainable yield of 100 million tonnes (OECD, 1991). The evidence indicates that producers do respond to high prices by economising on high cost inputs and finding substitutes. Worldwide resource shortages seem unlikely.

Nevertheless important commodities are in short supply in some countries. In particular, energy resources, water, timber and agricultural commodities are in short supply in many developing countries. Many valuable fish stocks are over-fished and fish harvests may exceed sustainable levels in a few years. Regrettably these natural shortages are frequently exacerbated not only by inefficient pricing policies, but also by administrative corruption, civil disorder and war.

Table 1.1 summarises the main environmental impacts. In developing countries, health and productivity impacts are usually more important than amenity. In developed countries, amenity effects are often the most important.

Table 1.1 Major forms of environmental degradation and main consequences*

Environmental degradation		*Main consequences*	
	Health	*Productivity*	*Amenity*
Water pollution and scarcity (including marine pollution)	Contribute to over 3 million deaths and billions of illnesses annually.	Shortages constrain economic output; fisheries decline; high costs to provide safe water.	Loss of recreation uses such as fishing, boating, swimming; offensive odours.
Air pollution	Causes many illnesses and deaths; many suffer from smoky indoor air.	High abatement costs; acid rain impact on forests and water bodies; corrosion of buildings.	Reduced visibility from smog; visual disamenity.
Global atmospheric changes	Risks from climatic natural disasters; possible shifts in vector-borne diseases; more skin cancer and eye damage from ozone depletion.	Damage to low-lying coastal assets; regional changes in agricultural output; disruption to marine food chain; threat to biodiversity; ecological impacts.	Species and ecosystems threatened by climate change.
Solid and hazardous wastes, including radiation	Toxic industrial and urban conditions; industrial accidents.	High collection costs; pollution of groundwater; high prevention costs.	Visual and odour disamenities.
Urban areas: congestion and noise	Infectious diseases; traffic accidents; hearing impairment.	Loss of productivity; costs of traffic management and noise abatement.	Overcrowding; stress; landlord oppression.
Rural areas: soil quality		Loss of productivity, especially in tropical soils; off-site siltation of waterways and bodies.	
Rural areas: forests		Losses of forest products, soil productivity, genetic resources; watershed instability; carbon emissions.	Reduction in biodiversity; loss of recreation uses.
Ecosystems, other natural areas		Losses of tourism, genetic resources; ecological impacts.	Reduction in wilderness experiences, biodiversity loss.
Depletion of raw materials and energy resources		Reduction in economic growth.	

*The format of this table and some points in it are based on a similar table in World Bank, 1992.

1.3 VALUATION ISSUES

Texts on environmental valuation tend to focus on methods for valuing amenity, and to a lesser extent health, and to ignore productivity. This is doubtless because amenity impacts are especially difficult to value. Also the valuation of productivity is described adequately in many basic cost–benefit texts.

However there are cogent reasons for including the valuation of productivity in environmental discussions. Firstly, productivity effects are often the most important consequences of environmental change. Secondly, many productivity effects are subtle and, in the writer's experience, are not always valued correctly. Thirdly, similar valuation methods may apply to productivity as to health or amenity. For example labour market data may be used to value productivity and health, and asset price data to value productivity and amenity. Valuation methods should be applied consistently across different kinds of impact.

As we shall see, most health impacts can be viewed in terms of loss of productivity or amenity (quality of life), or both. Even the value of life itself may be measured by productivity forgone, although this is not the preferred valuation method. However, because of the importance of health and the special treatment of life we will follow the convention of treating health impacts separately from productivity and amenity.

There are many kinds of amenity impact. These include recreational effects (on fishing, boating, swimming and so on), changes in wilderness experiences, and impact on the quality of residential life, including quality of view, visibility, noise and odours. These impacts usually occur outside normal markets. Consequently several methods have been developed especially to deal with non-market goods (see Chapter 4 and elsewhere). However it should be remarked that no firm line can be drawn between productivity and amenity. Where markets can be established and charges levied for services, services may be regarded as part of the productive sector.

Ecological changes are sometimes regarded as a separate class of impact. However, from a welfare perspective, ecological changes are usually intermediate impacts. It is generally health, productivity or amenity consequences that are of concern. Ecological impacts do not warrant a separate cost, or benefit, classification.

On the other hand the environment may be considered to have a non-use (existence) value. This important concept is discussed further in the next chapter.

1.4 CONCLUDING COMMENTS

Major environmental problems exist in all environmental media and most countries. In OECD countries the main local concerns appear to be outdoor air pollution, hazardous wastes, the shrinking of natural wilderness areas, and cities in which people are exposed simultaneously to several forms of environmental degradation. In developing countries the list of serious environmental problems is longer: it includes water pollution, indoor and outdoor air pollution, wastes of all kinds, urban slums, declining soil productivity, deforestation and resource shortages, including water scarcity. Globally the problems of greatest concern are probably the breakdown of long-established ecosystems and the rapid extinction of species, the risk of major industrial or military accidents, the pollution and over-exploitation of international water bodies, and the risk of major atmospheric and climatic changes. Increasingly the environment is a regional and global problem.

Environmental problems are closely related to social conditions and management and are sometimes indistinguishable from social problems. Indeed some so-called environmental impacts, such as resettlement caused by deforestation or large civil engineering projects, are essentially social impacts. Causes of environmental problems generally include a lack of property rights, inadequate pricing policies and a lack of public authority and social organisation. Social disorder, crime and inequality almost always exacerbate environmental problems.

Environmental challenges are increasing with the rise in population, consumption and mobility. Total global consumption and movement are likely to double in 25 years and treble in 50. The environment will not necessarily worsen. In the last 20 years, many OECD countries have achieved significant improvements in air and water quality, waste management and protection of natural habitats, including forests. In most developing countries people have more to eat and live longer than they did 20 years ago. But the likely size and speed of economic change will lead to more environmental challenges, more accidents and unforeseen environmental impacts, many of which will cross national boundaries.

Uncertainty and sheer lack of knowledge about the nature and consequences of environmental impacts are major constraints on the development of rational environmental policies. There are major uncertainties about the impact of air and water pollution on public health, of acid rain on crop productivity, of greenhouse gases on global warming and of deforestation on climate change, to name but a few examples. When there is considerable uncertainty about technical relationships between pollution and health and productivity, it is obviously not possible to make precise estimates of the cost of health or productivity impacts. Valuing amenity and existence benefits is almost always a difficult and subjective process.

Some experts believe that the answers to these environmental challenges and uncertainties are radical and simple. For example, Brown *et al.* (1992) argue that nothing less than an environmental revolution will meet existing and future global environmental challenges. According to Brown (ibid., p. 177) 'we know what we have to do'. There have to be dramatic changes in values, lifestyles and human reproductive behaviour. Carbon emissions, CFC emissions, air pollution, water pollution and toxic waste must be reduced. Deforestation must be stopped, soil erosion lessened and biodiversity protected.

Other authorities believe that the solution to the world's environmental problems is incremental and complex, and that the costs and benefits of alternatives need to be assessed. For example the OECD (1991) argues that environmental problems in OECD countries can, and should, be met by structural adjustment of the economies. Environmental policies should be integrated within sectoral polices, principally by means of economic instruments that ensure that environmental costs are fully taken into account by producers and consumers. To deal with international pollution, international cooperation and regulations are also required. The World Bank (1992) argues that economic development should be defined to include the welfare costs of environmental impacts; that development and environmental quality are properly regarded as complementary; and that poverty and lack of development are major causes of environmental problems.

This book adopts the OECD/World Bank stance that environmental policies should be based on detailed assessment of the benefits and costs of alternative policies rather than on calls for revolutionary action. The case-studies illustrate this approach and the benefits from it. But by itself a rational evaluation process achieves little. The case-studies also show that an efficient and accountable government is necessary for sustainable environmental quality.

2 Cost–Benefit Analysis

2.1 INTRODUCTION TO COST–BENEFIT ANALYSIS

In this book, project appraisal and cost–benefit analysis (CBA) are used as interchangeable terms. This reflects widespread international practice. Governments and international funding agencies use CBA as their main formal method of project appraisal. Also, as I argue below and elsewhere (Abelson, 1979; Applied Economics, 1995), CBA is the most systematic and consistent appraisal method available.

CBA is designed to show whether the total benefits of a policy or project exceed the costs, including environmental benefits and costs. As far as possible, all effects are measured as the persons affected would measure them.

Although this approach may appear reasonable and practical, there are concerns about fundamental evaluation objectives and principles of CBA and problems in application. For example, there are concerns about how costs and benefits are valued, the discounting of the future, the treatment of risk and the treatment (or lack of it) of distributional effects. There may also be concern that the environment is apparently regarded as a means to improve human welfare rather than as an end in itself.

These and other issues are addressed in this and the next two chapters. This chapter sets out the basic method of CBA. The chapter starts with the objectives of project appraisal and the main decision criteria employed in cost–benefit studies. We then consider how to identify relevant costs and benefits, the basic valuation principles, and the treatment of time, risk and distributional effects.

Chapter 3 describes the principles of valuation in more detail and elaborates on possible differences between developing and developed countries. The chapter concludes that CBA generally provides the best framework for valuing environmental impacts. Chapter 4 discusses the application of a wide range of valuation methods, especially for valuing environmental impacts.

2.2 BASIC OBJECTIVES OF PROJECT APPRAISAL

In project appraisal we aim to determine the action (*A*) that would maximise some overall measure of net social value. To do this we 'list all parties affected by the project and then value the effect of the project on their welfare as it would be valued in money terms by them' (Layard and Glaister, 1994, p. 4). Future costs and benefits are weighted according to individual preferences and equivalent present values are estimated. The affected parties should include not only the producers and consumers directly associated with the project, but also third parties who experience environmental impacts of the project. Moreover, insofar as future generations are deprived of scarce environmental resources, their loss should be taken into account (see Section 3.4).

If the net benefits of *A* are higher than those of the next best alternative, *A* is described as 'efficient' and doing *A* may be justified on three grounds. Firstly, doing *A* is unambiguously beneficial if its benefits are used fully to compensate the losers, so that some people will gain from *A* but no one will lose. Secondly, doing a large number of efficient projects produces more benefits for the community as a whole than doing a collection of efficient and inefficient projects. Thirdly, some advocates of CBA support the Hicks–Kaldor criterion (named after the two economists). This states that 'a project can be supported provided that the gainers could, in principle, compensate the losers, even if they do not' (ibid., p. 6).

In practice full compensation is not common and hypothetical compensation is not very attractive on ethical grounds. Therefore decision makers often have to consider the distributional effects of projects as well as their overall net benefit.

Moreover it is rarely possible to quantify all the impacts of a project, especially all the environmental effects, in money terms. In these cases the CBA report should include a description of the unquantified items and the decision makers will determine the weight to be given to these items in their policy determination.

Finally, we need to ask whether the objective of project appraisal (maximising the present value of net benefits) is consistent with the widely held objective of sustainable development. By sustainable development we mean that each new generation should be able to enjoy at least the standard of welfare of the previous generation. The answer is that maximising net project benefits and sustainable development are compatible providing that scarce natural resources are properly valued and any depletion of natural resources is compensated for by an increase in physical or human capital (Solow, 1993). On the other hand, if natural resources are undervalued or depleted without an offsetting increase in physical or human capital, future generations may suffer. The project report should recognise such a distributional impact.

2.3 TECHNICAL EVALUATION CRITERIA

Undoubtedly one of the most troubling aspects of project appraisal is the weighting of costs and benefits that occur at different points in time. As we shall see in more detail in Section 2.6, discount rates are used to estimate the present value equivalents of future costs and benefits. These discount rates are an essential part of the formal criteria used in project appraisal.

The principal evaluation criterion is the net present value (NPV) method. The NPV is the present value of estimated benefits net of costs:

$$\text{NPV} = \sum_{t=1}^{n} \frac{(b-c)_t}{(1+r)^t} \tag{2.1}$$

where b and c are benefits and costs in each period $t = 1 \ldots n$, and r is the selected discount rate. Suppose for example that a project with a capital cost of \$1000 in year one generates net benefits of \$600 in years two and three and that the selected discount rate is 10 per cent. The NPV is then

$$\text{NPV} = -1000 + \frac{600}{(1+0.10)} + \frac{600}{(1+0.10)^2} = 41 \tag{2.2}$$

A positive NPV indicates that estimated total benefits exceed total costs. Because benefits represent the value of consumption gained and costs are the value of consumption forgone, a positive NPV represents an increase in the total value of consumption. If there are several alternatives, the project with the highest NPV is preferred, other things being equal. But, as we have noted, many decisions depend also on the distribution of costs and benefits and on unquantified effects.

Two other closely related evaluation criteria are often used in project appraisal. One is the internal rate of return (IRR). The IRR is the rate of return that equates discounted net benefits to discounted capital costs. It is obtained by solving for i in Equation 2.3:

$$\sum_{t=1}^{n} \frac{C_t}{(1+i)^t} = \sum_{t=1}^{n} \frac{(b-c)_t}{(1+i)^t} \tag{2.3}$$

where C represents capital costs, i is the IRR, and the other symbols are as before. Using the same figures as in Equation 2.2, the IRR is 13 per cent per annum.

$$\$1000 = \frac{\$600}{(1+i)} + \frac{\$600}{(1+i)^2} = \frac{\$600}{(1+0.13)} + \frac{\$600}{(1+0.13)^2} \tag{2.4}$$

If the estimated IRR of a project exceeds the chosen discount rate (r), the NPV of the project is positive. In terms of net benefit, the project is acceptable.

The IRR provides a useful measure of project value for many people who are accustomed to rate of return concepts. However it may rank projects differently from the NPV measure. The IRR criterion favours projects with low capital requirements and high returns in early years and is biased against projects with high returns in the long run. Also, high IRRs can be misleading because project surpluses cannot be reinvested at the internally determined discount rate. Project benefits should be discounted by the chosen rate of discount rather than by an arbitrarily determined mathematical rate. In general, the NPV is the correct criterion and provides the preferred ranking.

The third evaluation criterion is the benefit–cost ratio (BCR). This is generally defined as

$$BCR = \frac{\sum_{t=1}^{n} \frac{(b-c)_t}{(1+r)^t}}{\sum_{t=1}^{n} \frac{C_t}{(1+r)^t}} \tag{2.5}$$

where all the symbols are as before. A project with a BCR greater than one has a positive NPV.

The BCR, like the IRR, favours projects requiring little capital and may rank projects differently from the NPV criterion. Where this occurs the NPV measure is usually preferred because it has no size bias: it ensures that the additional capital required for a large project is discounted at the appropriate rate; that is, the marginal opportunity cost of capital. However the BCR is relevant to decision making if the capital available to an agency is constrained and the marginal return on its investment exceeds the marginal return available elsewhere. In this instance projects should be selected 'in order of their present value per unit of constrained cost until the cost constraint is exhausted' (Layard and Glaister, 1994, p. 43).

2.4 IDENTIFYING RELEVANT COSTS AND BENEFITS

What effects should be included in a project appraisal? The answer is all the direct costs and benefits experienced by the producers and consumers of a product respectively plus the indirect costs and benefits (the externalities) borne by third parties. The externalities of concern are changes in real variables that affect the surpluses of producers or the well-being of individuals. These are known as *technological* externalities as distinct from *pecuniary* externalities. The latter refer to changes in price that simply transfer money from one group to another but do not change net income. As we shall see, difficulties can also arise with the concept of non-use benefits and with 'secondary benefits'.

All costs and benefits must be measured in relation to an alternative. The alternative most commonly employed is a projection of the existing situation. This is usually called the 'base case' or the 'do-nothing' case. Because the base case should include planned changes that will occur in any event, the do-nothing label can be misleading.

Project Costs and Cost Savings

The total costs of a project are the costs of resources employed by the producer(s) over the life of the project plus any costs imposed on third parties (who may be other producers or consumers). Resource costs typically include land and other property costs, infrastructure expenditures, plant and equipment, energy, materials and labour. External costs take many forms. Typical examples are water and air pollution from factories and air pollution and noise from transport sources. Of course, only incremental costs should be debited to the project. Fixed costs should not influence the project decision and should not be included in the appraisal.

All expenditures should be recorded in full when the cash payment is made. The discounting procedure captures the opportunity cost of the resources tied up in the project. Interest payments on borrowed capital should not be included as this would involve double counting. Likewise depreciation should not be included as this is an accounting device to spread capital costs over the life of assets, which would also involve double counting.

On the other hand, projects may produce savings in resource costs. Indeed cost savings are the main objective of many projects. For example road investment is intended to reduce vehicle operating costs and travel time. Rail electrification may save fuel costs. A soil conservation programme may reduce the need for fertiliser. All such cost savings count as a benefit in CBA.

Project Benefits

Project benefits are of two main kinds: use and non-use benefits. The word 'use' generally embraces all use benefits to man. It includes environmental benefits, such as clean air and wilderness, as well as conventional bread-and-butter goods.

Use benefits are sometimes subdivided into direct and indirect benefits. For example a dam may be built to provide electricity and irrigation to designated users, but may also provide indirect benefits in the form of recreational opportunities and reduced flooding. A forest provides timber and non-wood products, but may also provide a place of settlement, soil protection and catchment stability. In practice the distinction between the direct and indirect benefits is not always clear-cut. Any primary benefit from a project should count as a benefit.

Non-use values are so-called 'option' and 'existence' values. Thus, the total economic value (TEV) of a project (or asset) can be defined as:

$$\text{TEV} = \text{Direct and indirect use benefits} + \text{option values} + \text{existence values} \tag{2.6}$$

Option value is the premium, if any, that individuals are willing to pay for an asset over and above what they would be willing to pay for the services that they expect to use. Formally, option value (OV) is defined as

$$\text{OV} = \text{OP} - \text{EV} \tag{2.7}$$

where OP is option price (that is the total value of an asset to an individual) and EV is the expected value of use benefits. OV is similar to an insurance premium; it arises because people are uncertain about either the future availability of an asset or their use of it. Because option value is related to uncertainty, it is discussed in Section 2.7.

Existence value has been defined in various ways. However most definitions contain three main components: pure existence, altruistic and vicarious values. Pure existence value is the inherent value of the world independent of its use to man. It is widely held that man has a duty to preserve the natural environment and threatened animal and plant species for their own sake, even when they have no use to man. Altruistic values reflect our desire to preserve the environment, not only for relatives and friends, but also for all other people living today and future generations who may benefit from the conservation of environmental resources. Thirdly, we may obtain vicarious pleasure from thinking about the environment without using it in a conventional way. We may enjoy thinking of the Himalayan mountains or the Amazonian tropical forest even though we have no intention of climbing to the top of Everest or struggling through hot, humid, tropical forests.

There are two main difficulties with these definitions. Firstly, altruistic and vicarious values can be interpreted as use values. For example photo and TV tourism benefits may be regarded as vicarious existence values or as use benefits. In such cases what matters is that the benefits are counted once (and once only); whether they are considered use or non-use benefits is a minor issue of taxonomy. Secondly, and perhaps more importantly, it is not always clear what pure existence or its alternative (non-existence) mean. When does a natural environment lose its existence? Clearly there is a loss of existence value when a species becomes extinct. But some people consider that some existence value is lost with any degradation of the natural environment. In such circumstances our advice to the analyst would be to describe the likely changes to the environment but to avoid philosophical debate about whether these changes should or should not be described as losses of existence value.

Secondary Benefits

Secondary benefits are consequences of the primary benefits of a project. They arise when project expenditures and surpluses generate demands for goods and services that lead in turn to a secondary increase in output. A project may generate additional expenditures by employees (if they receive higher wages than they would in the alternative case) and by businesses that provide inputs to the project (if they make higher profits than they otherwise would). Also the expenditure of project surpluses, whether in the form of project profits or lower consumer prices, may lead to secondary benefits.

It is important to appreciate, however, that if a CBA uses appropriate shadow prices for labour and other project resources (as described in Chapter 3), the estimated NPV includes all primary benefits. That is, it includes the benefits obtained by labour and businesses that service the project as well as the surpluses associated with increased profits and lower prices.

Ignoring unquantified effects, the total benefit of a project (TB) can be expressed as the product of the estimated NPV and the secondary benefit multiplier (M):

$$\text{TB} = \text{NPV} \times M \tag{2.8}$$

where

$$M = 1/[1 - (X - I)] \tag{2.9}$$

X is the marginal propensity to spend and I is the marginal propensity to spend directly or indirectly on imported goods. Imports rise indirectly when existing local output is used to meet the new expenditure and this output is replaced by imports.

From a national perspective, X is generally about 0.85. The marginal propensity to spend in local areas is usually much lower. This is partly because the tax take has to be subtracted, but mainly because of the limited nature of local production. The size of the multiplier is very sensitive to the capacity of the economy to increase output. In a fully employed economy all *marginal* consumption is imported, so that $I = X$ and there are no secondary benefits. Also, in small local areas most goods are imported and the multiplier is low. In general the multiplier increases as the size of the study area increases and as unemployment rises.

The important general point, however, is that secondary benefits are usually not included in CBA. This is because similar benefits can generally be obtained by alternative uses of the project's resources. Indeed if the government were not to use these resources at all but were to cut taxes, there would be an expansionary (although doubtless slightly different) effect on output. Therefore secondary benefits are generally viewed as transfers between communities (depending on which projects are adopted) rather than as a net addition to community income.

Of course the argument for ignoring secondary benefits presumes that unemployed resources are distributed evenly across the country or that resources are completely mobile. If these assumptions do not hold, differences in secondary benefits may occur and may affect total output and incomes. In any case, secondary benefits almost always affect distributional results and may interest decision makers for this reason.

2.5 BASIC VALUATION PRINCIPLES

As we have seen, CBA aims to value the effects of a project as they would be valued in money terms by the individuals affected. The value of a resource is its marginal opportunity cost. The value of a benefit is the amount that someone is willing to pay for it. Because the marginal opportunity cost of a resource is the highest amount that someone would pay for it in an alternative use, valuation in CBA is based essentially on willingness to pay (WTP) values.

Although this may seem straightforward, there are several contentious issues. These include the definition of willingness to pay, whether compensation (willingness to accept) values are more appropriate for valuing losses, the reliance on individual preferences, and the measurement of existence value.

Willingness to Pay Values

When we talk about a willingness to pay value, we mean the maximum amount that an individual is willing to pay for a product. This is the sum of the product price (P) and an individual's consumer surplus (CS):

$$\text{WTP} = \text{P} + \text{CS} \tag{2.10}$$

All WTP values are represented by points along a demand curve for a product. These WTP values also represent the marginal benefits of individuals at each point along the demand curve. Consumer surplus is the excess that an individual is willing to pay for something over and above its price.

These concepts are illustrated in Figure 2.1, where Q_0 goods are purchased at P_0 price. The total WTP value is the whole area under the demand curve to the left of Q_0. This is the sum of producer revenues and all consumer surpluses.

Obviously, the lower the price the more important consumer surpluses are likely to be. In the case of non-market goods, all benefits are consumer surpluses. The measurement of consumer surplus is therefore a key issue in CBA, especially for environmental goods. Various ways of measuring what people are willing to pay for non-market goods are discussed in the next chapter.

But before we move on we should make a brief technical point about the definition and measurement of consumer surplus, partly because this foreshadows the discussion below about willingness to accept values. Consumer surplus is generally based on observed or estimated market

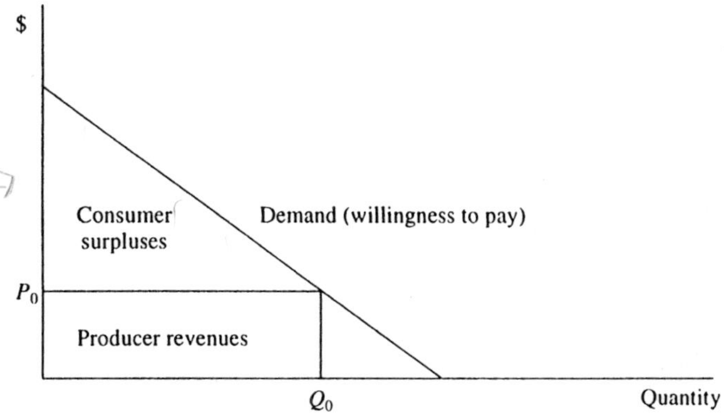

Figure 2.1 Willingness to pay

demand curves, which are described in the technical literature as Marshallian demand curves. In most markets, when prices fall individuals consume more goods and they are better off than before (their real income rises). On the other hand, when prices rise individuals are worse off. In other words, with a standard market demand curve, money incomes are constant but welfare changes with moves along the curve. Because welfare changes, these demand curves are described as uncompensated.

If we wish to estimate the maximum that individuals are willing to pay for a proposed change, or to avoid an unwelcome change, we should estimate the demand curve that is consistent with constant welfare. In technical terms, we should employ compensated (Hicksian) demand curves that notionally hold welfare (real income) constant as prices fall or rise. When prices fall or environmental quality increases a Hicksian demand curve produces a smaller benefit area than an uncompensated demand curve. Conversely, when prices rise or environmental quality falls a Hicksian demand curve produces a larger loss than a Marshallian demand curve.

In practice, when estimating project benefits most analysts ignore WTP differences between uncompensated and compensated demand curves for two main reasons. Firstly, the WTP differences are generally small (Feenberg and Mills, 1980; Pearce and Markandya, 1989). Secondly, it is much easier to work with observed or estimated market demand curves than with notional Hicksian demand curves.

Compensation and Willingness to Accept Values

That still leaves the issue of how to value costs that are imposed on people. Should these costs be valued by what individuals are willing to pay to prevent them from occurring? Or should they be valued by what individuals are willing to accept (WTA) as compensation?

Most people would probably consider that WTA values are fairer and more appropriate in these situations. This is consistent with the most common approach in the technical literature, which is known as the Hicksian compensation (or *compensating variation*) principle. Under this approach the existing situation and levels of individual well-being are taken as given, and the analyst estimates the maximum that individuals would be willing to pay for a benefit and the minimum they would be willing to accept for bearing a loss. These amounts ensure that individuals are as well off with the project as they are without it.

The *compensating variation* principle implies that the present situation is in some sense desirable. If the environment is degraded and the proposed project will enhance the environment, it might be argued that parties should be compensated if the project does not proceed. This is known as the *equivalent variation* principle. In this case the project, rather than the existing situation, is taken as the starting point. The analyst then estimates the minimum that the gainers would be willing to accept in compensation for the project not proceeding and the maximum that the losers would be willing to pay to stop the project. However this procedure is generally regarded as less fair and less practical than valuation based on the *compensating variation* principle.

In practice, for three main reasons most CBA studies use WTP values for costs borne unwillingly as well as for benefits. A practical reason is that it is easier to estimate WTP than WTA values. The latter are not observable in markets so that estimation of WTA values usually requires elaborate surveys and the results are subject to a wide value range. Secondly, differences between WTP and WTA values are small for most goods, including small environmental changes. Willig (1976) and Randall and Stoll (1980) show that WTP and WTA values are generally within 5 per cent of each other.

Thirdly, it is often not clear when people have a right to claim compensation. A claim for compensation implies that property rights can be identified. This is not easy to do for many common property resources and other environmental goods. For example individuals have a right to clean air, but they also have a right to electricity and to travel. Often the same individuals want all these goods. In such cases it makes sense to estimate how much people are willing to pay for each potential use of the environment rather than to start with a preconception about how it should be used and to weight the valuation procedure accordingly.

Clearly if all three of the above objections to WTA values were to hold, as was believed traditionally, there would be no case for using WTA values. However many economists (but certainly not all) have grown more confident that they can estimate WTA values reasonably accurately by using survey methods (see Chapter 4). More importantly, there is now substantial evidence that WTA values can be much higher than WTP values, especially when the loss is regarded as significant (Meyer, 1979; Schultze *et al.*, 1981; Knetsch and Sinden, 1984). There are various explanations. One is that possession of a property right, which is implied by the WTA measure, gives an individual a higher real income. Another is that most individuals are more attached to what they have acquired than to what they might purchase. A third explanation is that people require substantial compensation for the loss of commodities, such as some environmental goods, that are rare and difficult to replace (Hanemann, 1991).

In conclusion, the use of WTA values for losses of existing services or assets is consistent with the *compensating variation* approach to welfare measurement, which is a commonly accepted basis for CBA. This may apply not only to the loss of private property rights but also to the loss of access to public property, for example the loss of traditional access to forests, parks or beaches. However this does imply the value judgement that the present situation is desirable. Where this is not clearly so, where property rights are not well-established and where losses are relatively minor, WTP values are generally used.

Individual Preferences versus Expert Values

An important presumption of WTP and WTA values is that individuals are usually better judges of their own needs and of how to satisfy them than are governments and experts. This seems to be a reasonable presumption for most goods. Most individuals have a strong incentive to learn how to improve their own well-being.

Notwithstanding this general principle, people do not always know what is best for themselves especially with regard to the environment. For example they may not be aware of the links between water and air pollution and disease. Also, responses to survey questions about the value of the environment may depend on the information provided to the respondent. When individual values are evidently based on incorrect information they should be treated cautiously and may be modified (see the discussions of hedonic analyses and contingent surveys in Chapter 4).

Existence Values

In practical terms, if existence values are to be measured the analyst must estimate the amounts that people are willing to pay to preserve the natural environment and other species over and above what they would pay for any use benefits. This may appear an excessively human-centred approach to measuring the inherent values of the world. As Shin *et al.* (1992) point out, humans usually have higher WTP values for beloved monkey-like animals than for unloved rat-like creatures. But there is no practical alternative. In any case WTA values make no sense in this context.

Willingness to pay existence values may be discovered through surveys. However survey respondents often find it difficult to quantify their willingness to pay for the abstract notion of existence values and, especially, to distinguish between pure existence, altruistic and vicarious values. Therefore several writers (for example Brookshire *et al.*, 1983; Randall, 1991) propose that surveys should attempt to determine respondents' total (preservation) value for a specified environment and that analysts should infer existence values by deducting user values, which would be estimated separately.

There is a danger, however, that any such valuation approach will miss the main point of the environmentalist's argument that other species should have standing in their own right. There is therefore much to be said for the advice of Dasgupta and Maler (1994, p. 327): 'It is pretty much impossible to get a quantitative handle on "intrinsic worth", and so the right thing to do is to take note of it, keep an eye on it, and call attention to it whenever the stock is threatened'.

2.6 DEALING WITH TIME: CHOICE OF DISCOUNT RATES

Basic Concepts

Consistent with the principle that individual preferences matter, the future effects of a project should be valued as the parties affected would value them. It is clear from the fact that most people require a positive real rate of return for lending that they put a premium on present consumption and require a reward for forgoing consumption now. Taking typical figures for a developed economy, suppose that the nominal pre-tax return (nr) on lending is 10 per cent, the marginal tax rate (tr) is 30 per cent and the expected inflation rate (π) is 3 per cent. In this case, as shown in Equation 2.11, the discount on the value of marginal future consumption is 3.9 per cent. This is known as the private consumption rate of discount or the private time preference rate.

$$r = \frac{1 + nr(1 - tr)}{1 + \pi} - 1 = \frac{1 + (0.10 \times 0.7)}{1.03} - 1 = 3.9\% \qquad (2.11)$$

What exactly determines the private consumption rate of discount is something of a mystery, but appears to have two main components. One is a fall in the marginal utility of consumption as income rises. The second is the rate at which utility is itself discounted. The latter is sometimes described as 'impatience' and sometimes as a 'pure time preference rate'. Thus the discount rate can be represented formally as:

$$r = (g \times e) + p \qquad (2.12)$$

where g is the expected growth in consumption, e is the elasticity of the marginal utility of consumption with respect to consumption (that is the rate at which marginal utility declines as consumption increases), and p is the pure time preference rate.

How are the independent variables in Equation 2.12 estimated? Typically g is about 1.5, but it may be lower (and even negative) in some poor economies with low growth prospects. Unfortunately, as discussed in Layard and Glaister (1994, pp. 34–5), there is no easy way of estimating e. Work by Fellner (1967), Scott (1977) and Stern (1977) suggests that e is likely to be between 1 and 2.5. The pure time preference rate is also difficult to measure. The main rationale for it appears to be risk of death. Based on the probability of not surviving the year, Kula (1984, 1986) estimates that p varies from 1.0 to 2.0 in different societies. Assuming a mid-point value for e of 1.75 and assuming that g and p each equal 1.5, the private consumption rate of discount will be about 4.0, which happens to correspond to typical after-tax real interest rates.

A number of concerns have been raised, however, about the use of the private consumption rate of discount as reflected in market interest rates for public investments. One is that the pure time preference component is individualistic and 'myopic' and not relevant to social decisions. Another is that market interest rates may reflect precautionary saving motives rather than pure intertemporal consumption preferences. Perhaps most importantly, market rates do not reflect the interests of future generations.

To correct for these problems, the technical literature (for example Layard and Glaister, 1994) usually advocates that a social time preference rate (STPR) of discount equal to the social equivalent for $(g \times e)$ be adopted. In this case g should equal the forecast rate of growth of per capita income in the relevant community and the value of e has to be separately determined. Because the value attached to e involves interpersonal comparisons, its valuation involves a value judgement. This problem is often sidestepped by adopting the value of e that appears typical for individuals (that is, about 1.75). Assuming again a value of 1.5 for g, the STPR would be about 2.5 per cent.

Unfortunately we now have to confront the fact that the producer rate of discount, the marginal return on capital, is generally significantly higher than the consumer rate of discount. This would not be the case in a perfect capital market where producer and consumer rates of discount would be equal. However inflation and tax drive a wedge between the returns to producer and consumers. Using the earnings and inflation figures above (10 per cent and 3 per cent respectively), the real return on capital would be 6.8 per cent (which includes the return captured by government) compared with the private consumption rate of discount of 3.9 per cent.

How are we to choose between the producer and consumer rates of discount? Efficiency requires that the social return on each project should be at least as high as the return on the marginal alternative project, which is known as the social opportunity cost of capital (SOC). On the other hand the SOC heavily discounts future benefits and costs. For example the commonly recommended SOC rate of discount of 10 per cent per annum means that a benefit in 25 years time is worth only one tenth of the same benefit today. This appears to show a gross disregard for the welfare of future generations.

The Choice of Discount Rate

Despite the apparent attractiveness of the STPR, most public agencies recommend that the SOC be used for the discount rate. For example the World Bank (1991, p. 149) recommends that 'the standard opportunity cost of capital be used (e.g. 10 per cent) for environmental cost–benefit analyses, as it is for NPV calculations'. The Bank argues that a lower discount rate would cause more projects to pass the cost–benefit test and 'thus lead to additional environmental stress'. The UK Overseas Development Administration (ODA, 1988, p. 48) also recommends that the discount rate should be the opportunity cost of capital in the public sector, and that a real discount rate in the range of 8–12 per cent is appropriate in most countries. It is not clear to this writer whether these are *ex ante* rates, based sometimes on inflated forecasts of net benefits, which clear the market for investment funds in developing countries, or *ex post* rates which are actually achieved. I suspect the former.

The UK Treasury (1991, p. 24) recommends a real discount rate of 6 per cent for most purposes in the UK. This rate is described (ibid., p. 77) as both a rate of time preference and the cost of capital, based on the long-term, pre-tax cost of capital for low-risk projects in the private sector. However, the Treasury also proposes that an 8 per cent discount rate be used for roads and public enterprises operating in commercial markets, and that a 3 per cent rate be used for land acquisitions for new forestry plantations.

Can this official preference for using the SOC rate of discount for public projects be reconciled with the principle that, to maximise social welfare over time, future costs and benefits should be discounted by the lower STPR? Fortunately it can. Suppose that we have a project with a capital cost, C, and a stream of perpetual annual net benefits, b. Discounting these benefits by the STPR (r), the present value of these benefits is

$$\mathrm{PV}(b) = \sum_{t=1}^{\infty} \frac{b_t}{(1+r)^t} = b/r \qquad (2.13)$$

If we now turn to the capital cost and discount the stream of benefits forgone in an alternative project by the STPR, the present value of these costs is

$$\mathrm{PV}(C) = C \times \rho / r \tag{2.14}$$

where ρ is the SOC. Therefore a project has a positive NPV if

$$b/r - (C \times \rho/r) > 0 \tag{2.15}$$

which implies that

$$b > C \times \rho \tag{2.16}$$

In other words, in this simple case, if the STPR is applied to both the benefits (consumption obtained) and the costs (consumption forgone), a positive net present value requires that annual benefits exceed the product of the capital invested and the SOC.

In order to refine the appraisal procedure, some writers (for example Little and Mirrlees, 1974) propose that a project's consumption benefits be discounted by the STPR, and that a shadow price for capital be adopted. The latter would generally be equal to $C \times \rho/r$. This would be a theoretically superior procedure in that it would treat consumption and investment elements appropriately and allow for a premium to be attached to savings generated by projects and reinvested. This is often considered important for developing economies that are short of savings. However, for most practical purposes discounting future costs and benefits by the SOC and excluding a shadow price for capital gives similar results to the more refined procedure.

We should note however that use of the SOC rate of discount presumes that the capital employed does have an investment opportunity cost. This is not the case for environmental assets that provide mainly consumption benefits. For example natural forests provide fuel, food and wildlife benefits. Wilderness areas provide recreation benefits. In these instances the opportunity costs are the consumption benefits directly forgone. In order to assess options for such assets, the relevant benefit streams should be discounted by the STPR rather than by the SOC.

Also, where part of an investment is funded by forgone present consumption, a synthetic discount rate (*sr*) may be employed as in:

$$sr = (w \times \mathrm{SOC}) + (1 - w)(\mathrm{STPR}) \tag{2.17}$$

where w is the proportion of the capital employed in a project that would be invested elsewhere and $(1 - w)$ is the proportion that reflects consumption forgone. The usual, generally implicit, presumption is that all the capital employed represents investment forgone ($w = 1$), but this is not always the case.

2.7 DEALING WITH UNCERTAINTY

General Issues

Uncertainty is a key feature of environmental phenomena. For example, there is considerable uncertainty about the seriousness of the greenhouse effect, the damage to the ozone layer, the rate at which species are becoming extinct and the effect of widespread deforestation. Also, the risks of major accidents such as oil spills and nuclear fallout are difficult to quantify. How should we deal with such uncertainties?

Perhaps the first thing to note is that the difference between a quantified and an unquantified impact reflects the degree of uncertainty surrounding a variable rather than the kind of cost or benefit it represents. It is a matter for judgement as to when the value of a variable is so uncertain that it should be treated as an unquantified impact. In the writer's view, quantification should be attempted where there is some basis for it as this usually helps to clarify trade-offs and reduces the risks of wild exaggerations. Nevertheless in most studies, especially those involving environmental impacts, there are likely to be some unquantified impacts. Of course, these unquantified effects should be listed so that decision makers can decide whether they would outweigh the quantified results.

Turning to the quantified estimates, it is convenient to start by assuming that most people are risk neutral. In this case the *expected value* approach provides the most comprehensive method of accounting for the range of uncertain values. The expected benefit (Eb) from a project in any year is:

$$Eb = \sum_{i=1}^{m} p_i b_i = p_1 b_1 + p_2 b_2 + \ldots p_m b_m \tag{2.18}$$

where p_i represents the probabilities (adding up to 1) of different values of b occurring in $i = 1 \ldots m$ scenarios. Expected costs (Ec) are estimated in a similar way.

The expected net value (ENPV) of a project is then:

$$\text{ENPV} = \sum_{t=1}^{n} \frac{(Eb - Ec)_t}{(1+r)^t} \tag{2.19}$$

where $t = 1 \ldots n$ years and r is the selected rate of discount.

Given risk neutrality, the project with the highest ENPV should be preferred. For example, suppose we have to choose between project A, which has an expected value of \$2 million with a 50 per cent chance of a NPV of \$5 million and a 50 per cent chance of a NPV of –\$1 million, and project B, which has a certain NPV of $1.5 million? The expected value approach would lead us to select project A.

Needless to say, the full calculation of expected values requires a large number of assumptions. To avoid this, many studies adopt simple sensitivity tests to describe uncertainty. These tests show how the estimated NPV of a project (based on the estimated approximate mean values of variables) changes with variations in the values of particular inputs, such as forecast health costs due to air pollution. Sensitivity tests have the major advantage of simplicity and they may reassure decision makers that project outcomes are not sensitive to plausible changes in important variables. On the other hand they do not allow for the probabilities of high or low values of variables occurring. They may also fail to allow for interdependencies between variables. For example, in a commercial project, lower output may be offset by higher prices. Note, however, that given strict risk neutrality, a decision maker would not be influenced by the results of sensitivity tests.

But is risk neutrality a justified assumption and how should we proceed if it is not? Contrary to our starting assumption, most individuals are often risk averse. Therefore, in accordance with the general CBA principle that benefits and costs should be valued as individuals themselves would value them, it will be necessary to account for risk where risks are borne by individuals.

Fortunately, for the sake of simplicity at least, for many public sector projects the risks to individuals are small and can be ignored. There are two reasons for this: risk pooling and risk distribution. Risk pooling occurs where the government is carrying out a large number of projects. In this case, projects exceeding expectations can be expected to offset those that under-perform. Project selection based on expected values produces a higher aggregate return to society than does selection based on risk avoidance principles. In conjunction with the compensation principle, this produces more benefits for all members of the community. Risk distribution occurs where the government bears most of the costs and benefits of a project. In this case the impact on individual members of the community is small and can be ignored (Arrow and Lind, 1970).

For some major projects, however, the assumptions of risk pooling (and compensation) or risk distribution may not hold. This applies especially to large projects in regions where there are few alternative investment opportunities. In these cases there are three main ways to allow for risk. These are by sensitivity tests (as described above), by estimating the expected utility of a project, and by raising the discount rate.

To estimate *expected utility*, benefits (and costs) are weighted according to their utility (or disutility) as well as their probability. Thus the expected utility of a set of benefits, $Eu(b)$, is given by:

$$Eu(b) = p_1u_1(b_1) + p_2u_2(b_2)\dots p_mu_m(b_m) \tag{2.20}$$

where u_i are the utilities associated with each benefit and there are $1\dots m$ scenarios. The expected utility of a project, $Eu(P)$, is the sum of the utilities associated with all costs and benefits. More simply, it may be possible to attach utilities to the aggregate NPV results, as in:

$$\begin{aligned} Eu(P) &= \sum_{i=1}^{m} p_iu_i(\text{NPV}_i) \\ &= p_1u_1(\text{NPV}_1) + p_2u_2(\text{NPV}_2)\dots p_mu_m(\text{NPV}_m) \end{aligned} \tag{2.21}$$

If we could measure the attitude of either individuals or society as a whole toward the spectrum of risks that can occur, the expected utility approach would be an appropriate way to deal with risk: we would simply select the project with the highest expected utility. Alas matters are not that simple. Most commentators believe that it is quite impractical to derive risk utility weights for individuals or for society (see Mishan, 1982; Pearce, 1983). The fact is that the expected utility approach is rarely adopted.

A more practical approach is to allow for risk by raising the discount rate. This is common practice in the private sector where shareholders require a higher return for accepting risk. But it is a crude way of allowing for risk because it confuses time preference with risk aversion and is an imprecise way of representing individual attitudes towards risk.

Mention should also be made of the so-called *precautionary principle.* Unfortunately the principle has no agreed meaning. It may simply involve a presumption in favour of not taking risks, especially those that would harm the environment. More extremely, it may mean that no action should be taken that involves any risk of significant environmental damage. Unless such an extreme definition is adopted, which would imply very high, non-negotiable, costs for environmental protection, the precautionary principle does not have clear operational implications.

In conclusion, when risks are widely distributed, governments should seek to maximise net present values using risk-free discount rates. When risks are concentrated on particular community groups, potential sources of risk and their impacts should be identified. Studies should generally present sensitivity tests (and occasionally an estimated probability distribution of NPV results) to decision makers rather than a single NPV or ENPV figure. For publicly financed projects this approach is generally preferred to allowing for risk by modifying discount rates.

Option Values

As we saw above, an option value (OV) exists when an individual is willing to pay a premium in excess of expected use value to preserve an asset. This can occur when individuals are uncertain about the future supply of an asset or their demand for it, especially for assets such as environmental goods that are in scarce supply and not easily substituted. Allowing for option values would be consistent with the notion that most people are risk averse and that not all costs and benefits accrue to the government.

But even in these instances the complex technical literature shows that OV may be positive or negative. Risks attach to nearly all decisions. There is a risk that people may die if remote areas are not developed for energy production or if hospital services are not improved. Development may therefore have as much OV as preservation does. In his seminal article on demand uncertainty, Schmalensee (1972) concludes that OV should be assumed to be zero in applied studies. He points out there is a risk of paying for an option that could turn out to be worthless. Bishop (1982) shows that OV for risk averters facing uncertainty over the supply of an asset is usually positive. But subsequent analysis (for example Freeman, 1985) indicates that when there is uncertainty about both demand and supply, OV can be positive or negative. The general conclusions from the literature are that option values are very difficult to measure and that excluding them from CBAs does not generally bias the results.

There is an exception, which Arrow and Fisher (1974) term 'quasi-option value'. This may arise when development involves an irreversible transformation of the environment, hence a loss in perpetuity of the benefits from preservation. Although expected net benefits may indicate that development should occur, forecasts may change as new information becomes available. In this case development should be delayed or slowed down. With increasing knowledge, underinvestment can be remedied but mistaken overinvestment can not. This asymmetry means that the expected net benefits of irreversible development should be adjusted to allow for the loss of option it entails. On the other hand Fisher and Hanemann (1987) show that, if the benefits of development are uncertain, some development may be justified by the information it generates.

2.8 DEALING WITH DISTRIBUTIONAL ISSUES

As we have seen, CBA estimates the net benefit of a project regardless of the groups to whom benefits and costs accrue. There are three main reasons for using the net benefit criterion. Firstly, projects that maximise net benefits are likely to benefit more people than would less efficient projects. Secondly, project surpluses can be used to compensate losers. Thirdly, distributional objectives can be achieved more cost-effectively by fiscal instruments than by individual projects.

Unfortunately, fiscal policies frequently fail to produce a fair distribution of income. Moreover, losers from projects are often not compensated. Some projects with a positive NPV benefit the rich and disadvantage the poor. Moreover WTP values are based on the existing distribution of income. Because willingness to pay rises with income, the WTP measure biases projects towards richer households and is inequitable when goods are provided at below-cost prices. Therefore governments are usually interested in the distributional as well as the efficiency impacts of projects.

Distributional analysis has a descriptive and a normative component. The description of distributional effects shows the impacts on selected community groups. The normative component would show how the distribution of costs and benefits should affect decisions.

In order to describe the distributional impacts, the analyst must determine the social groups that matter to the government and how costs and benefits are borne or shifted between groups. Social groups must be selected because it is impractical to show the impacts on each individual. Discriminating group characteristics may include nationality, income, age, sex, health status or area of residence, to mention but a few. The choice can be difficult. Some currently poor people may have reasonable lifetime earnings expectations, some rich people may have poor health status, and so on. Inevitably the choice of social groups involves value judgements.

The shifting of impacts between groups matters because final impacts may differ from initial ones. In this regard, three points may be highlighted. Firstly, the distribution of project surpluses between producers and consumers depends on forecast prices. For example lower production costs initially benefit producers. But if the market is competitive, consumers will benefit from price reductions. Secondly, transfer payments (mainly indirect taxes and subsidies) affect the distribution of costs and benefits although they do not affect the net benefit of a project. Thirdly, secondary benefits can have substantial distributional effects, especially between areas.

In essence, incorporating distributional effects in an aggregate measure of project value means converting individual WTP values into utility values by the use of weights. Some experts (for example Little and Mirrlees, 1974; Pearce, 1983; Squire and van der Tak, 1989) propose that, instead of treating each dollar of benefit and cost equally, impacts on low income groups should be given greater weights. Using the same type of utility of income function that was discussed for the STPR, if the marginal utility of income is U_y, we can write:

$$U_y = Y^{-e} \qquad (2.22)$$

where Y is the level of income, and e is a parameter of the utility function. For example, if e is unity, the weight attached to marginal income is inversely proportional to income. Advocates of weights argue that this approach provides a measure of net social value based on equity as well as efficiency.

However there are several objections to the use of weights. Firstly, there is no generally acceptable set of weights available. Marginal tax rates may appear to provide an appropriate basis for weights. But they are not designed solely to maximise community utility. They also take into account the effects on the supply of labour. Secondly, the use of weights produces confusing results. An unweighted NPV measures the total value of consumption generally based on WTP values. A weighted NPV has no clear meaning. Weights can lead to inefficient projects being unwittingly adopted or to efficient ones being rejected. Moreover a project may have a weighted NPV that is greater than zero and still be harmful to poor households. Thirdly, practical problems may arise because the distributional analysis may include impacts such as secondary benefits that are not included in the CBA.

In summary, most governments require information on the distribution of impacts. It may be noted that a government may also seek an analysis of the financial implications for itself. A detailed distributional analysis may require data additional to those in a CBA. But the more contentious issue is the use of utility weights. These have been advocated most strenuously for project appraisals in developing countries (Little and Mirrlees, 1974; Squire and van der Tak, 1989). However it is now widely accepted that weights should not be used to factor impacts according to some hypothetical marginal utility of individuals because this confuses rather than clarifies the results for decision makers. Without conceding the argument, Little and Mirrlees (1994) recognise that it is standard practice to provide unweighted results in developing as well as developed countries.

2.9 SUMMARY

Cost–benefit analysis estimates the net consumption benefit attributable to a policy or project. Maximising net benefits and sustainable development are compatible providing that scarce natural resources are properly valued and any depletion of natural resources is compensated for by an increase in physical or human capital.

The values of both the benefits obtained from a project and the resources used (benefits forgone) are generally based on what individuals are willing to pay for the benefits and the resources, including environmental resources. In some cases it may be considered fairer to value losses using willingness to accept (compensation) values. Whether WTP or WTA values are used, the values generally reflect the preferences of the persons affected rather than government or expert values.

The basic CBA method applies in developing as well as in developed economies. However some differences may be noted. The real discount rate may be higher in developing countries, where there is often a severe shortage of savings and many poor people have a high time preference rate. Also, there may be greater aversion to risk and special concern about impacts on poor households in low income countries.

Cost benefit analysis has two important limitations. Firstly, it is not possible to value all impacts accurately, especially when physical impacts are difficult to predict or when quick practical studies are required. Secondly, the estimated net benefit of a project does not allow for the distribution of costs and benefits. In order to deal with these limitations, the cost–benefit report should generally show not only the estimated net present value of all quantified impacts, but also how changes in the quantified values affect the estimated NPV, the main elements (if any) excluded from the quantified analysis, and the estimated distribution of costs and benefits.

3 Valuation Methods: General Principles

3.1 INTRODUCTION

In this chapter we turn from the general principles of cost–benefit analysis to valuation issues. Specifically, we consider three main issues: the choice of valuation unit, or numeraire as it is sometimes called; the basic methods for valuing costs and benefits; and the strengths and weaknesses of the cost–benefit approach to valuation.

As we have seen, CBA uses monetary units of measure to transform all values into a single dimension. This creates two main technical problems. Firstly, domestic prices often differ from international prices. This has led to considerable controversy (albeit a rather sterile debate, as we shall see) over whether to use domestic or international prices as the numeraire for cost–benefit studies. Secondly, the value of monetary units varies over time with changes in price levels. In the following two sections we consider how to deal with these spatial and temporal variations in prices.

We then turn to the measurement of real economic values. In a perfectly competitive market, market prices would reflect economic (willingness to pay) values for goods and the opportunity costs of resources. There would be market prices for all services, these prices would equal the marginal costs of production and there would be little need for cost–benefit analysis as distinct from financial analysis. Such a competitive market requires, *inter alia*, marketable goods and transferable assets, many independent and informed sellers and buyers, freely determined prices with no government quantity or price controls on inputs or outputs, no taxes or subsidies and no impacts on third parties.

Not surprisingly, no market satisfies all these criteria completely and many markets fail on several counts. Common features of imperfect competition are monopoly or oligopoly pricing, government regulation of output or prices, indirect taxes and subsidies, externalities and unemployment. Sometimes there is no market at all for public goods, especially for natural environmental services.

In all such situations the analyst faces a problem of valuation: the real economic value of a benefit or cost must be estimated by adjusting the observed market price or, where there is no market price, by inferring willingness to pay values from other data. Formally, for some obscure reason, the real economic value is described as the 'shadow price'. The shadow price (SP) is given by

$$SP = MP \times CF \tag{3.1}$$

where MP stands for market price and CF for conversion factor. Importantly, the shadow price is a marginal concept. It is the value of an extra unit of output or the marginal cost of using an extra unit of a resource.

As Little and Mirrlees (1974) and many others point out, estimation of shadow prices is especially important in developing countries where markets are least formed and least competitive. Major features of market weakness or failure in developing countries are the often large subsistence sector, government controls of selected prices, imperfect labour markets associated with high levels of unemployment, overvaluation of the currency and associated restrictions on imports, and often a high rate of inflation in which time-lags or government controls, or both, distort relative prices.

The three middle sections of this chapter describe how to estimate shadow prices of resources and benefits respectively, including environmental impacts, and provide a classification of benefit valuation methods. The last part of the chapter briefly reviews criticisms of CBA valuation methods and alternatives to them.

3.2 DOMESTIC AND INTERNATIONAL PRICES

In any country it is natural to assess the costs and benefits of any proposed change in terms of local (domestic) prices. These prices should be corrected for economic distortions within the country, as discussed in the next sections. But first we consider how to deal with differences between domestic and international (border) prices. Given free trade and a freely determined exchange rate, domestic and border prices for internationally traded goods would be equal after allowance for internal transport costs. Valuation problems arise when trade or the exchange rate is regulated.

Trade regulations, such as import tariffs and quotas and export subsidies, are usually designed to protect local producers. Such regulations increase domestic prices relative to international prices. On the other hand some trade regulations assist consumers by lowering local prices, for example by restricting or taxing exports. All such distortions cause the domestic market price of a product to differ from its real economic value as expressed by its international opportunity cost.

Overall, trade regulations generally contribute to an overvalued exchange rate rather than the reverse as producer protection exceeds consumer protection. Protectionist exchange controls over capital flows, dividend payments and the like also produce an overvalued exchange rate. That is, the local currency is overvalued and foreign currency is undervalued. In these circumstances the analyst must deal both with inconsistencies between domestic and international prices and with the undervaluation of foreign exchange.

How do we deal with these issues assuming that consumption valued in domestic prices is the numeraire? A numeraire is the unit in which costs and benefits are ultimately measured. The first step is to distinguish between non-traded and traded goods (where trade means international trade) and to value them at their respective opportunity costs. Non-traded goods are valued at domestic willingness to pay prices, including shadow prices as required. Traded goods are valued at international (border) prices.

Secondly, an exchange rate is used to convert border prices from foreign currency to domestic currency units. If the official exchange rate undervalues foreign currency (or overvalues it), a shadow exchange rate (SER) is required. As discussed by Ward *et al.* (1991, pp. 35–6), the SER can be estimated in various ways. In World Bank work it is usually the estimated rate at which traded and non-traded goods exchange for each other on average. That is, the SER is the ratio of the weighted average of domestic prices of traded goods to a weighted average of border prices for the same goods. In the absence of a fully determined SER, it can be approximated by

$$\text{SER} = \text{OER} \times (1 + \text{WATR}) \tag{3.2}$$

where OER is the official exchange rate and WATR is the weighted average of import tariffs and export subsidies, with weights based on the shares of imports and exports in total trade.

Alternatively, following Little and Mirrlees (1969, 1974) and ODA (1988 and earlier editions), foreign exchange can be used as the numeraire. In this case all traded goods are again valued at border prices and non-traded goods at domestic prices, using shadow prices as required. Non-traded goods may also be separated into traded and non-traded components and valued accordingly. A standard conversion factor (SCF) is then used to convert domestic prices for non-traded goods into foreign exchange equivalents. The SCF is given by

$$\text{SCF} = \frac{\text{OER}}{\text{SER}} = \frac{1}{(1 + \text{WATR})} \tag{3.3}$$

Before comparing the numeraires, we should note two other points that apply to both numeraires. Some authors, notably Little and Mirrlees (1969), argue strongly that all tradeable goods (not just traded goods) should be valued at border prices because this shows the real opportunity costs of forgoing trade. However this approach has been criticised as impractical (Dasgupta *et al.*, 1972) and has not been widely adopted. Secondly, it is generally accepted that where specific project-based conversion factors (CFs) can be estimated, for example for the construction or transport sectors or even for products within these sectors, specific CFs should be used instead of economy-wide SCFs. However, in practice specific CFs are not often used.

Despite a huge literature on numeraires, the fact is that the choice of numeraire does not affect evaluation results. Advocates of the foreign exchange numeraire argue that it brings out the importance of international trade and discourages inefficient protectionist policies. On the other hand the UNIDO guidelines (Dasgupta *et al.*, 1972) argue that the domestic price numeraire should be preferred because most products and services are untraded, especially in developing countries. Ward *et al.* (1991), who demonstrate the equivalence of the two numeraires, consider that the choice is essentially one of convenience. The domestic price numeraire is usually more convenient when most goods are non-traded and the foreign exchange numeraire when most goods are traded.

Evidently the former case is much more common. As Little and Mirrlees (1994) acknowledge, most project appraisals over the past 15 years have used the domestic price numeraire. In this book, domestic prices are adopted as the unit of measure for each case-study. Traded goods are valued at border prices which are converted into domestic prices by using an appropriate exchange rate.

3.3 CONSTANT OR CURRENT PRICES

Project effects are generally valued in constant prices in cost–benefit studies. These are usually the prices prevailing at about the time of the appraisal. The alternative is to use forecast future prices, which are known as current (or nominal) prices. Constant prices are generally adopted because they are simpler to use, it is easier to make intertemporal comparisons using constant prices, and the inflation rate does not affect the real rate of return of a project. However we should note three implications of constant price valuations.

- The general use of constant prices presumes that the prices of all inputs and outputs will change at similar rates, so that price relativities are constant. If any price is expected to change relative to the general price level, this change in real value should be allowed for in the appraisal. For instance, if energy prices are expected to increase in real terms by 2 per cent each year, forecast energy costs and values of energy outputs should be inflated accordingly. As many writers have noted, the values of scarce environmental goods, especially those with a high income elasticity of demand, are likely to rise relative to other prices.

- Future effects should be discounted by the real rate of discount. As we saw in Chapter 2, this will generally be the real opportunity cost of capital, which is the marginal rate of return estimated in constant prices. Equation 3.4 shows that it makes no difference whether we discount a constant price benefit by the real rate of discount or a current price benefit by the nominal discount rate. The present value of the benefit, $PV(b)$, is the same:

$$PV(b) = \frac{b}{(1+r)} = \frac{b(1+\pi)}{(1+r)(1+\pi)} \tag{3.4}$$

where r is the selected real rate of discount and π is the rate of inflation.

- Unlike CBA, financial analysis may need to allow for expected inflation. Funding agencies may require a forecast of actual cash flows. Also, interest payments are made in nominal terms that include inflation.

3.4 VALUING RESOURCES

As a general principle, the value of a resource is its marginal opportunity cost (MOC). The MOC is the benefit forgone in the best alternative use. More specifically we can identify three distinct situations.

- If there is a market for a resource, the MOC is the maximum amount that another user would be willing to pay for it. In a competitive market this reflects the value of output forgone.
- In an exceptional case where there is no other potential user of the resource, for example because an input is produced especially for a particular project, the input should be valued on the basis of its constituent costs.
- If there is no market for a resource, such as public open space, the analyst has to estimate the benefits forgone by drawing on the benefit valuation principles described in the next section.

Let us now apply these valuation principles to the main resources, namely land and other natural resources, materials, energy and labour.

If land is marketable, its value is its market price adjusted for any government subsidies or taxes that affect its competitive economic value. If land is not marketable, its value is the present value of the estimated producer and consumer surpluses forgone as a result of the project. Similar valuation principles apply to the use of any natural resources (for example forests or wilderness areas).

In a competitive economy the opportunity cost of property (including housing and commercial property) is its market price. For non-commercial facilities, such as schools and hospitals, replacement costs may provide an approximate value. Likewise replacement costs may represent the approximate value of properties in non-market economies. We should note however that replacement expenditures may not reflect the full value of property to commercial owners and do not include possible losses of consumer surpluses.

The real costs of plant and equipment, materials and energy depend on how they are supplied. Let us consider four main ways of providing these inputs and the valuation implications.

- The inputs may be supplied by increased domestic production. In this case the real cost is the value of resources expended to produce the inputs. Generally, the cost is the price of the inputs net of indirect taxes and gross of subsidies (if any).
- The inputs may be supplied directly, or indirectly, by imports. An indirect increase in imports occurs when another user of a resource is forced to switch to an imported alternative. The real cost here is the import price less any tariff.
- The inputs may be supplied by reducing exports because the supplier diverts the inputs from the export market. In this instance the real cost is the export value forgone.
- When the total supply of inputs is fixed, inputs are diverted from another user. The opportunity cost in this situation is the highest price that another user would be willing to pay to obtain the inputs, gross of indirect taxes and net of subsidies.

The fourth scenario arises when a resource is controlled by a monopolist or when there is a natural resource constraint. The former case is relatively straightforward to deal with as we can usually identify the current value of a resource to an alternative user.

Valuation is more complex when the supply of a resource is fixed and consuming some of the resource now reduces the amount available to future users. The cost of present use of a unit of the resource is the net value of the unit later discounted to the present. The net value is the future gross value of the resource (its future price) less its marginal production cost (MPC). Suppose for example that the forecast price of a unit of a resource is \$10 in 10 years time, when it is expected to be exhausted. Using an 8 per cent discount rate its present value is just under \$4.6. The difference (if any) between this discounted net value and the marginal cost of producing a unit of the resource now is described as a marginal user cost (MUC) or depletion premium.

In formal terms, the marginal opportunity cost (MOC) of using a unit of a non-renewable resource is

$$\text{MOC}_1 = (\text{MPC} + \text{MUC})_1 = (\text{FP} - \text{MPC})_t/(1 + r)^t \tag{3.5}$$

where FP is the future price of the resource, subscript $_1$ represents the present year and t is the year in which the resource is exhausted. Of course, MUC is positive only when the forecast net value of the resource discounted to the present exceeds its present marginal production cost.

Finally we turn to the cost of labour. In a competitive market economy the real cost of labour is the wage required to attract workers. This reflects both the output forgone in other employment and the worker's preference for the job compared with alternative employment. In an imperfect market the project wage paid may exceed that required to attract labour, especially when the alternative is unemployment. In such situations some analysts use a shadow wage based only on the value of output forgone. This is zero when labour would be otherwise unemployed. However, to allow for some loss of informal earnings as well as for loss of leisure, the real cost of employing an unemployed worker is sometimes reckoned roughly to be half the nominal wage paid.

It should also be noted that there may be indirect costs of employing labour in a savings-short economy. This applies especially in some developing countries. The argument is that the use of labour instead of capital increases consumption and reduces the reinvestment of project surpluses and that the lower rate of reinvestment reduces the overall value of the project. Some writers, including the ODA (1988), have argued that the shadow price of labour should reflect this indirect cost. In our view, as Sen (1972) argues, it is not appropriate for each project evaluator to attempt to optimise savings in the economy. As a practical matter, few appraisals distinguish between alternative uses of project surpluses.

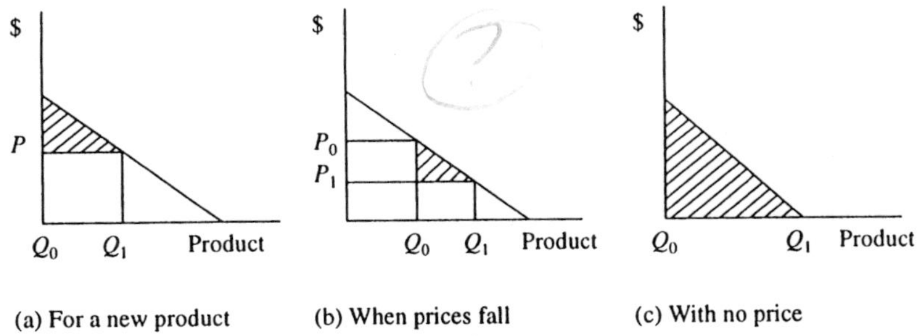

Figure 3.1 Consumer surpluses (shaded areas)

3.5 VALUING BENEFITS: GENERAL APPROACHES

Benefits may accrue as surpluses to producers or consumers. Producer surpluses are generally easier to forecast than consumer surpluses because they arise out of market transactions whereas consumer surpluses reflect non-market values. Therefore we focus below mainly on methods for valuing consumer surpluses.

As we saw in Chapter 2, the amount that individuals are willing to pay for goods corresponds to the area under part or all of the appropriate demand curve. In a perfectly competitive market, WTP amounts equal revenues. But when a new product is produced, prices change, or there is no price, WTP includes consumer surpluses. These surpluses are shown as the hatched areas in Figure 3.1.

There are broadly three ways of estimating what people are willing to pay for goods, including environmental benefits. These are:

- by observing the prices that people pay for goods in various markets;
- by observing individual expenditures of money or time to obtain goods, or to avoid their loss, and by inferring WTP amounts;
- by asking people what they are willing to pay for goods.

The first two approaches are based on observations of behaviour (revealed preferences). The third approach draws on stated preferences. The choice of valuation method depends on various factors, especially the availability of adequate data.

Using Market Data: Including Surrogate and Implicit Markets

Product markets are, of course, the main source of data for WTP values for products. However property and labour markets are also rich sources of information for many WTP values.

In a competitive market, domestic market prices inclusive of indirect taxes measure the value of goods to households. In imperfect markets, shadow prices are usually required. The following are some examples.

- When product prices, for example agricultural commodity prices or housing rents, are controlled, the analyst should estimate the full price that people are willing to pay for the product.
- Conversely, when producers are subsidised or receive higher prices from the government than they could obtain in the market, the real economic value is the producer price less the subsidy.
- When domestically produced goods are traded internationally, the relevant product value is normally the export price even if the output from the project is sold locally. The export price represents the marginal revenue obtained from increased domestic output.
- When a project is so large that it causes prices to fall, as in Figure 3.1b, the consumer surplus (CS) should be estimated. If, as is often assumed, the demand curve is linear,

$$\text{CS} = 0.5(q_1 - q_0)(p_0 - p_1) \tag{3.5}$$

where the subscripts 1 and 0 denote the quantities and prices with and without the project respectively. When price changes are large, the demand curve is more likely to be non-linear and the multiplier outside the brackets may be less than 0.5.

Even when a product is not itself marketed, its value may be inferred from the price of a marketed close substitute (a *surrogate* or *proxy price*). For example the value of unpriced water supply may be inferred from the price of water sold by private water carriers, the value of domestic fuel from woodlots inferred from the price of commercial energy substitutes, and the value of electricity for household lighting inferred from the price of paraffin (see Chapter 7).

Property prices provide considerable direct information about the effects of productive impacts on producers and amenity impacts on households. Labour markets provide data not only on labour costs but also on the value of time, the value of life itself, and the quality of the occupational environment.

Moreover many assets are composed of several attributes. For example houses have numerous attributes. Among other things they provide access to environmental services. These attributes usually have *implicit* prices that make up the total price of the asset. The technique for estimating implicit prices is known as hedonic price analysis and implicit prices are sometimes called hedonic prices. These implicit prices provide much evidence on WTP values for environmental quality. Likewise job occupations have many attributes, including various degrees of amenity and risk. When people choose between safe and risky jobs, there is usually an implicit price for safety (a lower wage). Hedonic wage-risk studies are an important source of value of life estimates.

Although product, property and labour markets provide many useful WTP data, they cannot provide useful data for non-marketed public goods, some externalities or existence values. Other data sources are needed in these cases.

Other Revealed Preference Approaches to Valuation

Households reveal their willingness to pay for environmental quality when they travel to obtain access to environmental resources or when they pay to avert or correct environmental degradation.

The *travel cost method* of valuation is based on the common observation that the use of environmental services varies inversely with the costs of access. In effect travel costs act as implicit prices for access to unpriced services. From variations in travel costs and use, we can deduce what individuals would be willing to pay for the services.

Environmental preferences can also be deduced from *defensive expenditures*. Averting expenditures are designed to prevent or mitigate environmental degradation *before* it occurs. Corrective expenditures abate or reduce the impacts of pollution *after* it occurs. Such expenditures include maintenance expenditures and, in extreme cases, the replacement or restoration of damaged assets. Defensive expenditures reveal the minimum amounts that producers and households are willing to pay to prevent environmental degradation.

The technical literature sometimes refers to the travel cost and defensive expenditure valuation methods as *household production function* valuation methods. This is because values are inferred from household expenditure on commodities that are complements or substitutes for environmental goods. Travel is a necessary complement to experience of a recreational benefit. A house insulated from noise is a substitute for a quiet environment.

Producers may also undertake defensive expenditure to avert, or correct for, environmental degradation. Although markets may provide information on defensive expenditure by the private sector, this expenditure is often not readily observable. Therefore estimates of private and public defensive expenditure may require special estimation exercises and be regarded as a distinct data source for benefit valuations.

Finally, collective valuations of environmental goods may be inferred from governmental (executive) or judicial decisions. Because such valuations are not usually based on individual preferences they are not consistent with CBA principles. Nevertheless they may provide a useful guide to community values.

Stated Preferences Methods

The stated preference approach to demand estimation draws on responses to surveys. Using the *contingent valuation* method, respondents are asked, among other things, what they would be willing to pay for an environmental attribute such as cleaner water or an unspoiled wilderness area. This provides a direct way of eliciting WTP values. Using *contingent ranking*, respondents are asked to rank a series of choices involving hypothetical money transactions and various goods. WTP values are deduced from the ordinal responses. Stated preference surveys are also the main method of determining WTA values and the only method of determining existence values.

The essence of the stated preference approach is its hypothetical nature (hence the adjective 'contingent' which is associated generically with the most commonly used application). The hypothetical nature means that stated preferences are not backed up by real economic commitments.

Analysts have attempted to make surveys economically realistic in two main ways. One is by proposing that an environmental improvement is contingent upon a hypothetical payment, such as a local property tax. Of course the realism of this depends on the credibility of the proposal. The second way is to construct markets in which payments actually take place (the *constructed market* approach). The valuation literature commonly treats constructed markets, as defined here, as an extension to the concept of contingent markets, and for convenience I follow this convention in the next chapter. However constructed markets could be regarded as closer in spirit to the revealed preference approach than to the stated preference approach.

3.6 CLASSIFICATIONS OF BENEFIT VALUATION METHODS

Unfortunately valuation authorities have used differing classifications for valuation methods. Although the methods described are similar, the variations in the classifications may cause confusion. To assist the reader, Table 3.1 shows a classification of valuation methods used by some authorities.

This book emphasises the information potential of markets. It regards substitute and implicit markets as close relatives of conventional markets, be

Table 3.1 Taxonomy of valuation methods

1. TAXONOMY ADOPTED IN THIS BOOK		
Revealed preferences		*Stated preferences*
*Market-based:**	*Other behaviour:*	
Product markets Property markets Labour markets	Travel costs Averting expenditures Corrective expenditures Public decisions	Contingent valuation Contingent ranking Constructed markets
2. OECD: PEARCE AND MARKANDYA (1989)		
Direct Methods		*Indirect Methods*
Revealed preference:	*Stated preferences:*	*Dose-responses resource costs:*
Surrogate markets Hedonic property Wage-risk Travel cost	Constructed markets Contingent valuation	Pollution – health Property damage Vegetation damage
3. WORLD BANK (1991 vol. III)		
Market-Based Methods		
Direct valuation:	*Surrogate markets:*	*Potential expenditures or WTP:*
Productivity changes Loss of earnings Defensive expenditures	Property markets Wage differences Travel costs	Replacement costs Shadow project Contingent valuation
4. WORLD BANK URBAN DIVISION: SHIN *et al.* (1992)		
Behavioural linkages		*Physical linkages*
Revealed preferences: Hedonic prices Travel costs Averting/mitigating expenditures	*Stated preferences:* Contingent valuation Contingent ranking	*Resource costs:* Productivity loss Costs of illness Human capital Replacement cost

Table 3.1 (continued)

5. WORLD BANK: MUNASINGHE (1992)

Conventional markets:	*Implicit markets*:	*Constructed markets*:
Actual behaviour Productivity changes Loss of earnings Defensive expenditures	Property values Wage differences Travel costs	Artificial markets
Potential behaviour Replacement costs Shadow project		Contingent valuation

*Including surrogate and implicit markets.

they product, property or labour markets. In contrast the World Bank (1991) distinguishes between direct market valuation and surrogate markets. Munasinghe (1992) distinguishes between conventional and implicit markets.

This book also emphasises the distinction between revealed and stated preference approaches, as do Pearce and Markandya (1989). Therefore valuations based on household production functions are linked to valuations based on markets. Some writers, such as Smith (1993), emphasise the distinction between market and non-market based methods and link valuations based on household production functions more closely to stated preference methods.

Writers such as Carson (1991) and Munasinghe (1992) use the phrase 'constructed markets' to describe all questionnaire methods of eliciting willingness to pay. Within this overall category, they describe contingent valuation surveys as a 'hypothetical' market method and surveys in which money actually changes hands as 'artifical' or 'simulated' market methods. In this volume and generally in the literature, the term 'constructed markets' refers only to the latter (artificially created) markets.

Finally, it may be observed that Pearce and Markandya (1989) adopt a separate category for dose response/resource costs. Shin *et al.* (1992) do likewise for physical linkages/resource costs. Pearce and Markandya regard dose response valuations as separate because they are applied mainly to damage estimates rather than to willingness to pay demand values. In this book we deal with the costs of damages partly in our discussions of market-based valuation methods, especially in product markets, and partly in our description of defensive expenditures.

3.7 CRITICISMS OF CBA VALUATION METHODS AND RESPONSES

Despite widespread official use of cost–benefit analysis, the technique has many critics (for example Adams, 1992; Green, 1992; Penning-Rowsell, 1992). This section lists the main criticisms in relation to environmental valuation, discusses alternatives to cost–benefit analysis and responds to the criticisms.

Criticisms of CBA Valuations of the Environment

The main criticisms of cost–benefit analysis in relation to valuing environmental impacts are as follows:

- Environmental phenomena have absolute, non-negotiable values in their own right. It is morally unacceptable to attempt to estimate non-use values. What is required is a fundamental shift in the underlying philosophy of value.
- People have such widely different attitudes to environmental attributes such as noise and visual beauty or ugliness that it is nonsense to try to estimate values for them.
- Many people are concerned about basic social issues such as the nature of 'progress', the type of cities they live in, and whether motorways are desirable or not. Cost–benefit studies about such issues as airport locations or motorway routes not only fail to resolve these basic arguments, they inflame them by their irrelevance.
- Everyone has an equal right to natural environmental assets. Willingness to pay values are based on income and are therefore irrelevant and unfair. It would be more appropriate for people to vote (one vote per adult person) on the use of environmental assets.
- Consumer sovereignty is an empirically false assumption. Many people do not know what is in their best interests, for example with respect to the consumption of alcohol, cigarettes and other drugs. For instance Gintis (1972, p. 276) argues that 'capitalism does not provide decent natural environments and hence city folk do not develop capacities to relate to natural environment. Thus decent environment becomes less 'preferred' and not a major priority in individual goal-orientations'.
- The whole of the environment is greater than its parts. The environment cannot be valued simply as a collection of discrete individual pieces of real property.

- Individuals may have different preferences in collective and individualistic situations. Therefore a collective decision may be different from the sum of individual decisions. People may individually have a high demand for a new motorway, but may nevertheless prefer public money to be spent on a national park or social welfare scheme.

Alternatives to CBA Valuations

There are two main alternatives to CBA valuations. One is to abandon environmental valuation altogether as too difficult. *Cost-effectiveness* and *environmental impact analysis* are leading examples of this approach. The other alternative is to adopt a *multi-criteria approach* that uses some other valuation procedure than that used in CBA.

In the cost-effective approach, project inputs are valued in monetary units and outputs in physical units. This is fine where a prior decision has been made to produce a particular good, for example a particular level of water quality, and the issue is how to produce this for least cost. However, as we will see in Chapter 5, cost-effectiveness cannot determine the level of water quality to be produced or compare different components of water quality. Whenever a project has more than one output or requires a decision about output quality, and most projects involve one or other of these, cost-effectiveness provides little assistance to decision makers.

Environmental impact analyses (EIAs) usually describe the physical and social impacts of projects in great detail. But the EIA process has several disadvantages. It provides no formal guide to the relative costs and benefits of the forecast environmental impacts; it is not based on any systematic theory of value; it frequently leads to double counting of environmental and social impacts ; and it provides no clear decision rule to decision makers. In the eyes of some, these limitations are a strength because an EIA is less likely than a CBA to make false claims or be misleading. I do not share such a sanguine conclusion.

The fundamental problem with these and other attempts to avoid valuations is that, when decisions are made, values are attributed implicitly to the environment. Without a common numeraire of value there is no basis for comparing environmental and other values, or even different environmental goods. In my experience, in the absence of a formal valuation procedure the implicit valuations of social and environmental impacts are often obscure.

On the other hand, multi-criteria analysis (MCA) evaluation methods are designed to value two or more criteria or impacts that have been measured in different units. The MCA approach applies weights to these impacts to determine a preferred project. Examples of MCA are utility value analysis (sometimes called decision analysis), planning balance sheets and goals-achievement matrices.

Utility value analysis, the most general form of MCA, consists of three main stages. Firstly, impacts are measured in physical units according to various criteria, such as electricity produced, air quality, visual impacts and so on. Secondly, value functions are used to transform these units into 'criterion–utilities', which indicate the extent to which the impacts fulfil the original objective, for example clean air. These criterion utilities are viewed as goal-achievement points. Thirdly, the individual criterion utilities are aggregated into one summary figure. The weights used reflect the relative importance of the criteria as judged by decision makers, experts or citizens. The weighted sum of the criterion utilities for each alternative is called utility value or project utility. If the criteria weights are agreed, the action with the highest utility value is chosen. Alternatively sensitivity tests would show how project utility (and the project decision) could change with variations in criteria weights.

MCA methods, such as utility value analysis, have some advantages compared with CBA. They are flexible. They can incorporate unquantified impacts more readily in the appraisal. Also, objectives can be weighted according to the values of decision makers, or in any other way, and are not based simply on individualistic WTP values. However this flexibility is obtained at a heavy cost: there is no consistent theory or practice for determining of weights within or between impacts or over time. Double counting is an endemic hazard. And, as noted by the Commission of the European Communities (1994, p. 31),

> There is much evidence, not all hearsay, to the effect that decision makers are remarkably adept at providing numerical weights where either there is no established unit of measurement (e.g. for a vague impact like 'Environment') or where the unit of measurement is misunderstood or forgotten. Weights derived in these circumstances are meaningless.

Responding to the Criticisms of CBA

In essence the criticisms of CBA revolve around two main points, namely that it is not reasonable or right to value all impacts using WTP values and that more weight should be given to the equity implications of actions. Both these issues were discussed in Chapter 2, so we will be brief here.

The first point to make is that, in the author's view, it would be wrong to compromise the integrity of the cost–benefit method by mixing up individual with expert or government preferences or efficiency with equity issues. CBA provides a systematic and consistent evaluation method. It is based on well-developed theoretical foundations: the principle of consumer sovereignty. As Mishan (1971) argues, whatever misgivings the analyst might have about the way preferences are formed, 'there are ultimate advantages in treating people as if in fact they do know what they want'. CBA promotes the efficient allocation of resources. It can also be applied to any action where impacts on individuals can be forecast. We should recognise however that it may be necessary to consider through surveys whether individuals value the environment as a whole differently from the sum of its parts and whether willingness to pay values may differ in collective and individualistic situations. Finally, CBA gives a clear result: whether the estimated total WTP benefits exceed the total costs.

This does not mean that a cost–benefit study, and in particular the quantified elements in the study, will provide a total picture of all impacts. As was argued in Chapter 2, it is generally desirable to provide a separate assessment of the distributional consequences of actions as well as a full description of unquantified impacts. Analysts can conduct useful CBAs that highlight the main trade-offs and opportunity costs while still recognising that non-use values may not be fully included, that many values have wide ranges, and that they do not have complete answers to some fundamental social controversies. In the final resort the political decision-making process can and often does provide an alternative weighting of impacts based more closely on the 'one person, one vote' principle than on the 'one dollar, one vote' approach. The technical evaluation does not need, and should not try, to second-guess the political decision.

3.8 CONCLUSIONS

Using cost–benefit analysis, costs and benefits are valued in one numeraire. Domestic and international price numeraires give similar results and the choice between them depends mainly on convenience. The use of domestic prices is generally more convenient when most goods are non-traded, which is a common situation with environmental resources. Using the domestic price numeraire, non-traded goods are valued in local WTP prices (corrected for domestic market distortions) and traded goods are valued in border prices (corrected for border distortions). The latter are converted into domestic currency units using the official or shadow exchange rate as appropriate.

Whichever numeraire is adopted, costs and benefits are usually valued in constant prices and discounted, as required, by an inflation-free discount rate. However CBA incorporates forecast changes in relative prices, which may be important for increasingly scarce environmental goods.

Resources are generally valued at the maximum amount that producers are willing to pay for them. If there is no alternative user, resources are valued on a cost basis. If resources are not marketed, as many natural environmental resources are not, their value is measured by what people would be willing to pay for benefits forgone. When resources are non-renewable the marginal opportunity cost is the higher of the present cost of extraction or the future net value discounted to the present.

Benefits may accrue as savings to producers or as final goods to households. In the latter case, benefits can be valued using revealed or stated preference valuation techniques. Revealed preference methods draw heavily on prices observed in product, property or labour markets. In the absence of directly observable prices, WTP values can often be inferred from surrogate prices or estimated implicit prices. WTP values can also be deduced from household travel behaviour, from defensive expenditure by households or producers, and occasionally from governmental or judicial decisions. Stated preference techniques involve asking people what they would be willing to pay, or accept, for environmental and other goods, usually in hypothetical situations. The strengths and weaknesses of these valuation methods are discussed in the next chapter.

Despite, or perhaps because of, the comprehensive nature of cost–benefit methodology, there are many critics of the valuation processes. Some critics, many of whom are not economists, are concerned more with broad philosophical issues of valuation than with detailed problems. These critics argue *inter alia* that it is inappropriate to attempt to measure non-use values; that CBA deals inadequately and unfairly with income differences; that CBA valuation methods are too limited to deal with fundamental social choices about the kind of society we want to live in; and that the valuation methods do not deal adequately with holistic problems of the environment and collective decisions.

In response, two main points have been made in this chapter. Firstly, despite its limitations cost–benefit analysis is the most systematic and consistent evaluation method available. Valuation of impacts is unavoidable and other analytical techniques, such as environmental impact analysis or utility value analysis, either fail to provide any valuation method at all or, in practice, adopt arbitrary and inconsistent weights. Secondly, the integrity of the cost–benefit method should not be compromised by mixing up individual with expert or government preferences or efficiency with equity issues. CBA gives a clear result: whether the estimated total WTP benefits exceed the total costs.

Nevertheless the results of CBA studies, and the value judgments and the data on which they are based, should be presented as transparently as possible. In particular it is generally desirable to provide a separate assessment of the distributional consequences of actions and a description of the unquantified impacts. Governments may weight impacts according to their own preferences, but they should be well informed of the opportunity costs of their decisions.

4 Valuation Methods for the Environment

4.1 INTRODUCTION

This chapter describes in more detail the main valuation methods for the environment, their strengths, weaknesses and applications. Sections 4.2 to 4.5 discuss *market-based methods*, that is valuations based on product and property markets, hedonic analysis and labour markets respectively. Sections 4.6 to 4.8 deal with *other revealed preference valuation methods*, namely travel costs, defensive expenditures, and inferences from political and judicial decisions. Sections 4.9 and 4.10 describe *stated preference methods* using contingent valuation, contingent ranking and constructed markets.

Finally there are two summary sections. The first of these summarises the relationship between the major environmental impacts identified in Chapter 1 (productivity, health, amenity and existence impacts) and the main valuation methods. The second provides some general conclusions about environmental valuation.

4.2 VALUING THE ENVIRONMENT IN PRODUCT MARKETS

Most economic effects of productivity changes can be deduced from changes in revenues and costs in product markets, even in developing countries. When goods are not marketed, their values can often be inferred from the prices of close market substitutes. Of course such valuations are essentially applications of standard cost–benefit procedures. However complications may occur when an environmental impact causes producers to change outputs or inputs, or prices, in which case consumer surpluses are also affected.

The benefit (b) of an environmental change to producers is the change in the net value of output:

$$b = \left(\sum_{i=1}^{k} p_i q_i - \sum_{j=1}^{l} c_j q_j \right)_x - \left(\sum_{i=1}^{k} p_i q_i - \sum_{j=1}^{l} c_j q_j \right)_y \tag{4.1}$$

where p, c and q denote prices, costs and quantities; there are $i = 1 \ldots k$ outputs and $j = 1 \ldots 1$ inputs; and the subscripts x and y denote the environment with and without change respectively. To estimate the net benefit to the community, the prices and costs should reflect shadow prices, as described in the previous chapter.

Examples of productivity changes associated with the environment are given in Table 4.1. As shown, there is a double benefit if output increases and inputs fall, or a double loss in the reverse case. On the other hand, output and inputs may both rise (or both fall) and to some extent offset each other.

To estimate Equation 4.1 three complications should be noted:

- *All* changes in net output, direct and indirect, associated with the environmental change should be valued. For example deforestation may open up agricultural land, but also cause soil erosion and increase sedimentation in waterways.
- To value output changes, we generally need to forecast both the impacts of the proposed action on the environment and the relationship between this environmental change and output. For example, in order to value the effects of a power station we need to forecast its impact on air quality and the impacts of marginal changes in air quality on vegetation, structures and human health. Robust technical estimates are essential prerequisites for valuations of productivity changes.
- Producers may respond to environmental changes by altering their output or their method of production, for example by changing their crop or their mix of inputs.

Table 4.1 Productive effects of some environmental changes

Environmental changes	*Output*	*Inputs*
Improvement in soil quality	Increases	Fall
Reduced pollution of fisheries	Increases	Constant
Conservation of forests	Increases	Increase
Improved water quality for industry	Constant	Fall
Soil erosion	Falls	Increase
Increased pollution of fisheries	Falls	Constant
Loss of forests	Falls	Fall
Degraded water quality for industry	Constant	Increase

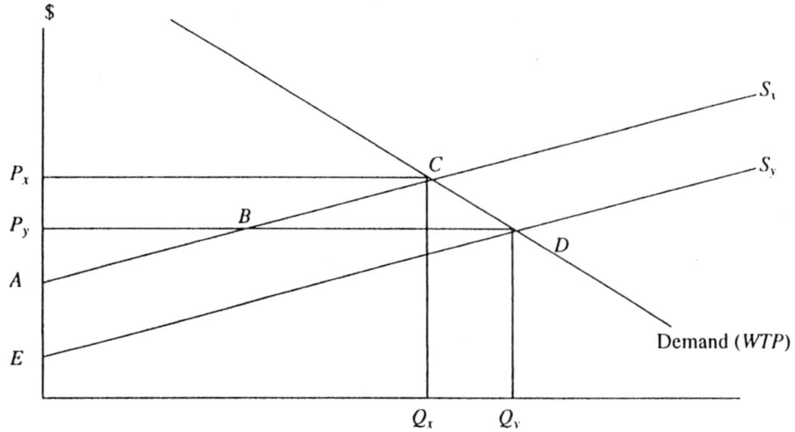

Figure 4.1 Project surpluses when costs and prices fall

Figure 4.1 illustrates producer and consumer surpluses when costs and prices change. In this figure, supply costs fall from S_x to S_y and prices from P_x to P_y. The total increase in consumer surpluses is given by area P_xCDP_y. However the part shown as P_xCBP_y offsets an equal loss of producer surplus. The sum of producer and consumer surpluses due to the fall in costs is given by the area *ACDE*.

4.3 VALUING THE ENVIRONMENT IN PROPERTY MARKETS

In a competitive market, rent reflects the periodic value of all services from a property and the asset price reflects the present values of the stream of services less maintenance costs. Given the long life of most property, asset price (P^a) and net rent (NR) measured in constant prices are related approximately by

$$P^a = \text{NR}/r \tag{4.3}$$

where r is the real rate of interest.

Therefore the short-and long-run values of land for productive or residential purposes are reflected in land rents and asset prices respectively. Also, changes in the productivity of natural resources or the amenity of the residential environment are reflected in changes in rents and prices. For instance improved soil quality should increase farm land prices.

Improvements in coastal water quality should increase the price of coastal land for tourism and residential purposes.

The values of commercial and amenity services can also be inferred from the rents and prices of developed property. For example residential property prices generally increase with reductions in traffic noise and congestion. Commercial property values are enhanced by improvements in air quality that reduce soot and corrosion.

However changes in property values may not reflect the full welfare effects of environmental changes. As we shall see, an environmental change may affect not only the principal property owner(s), but also other producers, consumers and the labour force. In these situations the welfare effects are valued by the sum of changes in all producer and consumer surpluses, including changes in real wages.

Consider, first, changes in *producer surpluses*. Two producers need to be considered: the agency that supplies the environmental change and the government in its role as tax collector. If a supplying agency charges for an improvement, for instance for improved water quality to households, the value of the improvement is reflected partly, or even wholly, in agency revenues. Also, when a property owner pays a property tax, the government gains revenue from enhanced property values. In these cases, the total willingness to pay for an environmental improvement is the sum of the changes in property values, the revenue of the supply agency and government revenue.

Secondly, changes in *consumer surpluses* must also be taken into account. We have seen that an environmental change may affect product prices as well as producer surpluses. Thus, suppose that an improvement in air quality raises agricultural productivity. If the increased output reduces product prices, the total value of the improved productivity is the increase in land rent plus the increase in consumer surplus.

A similar argument applies where an environmental change affects residential amenity. Suppose that an improvement in air quality enhances residential amenity in polluted suburban area *u*. The rent increases fully measure the improved amenity in *u* if the increases paid to landlords absorb all the benefits and renters gain no residual consumer surplus. As Polinsky and Shavell (1976) show, this occurs when the improved area is small and households can move freely within and between cities. This is the so-called 'open city' model, which is analagous to a competitive economy with mobile resources and costless transactions. At the other extreme, if households are totally immobile, rents will remain the same and all amenity improvements will accrue in surpluses to the renter. In the in-between case, in which the improved area is quite large and moving house is a significant cost, the amenity improvement is valued by the sum of the increases in rents and consumer surpluses in the improved area. We should also note that rents *outside* the improved area may fall because some demand for housing switches to *u*. But this fall in rents would be a welfare transfer from landowner to tenant in the unchanged area (a pecuniary externality) and not a net cost to society.

Thirdly, environmental conditions are likely to affect labour, as well as land, markets. Because desirable locations attract labour, environmental quality *reduces* wages as well as *increasing* rents. This was confirmed in a major US study of 253 counties by Blomquist *et al.* (1988). If the labour supply in an area is fixed, a property market study shows location-based environmental values within the area. But when labour supply and wages adjust to changes in environmental conditions, improvements in environmental values are equal to the sum of the increase in rents and the fall in wages. The valuation of location-based environmental features would then be understated if only the property market were to be considered.

To summarise, changes in property prices or rents fully and precisely reflect changes in environmental quality only when prices and rents are determined in competitive markets, other producer and consumer surpluses are constant, and the labour supply is fixed. Moreover capitalised private willingness to pay values equal social values only if private and social time discount rates are similar. These conditions are restrictive. However, as shown in Chapters 5 and 7, property values can provide rough values for some environmental changes even when strict competitive conditions do not prevail. In more sophisticated studies it should be possible, where necessary, to take into account other changes in producer and consumer surpluses and wages. Of course we have assumed that the impact of the environment on property prices can be readily identified. Professional valuers and real estate agents do this daily. However professional judgement may have to be supplemented by statistical analysis as in hedonic analysis of property prices.

4.4 HEDONIC PRICE ANALYSIS

Hedonic analysis is widely used to estimate the implicit prices of the attributes of goods. A common application is estimation of the value of environmental attributes in the housing market. This means finding the house price or rent differential associated with differences in the environmental attributes of the house. This is usually done by a cross-section, multiple regression study of house prices and the large number of variables that may influence house prices. Wage-risk studies also use the hedonic method as a basis for estimating the value of life (see next section). Implicit hedonic prices are often reasonable proxies for the amounts that people are willing to pay for environmental goods. However an implicit price represents only one point on an individual's demand curve. Therefore we need to consider when implicit prices can be used as WTP values. The rest of this section describes the derivation of implicit prices, the estimation of demand curves and the uses of hedonic pricing.

Let us consider a simplified relationship between house prices (P^h) and environmental and other variables:

$$P^h = P(S, A, E) \tag{4.4}$$

where S, A and E are sets of structural, access and environmental attributes of houses. The partial derivatives, dP^h/dS and so on, show the implicit price for each attribute.

In order to estimate a hedonic price equation such as Equation 4.4, three main problems must be resolved.

- *Variable selection.* Ideally the data set will contain sufficient size and variation to include all relevant variables. If a relevant variable is omitted, the estimated effects of included variables may be biased. On the other hand inclusion of all relevant variables may lead to multicollinearity (for example between traffic noise and air pollution or between various forms of air pollution) and the impact of each pollutant on house prices is difficult to measure.
- *Variable measurement.* Collection of measures for the variables for each property generally requires a special survey. Pollution data are often not readily available. We should also note that objective measures of pollution may not reflect the household perceptions of pollution that determine their demand for houses.
- *Functional form.* Implicit environmental prices are often sensitive to the choice of functional form. A linear hedonic equation implies that house prices fall by a constant amount per unit of pollution. But house prices may also fall by decreasing or increasing amounts as pollution increases. Some functional forms and their implications for environmental prices are illustrated in Figure 4.2. Statistical criteria are generally used to select the preferred form of the hedonic equation. However they do not always provide clear guidance to the most appropriate functional form.

Moreover house prices are determined by expected future levels of environmental quality as well as by present levels. Failure to allow for

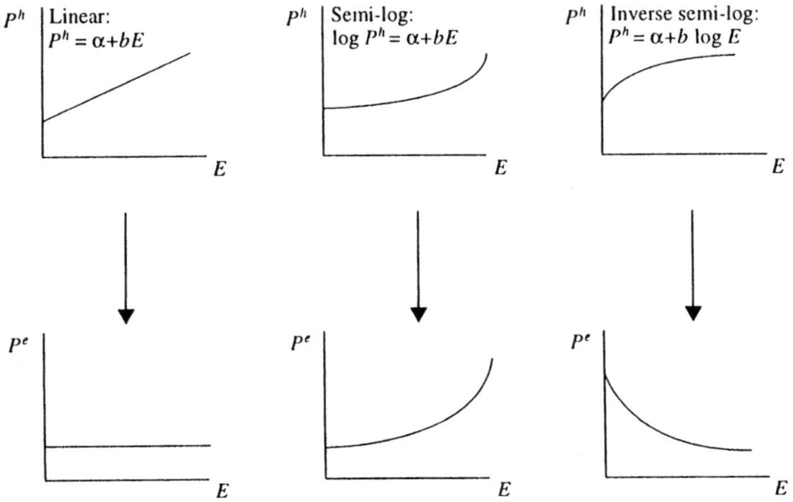

Notes: P^h = house price; E = environmental attribute such as air quality;
P^e = price of a unit of environmental attribute.

Figure 4.2 House prices and implicit environmental prices

expectations biases estimates of environmental values. Suppose that a household expects traffic noise to increase, but this is not allowed for in the analysis. The implicit price of a unit of noise would be overestimated because the property price depreciation would be associated with the current low level of noise but not with the expected higher level of noise. Abelson and Markandya (1985) discuss some valuation implications of changes in environmental quality and household preferences.

In their review of the application of hedonic studies to air quality, Graves *et al.* (1988) conclude that econometric problems make the results 'misleading at worst and unconvincing at best'. Despite these problems, surveys by Goodman (1989) and Pearce and Markandya (1989) show that the hedonic method has been applied extensively to residential property prices. Various studies indicate that a one unit increase in traffic noise (measured by L_{eq}) causes house prices to fall by between 0.14 per cent and 1.26 per cent. Others show that a 1 per cent increase in suspended particulates (air pollution) causes house prices to fall by between 0.05 per cent and 0.14 per cent. Some variation in the results is probably attributable to differences in econometric practices. The variations also reflect differences in local demand and supply conditions.

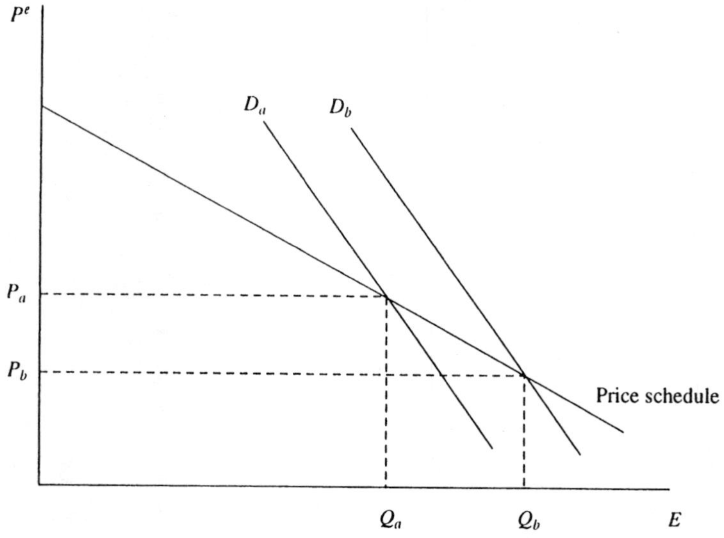

Figure 4.3 Environmental prices and the demand for environmental quality

To what extent do these implicit prices reflect WTP values? To answer this question we should note that the implicit price schedule is generally not a demand curve, but a locus of points on the demand curves of many households. Figure 4.3 shows two household (inverse) demand curves (D_a, D_b) for an environmental good with a declining price. They are inverse demand curves because price is a function of quantity demanded. In equilibrium, each household chooses a location where its marginal willingness to pay for the environmental good equals the marginal implicit price of the good. Only if all households have similar demand functions (that is, similar incomes, preferences and so on) will the implicit price curve be the same as the (inverse) demand curve.

If household demands for environmental goods differ, the benefits of non-marginal changes in the supply of environmental goods are the sum of the appropriate areas under the demand curve for each household. This is generally different from the product of the estimated hedonic price per unit of the environmental good and the change in the number of units provided. Ideally we should then estimate the aggregate demand schedule for the environmental good. If the supply of attributes in each location is fixed, the inverse demand curves can be estimated by regressing the implicit prices paid by each household (or groups of households) on observed quantities of the environmental good and various socio-economic variables. If the supply of attributes adjusts to relative prices, supply and demand equations for environmental attributes have to be estimated simultaneously.

Few studies have attempted to estimate formal demand functions for environmental attributes. The resources required are considerable and the benefits small. In lieu of estimated demand functions, implicit price schedules are commonly used as measures of WTP values. This is a reasonable approximation when the prices do not vary with environmental quality, when changes in environmental quality are small, or when households are similar.

Also, implicit environmental prices reflect WTP values only when households are well informed about both environmental quality and likely changes. For example, if purchasers are not aware of an environmental disamenity or its health impacts its implicit price will be an underestimate of its true cost. Moreover, when large changes are announced (for example that a major road will be constructed close to a residential area) housing markets need time to adjust. There may be transition costs as households change locations. The welfare costs are then the sum of the fall in property values, losses of householder surpluses (if any) and household movement costs (Abelson, 1981).

Our discussion presumes that local estimates of Equation 4.4 are available or can be made. This is often not the case. Shin *et al.* (1992) emphasise that the data requirements for hedonic price studies are large and despite an extensive review of valuation studies they found 'no application of this technique to valuation of environmental variables in developing countries'. We must ask therefore whether a simple variation of Equation 4.4 can be readily estimated. If not, to what extent (if at all) can the results of hedonic studies be transferred from the study area to other areas?

A full hedonic price study cannot be done quickly and simply as part of a standard project appraisal. In a quick study, sample size is likely to be small, important variables excluded and included variables measured incorrectly. Nevertheless the hedonic price *approach* can be used to estimate approximate WTP values (see Chapters 5 and 7). Expert valuers are accustomed to estimating marginal differences between property prices, and can be asked to estimate the impact of an environmental amenity on property prices, holding other factors constant. The accuracy of the answers depends on the precision of the questions and the seriousness with which valuers answer them. In any case the answers should be checked carefully for consistency and realism.

Transferring results is made difficult by the wide ranges found in hedonic price studies. Like other prices, implicit environmental prices depend on demand and supply. Prices are high when demand is high or supply scarce.

There has been little attempt to date to explain the estimated ranges in prices. Consequently, when analysts draw on the results of other studies they often adopt an average figure. To ensure a relevant valuation, analysts should transfer results from case-studies with similar demand and supply characteristics to the policy area.

In summary, there have been many hedonic price studies in developed economies. These provide estimates of the implicit prices of many environmental goods. These prices are based on actual behaviour and can usually be regarded as approximate WTP values. Estimated values can be transferred from research studies to policy areas if the environments have similar demand and supply characteristics.

On the other hand the results are sensitive to the econometric assumptions used. Full hedonic price studies require considerable data and cannot be done quickly. Also the implicit environmental price schedules may not represent WTP values for large environmental changes.

4.5 VALUING THE ENVIRONMENT IN LABOUR MARKETS

Labour markets provide useful information on what producers are willing to pay for labour and on the wages for which labour is willing to work. These data can be used to value productivity, or the loss of productivity due for example to ill-health or travel time, health and safety in the workplace, and even life itself. Of these topics, the value of life is most contentious and is discussed at greater length below.

In a competitive market, employer payments for labour (that is, gross wages plus related on-costs) reflect the value of a worker's marginal product. Of course many markets have imperfect elements, including government regulations, monopsonistic firms or powerful unions, which may cause employer payments to diverge from the value of a worker's marginal product. Shadow prices should be used to correct for such distortions when they are large.

Valuing Life

Traditionally the value of life was assumed to be the present value of future output or consumption forgone. The loss of output was measured by loss of earnings and this was known as the human capital method of valuation. This method produced an average value of life of around $350 000 in Europe and the US in the mid-1980s (Quinet, 1990; Rice *et al.*, 1989). The results are sensitive to age, earnings and choice of discount rate. The present value of average consumption forgone is usually similar to that for average output forgone.

Although the output and consumption forgone methods generally produced politically acceptable estimates of the value of life, both methods are flawed. Neither is consistent with the CBA principle that things are worth what individuals are willing to pay for them. Some lives (for example those of non-producers) would have little or no value. Also, the valuations are not relevant to most decisions, which are concerned with the benefits of reductions in the risk of death for many unknown people rather than the certain saving of a particular life.

At first sight it might seem that WTP or WTA values are irrelevant to valuing life. Most people would be prepared to spend virtually all their wealth to save their life. On the other hand most would refuse even higher values in compensation for the loss of their life. However it turns out that in many labour markets workers do accept higher wages to compensate for risk, or alternatively they accept lower wages for safer occupations. Thus wage differentials indicate what individuals are willing to accept for risk of death.

To estimate the relationship between wages and risks we must control for other variables that influence earnings as in the general hedonic wage equation:

$$W = W(S, X, R) \tag{4.5}$$

where W is wages in each occupation, S denotes skills such as education and experience, X represents other job attributes such as unionisation or job desirability and R is risk of death. The partial derivative (dW/dR) is the wage premium for accepting an extra risk of death (say 1 in 1000). To estimate the WTA value of life, the premium is factored up by the risk (in this case by 1000).

The hedonic wage method requires that all important independent variables can be identified and measured. The measurement of risk of death is critical. It is not easy to measure the risk of death in different occupations, especially in the post-work period, and many studies rely on death from accidents during work. Moreover dW/dR can be interpreted as a risk premium only if workers perceive the same risks as do econometricians. Another problem is the measure of job attractiveness as some risky jobs may appeal to risk-loving people.

Despite these difficulties, many wage/life-risk studies have been conducted. Cropper and Freeman (1990) report 11 studies with estimated values for life, based on reductions in risk of accidental death, ranging from \$0.44 million to \$14.9 million in 1986 prices. Most of these values are significantly higher than those estimated in human capital studies. The range in results reflects partly differences between individuals, for example in income or risk aversion. To explain why risk premia vary, it would be necessary to regress the premia on the levels of risk assumed and individual characteristics.

The range of results also indicates estimation difficulties in the hedonic-wage approach. Dickens (1984) estimates that for some workers there is a negative relationship between wages and risks and concludes that the available data do not always provide sensible wage/life-risk relationships. Pearce and Markandya (1989) note that studies show that more compensation per unit of risk is required at low levels of risk than at high levels, which is contrary to what might be expected.

Given the variation in the results and the estimation and interpretation difficulties in wage/life-risk studies, can the results be used in project analysis? In the writer's view, excluding the extreme results they indicate an appropriate order of magnitude value. The results should be combined with those obtained from other methods, mainly contingent valuation. The most relevant applications are accident reductions in occupational situations from which most wage/risk results are derived. Higher values may apply when risks are imposed on people than when they voluntarily take on risk.

It should also be possible to infer values for occupational amenity, health and safety (other than life) from hedonic wage-risk studies. However there appears to be little work of this kind.

4.6 VALUATIONS BASED ON TRAVEL COSTS

The travel cost method of valuation enables us to value many unpriced amenities. From travel costs, we can infer consumer surpluses and derive demand curves. However travel costs should not be confused with actual WTP prices or consumer surpluses.

Figure 4.4 illustrates how consumer surpluses and the value of an amenity can be estimated from travel costs. Suppose that the residents of two zones (x and y) face travel costs to a park of C_x and C_y and make an average T_x and T_y trips per capita to the park each year. Given enough zones, a negative *visitation relationship* (V_0) between trips and travel costs can be estimated. Assuming a linear relationship, a visitor to the park from x has an average surplus per trip of 0.5 ($C_n - C_x$), where C_n is the travel cost that deters all visits. A visitor from y has an average surplus of 0.5 ($C_n - C_y$). The total value of the park is obtained by summing the consumer surpluses over the populations in all relevant zones.

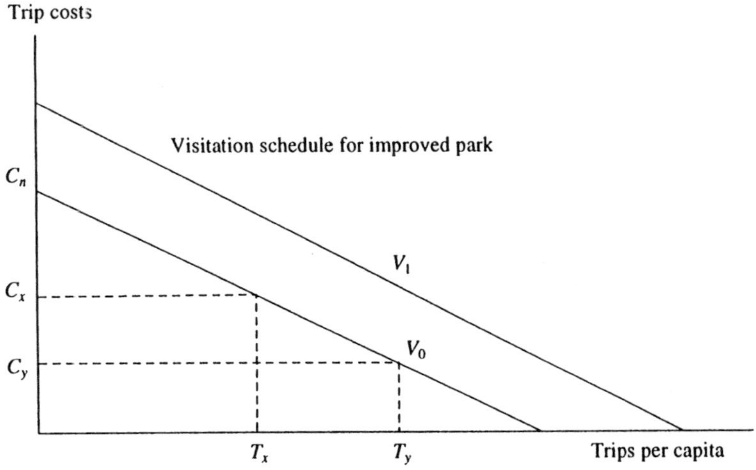

Figure 4.4 Park visits and consumer surpluses

The travel data, which are generally obtained by a visitor survey, can also be used to derive a *demand curve* for the park. The key assumption is that visitors respond to admission fees as they do to increases in travel costs. For example if a fee equal to $(C_x - C_y)$ were charged, trips from y would fall from T_y to T_x. Summing over all zones, the total number of visitors prepared to pay a fee equal to $(C_x - C_y)$ is estimated. Other points on the demand curve are found by further notional variations in the admission fee. In this case the total consumer surplus for the park is equal to the whole area under the demand curve.

In general terms, trips from zone i to site j (T_{ij}) depend on several variables, as in

$$T_{ij} = T(C_{ij}, \text{POP}_i, \text{SE}_i, X_j) \tag{4.6}$$

where POP is population, SE are the socio-economic characteristics of households, X is a vector of site attributes, i indexes origin zones and j indexes sites. The dependent variable may be expressed as average trips per person in an area or as the number of trips by each person. The literature provides no clear preference for one or other. Here we use average trips per capita, which is the more commonly used variable.

The travel cost method depends critically on accurate measures of travel costs. These include vehicle operating and travel time costs. Both components should be based on individual perceptions of marginal travel costs, because it is these perceptions that influence behaviour. Many studies have shown that commuters are prepared to pay at least a third of their hourly income to save an hour of commuting time (Button, 1993). However travel time on a recreational trip through attractive country generally has a lower cost than commuting time. In order to estimate specific travel cost values it may be necessary to obtain data on travel and vehicle operating costs in the visitor survey. This complicates the survey and is often not done. Moreover a critical assumption of the travel cost method is that the trip has a single purpose. If a trip has several purposes, travel costs must be allocated between them.

The following simple example illustrates some basic points in the travel cost method. Suppose that a simple visitation relationship is obtained from the visitor survey:

$$T_i = 200 - 10C_i \tag{4.7}$$

where T_i is annual park trips per 1000 persons in zone *i*. There are three origin zones, *x*, *y*, and *z*, with visitation rates and travel costs (C_i) as in Table 4.2. The consumer surplus per visitor from *z* (the zone furthest from the park) is \$2.5 = 0.5(\$ 20 – \$15), where \$20 is the maximum travel cost that any visitor is willing to bear and \$15 is the average cost from *z*. Similar surplus calculations can be made for *x* and *y*. The example shows the inverse relationship between travel costs and consumer surpluses. The estimated total consumer surplus of \$27 500 is the annual preservation value of the park based on existing use patterns. In order to estimate the total preservation value of the park, future surpluses must also be forecast and discounted.

However governments are more often concerned with changes in the quality of a natural asset than with losing or recreating it in its entirety. In

Table 4.2 Estimates of consumer surplus

Zone	*Trips per thousand persons per annum*	*Average travel costs (\$)*	*Average consumer surplus (\$)*	*Population (thousand)*	*Trips per annum*	*Total consumer surplus (\$)*
x	150	5.0	7.5	10	1500	11 250
y	100	10.0	5.0	20	2000	10 000
z	50	15.0	2.5	50	2500	6 250
All	75	10.9	4.6	80	6000	27 500

this case the analyst has to estimate another visitation relationship (see Schedule V_1 in Figure 4.4) and estimate the total change in consumer surplus.

The above example deals with only one site and one explanatory variable. Many recent studies estimate visitation models with many sites and multiple variables to represent individual characteristics. This enables the analyst to estimate the benefits of new sites and quality changes either directly from the estimated equations or by analysis of the estimated coefficients. For example Desvouges *et al.* (1983) explain the variations in the coefficients on travel costs for 46 sites in the US, using variables such as number of shore miles on the site, the number of recreation areas, the ratio of water to land area, and the mean and variance of the dissolved oxygen levels in the water. Smith and Karou (1987) examined 77 US travel-cost studies and found that the consumer surpluses vary consistently with type of recreation site (lake, forest, state or national park).

Based on a survey of over 200 recreational studies in the US, Walsh *et al.* (1992) estimate that the average value of a recreation day at a site of low or average quality is \$33. At a high quality site, the average value rises to \$72. The highest values are for salt water and anadromous fishing and non-motorised boating. The lowest values are for camping, picnicking and swimming. On the other hand Willis (1991) finds that the average recreational surplus per visitor day to 15 UK forests is only about \$4. Nearly all these results are sensitive to the treatment of travel time, the effects of substitutes and the selection of functional form.

In conclusion, the travel cost method has several advantages. The method is based on observable behaviour. It can be applied effectively and relatively inexpensively to single sites when conditions at alternative sites are expected to stay constant. It is a well-tried technique that produces plausible results. Also, there is some evidence that the results are similar to contingent valuation results (Johansson, 1987).

The travel cost method has significant disadvantages, too. It has limited applications. Even in the valuation of natural amenities, for which it is most appropriate, it does not provide estimates of existence values. In complex situations, especially where environmental quality changes are being considered, the data requirements are considerable. Moreover, as Bockstael *et al.* (1991, p. 238) point out, 'a whole host of issues arises in the specification and estimation of the model and subsequent calculation of consumer surplus, all of which have enormous bearing on the final benefit estimates'. These issues include the development of a multi-site model, the valuation of travel time and the treatment of non-visitors. Consequently, except for some simple cases, travel cost studies are usually conducted as self-standing research studies, or as part of large consultancy studies, with sufficient resources to address these complex issues.

4.7 VALUATIONS BASED ON DEFENSIVE EXPENDITURES

As we have seen, defensive expenditure includes averting expenditures that are intended to mitigate or eliminate the impact of pollution *before* it occurs and corrective expenditures that are designed to reduce or eliminate the impact *after* it has occurred. Examples of both kinds of expenditure are given in Table 4.3.

How can environmental values be inferred from such defensive expenditures? The answer is by assuming that profit-making producers and rational households purchase averting inputs and make corrective expenditures to the point where the marginal cost of an input is equal to the marginal cost of pollution. For example, if each L_{eq} unit of noise reduces household welfare by \$1000, the rational household will spend on noise insulation to the point where it costs \$1000 to reduce noise by one L_{eq} unit. Thus the unpriced marginal benefit of an environmental improvement (noise reduction in this case) can be inferred from the observed marginal expenditure of households and producers.

Of course defensive expenditures rarely eliminate pollution impacts completely. Therefore, where defensive expenditures are considered a reasonable measure of the pollution costs avoided, the total costs of pollution are the sum of defensive expenditures and residual pollution costs.

Table 4.3 Examples of defensive expenditures

Averting expenditures:	
Producers	Purchase of equipment to reduce toxic air emissions
	Treatment of industrial wastewater before releasing it
	Construction of earthworks to prevent adverse drainage.
Households	Health care expenditures to reduce morbidity risks
	Purchase of seat belts to reduce mortality risks
	Noise insulation expenditure to reduce noise impacts.
Corrective expenditures:	
Producers	Expenditure on fertilisers to offset soil loss
	Replacement of buildings taken in infrastructure projects.
Households	Cleaning costs for household soiling from air pollution
	Health expenditures to restore personal health.

There have been many studies of defensive expenditure by households. For example Blomquist (1979) studied the use of seatbelts (before seatbelts were mandatory) and Dardis (1980) analysed the use of smoke detectors to reduce the risk of death. Both studies valued an individual's willingness to pay to reduce his risk of death by assuming that the marginal cost of the activity equalled the marginal value of reduced risk of death. Gerking and Stanley (1986) used defensive expenditures on medical care consumption to value the health costs of air pollution. Harrington *et al.* (1989) estimated averting and mitigating expenditures as well as lost work time to measure the cost of polluted water supplies. Starkie and Johnson (1975) estimated the value of quiet in the UK from household expenditures on insulation from external noise.

Studies have also been made of defensive producer expenditures required to reduce pollution. For example Koomey (1990) reviewed several studies of abatement expenditures as proxies for the cost of air pollution from electricity generating plants. Convery (1991) estimated the replacement cost of nutrients to measure the cost of soil erosion in Ghana. Ottinger *et al.* (1990) used the cost of tree planting to value the costs of CO_2 releases.

In practice, defensive producer expenditures are routinely included in project appraisals. Nearly all major engineering projects include measures to mitigate environmental impacts. For instance most major civil projects involving earthworks are designed to prevent significant adverse changes in drainage or soil erosion. Most new power stations are designed to reduce noxious emissions, such as sulphur. Nevertheless residual pollution almost invariably occurs and may require corrective action. For example polluted waterways may have to be cleaned and corroded buildings maintained. In some cases major restoration works are required, for instance when mining companies devastate a landscape and are required to restore it to resemble the pre-mining state.

Defensive expenditures have several advantages as measures of environmental benefits. The inferred values are generally based on observable behaviour. There are many cases where expenditures can be interpreted as WTP values. Also the data, at least for producers, are often accessible and easy to incorporate into appraisals.

On the other hand the defensive expenditure valuation method has important drawbacks, especially in relation to households. Firstly, the marginal defensive expenditure associated with a unit reduction in pollution is generally difficult to estimate. As with the travel cost method, the value of household time is often a critical variable in production costs. Secondly, some expenditures, for example noise insulation or air conditioning, are lumpy and households may not be able to make marginal optimising adjustments. Thirdly, some averting activity provides joint benefits. For example water purifiers may reduce health risks and improve water quality. Fourthly, when expenditures are precautionary, the expected benefits depend on the individual's subjective probability of reduced risk, which may vary from objective probability.

Moreover the defensive expenditure method is easily misused, partly because it is relatively easy to use. Engineers frequently use abatement costs in design work without showing that the benefits therefrom exceed the costs. Caution is also required when using hypothetical replacement expenditures, such as nutrient replacement for soil loss or tree planting expenditure to avoid greenhouse effects, when the cost of the 'cure' far exceeds the cost of the disease. Basing values on hypothetical, irrational behaviour is a departure from the basic idea that defensive expenditures should be based on observable and rational behaviour.

4.8 VALUATIONS BASED ON PUBLIC DECISIONS

Governments make many decisions that imply environmental values. For instance zoning land as open space in an urban area implies that the land is at least as valuable to the community as open space as it would be in its commercial alternative. The decision by the Australian government to veto the Franklin hydro-electric dam in Tasmania implied that the preservation value of the wilderness area that was saved was at least as great as the profits forgone. Also, just as the benefits of safety have been inferred from individuals' willingness to pay for safety belts in cars, so too could the benefits of safety be inferred from government regulations on the use of safety belts, or possibly from speed limits.

However there are concerns about inferring values from government decisions. To start with, environmental values cannot be readily inferred when a decision has several consequences. For example speed limits not only save lives, they also reduce health care costs and conserve energy. Secondly, government decisions are not always consistent and based on good information. Moreover valuations implied by government decisions may be inconsistent with those based on individual preferences. This is the government's prerogative. Nevertheless there are advantages in maintaining a clear distinction between technical analysis, based on individual preferences, and political prerogative. There is also a risk of circular argument. For example if a government supports public transport, this implies that the government places an environmental value of X on air quality; because clean air is valued at X, public transport is justified. A consultant used just this approach to try to persuade the writer that the proposed investment in Lagos rail (Chapter 8) should be justified on environmental grounds.

In many countries, law courts give judgments on compensation for accidental death and injuries, often including amounts for pain and suffering. Shin *et al.* (1992) cite some interesting pollution-related court cases in Japan with regard to sea-food poisoning and air pollution. From these cases it appears that serious damage to the nervous system may be valued at about \$150 000 and respiratory problems between \$14 000 and \$42 000. Unfortunately the basis for such judgements is not always explained clearly and is rarely related to individual WTP values.

In conclusion, inferring environmental values from political and judicial decisions should be done cautiously. However there is scope for research in these areas. Also, there are cases where the inferred environmental values are broadly consistent with individual preferences and can be used in economic studies.

4.9 STATED PREFERENCES: CONTINGENT VALUATION METHOD

The contingent valuation method (CVM) uses surveys to elicit the values that people place on hypothetical changes in environmental resources. Although many economists are wary about the accuracy of answers to hypothetical questions, CVM has been used increasingly over the last 15 'years. Carson (1991) lists 10 CV studies on each of the following subjects: water quality, air quality, risk studies associated mainly with environmental accidents and the value of life and health, recreational facilities, and wildlife and hunting.

There have been a few CV studies in developing countries. These include a study of an urban park (Grandstaff and Dixon, 1986), water quality (Hsu and Liu, 1990) and water supply (Whittington *et al.*, 1990; Briscoe *et al.*, 1990). These studies suggest that CV surveys can obtain reasonable, consistent answers even from poor, illiterate respondents. However in the Taipei water quality study, Hsu and Liu (1990) deemed one quarter of the responses to be invalid and excluded them from the results, mainly because the respondents thought someone else (usually government or business) should pay for improved water quality.

The following subsection describes the basic CVM, discusses several contentious issues, considers the accuracy of CVM studies and summarises the strengths and weaknesses of the method.

Contingent Valuation: Basic Method and Some Problems

A contingent valuation survey generally asks a sample of households what they would be willing to pay to support an environmental improvement or prevent a deterioration. Alternatively households may be asked to state the minimum amount they would be willing to accept to forgo an improvement or compensate for a deterioration. These questions are usually asked in situations where payments are not made or received.

Surveys may seek to determine total WTP or WTA amounts for an environmental change, including non-use values, or attempt to identify the main separate components of total value, for example use, option and existence values. Experience has shown that asking respondents to bid for separate amounts for each element of benefit risks double counting, and that asking them to break down a stated total bid into bid categories tends to cause misattribution of elements (Hanley and Spash, 1993).

In order to elicit accurate answers, a CV survey must first establish the nature of the environmental benefit to be 'paid for' and the 'bid vehicle'. The bid vehicle is the way in which payment would hypothetically be made, for example in user fees, higher local taxes, contributions to a non-profit environmental fund and so on. Information and bid vehicle problems are discussed below, but first we consider how WTP and WTA values can be elicited:

- By an *open-ended question*. Individuals may be asked to state their maximum WTP or minimum WTA amount, with no value being suggested to them. It appears, however, that many people find it difficult to answer such a direct question, especially when they have no previous experience of the issue. Analysts have therefore tended to use other elicitation methods.
- The *payment card method*. Interviewers present respondents with a range of values from which to select. Payment cards have the drawback that they provide implied cue values, including minimum, average and maximum values, which may bias responses.
- The *bidding game technique*. Individuals are asked to respond to increasing figures until they reach their maximum WTP amount or to reducing figures if they are unwilling to pay the initial figure suggested. In this case responses may be influenced by the starting figures provided. *Starting point bias* is generally viewed as a serious problem (Cummings *et al.*, 1986).
- *Close-ended bidding technique* or *referendum model*. In this case individuals are usually presented with a single payment, which they are asked to accept or reject.

Potential biases with payment cards and starting points can be largely overcome at a cost by administering questionnaires with different payment ranges or starting points to separate households. For example different payment cards were used for the CV study of the impacts of a mining proposal in the Kakadu National Park in Australia (Imber *et al.*, 1991).

Calculation of an average value from answers using the first three methods is straightforward. However before an average is calculated, extreme low and high responses may be eliminated (see discussion below). Estimation of an average value in the referendum model is more complex because respondents have not given their maximum WTP figures. In this case a logit equation relating the probability of a 'yes' answer to each proposed amount is estimated. The area under the logit curve gives the total WTP amount.

In designing and using a CV survey, three statistical issues should be noted. Firstly, there is the question of sample size. The required sample size depends on the expected variation in responses, the desired degree of accuracy and the expected non-response rate. Table 4.4 shows some required sample sizes based on usable responses. In addition, extensive pre-testing of the questionnaire is usually necessary. Also, extra questionnaires and increased sample size are often required to reduce response biases, which are a separate problem from sampling error, and larger samples are needed for close-ended elicitation methods than for the other survey methods.

The second issue is the treatment of outliers. Extreme bids are usually eliminated on the grounds that they reflect untruthful or erroneous responses. This may be done by culling extreme answers, for example by using a 5 per cent or 10 per cent cut-off point, or by using regression techniques to estimate a bid curve (Desvouges *et al.*, 1983). The elimination is often based more on judgement than on statistical science.

The third issue relates to aggregation. Total willingness to pay may be estimated simply by multiplying the estimated mean WTP by the relevant population. Hopefully the survey will identify the population likely to value the environmental resource. However if the sampled population is not representative of the total population, the relationships between WTP (or WTA) bids and a range of independent variables, such as income, age or household size, should be estimated and used to calculate the total WTP of the population.

More Issues in Contingent Valuation

Several other problems can arise in CV studies. These include biases caused by survey design (namely information, payment vehicle and part–whole

Table 4.4 Required sample sizes based on usable responses

Values of V, a	*Maximum deviation as % of true mean* 10%	20%	30%
$V = 1.5;\ a = 0.10$	643	161	72
$V = 1.5;\ a = 0.05$	865	217	97
$V = 2.0;\ a = 0.10$	1143	286	127
$V = 2.0;\ a = 0.05$	1537	385	171
$V = 2.5;\ a = 0.10$	1786	447	199
$V = 2.5;\ a = 0.05$	2401	601	267

Notes: V = coefficient of variation; $a = 0.05$ (or 0.10) means that estimated WTP amount is within the maximum deviation 95% (or 90%) of the time.

Source: Mitchell and Carson, 1989.

biases); biases caused by respondent behaviour (strategic bias); and random error due to the hypothetical nature of the survey (sometimes described as hypothetical bias).

Information bias arises when answers depend on the information provided about the environment. In Australia, respondents' WTP values for preserving the Kakadu National Park from mining varied significantly depending on whether information presented about possible damage to the park reflected the views of the mining group or a leading conservation lobby (Imber *et al.*, 1991). A German study of willingness to pay for better air quality in Berlin (OECD, 1987) found that respondents were ignorant about the harmful substances of air pollution and increased the WTP amount of the less well-informed to allow for this information deficit. This nearly doubled the estimated benefits from improved air quality. Unfortunately WTP values cannot always be adjusted using agreed, objective criteria.

Payment vehicle bias occurs when respondents' bids vary with the payment vehicle. For example, to preserve environmental quality most individuals prefer to donate funds to non-profit conservation agencies rather than pay higher entry fees. Rowe *et al.* (1980) found that, to preserve landscape quality, individuals were willing to pay more in income tax increases than in entry fees. Pearce and Markandya (1989) state that choice of a 'neutral' vehicle is a 'research issue'. Other commentators conclude that there is no true unbiased payment vehicle. Rather the payment process should be regarded as an integral part of the provision process.

Another potentially important survey bias is *part–whole* bias. This bias occurs when a respondent fails to distinguish between the value of a particular environment, say a bird sanctuary, and the value of the wider group of environments (all bird sanctuaries) of which it is part. For example many critics argued that respondents would have placed a lower WTP value on the mining area in the Kakadu National Park if they had taken into account all the other parts of the park and indeed of Australia that they wanted to preserve (Resource Assessment Commission, 1991). Kahneman and Knetsch (1992) reported no significant difference between mean WTP for a small number (1 per cent) of lakes in Ontario and mean WTP for all lakes in the province. Similarly Carson (1991) notes that there can be a sequence problem: respondents may state a high WTP for the first environmental good and progressively lower values for subsequent goods. However surveys can be designed to bring out the budget constraint. For example Willis and Garrod (1991) identified the respondent's total recreation budget before asking WTP values specifically for the Yorkshire Dales national park.

Strategic bias occurs when respondents lie about what they are willing to pay or accept for environmental changes. In the traditional model of public good provision where each good is separately funded, it was expected that, to reduce their liability to pay, respondents would understate what they would be willing to pay for a public good. However when public goods are funded from general funds and proposed payments are notional, potential beneficiaries are more likely to overstate their WTP amounts. Exaggeration of WTA amounts is also rational behaviour for many respondents.

Despite these incentives to lie, many commentators conclude that strategic bias is not a major problem and that it can be contained by careful survey design. Based on experimental research, Bohm (1972) argues that most people are inclined to answer questions honestly. Hoehn and Randall (1987) argue that with close-ended bidding, honesty is the respondents' best strategy. Freeman (1986) contends that there is little evidence of free-rider behaviour. Mitchell and Carson (1989) propose that strategic bias can be minimised by removing all outliers, by not revealing other respondents' bids, by stressing that payments by others are guaranteed and by making the environmental change dependent on the bid.

However the last two conditions are rarely practical. In real negotiating situations, for example in labour market negotiations and in market bazaars around the world, most parties overstate their true position. This writer's view, based partly on eight years as an elected representative in local government in Australia, is that people are prone to exaggerate their needs if they believe that this will influence the outcome. Consistent with this view, WTP values quoted in surveys often appear high (Hanley and Spash, 1993).

Hypothetical bias may occur simply because, in a CV survey, individuals respond to hypothetical market questions rather than real ones. It has been found that inaccuracy increases when respondents are asked to value unfamiliar and non-marketed goods (Kneese, 1984; Cummings *et al.*, 1986). In such cases individuals cannot learn from the experience of regular purchases. Even if they try to give an accurate answer, they may fail.

Attempts have been made to test for hypothetical bias by comparing survey results with actual payments. In a much-quoted study, Heberlein and Bishop (1986) tested whether hypothetical and actual payments for goose hunting permits were similar. Unfortunately, despite extensive analysis of their data, commentators cannot agree on the implications. Another comparison of hypothetical and actual payments by Coursey *et al.* (1986) concluded that hypothetical bias did exist. Of course if the hypothetical nature of the survey only increases errors, but does not cause bias, the problem may be overcome by increasing sample size.

A more fundamental issue (which is often overlooked in the literature) is the willingness or otherwise of households to accept the basic premise of a CV survey that households may be required to pay for an environmental change. This may be a plausible assumption in the US, where most CV studies have been done, but even in developed market economies people are sometimes reluctant to accept this premise. For example many elderly people eligible for medical benefits in the UK and Scandinavian countries are very reluctant to state their willingness to pay for health services that they are accustomed to receiving free of charge – many responded to CV questions with protest zeros (communication with Dr Rushby, London School of Tropical Medicine). It was noted above that some Taiwanese were reluctant to state what they were willing to pay for water quality. In another example of this problem, Jim Winpenny (Overseas Development Institute) told me that he had considered trying to run a CV survey of WTP amounts for beach facilities in Barbados where, as in many places, the beach is a free public good. The likely political uproar made this totally impractical. Generally, CV studies are of limited use where there are highly entrenched property rights, or where there are acrimonious disputes about the allocation of property rights and income. Some examples are reported in the case-studies in this volume.

To summarise, each of the above biases is a potentially serious problem. The three survey biases (information, payment vehicle and part–whole biases) can be overcome to some extent by extensively tested survey design and by administering different questionnaires to separate groups. Strategic bias is more difficult to test for, especially in hypothetical situations.

Hypothetical bias may be reduced by increasing sample size. Considerable resources are required to eliminate excessive bias from CV surveys and to obtain accurate answers.

How Accurate is Contingent Valuation?

How does the analyst know whether accurate answers have been obtained? Responses are usually considered accurate if they correspond to market values. This is not easy to demonstrate in the absence of markets, which is where contingent valuation is intended to be useful.

The accuracy of CV results is tested most commonly by comparing the results with those obtained using other valuation techniques, especially hedonic property price and travel cost studies. Of course this test presumes that the results of the comparison studies are correct. Pearce and Markandya (1989) reviewed the results of eight studies containing 15 such comparisons and conclude that all the CV results are within plus or minus 60 per cent of the estimates in the comparison studies. They argue that these are familiar ranges of error in demand estimates. The World Bank (1991) acknowledges that these results are not very precise, but regards them as 'reasonably reassuring' and indicative of the potential use of CV studies.

Smith (1993) outlines another six tests of CVM, including the use of constructed markets in which goods are actually purchased, consistency with demand theory (for example stated WTP should rise at a plausible rate with household income), stability of CVM results in test/retest comparisons, laboratory experiments, and comparisons of purchase intentions revealed in surveys with actual purchases. He quotes 10 studies that draw on one or other of these tests. Smith concludes that CVM can provide plausible measures of individuals' values for some types of environmental resources. However we have not yet identified the characteristics of the resources that can be so valued, the attributes of the people whose values are to be measured or the features of the survey that most influence the reliability of CVM results.

It is important that criteria for the acceptability of a CV study be established because, notwithstanding the general acceptability of CVM, particular CV studies may produce misleading results. Project economists can rarely compare the results of a CV study in the field with results from another valuation technique in the same geographical area. The main practical criteria for the acceptability of a one-off CV study are internal consistency of responses, consistency with the predictions of economic theory, and consistency with the results of other credible studies dealing with a similar topic in a not dissimilar environment. For example the consultants in the Lagos rail study (Chapter 8) conducted a CV study of 600 bus users to try to discover local value(s) of travel time savings. They discarded the results because the responses were internally inconsistent and the reported values were unbelievably high relative to capacity to pay. On the other hand, in their study of WTP for water services in Haiti, Whittington *et al.* (1990) found that the explanatory variables conformed with standard expectations as defined by economic theory.

A special problem has arisen over the acceptability of reported WTA values because these have often been several times higher than estimated WTP values. In a seminal article Willig (1976) concludes that, based on the marginal utility of income, WTA values lie within 5 per cent of WTP values unless the WTP amount for the demanded good is a high percentage of income. The high WTA values have created a suspicion that CV surveys have been subject to strategic bias. On the other hand, psychologists (such as Kahnemann and Tversky, 1979) argue that people value owned assets much more highly than similar unowned assets.

More recently, Hanemann (1991) has shown that the WTA/WTP ratio is inversely related to the substitutability of the demanded good. He concludes that the WTA/WTP ratio can exceed five when the subject good is unique or has a very low degree of substitutability or when the WTP/income ratio is high. However he confirms that the WTA/WTP ratio should be close to one when the WTP/income ratio is low and the elasticity of substitution for the subject good is not low.

Advantages and Disadvantages of Contingent Valuation Studies

CVM can be applied to most environmental resources. It is the only method that can measure non-use benefits and WTA values. Although there are several sources of bias in CVM, most of these can be dealt with by appropriate survey techniques. Also, the results of CV studies have been shown to be broadly consistent with the results of market-based valuation studies.

On the other hand the very facility with which CV can be used represents a risk. Bad CV studies are easy to do. CVM is least useful in hypothetical situations where people are unfamiliar with the subject environment, where it is usually most needed. Validation of one-off surveys is a problem. CV surveys usually produce only one point on an (inverse) demand curve; complex surveys are required to estimate more than one point. Finally, it is questionable whether accurate answers can be obtained from CV studies when property rights are bitterly disputed or when major changes in established property rights are proposed.

4.10 CONTINGENT RANKING AND CONSTRUCTED MARKETS

Contingent Ranking Method

The contingent ranking method (CRM) is an alternative technique used occasionally to elicit values in hypothetical markets. CRM is based on asking people how they rank alternatives rather than how much they would be willing to pay for goods. Because the method uses discrete choices, it is sometimes described as a referendum method (Bockstael *et al.*, 1991).

For example, in order to estimate the toll that people would be willing to pay to use a new freeway a CR survey might ask respondents to rank the following:

(a) Saving 10 minutes of travel time – at a cost of $0.50
(b) Saving 20 minutes of travel time – at a cost of $1.50
(c) Saving 30 minutes of travel time – at a cost of $2.20
(d) Saving 45 minutes of travel time – at a cost of $3.00

From such a ranking a maximum likelihood estimator routine can be used to estimate an indirect utility function:

$$U = u(T, C, Y) \tag{4.7}$$

where u is utility, T is travel time, C is the cost of the toll and Y is income. Holding utility constant, a trade-off between travel time and toll cost can be estimated. Cameron and James (1987) describe how the parameters of the utility and expenditure functions can be estimated.

Contingent ranking has the advantage that respondents often find it easier to rank non-market alternatives than to state what they would pay for them. On the other hand respondents can be confused by a choice of more than about five similar options. Because CRM uses only ordinal information it requires a larger sample size than CVM. Also, CRM estimates are subject to vehicle bid bias, the estimates are sensitive to the number and kind of alternatives ranked and to econometric specification, and CRM is more demanding econometrically than other valuation methods.

Constructed Markets

As defined in Chapter 3, constructed markets refer to any market in which money actually changes hands for a usually unmarketed good. Carson (1991) cites 10 such studies including five laboratory studies and five mail surveys (whereas most CV studies employ the more expensive personal interview method).

Constructed market studies have been designed mainly to test the performance of CV studies, for example the importance of free riding and the differences between WTP and WTA values. They have therefore been complements, not alternatives, to CV studies. Obviously, if substantial money were to change hands there would be no difference between constructed and real markets, other than any difference due to the one-off nature of the constructed market.

4.11 ENVIRONMENTAL ISSUES AND VALUATION METHODS

Table 4.5 shows the main environmental impacts identified in Chapter 1 along with the main valuation methods discussed above. To condense the matrix, 'standard markets' includes product, property and factor markets, and proxy prices. A tick indicates that the valuation method can generally be applied to the relevant impact; a question mark means that the valuation method may apply; a cross means that the valuation method generally does not apply.

Not surprisingly, *productivity changes* are generally valued using data from product markets. Even when markets do not exist, as for some public sector activities, changes in production costs may be the relevant measure of benefit or cost. Product market data also provide the basis for estimates of consumer surpluses when prices change.

Productivity impacts may also be measured by changes in property values, when private property rights exist. Averting or corrective expenditures can provide a measure of damage avoided in many cases of productivity impact. Travel cost and contingent valuation methods are rarely used to value productivity changes.

Health impacts require different valuation methods. Loss of life has been valued using hedonic wages, averting expenditures and contingent valuation. To cost illness, labour market data can be used to value work days lost, corrective expenditures to value medical expenses, and contingent valuation to value the costs of restricted activity days and pain and suffering.

Contingent valuation is the main technique used to value *non-market amenity goods*. CVM can deal with qualitative aesthetic changes, it can generate the necessary data for most goods and it can be used to obtain values from non-users. However there are problems of accuracy and validation. The travel cost method has been widely used to value the benefits of recreational sites. However TCM has limited application outside

Table 4.5 Applications of valuation methods

	Standard markets[1]	*Hedonic property*	*Hedonic wages*	*Travel costs*	*Averting*[2] *expenditure*	*Corrective expenditure*	*Contingent valuation*
Productivity:							
Soil loss	√	?	x	x	√	√	x
Crop damage	√	?	x	x	√	√	x
Forest loss	?	x	x	x	√	√	?
Habitat/species loss	?	x	x	?	√	√	?
Fisheries depletion	√	x	x	x	√	√	x
Water quality loss	?	x	x	x	√	√	x
Property/materials damage	√	?	x	x	√	√	x
Other resource depletion[3]	√	?	x	x	√	√	x
Health:							
Loss of life	?[4]	x	√	x	√	x	√
Illness –							
Work days lost	√	x	x	x	x	x	x
Restricted activity days	x	x	x	x	x	x	√
Pain and suffering	x	x	x	x	x	x	√
Medical expenses	x	x	x	x	x	√	x
Amenity:							
Recreation losses[5]	x	?	x	√	?	?	√
Habitat/species loss	?	x	x	?	√	√	√
Aesthetic damages[6]	x	√	x	x	√	x	√
Noise	x	√	x	x	√	x	√
Other:							
Existence values	x	x	x	x	?	x	√
Occupational environment	x	x	√	x	x	x	√
Access to water supplies	?	?	x	√	x	x	√
Sanitation services	?	√	x	x	x	x	√
Travel time savings	√	√	x	x	x	x	√

Notes:
1. Including product, property and labour markets, and surrogate prices.
2. Including averting expenditures required by government, for example policies to reduce CO_2 emission.
3. Depletion of energy and mineral resources.
4. Human capital approach.
5. Loss of recreational opportunities or quality, for example in lakes, parks and so on.
6. Visual, odour (scenery) degradation.

recreation. The hedonic property price method can be used to value aesthetic effects, air pollution and noise in residential areas. But it cannot value aesthetic goods that are located away from residential areas. Also, averting or corrective expenditures may provide indicators of value for many forms of amenity.

The 'Other' category shown in Table 4.5 includes existence values and some impacts that do not fall wholly in one of the three major categories (productivity, health or amenity). CVM is again the main technique used, especially for existence values. Apart from CVM, a range of techniques can be used according to requirements. Hedonic wages could be used to value the environmental quality of the occupational environment, TCM to value access to water supply, hedonic property prices to value provision of sanitation services to homes, labour markets and hedonic property prices to value travel time savings.

Clearly valuation methods must be selected to suit the purpose. However, sometimes only two or three methods may be appropriate. Therefore to value all effects of a complex project, a mixture of valuation methods is generally used. Care is then required to avoid double counting. Summing the values of specific classes of use and non-use across all categories may fail to allow for interactions among categories and result in overcounting of demands (Randall, 1991). The alternative is a composite evaluation of impacts, in which case contingent valuation is usually the sole option.

4.10 CONCLUSIONS

This chapter has described the main valuation methods, their strengths, weaknesses and applications. In concluding, I make some general points that affect most valuation methods rather than repeat points about specific methods.

Firstly, most valuations are information-intensive irrespective of the valuation method employed. Many valuations require considerable technical input. Productivity valuations require data on price and behaviour responses. Health valuations require information on the nexus between the environment and health. Revealed preference valuations of amenity impacts require data on individual perceptions of the environment. CVM studies of amenity must usually present detailed information to respondents. Generally, much is still unknown about environmental impacts, especially complex ecological changes.

Secondly, markets are important for all valuation methods, not just for those that draw directly on market data. The less familiar people are with markets, the less accurate willingness to pay responses are likely to be. WTP responses in CV surveys are likely to be especially wild when there are major disagreements about property rights.

Thirdly, all valuation methods have serious, though surmountable, problems. No method is cheap or simple. There are many unreported failures for each valuation method. Validation of each study is therefore essential. The main criteria of study validity are theoretical soundness of method, results that are consistent with economic theory, and results that are not inconsistent with those found by reputable studies in other similar situations.

Fourthly, it is often too expensive to conduct valuation studies *de nuovo*. The transferability of results from one context to another is therefore a critical issue. Transferability is complicated by the wide variation in results for similar environmental goods, for example for air pollution and noise. Also, most valuation studies produce estimates of willingness to pay amounts rather than estimates of demand functions. The analyst must then assess how much of the variation in WTP estimates is due to study errors and how much to differences in demand and supply. Often analysts simply transfer the average results of other studies, which implies that the variations are due only to errors. Alternative procedures for transferring results from one context to another are discussed in Chapter 11.

Fifthly, there are two main aggregation problems. One is the risk that impacts will be double counted unless they are valued within the discipline of a total value framework and income budget constraint. The second problem is the more fundamental one of aggregating benefits and costs over all individuals. Standard practice is to use average values even when individuals hold a wide range of values, and to aggregate values although some individuals may gain and others lose from an environmental change. Generally, the analyst should explicitly present the distributional consequences of possible changes rather than conceal them.

Finally, as the reader will appreciate, the voluminous and growing literature on valuation methods treats many issues in greater detail than has been possible here. For further reference, the reader may find especially useful the short surveys on valuation methods by Pearce and Markandya (1989), Shin *et al.* (1992) and Smith (1993). Excellent, more detailed texts on valuation methods include Pearce (1978), Freeman (1979), Hufschmidt *et al.* (1983), Dixon and Hufschmidt (1986), Johansson (1987), Braden and Kolstad (1991) and Hanley and Spash (1993).

5 Valuing Water Quality in Wuxi, China

5.1 INTRODUCTION

In many countries, water pollution is the most pressing environmental problem. Water pollution reduces the quantity of useable water, increases the costs of supplying water, is a major cause of human disease, adversely effects aquatic species and reduces recreational opportunities.

In urban areas, industrial and domestic wastewater are major causes of water pollution. Urban water quality can be improved by raising the quality of wastewater, by redirecting wastewater away from sensitive locations, or by collecting and treating wastewater. However wastewater management is expensive. In developing countries, total public investment in water supply, sanitation and wastewater systems accounts for 10 per cent of all public investment. In order to allocate resources efficiently, measures of the benefits of water quality are required.

To illustrate these points, this chapter evaluates proposed investments in wastewater collection and treatment in Wuxi, China. Wuxi City (population 930 000) is a substantial industrial, trading and tourist centre 128 km to the north-west of Shanghai (see Figure 5.1). It is also the administrative centre for the Wuxi Administrative District (total population 4.3 million), which includes three counties (Jiangyin, Yixing and Wuxi County). The city itself is laced with over 200 km of waterways, has many wide tree-lined streets and much solid housing. Hills to the north and west provide a scenic backdrop and the extensive Lake Tai (2200 square kilometres) to the south-west is a major recreational attraction. Average annual household wage income in Wuxi in 1992 was about US$1000, but many goods and services, including housing, are heavily subsidised from public enterprise taxes or surpluses, so that real income substantially exceeds wage payments. Most households have refrigerators, over a half have colour televisions and one third have video players.

Over the last thirty years water quality in Wuxi has deteriorated greatly. In the 1960s the water in the city canals was suitable for swimming, washing and fishing. Today much of the water is septic and malodorous. Lake Tai is suffering from eutrophication and is deteriorating as a water

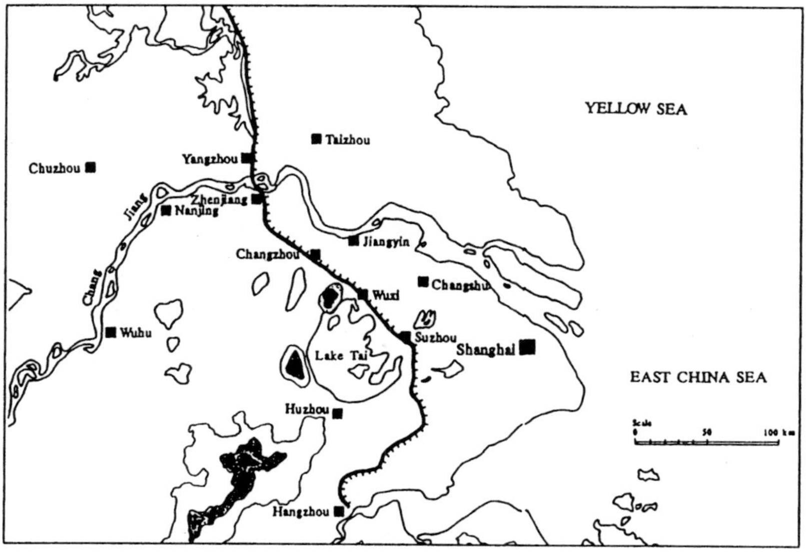

Source: Watson Hawkesley, 1992

Figure 5.1 Location plan

supply source, habitat for fish and recreational amenity. In order to reduce the pollution the Wuxi authorities implemented several initiatives in the 1980s, including standards for discharge of effluent into waterways and wastewater collection and treatment facilities. In 1991–92 consultants Watson Hawksley, together with the local authorities, developed a wastewater masterplan that proposes greatly to augment these wastewater facilities. The consultants were funded by the UK Overseas Development Administration as part of a programme of pollution control in the Wuxi Grand Canal. The fundamental objective of the masterplan is to improve water quality in and around Wuxi. This masterplan, and its prospective costs and benefits, are the subject of this chapter.

To provide a general perspective, we start with an overview of the main general issues in urban water quality and the provision of wastewater services. The chapter then describes water quality issues in Wuxi, the wastewater masterplan and the main alternatives. The following sections describe forecast improvements in water quality, discuss and quantify the main benefits of improved water quality in and around Wuxi, and present the cost–benefit results. There is a brief concluding section.

5.2 WATER QUALITY: GENERAL ISSUES

Uses of Water and Costs of Polluted Water

Water quality matters mainly because people want to use water. There are two major categories of water use – instream and withdrawal uses. Instream uses include fishing, swimming and boating, washing clothes and food, as well as more indirect uses such as riverside walks and picnics. Polluted water reduces the quantity and quality of recreational use and affects aquatic and marine life. Also, ingestion of polluted water is a major cause of gastrointestinal diseases, including cholera and typhoid.

Withdrawal uses include the use of water for domestic, industrial, agricultural and maricultural purposes. Polluted water increases the cost of treating withdrawn water. When water quality deteriorates too much the cost of treatment becomes prohibitive and the supply of water declines. Polluted water may also reduce agricultural and mariculture productivity. If polluted water is withdrawn without adequate treatment, water supplies and the food chain may be contaminated and disease may result.

Some studies have found that water quality is also important to households who do not use it. For example Kneese (1984) found that non-recreationalists in the US were willing to pay 45 per cent of the amount that recreationalists were willing to pay for water quality. Kneese argued that this reflected the 'intrinsic' value of water quality and that, when the willingness to pay amounts of all respondents were consolidated, the intrinsic value amounted to 55 per cent of the total instream value of water. The UK Water Research and Flood Hazard Centres (1989) also found that many people attach a high importance to the intrinsic benefit of water quality.

Measures of Water Quality

Water quality has numerous attributes and there are correspondingly many measures of water quality. A waterway may score well on one measure and poorly on another. Therefore we need to know which attributes are most important and why. For practical purposes it is convenient to distinguish between degradable and non-degradable substances, although the distinction is not absolute. Whereas degradable substances (most organic wastes) are gradually reduced by natural biological processes, non-degradable substances remain intact or degrade very slowly.

The degradation of organic substances (by bacteria in waterbodies) depletes the dissolved oxygen (DO) content of the water. If a waterway is overloaded with degradable discharges it can become completely anerobic, with DO falling to zero. At low DO levels below about 2 ppm waterways develop an offensive odour, organic wastes are merely diluted and carried downstream, fish and other aquatic life cannot survive and the water becomes unusable for most purposes. Biochemical oxygen demand (BOD) and chemical oxygen demand (COD) are also useful measures of the quantities of degradable (biological and chemical) substances in waterways. Clearly, high levels of BOD and COD are undesirable.

Non-degradable discharges include many hundreds of chemicals for which there is no simple classification. Suspended solids reduce the transparency of water; this interferes with natural processes and makes water unattractive. Nutrients such as phosphorous and nitrogen fertilise waterbodies and accelerate eutrophication. Non-degradables also include toxic substances such as pesticides and heavy metals, which may affect drinking water and enter the aquatic food chain.

Sources of Water Pollution

In developing countries the major sources of BOD discharges into waterbodies are wastewaters carrying domestic sewage and organic discharges from industries that are not served by municipal sewage systems. Runoff from urban areas and agriculture can also substantially contribute to BOD loads.

Most toxic substances in water bodies come from untreated industrial wastewater. Suspended solids are discharged into water bodies from construction activity, agriculture, households and natural erosion. Nutrients are discharged from industry, agriculture and municipal sewage systems.

Policies for Water Pollution Abatement

Industrial water pollution can be reduced directly by improving the quality of wastewater before it is discharged into public waterbodies or waste disposal systems. This can be done by reducing the quality of noxious materials in production processes, by treating wastewater in-house before disposal and by separating out hazardous materials from less harmful effluents. Effluent taxes can encourage these practices. Nevertheless residual amounts of wastewater are likely to require collection and treatment before they can be returned to public waterbodies.

When dealing with domestic wastewater in cities there is often no effective alternative to expensive waterborne wastewater systems costing several hundred dollars per household. Depending on circumstances, these systems may involve 'conduits for collection and conveyance of wastewater, pumping stations, conventional and innovative treatment works, wastewater reclamation and reuse projects, ocean outfalls, wastewater treatment sludge management facilities, a variety of small-scale sanitation systems for rural and urban areas, and urban stormwater drainage projects' (World Bank, 1991, Vol. II, p. 231). In outer urban areas, cheaper technologies of waste disposal – including package sewage and collection treatment systems, mixed septic tank-conventional systems and smaller sewers with fewer manholes – may be appropriate.

Wastewater systems may also have negative impacts, including the shifting of waste from one area to another with varying degrees of treatment, so that the recipient area bears some costs and suffers sewer overflows and treatment process failures. Treatment plants may be a local nuisance as treatment processes and sludge disposal operations may cause unwanted odours and noises. Worker accidents may be caused by gas accumulation in sewers and other confined spaces, hazardous materials discharged into sewers and chlorine accidents.

Comprehensive wastewater system planning requires full consideration of technological alternatives for collection systems, treatment works, waste disposal and sludge management; effective treatment of toxic industrial wastes before they enter the municipal waste system; full consideration of the socio-economic impacts of the alternatives; and effective operation and maintenance procedures (World Bank, 1991, Vol. II, pp. 232–8).

Evaluation of Water Pollution Abatement

Traditionally engineers have justified pollution abatement projects on cost-effective grounds. They have sought to show that proposed projects can achieve the desired water quality standards at least cost. This presumes that the standards are appropriate and can be determined independently of the costs and benefits of wastewater treatment.

In their seminal contribution, Feenberg and Mills (1980, p. 3) show that 'a coherent body of theoretical tools is now available' to measure the benefits of water quality. Instream benefits accrue mainly to consumers. Although these benefits are often in the nature of public goods, consumer willingness to pay for water quality can be assessed through contingent valuation surveys, travel cost studies and property value studies. Withdrawal benefits generally accrue in the first instance to producers through cost savings. These savings can be estimated with enough knowledge of production functions and of the ways in which producers can respond to changes in input quality and costs. However Feenberg and Mills also note (p. 3) that 'there are still disturbingly few high-quality empirical studies of benefit measurement available' and conclude (p. 169) that 'there is a nearvacuum of empirical studies of benefit of water pollution abatement'. The key difficulty, they contend, is the scarcity of useable data. Many visitor surveys are poorly conducted and there are few data on the impacts of water quality on production costs and health.

In the late 1980s the UK Water Research Centre and Coopers and Lybrand (1989) developed investment appraisal techniques for sewerage schemes, mainly renovation schemes. They evaluated three main benefits: the benefits arising from flood alleviation, the reduced risk of disruption from sewer rehabilitation or collapse, and recreational benefits arising from water quality improvement. The latter were estimated through a contingent valuation survey.

The World Bank has encouraged economic evaluations of water pollution abatement programmes in developing countries. However these studies are often based on crude estimates of production cost savings and property value increases using data of doubtful reliability (see Section 5.8).

5.3 WATER QUALITY IN WUXI

Water Supply and Uses in Wuxi

Wuxi has a plentiful supply of water. The city is located in the Yangtse River delta, 40 km south of the Chang Jiang (Yangtse River) on the northern shores of Lake Tai. The Wuxi area is low-lying, and receives a plentiful supply of rainwater (between 100 centimetres and 150 centimetres annually). Many waterways run through the area, including the Grand Canal and the Liangxi and Xicheng rivers, which connect with the Yangtse (see Figure 5.2).

Water flows down from the north into the extensive Wuxi canals. The canals, especially the Grand Canal, provide a major transportation system in and through Wuxi. There are 12 400 registered barges in Wuxi. There are also numerous links between the canal system and Lake Tai. For two thirds of the year the water flows east from Lake Tai into the Wuxi canals; at other times it flows in the reverse direction.

The Wuxi Water Supply Company annually supplies about 190 million cubic metres of piped water to the Wuxi urban area. Industry takes two thirds and households the other third. Three quarters of the water comes from Lake Tai; the rest comes from the Xibei Canal and boreholes.

In addition, industry in Wuxi takes about 50 million cubic metres of water each year from the canals. Industry used to take more water from the canals, but pretreatment costs make canal water more expensive than tap water for many uses. Agriculture and fish farms also draw water from the canals.

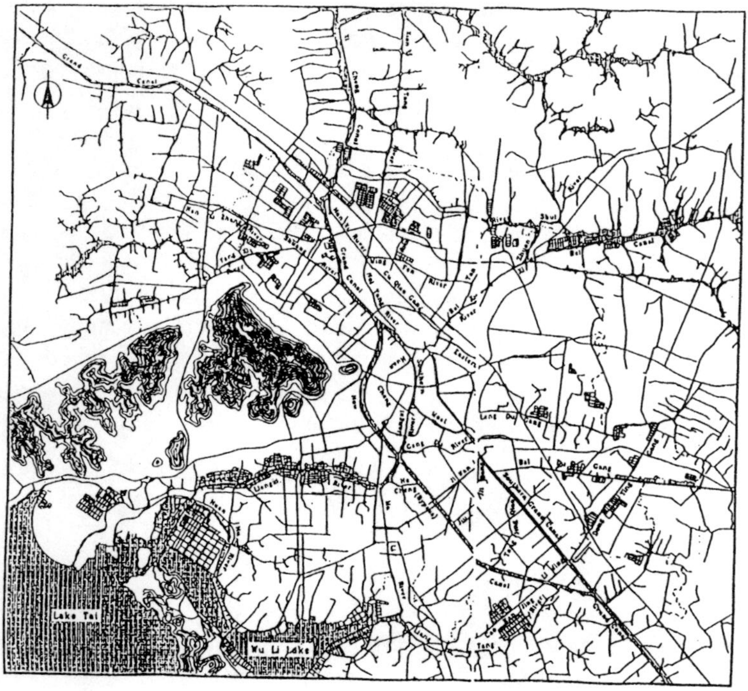

Source: Watson Hawkesley, 1992

Figure 5.2 Waterways around Wuxi

Wuxi households rely almost entirely on tap water. The water company supplies tap water to virtually all (330 000) households in the city and to about 40 per cent of households in the surrounding counties. Lake Tai provides recreational facilities for boating, swimming and fishing as well as many walking and sight-seeing spots. However algal growth makes swimming unattractive in many parts of the lake. The city waterways provide some opportunities for boating. However it is no longer safe to eat fish caught in these waterways, nor to swim, although a few foolhardy persons still swim in the canals in high summer.

Water Quality in Wuxi

The water in most Wuxi canals is heavily polluted and suitable only for agricultural use (Class 5 in terms of national Chinese standards under Regulation GB 3838-88). Water in the Liangxi River and the New Canal is less polluted and is generally Class 4 (suitable for industrial use and boating) due to the inflow of better quality water from Lake Tai. Water quality in Lake Tai is mainly quite good (Class 2) but has deteriorated to Class 3 around its margins (suitable for potable water and swimming).

Table 5.1 shows measures of average water quality in Wuxi waterways, along with Chinese class standards. The measures are based on monthly or bimonthly readings of water quality at 21 survey points in the canals taken by the Wuxi Environmental Protection Bureau (WEPB). Of course water quality depends on many factors, including water temperature, water velocity and flow direction, and varies significantly by place and time.

As shown in Table 5.1, the DO level in the city waterways is often close to zero and averages below the concentration of 2 mg per litre considered desirable for aesthetic reasons in crowded residential areas. In the populated inner city areas, canal water frequently appears deep black and stinks in summer. COD, BOD and NH_4-N (ammonia) levels are often well above acceptable standards. Oil, garbage and various debris float on the water surface. However, because of source controls the canal waters generally have low concentrations of heavy metals.

Table 5.1 Average water quality in Wuxi waterways

Element	*1986 (mg/l)*	*1990 (mg/l)*	*WEPB standards Class 3*	*Class 4*	*Main problems*[1]
DO	1.40	1.68	>5.0	>3.0	Malodour; fish
BOD	14.25	10.15	<4.0	<6.0	Ind.; health; fish[2]
NH_4-N	5.47	5.45	<1.0	<2.0	Ind.; health[2]
COD	30–50	30–50	<15.0	<20.0	Health; fish
SS[3]	12.50	10.00	<5.0	<7.5	Ind.; aesthetic
Oil	0.84	1.34	<0.05	<0.5	Health; fish; ag.
Phenol	0.04	0.07	<0.005	<0.01	Health; fish; ag.
CN	0.02	0.02[4]	<0.2	<0.2	Health; fish; ag.
AS	0.01	0.01[4]	<0.05	<0.1	Health; fish; ag.

Notes:
1. Industry (Ind.) includes the Wuxi Water Supply Company.
2. High NH_4-N and BOD are good for agriculture (ag.)
3. The SS standards shown here are indicative, not WEPB standards.
4. 1989 figures.

Source: Wuxi Environmental Protection Bureau.

In contrast Lake Tai has mostly fair-quality water. The DO in most parts is usually above 8 mg per litre and the BOD under 3 mg per litre. COD levels are acceptable and total phosphorus meets Class 3 standards. However effluent from the city affects sources of drinking water and increases the cost of municipal water supply. The water in Lake Tai is eutrophic because of excessive concentrations of nutrients (phosphorous and nitrogen). Eutrophication adversely affects the lake as a water supply source, as a habitat for fish and as a recreational resource (in places the water is green, slimy and quite unappealing).

Causes of Water Pollution in Wuxi

The deterioration in water quality in the city waterways over the past 30 years has been caused by increased population and industrial activity in Wuxi, construction of the New (Bypass) Canal in 1982, which greatly reduced flows through other city canals, increased barge traffic and increased development in areas upstream of Wuxi. Between 30 per cent and 40 per cent of the pollution in Wuxi is attributable to effluent entering from the north.

Industry is responsible for three quarters of all wastewater discharged to the waterways within Wuxi. Most factories discharge their wastewater into the canals. However a small number (about 30) are responsible for over 90 per cent of the industrial water pollution. Half the industrial wastewater can be discharged into the receiving watercourse without treatment and any adverse impact. Another 100 factories have wastewater treatment works and discharge a further 30 per cent of industrial wastewater into the waterways after treatment with little adverse effect. This leaves a relatively small amount of wastewater (about 32 million cubic metres, including some treated wastewater) that does not meet Wuxi's discharge standards.

Household wastewater accounts for most of the other effluents discharged into the waterways. Most households in Wuxi use flush toilets. A high proportion of household waste is discharged untreated into the canals via reticulation sewers or combined stormwater and wastewater sewers.

The main causes of pollution in Lake Tai are wastewater from the city, which passes through various inlets to the lake, chemical fertilisers and insecticides used in agriculture, wastewater discharges from hotels and factories at the lakeside, and wastewater from the ships and barges that regularly use the lake.

Water Pollution Abatement Policies in Wuxi

The Wuxi authorities have implemented several initiatives to reduce water pollution. Between 1983 and 1992, 23 factories were moved and upgraded with new pollution control facilities. Nearly half the factories in Wuxi now have primary treatment facilities for wastewater; all factories whose effluent exceeds national limits pay a monthly discharge fee to the WEPB; and new and extended factories require an environmental impact assessment report. In 1991–92 water quality improved significantly because four factories (two paper mills, a solvent factory and a titanium factory), which accounted for a quarter of the COD load, were closed down. These actions show that water quality can be improved by pollution abatement policies as well as by investment in wastewater treatment.

In recent years most new sewers have been designed to supply wastewater to the Lucun Sewage Treatment Works (LSTW) in the south of Wuxi, which started operations in 1990. By the end of 1992 the sewerage system servicing the LSTW comprised 29 km of trunk sewers, 7 km of connecting sewers and seven pumping stations. The works had a capacity to provide primary treatment to 100 000 cubic metres per day and secondary treatment to 50 000 cubic metres per day. In primary treatment 30 per cent of BOD and suspended solids are removed; in secondary treatment 80 per cent of BOD and suspended solids are removed. However the LSTW was receiving mainly domestic waste and was treating only 25 000 cubic metres per day. This reflected the poor state of the reticulation system in Wuxi and the poor connections with the trunk sewers.

5.4 THE PROPOSED WASTEWATER PROGRAMME, ITS COSTS AND ALTERNATIVES

The Proposed Programme

The proposed wastewater programme has two main components: sewerage and treatment. The sewerage component involves collection of wastewater from all households and water-polluting small and medium factories in the Lucun catchment area and transporting the captured wastewater by main trunk sewers to the LSTW. The Lucun catchment includes the south, centre and north-east of the city and accounts for four out of five households and factories in Wuxi. This component comprises the reconstruction or renovation of 205 km of reticulation sewers, 14 pumping stations and 44 km of new trunk sewers by the year 2000. The wastewater treatment will upgrade the LSTW to provide a daily capacity of 200 000 cubic metres of primary treatment and 100 000 cubic metres of secondary treatment by the year 2000. Secondary capacity will be increased to 200 000 square metres per day and tertiary treatment (nutrient removal) will be introduced after 2000.

The total programme should meet all the forecast needs of the Lucun catchment area. The plan is that the treatment works will deal with all household wastes by the year 2010; that the 27 major industrial polluters have or will install adequate in-plant wastewater treatment facilities and discharge the treated waters directly into the canals; and that the north-eastern Shanbei catchment, which includes the other one fifth of households and factories in Wuxi, will be treated as a separate problem after 1995.

The sewerage programme will chiefly improve water quality in Wuxi and benefit users of this water. Upgrading the LSTW will mainly improve water quality in the Grand Canal south of Wuxi and benefit other water users. Both components will improve water quality in Lake Tai.

Table 5.2 summarises the capital and operating costs of the sewerage and treatment works to the year 2000. In order to convert financial costs to real

Table 5.2 Summary of capital and operating costs to year 2000[1] ($ million, 1992 prices)

Capital costs	*Sewerage costs*		*Augmented treatment works*	
	Fin. costs	*Econ. costs*	*Fin. costs*	*Econ. costs*
Land acquisition	0.24	0.24	0.31	0.31
Retic. sewers	8.57	9.00	–	–
Pumping stations	1.34	1.41	–	–
Trunk sewers	5.69	5.97	–	–
Treatment works	–	–	9.87	10.66
Equipment	0.70	0.70	–	–
Tech. assistance	0.46	0.46	0.35	0.35
Total	17.04	17.78	10.53	11.32
Annual operating costs	0.39	0.48	1.04[2]	1.41[3]

Notes:
1. Including contingency allowance of 10 per cent.
2. The increase in financial costs = $0.55m.
3. The increase in economic costs = $0.75m.

Source: Watson Hawksley, 1992.

economic costs, consultants Watson Hawksley (WH) used conversion factors for labour, plant and equipment and materials provided by the World Bank. For example, estimated real unskilled labour costs are 55 per cent of wages, but real electricity costs are 72 per cent higher than electricity charges. Electricity accounts for one third of the operating costs of the sewage system and for nearly half the operating costs of the treatment works.

Some Options

WH concentrated on a conventional sewerage and wastewater treatment scheme and considered three main alternatives and two complementary schemes. The alternatives were pumping water from Lake Tai through the Wuxi canals to flush the effluent out of the city, additional sewage treatment plant locations and sizes, and pumping wastewater treated in the LSTW to the Yangtse River instead of down the Grand Canal. The main complementary options would be the introduction of aeration plants into the worst Wuxi canals to increase DO concentrations to above 2 mg per litre where the proposed scheme is not sufficiently effective (partly to deal with effluents arriving from the north), and providing sewer connections to another six large factories discharging effluent into the Yan Tang River north-east of Wuxi. These options are considered further in Section 5.8.

5.5 FORECAST IMPROVEMENTS IN WATER QUALITY

Water Quality Improvements from Wastewater Collection

Table 5.3 gives current and projected standards for major sections of the Wuxi waterways. The WEPB predicts that water quality standards will decline by one class by the year 2000 if no remedial actions are taken. On the other hand the proposed sewerage scheme is expected to improve water quality by about one class compared with present standards.

In order to obtain a more precise assessment of water quality, WH developed a water quality model for Wuxi. Modelling the many attributes and causes of water quality is a complex process. The causal factors include effluent from outside Wuxi, industrial effluent policies in Wuxi, the direction and strength of water flows to and from the Grand Canal (especially to and from Lake Tai) and water temperature. Ascribing improvements in water quality to particular wastewater programmes, which is essential for evaluation, is tricky. The following comments are a bare summary of the model's results (Watson Hawksley, 1992).

Table 5.3 Class summary of canal water quality*

Location/river	*No project* *1992*	*2000*	*Project* *2000*
North Wuxi: Grand Canal	5	>5	4
North Wuxi: Nan Xu/Nei Tang Rivers	5	>5	4
NW Wuxi: Xinbei Canal	5	>5	4
West Wuxi: Liangxi River	4	5	3
West Wuxi: New (Bypass) Canal	4	5	3
Centre Wuxi: Grand Canal	>5	>5	4
East Wuxi: Eastern Moat	>5	>5	4
South Wuxi: Grand Canal	5	5	4
Lake Tai	3	4	2

*Using Chinese standard GB 3838-88.
Source: Wuxi Environmental Protection Bureau.

The consultants predict that the wastewater collection will significantly reduce BOD and COD concentrations in most conditions. By 2005, BOD concentrations will fall by about 2 mg per litre in most canal reaches. Depending on flow direction, between 70 per cent and 85 per cent of the network will be under 10 BOD mg per litre. COD concentrations will fall by 3–10 mg per litre and 80 per cent of the canal network will comply with a suggested COD standard of under 40 mg per litre.

There will also be a substantial reduction in anaerobic conditions. In typical flow conditions in winter, the proportion of the canal system with DO less than 0 mg per litre will fall from 25 per cent to 7 per cent. However half the network will still have a DO of less than 2 mg per litre. In summer, the proportion of the canal waters with a DO of less than 0 mg per litre will only fall from 55 per cent to 45 per cent.

The scheme will have only a minor impact on NH_4-N concentrations. A few reaches could show significant reductions in NH_4-N concentrations, but usually of less than 0.2 mg per litre.

Overall, WH's model suggests that the proposed sewerage scheme will provide significant improvements but will not achieve the desired Class 4 standards in many canal reaches, mainly because of effluent entering the city from the north. This should decline as effluent discharge standards upstream are improved. In addition, sewering the six major industrial effluent sources in north-east Wuxi will greatly reduce COD levels. However the consultants also noted that the WEPB standards for COD and NH_4-N may be unreasonably high. Finally, in order to increase DO levels the consultants proposed that canal aeration should complement the sewerage scheme.

Water Quality Improvements from the Expanded Treatment Works

Currently, most water in the Grand Canal downstream of the LSTW is Class 3 quality, although this depends on distance downstream and water flow to or from Lake Tai. At the survey station 5 km south of the LSTW, the DO level varies from 2.5–4 mg per litre; BOD and COD concentrations are usually about 8 mg per litre, but can rise to 20mg per litre; NH_4-N is about 1 mg per litre. The suspended solid concentration can also be high, but this is caused partly by boats disturbing silt in shallow water. Water quality improves further downstream, but some pollution impact from Wuxi City is probably experienced as far away as Suzhou, 50 km to the south.

The proposed development of the LSTW will improve water quality in the Grand Canal and Lake Tai (which receives effluent from the Grand Canal south of the LSTW) by removing 66 tonnes of suspended solids and 54 tonnes of BOD from the daily discharged flow and by reducing bacteria by adding chloride before discharge. Immediately downstream of the LTSW there will be large reductions in BOD and COD and a significant increase in DO. WH predict that increasing secondary treatment from 50 000 cubic metres to 100 000 cubic metres daily will reduce the BOD concentration from 60 mg per litre to 30 mg per litre and increase DO from less than 1 mg per litre to over 2 mg per litre. The impact will be lower 15–20 km to the south, where natural dilution processes have already reduced the BOD concentrations – usually to less than 20 mg per litre.

5.6 BENEFITS OF THE PROPOSED WASTEWATER COLLECTION SCHEME

The estimated productivity, health and amenity benefits from the proposed wastewater system are described below. Productivity benefits include savings to the Wuxi Water Supply Company (WWSC), industrial users of water and the Wuxi Drainage Company, and gains to fish farmers. Amenity benefits include benefits to residents adjacent to canals, swimmers and tourists. In each case benefits are assumed to have started in 1994, shortly after the programme was scheduled to start, and full benefits are assumed to accrue in 2000, when the major works evaluated in this study will be complete. Non-user benefits are also discussed briefly.

Savings to the Wuxi Water Supply Company

In 1992 the WWSC supplied 170 million cubic metres of water from surface water sources. This quantity is expected to increase by 3 per cent annually to 2005. The estimated average processing cost is $0.03 per cubic metre. Separate plant costs are not available.

Improved water quality will lower processing costs by reducing the company's own use of water and chemicals. The WWSC currently uses 30 per cent of its output to wash its own plant, filters and tanks. The company estimates that the sewerage scheme will reduce processing costs by 7 per cent. This is an important estimate, which WH considered plausible but not readily checkable. To check whether the estimated cost savings are accurate it would be necessary to estimate the marginal costs of production for various input combinations. This would require considerable time by economists, accountants, engineers and interpreters.

Poor water quality also causes pipe deterioration because the required high disinfection levels (of chloride) cause corrosion. To reduce corrosion the pipes need adequate lining, usually cement or zinc, which is an additional construction cost. This can be avoided with improved water quality, but this saving is difficult to quantify and is not included below.

Savings to Industry

Industry currently takes 120 million cubic metres of tap water and 50 million cubic metres of canal water per annum. These amounts are assumed to increase by 3 per cent annually to 2005. Tap water costs industry $0.08 per cubic metre, which is well above the WWSC's estimated unit cost. Industry treats 40 per cent of all water taken at a cost ranging from $0.035 to $0.09 per cubic metre. Improved canal water quality will reduce these treatment costs and enable some factories to switch from tap to canal water.

WEPB experts and the managers of five major industrial plants in Wuxi consider that the savings from improved water quality could be substantial. The savings are difficult to forecast because the wastewater collection scheme will only partially improve water quality. Also, the heterogeneous nature of industrial plants and their water quality requirements make generalisation from a few observations hazardous. Based on the interviews, the evaluation assumes that the sewerage scheme will save industry $0.02 per cubic metre on one fifth of its water intake, principally by saving on treatment costs, but also in some cases by switching from tap to canal water.

In addition some factories will reduce wastewater treatment costs because, instead of discharging the wastewater to the canals, they will be able to discharge it with less treatment into the municipal sewerage system. It is estimated that factories will save $0.035 per cubic metre on one tenth of their treated wastewater. Half the savings will be due to the sewerage system and half to the treatment works.

Again the data are flimsy. Unfortunately the step from working with the best estimates of industrial managers, subject to plausibility checks by independent engineers, to a detailed investigation of cost functions is a large one.

Savings to the Wuxi Drainage Company

Substantial renovation work on existing reticulation sewers (estimated cost $9.0 million) will be required if there is no major project. Many sewers are old or poorly constructed, or both, and are prone to blockages; some pipes or connections between pipes leak; and some sewers have to be reconstructed to connect with recently established trunk sewers. The evaluation assumes that the sewerage project will save the drainage company $4.5 million on work that would otherwise be required between years 2000 and 2010.

Fishery Benefits

Currently 10 000 tonnes of fish are produced annually in the Wuxi urban area and Lake Tai at an ex-farm price of $1100 per tonne. About 60 per cent of fish farms draw water from the canal system and the others draw water from Lake Tai.

Improved water quality will increase the quantity and quality of fish produced in Wuxi fish farms and Lake Tai and reduce production costs. Alas the improvements will not lead to the harvesting of fish from the Grand Canal itself, once famous for the quality of its fish but now suffering from excessive pollutants, including toxins and high nitrogen concentrations. Allowing for some Lake Tai farms to gain from improved water quality, 70 per cent of fish farms are expected to benefit from improved water quality.

In the past regular water exchanges to the fish farms provided new oxygen. Now the low DO in the canals increases fish disease and mortality and makes frequent exchanges unproductive. In 1989–90 1.7 million kilos of cultivated fish were found dead in rivers off the main canals. The Chief of the Aquatic Products Division of the Wuxi Multi-Business Bureau estimated that poor water quality has increased fish production costs by 15 per cent (to $1.0 per kilo) since the 1970s, due for example to increased fish medicine requirements. On the other hand aquaculture can itself contribute to poor water quality and initial improvements in water quality could be partially offset by pollution from the fish stock itself. The evaluation allows that the sewerage scheme will increase fish output and lower costs and that the combined effect will equate to a 7.5 per cent increase in net income for 70 per cent of fish farms in Wuxi (which will recoup half the estimated cost increase due to poor water).

Agriculture

In Wuxi City 273 hectares are under agriculture, producing an average 5.4 tonnes of output per hectare, mainly rice and vegetables. Some local people believe that the deterioration in water quality has reduced rice quality, but this has not been substantiated. Conceivably, the silt taken from canals for construction purposes on farms may dissolve in heavy rains and the currently low heavy metal content may increase.

Experts in the Wuxi Agricultural Bureau consider that water quality is not affecting agricultural output and is unlikely to do so. As noted, the canals have low concentrations of heavy metals. Some traces of heavy metals have been found in rice and vegetables, but below designated limits. Although high organic substances and nitrogen can reduce crop productivity, moderate amounts can be useful to crops. Accordingly this evaluation includes no agricultural benefits.

Public Health Benefits

There are no data on diseases caused by poor water quality in Wuxi. Nor have there been any surveys of the health status of residents or workers (for example barge owners) especially exposed to canal water. Therefore this study relies on the views of local health experts.

According to the division chief of epidemic prevention of the Wuxi Public Health Bureau, the health status of most Wuxi residents is high, very few people are hospitalised due to illness from poor water and water-related diseases are not now a serious problem. Nevertheless poor water quality does apparently produce some minor stomach disorders.

In the early 1950s epidemic disease was a major cause of death. However it is now only a minor cause and cases of diarrhoea and intestinal diseases have declined. In 1991, when a one in 100 year flood occurred, intestinal diseases were 8 per cent lower than in the previous year. Local experts also point out that even if data on stomach diseases existed there would be many possible causes, including non-water sources of poison, rotten food and stress.

There are several reasons for this good health. Virtually all households in Wuxi receive good quality tap water and drink and food companies must conform to high standards. Moreover many households take measures to prevent disease, including protecting against mosquitos and flies, the use of water filters, and the boiling of water. However problems may arise through the food chain, stomach complaints often being attributed to inadequate preparation (washing) of foodstuffs.

Improved water quality in Wuxi will have two main benefits: it will reduce the public and private expenditures required to prevent disease and it will reduce working days lost due to minor stomach disorders. It will not reduce health treatment costs significantly because of the low incidence of serious water-related disease.

The Public Health Authority in Wuxi currently spends $75 000 annually on public sterilisation programmes to obviate disease caused by the increased breeding of mosquitos and flies that is encouraged by water pollution. Some departments and business agencies also spend money on controlling the breeding of mosquitos and flies. Many families spend $7–$10 a year on preventing mosquito or fly-borne diseases. Increasingly families spend $20–$30 on water filters (a capital expenditure). Also most families use energy to boil water before drinking it, although this partly reflects a cultural preference for tea. For the evaluation it is assumed that families spend an average of $8 per annum to prevent water-related diseases and that improved water quality will reduce these expenditures and public health prevention expenditures by one quarter.

It is also assumed that 2 per cent of barge operators and residents close to waterways lose an average of two days work a year due to stomach disorders; that the value of daily output lost is $3.5; and that improved water quality will cut these losses by 75 per cent. It may be noted that these estimated productivity gains from improved water quality are far lower than those estimated for a similar sewerage project in Beijing (see Section 5.8).

Possible Savings During Floods

When heavy flooding occurs, canals overflow and wastewater floods back into streets and housing. In the one in 100 year flood in Wuxi in 1991, 200 000 households, 280 public toilets and 5000 factories were flooded, and the estimated total damage was $0.6 million. Other major floods occurred in 1954, 1962 and 1983. After these, suspended solids and ammonia/nitrogen levels rose considerably in many canals. An improved sewerage system will marginally reduce foul-water flooding during major floods but the benefits will be small and are not allowed for in this evaluation.

Amenity Benefits for Residents

As discussed in Chapter 4, increases in land (or house) values are often used as measures of improvements in amenity. For example Feenberg and Mills (1980) used a property price model to estimate the benefits of improved (ocean) water quality in Boston (USA), but the estimated benefits were much lower than those found in their travel cost model. Also, the World Bank has adopted imputed values of property price increases as measures of improved water quality in China and elsewhere. Typically an average land value increment factor is applied to all land within some distance (often 100 metres) of the improved waterways. This approach has a considerable advantage in that it requires few assumptions.

However such an all-inclusive approach to amenity benefit estimation may not provide accurate results. One problem concerns the amount of land that would benefit. In Wuxi, many canals are bordered by public open spaces and roadways where little, if any, increase in land values would occur. Although parts of Wuxi are densely developed, less than one eighth of the total urban area (35 square kilometres out of 400 square kilometres) is built up with commercial or residential development. Secondly, property values are used mainly because they are expected to reflect willingness-to-pay values and because, in market economies, property values are often observable when other willingness-to-pay values are not. But this is not the case in Wuxi where the property market is highly regulated. Thirdly, the land value approach incorporates benefits to commercial activities, including tourist facilities, as well as to local residents. Generally, it is desirable to focus as directly as possible on the benefits to specific beneficiaries rather than use a loosely defined global surrogate measure of benefits. Accordingly, this study makes separate estimates of the amenity benefits (reduced malodour and improved visual quality) of local residents and workers; the improved recreation (swimming) benefits available to all residents of Wuxi; and the consumer and producer benefits associated with domestic and international visitors to Wuxi.

Water quality is expected to improve in 200 kilometres of waterways in Wuxi. Allowing for 100 metres on each side, the total affected land area will be 40 square kilometres , which represents one tenth of the city area. Based on a sample survey of affected areas and discussions with WEPB officers, the evaluation allows that 7.5 per cent of Wuxi households, 5 per cent of Wuxi land-based workers, and 12 400 barge operators and assistants will experience improved amenity.

What these groups will be willing to pay for the amenity improvements depends on subjective valuations of odour and visual quality, on which, not

Table 5.4 Survey record: observations of amenity quality*

		1982	*1983*	*1984*	*1985*	*1986*	*1987*	*1988*	*1989*	*1990*	*Per cent*
Jan.	Bad	0	0	0	0	5	2	4	3	3	16
	Not bad	5	5	7	7	9	13	14	15	17	84
March	Bad	1	2	1	0	5	0	0	9	2	18
	Not bad	4	3	6	7	9	15	18	9	18	82
May	Bad	1	1	0	–	7	4	6	4	9	31
	Not bad	4	4	7	–	7	11	12	14	11	69
July	Bad	2	2	2	3	7	0	12	6	14	45
	Not bad	3	3	5	4	7	15	6	12	6	55
Sept.	Bad	0	0	0	1	6	0	2	3	6	16
	Not bad	5	5	7	6	10	15	16	15	14	84
Nov.	Bad	1	0	0	2	3	1	5	2	1	13
	Not bad	4	5	7	5	13	14	13	16	19	87
Total (%)											
	Bad	16	17	17	7	17	37	8	27	25	29
	Not bad	84	83	83	93	83	63	92	73	75	71

*'Bad' indicates that the surveyed point was either malodorous or black, or both.

Source: Wuxi Environmental Protection Research Institute.

surprisingly, there are few data. However since 1982 five officers from the Wuxi Environmental Protection Research Institute have inspected up to 20 points in the Wuxi canal system on the 10th of each month and recorded whether these points were malodorous or black (or both). Table 5.4 summarises the results for six months each year to 1990. From this, three conclusions can be drawn. Firstly, pollution varies considerably around the canal system. Secondly, pollution increased in the 1980s. The points considered black or malodorous rose from under one fifth between 1982 and 1985 to over a quarter between 1988 and 1990. However COD levels have fallen recently as four factories responsible for 25 per cent of COD levels in the canals have closed. Thirdly, most pollution occurs in the summer from May to August.

Drawing on international literature on amenity values (for example Freeman, 1979; Abelson, 1979; Pearce and Markandya, 1989), it is evident that people in developed countries are willing to pay up to about 25 per cent of house rents or prices to live in a high-quality environment free of all disamenities (noise, air pollution, unpleasant odours, visual blight and so on) compared with a severely blighted environment. In a discussion with WEPB officers it was agreed that the benefits from reduced canal malodours and improved visual amenity, mainly in summer, will be comparatively minor. Correspondingly it was judged that, in a market situation, affected households would be willing to pay 0–5 per cent of house rents or prices for improved water quality (depending on whether the perceived improvement is almost imperceptible or quite significant) and the study adopted an average 2.5 per cent increase in willingness-to-pay rents.

In the absence of a housing market, market rents must be imputed. For this purpose real income inclusive of free and subsidised goods and services was taken to be $1250 per worker and $2500 per household. Of this a household was assumed to be willing to pay one quarter ($625) in housing rent. On these assumptions, households living close to the canals would be willing to pay an average $15 per annum for year-round removal of malodours and water blackness. WEPB officers confirmed that this is realistic. It was also estimated in a discussion with these officers that barge operators would be willing to pay $9 per annum and that workers employed close to the canals would be willing to pay $2 per annum for these benefits.

However even with an aeration programme, the sewerage scheme will not fully clean up the canals. The evaluation therefore allows that 75 per cent of the potential amenity benefits will be achieved. Of this, half the improvement will be attributable to sewerage and half to aeration.

Local Recreation Benefits

Using a travel cost model, Feenberg and Mills (1980) showed that improved water quality would have substantial recreation benefits in Boston, USA. But where existing water quality is poor, recreational usage is low and latent demand is difficult to estimate (UK Water Research Centre and Coopers and Lybrand, 1989).

Traditionally, swimming was common in the Wuxi canals. Today, understandably, few people swim in the canals and few swim in Lake Tai, much of which is green and slimy with algae growth, especially close to the shores. On the other hand the public swimming pools are crowded. Lake Tai, a popular area for health resorts, has considerable recreational potential.

For the evaluation it is assumed that improved water quality will enable one in ten Wuxi residents to swim in Lake Tai or other waterways an average of eight times a year (twice a month in the four hot summer months) and that residents will be willing to pay $0.20 for each swim (which is the entrance cost to a public swimming pool). It was not possible within the study constraints to conduct a survey that might have improved the accuracy of these estimates.

Visitor Benefits

Wuxi currently attracts 150 000 foreign tourists and a million local Chinese visitors a year. Most foreign tourists visit Wuxi for one day (and spend $75) as part of a seven-day tour from Nanking to Shanghai. Most of these take a Lake Tai boat trip and a few take a canal tour (the price of each is $2.75 to foreigners).

A common local view is that improved water quality will attract significantly more tourists to Wuxi, encourage them to stay longer and spend more and bring substantial economic benefits which should be included in the cost–benefit analysis. There are two main problems with this argument. Firstly, Wuxi faces considerable competition for tourist time. Until it provides active water-based recreational activities and associated tourist services (which will not happen for many years), water quality will have little impact on total tourist days in Wuxi. Secondly, even if tourism in Wuxi does increase, the net benefit to China will be less than to Wuxi as some tourist expenditure will simply be transferred to Wuxi from another Chinese city.

What then are the visitor benefits from improved water quality in Wuxi? They are the net increase in consumer and producer surpluses that are directly attributable to the improved water. That is, they are what foreign and local visitors will be willing to pay for better water quality plus what local businesses will be willing to pay for improved commercial land by the canals (in part to serve local residents as well as tourists).

For the evaluation, foreign visitors are assumed to be willing to pay an average $1.0 extra for one boat trip and local visitors to be willing to pay an average of $0.2 extra for improved water quality. The latter figure is equivalent to a park entry price or the price of a swim.

At present, little land around the canals is used for services. Although some of this land could be converted from manufacturing to services, the demand for service land is limited and there are social constraints on land use changes. This evaluation assumes that 20 000 square metres of land will be taken up primarily for tourist facilities and that the average value of such land will rise by 10 per cent from $7.25 per square metre. (Currently commercial land is usually rented to joint foreign/Chinese ventures in Wuxi for between $4 and $11 per square metre.)

Non-Use Benefits

We saw above that people often place an intrinsic (non-use) value on water quality. This may also occur in Wuxi, which is known traditionally as 'The Land of Rice and Fish'. It may also be argued that the high water quality standards set by the Chinese government reflects the importance attached to water quality by the Chinese people. However, in the absence of survey data on the possible intrinsic benefits of water quality the evaluation includes no such benefits.

Conversion Factors for Financial Benefits

Drawing on World Bank conversion factors, financial benefits are converted to economic benefits using the following factors: 1.14 for the water company and industrial benefits; 1.05 for the drainage company (savings on reticulation sewers); and 0.90 for public health benefits.

5.7 BENEFITS FROM THE EXPANDED TREATMENT WORKS

Benefits from the expanded treatment works will be experienced downstream as far as Suzhou as well as by Lake Tai water users. Allowing for some beneficial impact on the outer suburbs of Suzhou, WEPB officers estimate that 100 000 families reside in the affected area.

Unfortunately the consultants were commissioned to model the waterways only in Wuxi Administrative Area, which extends 15 km south of Wuxi City. The water quality impacts further south and in Lake Tai were not modelled and little information is available on the households and activities that might benefit from water quality improvements. The benefit estimates below are based on information provided by WEPB officers and other Wuxi sources. Previous discussions of valuation principles are not repeated.

Savings to the Wuxi Water Supply Company: the company estimates that the expanded treatment works will reduce its processing costs by 2 per cent due to improved water quality in Lake Tai.

Savings to industry: industry in Wuxi is expected to save $0.004 per cubic metre on treatment costs for one fifth of its water intake due to improved water quality in Lake Tai. Also, factories are expected to save $0.035 per cubic metre on wastewater treatment costs for one tenth of their treated wastewater, with half the savings attributed to the LTSW.

Savings to fisheries: fish farms downstream of the treatment works and around Lake Tai are expected to increase their output of 10 000 tonnes by 3.5 per cent.

Agricultural benefits: no agricultural benefits are included. The treated effluent could possibly be used as fertiliser, but this is not likely.

Public health benefits: stomach disorders are much more common downstream of Wuxi City because only 40 per cent of rural households receive tap water. Many people wash clothes and vegetables in canal water. An estimated 2 per cent of the rural population suffer a water-related stomach disorder for an average of two days a year and one in 40 of these attends hospital for an average of three days. The estimated average value of lost output in the rural areas is $2 per day and the estimated hospital cost is $20 per day. The Wuxi Health Department spends $50 000 annually on medicines and doctors in relation to water-related disease in rural areas. Also, households in rural areas spend an estimated $1.0 per household on leaching powder to sterilise water before use. It is assumed that improved water quality will halve the work days lost, the hospital days and public and private preventive expenditures associated with water-related disorders.

Resident amenity benefits: an estimated 10 per cent of the 100 000 households in the affected area will experience a small amenity (odour and visual) benefit valued at $3.5 per family. A benefit of $2 per barge operator is allowed for 6000 barge operators.

Resident recreation benefits: one in ten of the local population is assumed to recreate in the canals an average of 16 times per annum due to improved water quality and to be willing to pay $0.1 per swim.

Tourist benefits: tourist benefits will arise indirectly due to the improved water quality in Lake Tai. Foreign tourists are assumed to be willing to pay an average of $0.2 and domestic tourists $0.04 for the improvements, which is about one fifth of those due to wastewater collection in Wuxi.

However these estimated benefits may not capture all the benefits of the downstream tributaries of the Grand Canal and in Suzhou. To allow for possible major underestimation of benefits, *other possible benefits* are included below at 50 per cent of estimated benefits. The impact of this allowance on the results is not significant.

5.8 EVALUATION OF PROPOSED WATER QUALITY PROGRAMMES

Main Results

Tables 5.5 and 5.6 show the evaluation results for the wastewater collection system and expanded treatment works in 1992.

Table 5.5 Cost–benefit analysis of wastewater collection in Wuxi (US$ m, 1992 prices)

	Capital costs	*Increased operating costs**	*Total costs*	*Water company savings*	*Industry savings*	*Drainage company savings*	*Fishery benefits*	*Public health benefits*	*Resident amenity benefits*	*Resident recreation benefits*	*Tourist + comm. benefits*	*Total benefits*	*Net benefits*
1993	0.84	0.00	0.84	0.00	0.00	0.00	0.00	0.00	0.00	0.00	0.00	0.00	–0.84
1994	4.23	0.07	4.30	0.04	0.09	0.00	0.06	0.06	0.04	0.01	0.04	0.34	–3.96
1995	3.32	0.14	3.46	0.04	0.09	0.00	0.06	0.06	0.04	0.01	0.04	0.34	–3.12
1996	3.50	0.25	3.75	0.09	0.18	0.00	0.12	0.12	0.08	0.03	0.08	0.70	–3.05
1997	3.54	0.30	3.84	0.18	0.37	0.00	0.23	0.25	0.17	0.06	0.17	1.42	–2.42
1998	1.55	0.35	1.90	0.27	0.57	0.00	0.35	0.37	0.25	0.09	0.26	2.17	0.27
1999	1.23	0.40	1.63	0.38	0.79	0.00	0.46	0.49	0.33	0.12	0.3	2.94	1.31
2000	0.32	0.45	0.77	0.49	1.01	1.57	0.58	0.62	0.41	0.15	0.48	5.32	4.55
2001	–	0.48	0.48	0.50	1.05	0.00	0.58	0.62	0.41	0.15	0.51	3.81	3.33
2002	–	0.48	0.48	0.52	1.08	0.00	0.58	0.62	0.41	0.15	0.53	3.8	3.40
2003	–	0.48	0.48	0.53	1.11	0.00	0.58	0.62	0.41	0.15	0.56	3.96	3.48
2004	–	0.48	0.48	0.55	1.14	0.00	0.58	0.62	0.41	0.15	0.58	4.03	3.55
2005	–	0.48	0.48	0.56	1.18	1.57	0.58	0.62	0.41	0.15	0.61	5.68	5.20
2006	–	0.48	0.48	0.56	1.18	0.00	0.58	0.62	0.41	0.15	0.61	4.11	3.63
2007	–	0.48	0.48	0.56	1.18	0.00	0.58	0.62	0.41	0.15	0.61	4.11	3.63
2008	–	0.48	0.48	0.56	1.18	0.00	0.58	0.62	0.41	0.15	0.61	4.11	3.63
2009	–	0.48	0.48	0.56	1.18	0.00	0.58	0.62	0.41	0.15	0.61	4.11	3.63
2010	–	0.48	0.48	0.56	1.18	1.57	0.58	0.62	0.41	0.15	0.61	5.68	5.20
2011	–	0.48	0.48	0.56	1.18	0.00	0.58	0.62	0.41	0.15	0.61	4.11	3.63
2012	–	0.48	0.48	0.56	1.18	0.00	0.58	0.62	0.41	0.15	0.61	4.11	3.63
2013	–	0.48	0.48	0.56	1.18	0.00	0.58	0.62	0.41	0.15	0.61	4.11	3.63
2014	–	0.48	0.48	0.56	1.18	0.00	0.58	0.62	0.41	0.15	0.61	4.11	3.63
2015	–	0.48	0.48	0.56	1.18	0.00	0.58	0.62	0.41	0.15	0.61	4.11	3.63
2016	–	0.48	0.48	0.56	1.18	0.00	0.58	0.62	0.41	0.15	0.61	4.11	3.63
2017	–	0.48	0.48	0.56	1.18	0.00	0.58	0.62	0.41	0.15	0.61	4.11	3.63
2018	–	0.48	0.48	0.56	1.18	0.00	0.58	0.62	0.41	0.15	0.61	4.11	3.63
2019	–	0.48	0.48	0.56	1.18	0.00	0.58	0.62	0.41	0.15	0.61	4.11	3.63
2020	–	0.48	0.48	0.56	1.18	0.00	0.58	0.62	0.41	0.15	0.61	4.11	3.63
PV 10	13.00	3.04	16.04	2.99	6.24	1.47	3.31	3.54	2.37	0.85	3.11	23.88	7.85
NPV 10%		7.85											
NPV 12%		4.40											
IRR		0.157											

*Compared with operating costs in 1992.

Table 5.6 Cost-benefit analysis of expanded Wuxi sewerage treatment works (US$m 1992 prices) [1]

	Capital costs	*Increased operating costs*[2]	*Total costs*	*Water company savings*	*Industry savings*	*Fishery benefits*	*Public health benefits*	*Resident amenity benefits*	*Resident recreation benefits*	*Tourist benefits*	*Other possible savings*[3]	*Total benefits*	*Net benefits*	*Both projects*
1993	0.53	0.00	0.53	0.00	0.00	0.00	0.00	0.00	0.00	0.00	0.00	0.00	–0.53	–1.37
1994	2.69	0.08	2.77	0.03	0.05	0.05	0.02	0.01	0.01	0.02	0.09	0.28	–2.50	–6.46
1995	2.12	0.16	2.28	0.03	0.05	0.05	0.02	0.01	0.01	0.02	0.09	0.28	–2.00	–5.12
1996	2.23	0.25	2.48	0.05	0.10	0.11	0.04	0.02	0.02	0.03	0.18	0.55	–1.93	–4.98
1997	2.25	0.35	2.60	0.08	0.15	0.16	0.05	0.03	0.03	0.05	0.28	0.83	–1.77	–4.19
1998	0.98	0.45	1.43	0.10	0.21	0.22	0.07	0.04	0.04	0.07	0.38	1.14	–0.30	–0.03
1999	0.78	0.55	1.33	0.12	0.24	0.24	0.08	0.04	0.05	0.08	0.43	1.29	–0.04	1.27
2000	0.20	0.65	0.85	0.14	0.27	0.27	0.09	0.05	0.06	0.09	0.49	1.46	0.60	5.15
2001	–	0.75	0.75	0.14	0.28	0.27	0.09	0.05	0.06	0.10	0.49	1.48	0.73	4.06
2002	–	0.75	0.75	0.15	0.29	0.27	0.09	0.05	0.06	0.10	0.50	1.51	0.76	4.16
2003	–	0.75	0.75	0.15	0.30	0.27	0.09	0.05	0.06	0.11	0.51	1.54	0.79	4.26
2004	–	0.75	0.75	0.16	0.31	0.27	0.09	0.05	0.06	0.11	0.52	1.56	0.81	4.37
2005	–	0.75	0.75	0.16	0.32	0.27	0.09	0.05	0.06	0.12	0.53	1.59	0.84	6.05
2006	–	0.75	0.75	0.16	0.32	0.27	0.09	0.05	0.06	0.12	0.53	1.59	0.84	4.48
2007	–	0.75	0.75	0.16	0.32	0.27	0.09	0.05	0.06	0.12	0.53	1.59	0.84	4.48
2008	–	0.75	0.75	0.16	0.32	0.27	0.09	0.05	0.06	0.12	0.53	1.59	0.84	4.48
2009	–	0.75	0.75	0.16	0.32	0.27	0.09	0.05	0.06	0.12	0.53	1.59	0.84	4.48
2010	–	0.75	0.75	0.16	0.32	0.27	0.09	0.05	0.06	0.12	0.53	1.59	0.84	6.05
2011	–	0.75	0.75	0.16	0.32	0.27	0.09	0.05	0.06	0.12	0.53	1.59	0.84	4.48
2012	–	0.75	0.75	0.16	0.32	0.27	0.09	0.05	0.06	0.12	0.53	1.59	0.84	4.48
2013	–	0.75	0.75	0.16	0.32	0.27	0.09	0.05	0.06	0.12	0.53	1.59	0.84	4.48
2014	–	0.75	0.75	0.16	0.32	0.27	0.09	0.05	0.06	0.12	0.53	1.59	0.84	4.48
2015	–	0.75	0.75	0.16	0.32	0.27	0.09	0.05	0.06	0.12	0.53	1.59	0.84	4.48
2016	–	0.75	0.75	0.16	0.32	0.27	0.09	0.05	0.06	0.12	0.53	1.59	0.84	4.48
2017	–	0.75	0.75	0.16	0.32	0.27	0.09	0.05	0.06	0.12	0.53	1.59	0.84	4.48
2018	–	0.75	0.75	0.16	0.32	0.27	0.09	0.05	0.06	0.12	0.53	1.59	0.84	4.48
2019	–	0.75	0.75	0.16	0.32	0.27	0.09	0.05	0.06	0.12	0.53	1.59	0.84	4.48
2020	–	0.75	0.75	0.16	0.32	0.27	0.09	0.05	0.06	0.12	0.53	1.59	0.84	4.48
PV 10%	8.27	4.39	12.67	0.93	1.84	1.70	0.57	0.31	0.35	0.66	3.18	9.54	–3.13	4.72
NPV 10%		–3.13												IRR
NPV 12%		–3.59												0.125
IRR		0.046												

Notes
1. Assumes 200 000 m3/day primary treatment, 100 000 m3/day secondary treatment.
2. Increase in operating costs compared with 100 000 m3/day primary and 50 000 m3/day secondary treatment.
3. See text for explanation of these estimated savings.

The wastewater collection system has significant net benefits. The estimated net present value is $7.9 million with a 10 per cent discount rate and the estimated internal rate of return is 15.7 per cent. Moreover the benefits are broadly based: water company and industry savings, fishery benefits, public health benefits, resident amenity and visitor benefits each account for 10 per cent or more of total benefits. This makes more robust the conclusion that the wastewater collection system is justified.

On the other hand, expansion of the treatment works has a poor rate of return. Even after factoring up estimated benefits by 50 per cent to allow for possible underestimation, there is a substantial negative net present value with a 10 per cent discount rate and the estimated internal rate of return is only 4.6 per cent. These results reflect the relatively low level of population and activity in the affected areas downstream of the LTSW and the high operating costs of the treatment works (total discounted operating costs are half the discounted capital costs).

Together, the wastewater collection system and the treatment works have an estimated internal rate of return of 12.5 per cent and a modest net present value with a 10 per cent discount rate. However consolidating the two projects into one overall programme should not be allowed to disguise the relative benefits and costs of the component parts.

Consideration of Alternatives

The consultants (WH) considered but dismissed some alternative schemes and recommended a supplementary aeration scheme, but they did not consider management and pricing issues in any detail as they were outside the formal scope of the study. To clean up water quality in Wuxi City, WH examined the possible transfer of surface water from a tributary of Lake Tai through the city. However this would be nearly as costly as the proposed scheme, would be less effective and would cause side problems such as algal bloom and increased BOD in the Grand Canal. The consultants also analysed the possibility of exporting wastewater to the Yangtse – a Class 2 river. The Yangtse has an average flow of 30 000 cubic metres per second, which far exceeds the average flow of 50 cubic metres per second in the Grand Canal downstream of the LTSW. The flow from the Lucun treatment works is three cubic metres per second. However discharging effluent into the Yangtse is not permitted under national regulations. The Yangtse alternative was also discarded because of the high capital costs of the pipelines and pumping stations and the projected need for secondary treatment in the medium term. The consultants did not examine low-cost sewerage options. They considered that a conventional sewerage system would be appropriate and affordable in such a middle-income society.

WH recommended the aeration scheme because this is required to meet national water quality standards for DO in Wuxi. The consultants also showed that the return from the total Wuxi wastewater programme would continue to exceed 10 per cent with the inclusion of the aeration project. However using the valuation assumptions outlined above, aeration has an estimated benefit–cost ratio of only 0.4. Annual amenity and recreation benefits would be less than the annual economic operating costs of $0.5 million and would make no contribution to the capital cost ($1.6 million) of aeration. Aeration can be justified only by invoking high non-user benefits or by the argument that national water quality standards must be achieved.

Water quality could also be improved by effluent charges to encourage industry to treat wastewater before discharging it into the canals. The Wuxi municipal authorities plan to introduce wastewater charges for industry. But at the time of writing it appears that they will copy Shanghai and base wastewater charges on hydraulic load rather than on the attributes of the wastewater.

Benefit Comparisons with Some Other Results

Table 5.7 compares the benefit percentages estimated in this study with those estimated in WH's draft report for the whole scheme before the present results were available and those in three other Chinese studies. Of course the percentages should vary by scheme and place. Nevertheless the contrasts are interesting.

Firstly, our results and those of the Shanghai and one Beijing study suggest that industrial savings are usually a large part of total benefits of wastewater projects in China. In contrast, in developed countries industrial savings are generally less important than amenity benefits (Feenberg and Mills, 1980).

Secondly, based on untested local advice, water quality was considered important for fish industry productivity in Wuxi; this was not found in Shanghai or Beijing. On the other hand, poor water quality is not considered to affect health significantly in Wuxi. This was in marked contrast to WH's initial assumptions that improved water quality would produce large health benefits in Wuxi and the high health benefits estimated in one of the Beijing studies.

Thirdly, other studies have found that increased land values would be a major benefit (or measure of benefit) of improved water quality. This evaluation estimated specific consumer and producer surpluses related to

Table 5.7 Benefit percentages in various studies (per cent)

		Wuxi		*Shanghai*	*Beijing*	
Benefit	*(1)*	*(2)*	*(3)*	*(4)*	*(5)*	*(6)*
Water company	12.5	9.7	5.2	[34.5]	52.6	–
Industry	26.1	19.3	([7])		33.3	–
Drainage company	6.2	–	–	–	–	–
Fisheries	13.9	–	17.8	7.4	–	–
Agriculture	0.0	0.0	0.1	3.0	–	–
Health	14.8	6.0	35.8	–	–	67.3
Resident amenity	9.9	3.2	–	–	–	–
Resident recreation	3.6	3.7	–	–	1.2	–
Visitors/tourism	13.0	6.3	12.7	–	–	–
Land values	([8])	([8])	38.8	62.5	12.9	32.7
Other	–	33.3[9]	–	–		

Notes
1. Sewerage project analysed in this study.
2. Expansion of treatment works analysed in this study.
3. Initial consultant estimates of benefits of whole Wuxi scheme.
4. Shanghai sewerage project.
5. Beijing South sewer interceptor.
6. Beijing sewer interceptors in No.3 water plant area.
7. Recognised as significant but not estimated.
8. Land values will increase due to increased resident amenity and recreation benefits and visitor benefits, but are not estimated separately, see text.
9. Large contingency item, see text.

Sources: This study; Watson Hawksley, 1992: World Bank reports.

improved amenity (including some estimates based on property values) rather than rely on an aggregate land value proxy for all amenity benefits.

Finally, in this study water quality improvements were found to bring a range of significant benefits. In other studies, a few items make up very high proportions of estimated total benefits.

5.9 CONCLUSIONS

Engineers have traditionally sought to achieve water quality objectives at least cost. Wastewater disposal requirements have been taken as given and solutions designed to meet projected requirements. There have been few attempts to quantify the benefits of water quality objectives or to analyse the scope for reducing wastewater disposal requirements.

However a cost-effectiveness appraisal has several disadvantages. Predetermined water quality objectives may not be economically justified. In particular the costs of achieving the objectives may exceed the benefits. As Kneese (1974) has pointed out, uniform water quality or effluent standards are inefficient because the costs of water pollution vary greatly with location. Moreover a cost-effectiveness appraisal cannot cope with the fact that water quality has many elements, so that benefits often vary with alternative pollution abatement projects.

In recent years techniques for valuing the benefits of water quality have been developed and there have been several attempts to estimate these benefits in developed and developing countries. However many of these studies have been based on crude data.

The development of the wastewater masterplan in Wuxi contained elements of the traditional approach. The study was designed to achieve the Chinese government's water quality objectives at least cost. Only near the end of their study were the consultants asked to estimate the benefits of the proposed wastewater facilities. Also, limited attention was paid to non-engineering solutions such as effluent charges.

The study reported in this chapter quantified the benefits of the wastewater masterplan using best available data. There were few hard data and many estimates were speculative and untested. Regrettably this is common in consultant studies. If benefit valuation had been part of the consultant's brief from the outset, there would have been time critically to examine, amongst other things, the value of water quality to industry, the relationship between water quality and health, the amenity value of water to households and the intrinsic non-use value (if any) of water to the local community.

Nevertheless the study produced several interesting findings. In terms of content, water quality in Wuxi was found to provide a wide range of benefits. Industry savings were relatively important. But health savings were less important than expected. In terms of procedure, several valuation methods were found to be useful. These included production cost estimates, defensive expenditures, proxy prices and the property value approach. Also, it was important to distinguish carefully between, and value separately, the various classes of amenity benefit.

Although crude, the benefit estimates enabled us to estimate the returns to separate parts of the wastewater programme. The study results indicate that there are high net benefits to moving wastewater out of the highly populated urban area of Wuxi. On the other hand the estimated benefits from treating wastewater before discharging it into the waterways in the less populated rural areas downstream of the Lucun Sewage Treatment Works are low and do not justify the high capital and operating costs of the expanded treatment works. It is also doubtful whether the proposed aeration programme in Wuxi can be justified. These results demonstrate the important general principle that the major components of wastewater (and other) programmes should be identified and evaluated separately.

6 Valuing Electricity and the Environment in Bangladesh

6.1 INTRODUCTION

Electricity is widely considered essential for economic development. Consequently aid agencies have financed large numbers of electricity supply projects in developing countries. However the supply of electricity almost always involves sensitive environmental issues. Depending on the technology adopted, these issues may include the use of non-renewable energy resources, local and regional air pollution from thermal power stations, occupational hazards, site-specific impacts of power stations, ecological and social impacts of hydro projects, the risk of nuclear accidents and greenhouse effects.

This chapter evaluates the benefits and costs of electricity supply in Bangladesh. Of the world's mega-populated countries, Bangladesh is the most densely populated and the poorest. In 1990 Bangladesh had an estimated population of 107 million living at an extraordinary density of 740 persons per square kilometre. One fifth of urban households live in a single room of 100 square feet with an average occupancy of 4.5 persons (Mahtab *et al.*, 1991). The World Bank (1992) recorded that average per capita income was only US$210 in 1990, having increased by only 0.7 per cent per annum since 1965. Commercial energy consumption per capita was 57 kg of oil equivalent compared with an average of 339 kg in the 43 lowest income countries in the world and an average of 5158 kg in the 24 richest countries.

To promote economic development in Bangladesh, the World Bank, the Asian Development Bank and the UK Overseas Development Administration (ODA) have invested heavily in electricity supply since Independence in 1972. The ODA concentrated on improving transmission and distribution in Dhaka (the capital with eight million residents). In June 1992 I participated in a retrospective evaluation of the ODA programme (Barnett *et al.*, 1994). The field trip also provided a brief opportunity to consider environmental issues in national electricity generation.

To place the discussion in Bangladesh in a wider perspective, the following two sections outline the main environmental problems and valuation issues encountered worldwide in electricity supply. The focus is on fossil fuels as these provide most of the electricity in Bangladesh. Section 6.4 describes the development of electricity in Bangladesh. Sections 6.5 and 6.6 describe the costs and benefits of electricity generation in Bangladesh, including environmental effects. Sections 6.7 and 6.8 deal with the costs and benefits of improved transmission and distribution in Dhaka, again including environmental impacts. The final section summarises the main conclusions.

6.2 GENERAL ENVIRONMENTAL ISSUES IN ELECTRICITY SUPPLY

Energy Resources

Non-renewable energy sources provide 80 per cent of the primary energy consumed worldwide (WCED, 1987). Most of these are fossil fuels: oil accounts for about 32 per cent of global primary energy use, coal 27 per cent and natural gas 17 per cent. Nuclear power provides only 4 per cent. Of the supposedly renewable energy sources, biomass (mainly fuelwood) provides about 14 per cent of primary energy use and hydropower 6 per cent. Other renewable sources such as solar and windpower make very small contributions to primary energy consumption.

Even assuming a modest rate of growth of world GDP of 2.5 per cent per annum and some continuing fall in the primary energy to GDP ratio, the demand for primary energy will double in 30 years and quadruple in 60. Despite such a growth in consumption, fossil fuel reserves are sufficient to meet demands for over 100 years (World Bank, 1992). On the other hand, critical shortages of biomass material already exist in many countries. The scope for major hydro-power projects is limited. Nuclear power presents great risks from accidents and long-term waste storage problems. Power from other renewable sources is produced at high capital cost, therefore fossil fuels will remain the main source of electricity for at least 30 years and probably much longer.

Environmental Impacts of Energy Production

The production of oil and natural gas has various environmental impacts (Winpenny, 1991). These include impacts from construction of supporting facilities (such as tanks, pipelines, terminals), occupational hazards, accidental oil spills and air pollution (for instance sulphur emissions). Oil spills during marine transportation are a major ecological threat – over

200 000 tons of crude oil were spilled off the Brittany coast in 1978 and the Alaska coast in 1989. Significant leakage of methane can occur during the transportion of natural gas. Oil refineries emit airborne effluents (for example sulphur oxides, nitrogen oxides, carbon monoxide and particulates) and liquid pollutants (such as oil and grease, phenols, ammonia and various solids). However these wastes are usually treated and the pollutants are discharged in low concentrations.

Coal mining, processing and transport also have substantial environmental impacts. During mining the impacts include occupational hazards (a high risk of lung disease and even death), effects on local water quality and landscape impacts. Coal cleaning, which separates refuse and sulphur-containing pyritic material from coal, creates water and air pollution. Coal transport by road degrades any affected residential environment.

Environmental Impacts of Electricity Generation, Transmission and Distribution

Both construction and operation of thermoelectric plants can damage the environment. Construction impacts are caused by clearing land, earth moving, dredging and/or impounding water bodies, and the building process itself. Impacts during operation may be site-specific (local), regional, international or global. Site-specific impacts are visual, noise, road and rail traffic, water pollution and solid waste impacts. In the UK, concern about noise and traffic outweighs concern about water pollution and visual disamenity (Lockwood, 1992). However liquid effluents often include some trace metals, acids and other chemicals and may affect water quality. Abstraction of water for cooling purposes can damage animal organisms. Also, the return of heated water can affect aquatic animal and plant communities. Disposal of solid waste is a problem for coal-fired power stations.

Thermoelectric plants using coal or fuel oil are often a major source of regional or global air pollution. Pollutants include particulates, sulphur oxides (SO_2, the major source of acid rain), nitrogen oxides (No_x) and carbon dioxide (CO_2, the major greenhouse gas). On the other hand power plants using natural gas emit virtually no particulates or SO_2, only half the NO_x and CO_2 emitted by coal-based plants, few liquid effluents, and create no solid wastes (World Bank, 1992).

Various measures can mitigate adverse environmental impacts (World Bank, 1991, pp. 79–82). Site-specific effects are highly sensitive to site location. Air pollution can be mitigated by locating power stations further away from sensitive air quality receptors, higher stacks that reduce ground level concentrations, cleaner fuels (for instance low sulphur fuel) and air pollution control equipment. To reduce water pollution, discharges can be treated chemically or mechanically on site, groundwater contamination prevented by the use of liners, deep well injection used below potable zones and effluent diluted at the point of discharge.

Most aid donors adopt loosely defined 'international standards' for new power plants. For example the ODA requires that all aid-assisted industrial plants, including power plants, should meet the higher of EC or local environmental standards. Barnett *et al.* (1990) reviewed eight power plants constructed with UK assistance in the late 1970s and early 1980s and found that they generally conformed to ODA policy standards, although the review noted shortcomings in plants in Botswana and Sudan. All the plants were designed so that pollution control facilities could be upgraded to meet more stringent environmental standards. In 1992 the UK provided an additional grant of $3 million for limestone injections to the top of the furnace in the Fushan power station (China) to ensure that sulphur emissions met ODA requirements.

Electricity transmission and distribution may also have damaging impacts. As catalogued by the World Bank (1991), these impacts include vegetation damage; habitat loss and fragmentation; runoff and sedimentation from grading for access roads, tower pads and substation facilities; loss of land use and population relocation due to placement of towers and substations; chemical contamination from chemical maintenance techniques; aircraft and avian hazards from transmission lines and towers; induced effects from electromagnetic fields; and visual impacts. The distribution of electricity may also have a significant impact on land uses.

Concluding Points

In conclusion, four points should be noted.

- Environmental impacts of the full fuel cycle should be considered. For instance, in order to evaluate electricity generation, impacts of energy production and electricity transmission and distribution also need to be considered.
- All forms of electricity production have some environmental costs. Indoor combustion of biomass in confined areas is unhealthy and the use of woodfuel depletes forests. Burning diesel or paraffin creates air pollution and depletes non-renewable resources.
- To conserve primary energy resources and reduce pollution, energy should be used as efficiently as possible. As pointed out by the World

Bank (1992), China uses four times as much energy per unit of output as Germany or Japan. A major cause of wasteful energy use is the underpricing of energy.

- Relatively clean forms of energy such as natural gas and solar energy should be encouraged. However the optimal energy source and transformation process varies from place to place depending upon local primary energy costs, power generation costs, pollution concerns and possible mitigating measures.

6.3 VALUING ENVIRONMENTAL IMPACTS

Valuation Applications

Environmental impacts over the fuel cycle can be classed as damage to property and productive capacity, to health and to household amenity. These impacts are not easy to value in monetary terms. The Technical Research Centre of Finland (1986) reviewed various energy–environment models and concluded that 'the economic consequences of environmental impacts cannot be adequately defined (in money terms)'. Markandya (1990) surveyed 30 power system planning models and concluded that only two models included environmental damage costs and that these had not been applied effectively in any practical case. However some research studies (Koomey, 1990; Lockwood, 1992) have attempted to cost the environmental impacts of power supply, especially of power generation. We draw on these below.

In the absence of estimated damage costs, the environmental impacts of a power system are usually considered in, and justified by, an environmental impact assessment (EIA) rather than by cost–benefit analysis. An EIA provides forecasts of physical impacts, such as impacts on water quality and air emissions, but not monetary evaluations. It may also show how the forecast impacts and emissions meet, or can be mitigated to meet, official public standards.

Costing Site-Specific Impacts of Electricity Generation

Few studies have costed the site-specific impacts of electricity generation. Lockwood cites only two such studies: Ottinger *et al.* (1990), which surveys several US studies, and Ferguson (1990). Ottinger *et al.* considered the costs of abstracting water, thermal pollution, and pollution from waste water contamination. The authors estimated low costs of losses of fish stock due to entrapment/entrainment. However they concluded that the technical data on thermal pollution and waste water contamination were too crude to permit useful monetary calculations. They did not attempt to cost noise or visual impacts. Ferguson used a land-value approach to estimate visual impacts. More contentiously, in order to estimate thermal pollution he assumed that rivers have similar values to land and that these values will fall to zero with a 15°F rise in water temperature. On the other hand Hohmeyer (1988) made a detailed monetary study of air pollution impacts of electricity generation in West Germany and concluded that the site-specific impacts could not be monetised for lack of data.

Costing Air Pollution and Global Warming from Electricity Generation

Table 6.1 summarises several estimates of air pollution and global warming costs of existing power plants. Taking averages, air pollution costs range from 6 per cent of electricity price for gas-fired plants to just over 40 per cent of electricity price for coal-fired stations. Global warming costs range from 15 per cent of electricity price for gas-fired plants to 30 per cent for coal. The externality costs of oil-fired plants are closer to those for coal than for gas.

However several important caveats about these figures must be entered and conclusions modified accordingly. First, estimates of air pollution and CO_2 costs vary greatly. Views diverge widely on the relationship between acid rain and forest decline; few studies quantify the relationship between sulphur deposition and fish stocks; the critical relationship between SO_2 and NO_x and morbidity and mortality is not known; estimates of the value of life vary widely (Ottinger *et al.*, 1990, use a very high figure); also, costs of lost visibility are difficult to estimate. Moreover there is great uncertainty about global warming costs (see Chapter 9).

Secondly, only a few of the estimated costs are damage estimates. Most estimates, including all CO_2 costs, are based on abatement expenditure. These are maximum figures because society should not incur abatement expenditures when they are higher than estimated damage costs. As discussed in Chapter 9, if a few cost-beneficial abatement measures were to be taken, damage costs from global warming would probably be lower than abatement costs.

Thirdly, as shown in Table 6.2, new power plants (constructed to higher environmental standards) approximately halve air pollution costs for each energy source and slightly reduce CO_2 costs. External costs fall further if the less polluting processes (gas or combined-cycle oil-fired plants) are adopted.

Table 6.1 Estimated externality costs of electricity generation in existing power plants (1989 c/kWh)[1]

Study	*Method*[2]	*Problem*	*Gas*	*Oil*	*Coal*
EPRI (1987)	DE	SO_2	0.00	0.53	1.05
	DE	NO_x	0.03	0.03	0.06
		$SO_2 + NO_x$	0.03	0.56	1.11
Hohmeyer (1990)	DE	SO_2	0.00	0.80	1.60
	DE	NO_x	0.38	0.35	0.78
	AC	CO_2	1.10	2.20	2.40
		Total	1.48	3.35	3.78
Ottinger *et al.* (1990)	DE	$SO_2 + NO_x$	0.37	6.00	4.62
	AC	CO_2	0.69	1.23	1.38
		Total	1.06	7.23	6.00
Chernick (1989)	AC	SO_2	0.00	1.00	2.00
	AC	NO_x	0.63	0.60	1.33
	AC	CO_2	1.38	2.14	2.60
		Total	2.02	3.74	5.93
CEC Staff (1989)[3]	AC	SO_2	0.00	6.27	12.50
	AC	NO_x	2.34	2.20	4.90
	AC	CO_2	0.43	0.66	0.81
		Total	2.76	9.13	18.21
Schilberg *et al.* (1989)[4]	AC	SO_2	0.00	0.55	1.09
	AC	NO_x	0.54	0.51	1.14
	AC	CO_2	0.89	1.37	1.67
		Total	1.43	2.43	3.90
Average[5]		$SO_2 + NO_x$	0.39	2.07	2.74
		CO_2	1.02	1.74	2.01
		Total	1.41	3.81	4.75
US electricity price			6.6	6.6	6.6
Costs as per cent of price		$SO_2 + NO_x$	5.9	31.4	41.5
		CO_2	15.5	26.4	30.4
		Total	21.4	57.8	71.9

Notes

1. Estimated mean costs. Some authors give wide cost ranges.
2. DE: damage estimates; AC: abatement costs.
3. In California by California Energy Commission.
4. In US, outside California.
5. Excluding high-cost CEC abatement requirements.

Sources: Koomey, 1990; Lockwood, 1992.

Table 6.2 Estimated externality costs of electricity generation in new power plants (1989 c/kWh)[1]

Study	*Method*[2]	*Problem*	*CC Gas*	*CT Gas*	*CC Oil*	*CT Oil*	*Coal*
EPRI (1987)	DE	SO_2+NO_x	0.01	0.02	0.10	0.16	0.34
Chernick	AC	SO_2+NO_x	0.28	0.46	0.44	0.73	1.53
(1989)	AC	CO_2	1.13	1.86	1.73	2.72	2.45
		Total	1.41	2.32	2.17	3.46	3.98
CEC staff	AC	SO_2+NO_x	1.04	1.11	2.07	3.40	7.09
(1989)[3]	AC	CO_2	0.35	0.57	0.53	0.84	0.76
		Total	1.39	1.69	2.60	4.25	7.85
Schilberg	AC	SO_2+NO_x	0.24	0.40	0.33	0.55	1.14
(1989)[4]	AC	CO_2	0.72	1.19	1.11	1.75	1.58
		Total	0.97	1.59	1.44	2.30	2.71
Average[5]		SO_2+NO_x	0.18	0.29	0.29	1.44	1.00
		CO_2	0.92	1.52	1.42	2.23	1.97
		Total	1.10	1.81	1.71	3.67	2.97
Average[6]		Total	0.64	1.05	1.00	2.56	1.98
As per cent of price (6.6c\kWh)			9.7	15.9	15.1	38.8	30.0

Notes:
1. Estimated mean costs. Some authors give wide cost ranges.
2. DE: damage estimates; AC: abatement costs.
3. In California by California Energy Commission.
4. In US, outside California.
5. Excluding high-cost CEC abatement requirements.
6. Including damages from CO_2 equal to 50 per cent of estimated AC.

Sources: Koomey, 1990; Lockwood, 1992.

However most of the externality costs are based again on abatement expenditures. Assuming plausibly that actual damages from CO_2 are half abatement expenditures, the externality costs for existing plants range from 0.90 cents (c) per KWh for gas-fired plants to 3.74 c per KWh for coal plants. The externality costs for new plants range from 0.64 c per kWh for combined-cycle gas plants to 2.56 c per kWh for combined turbine and oil plants. That is, they range from 10–30 per cent of electricity price respectively.

6.4 THE ELECTRICITY SECTOR IN BANGLADESH AND DHAKA

Power Generation and Transmission in Bangladesh

The Bangladesh Power Development Board (BPDB), a public authority, generates and transmits electricity throughout Bangladesh. The private sector provides minor additional generating capacity to own-users. The BPDB also distributes most of the electricity in Bangladesh. The main exceptions are some rural areas served by rural electricity cooperatives and the Greater Dhaka area, served by the Dhaka Electricity Supply Authority (DESA). Table 6.3 shows some summary data for electricity generation and use in Bangladesh.

Between 1972 and 1982 energy generated and sold by the BPDB increased at high rates of about 15 per cent per annum. By mid-1983

Table 6.3 Summary of system statistics for Bangladesh

	1982–83 Actual	*1989–90 Planned*	*1989–90 Actual*	*1991–92 Estimate*
Installed generating capacity*				
East zone (MW)	616	1934	1907	1939
West zone (MW)	292	534	445	445
Total (MW)	908	2468	2352	2384
Transmission lines (circuit km)	2820	5271	3933	na
Peak demand (MW)	709	1823	1604	1800
Gross energy generation (GWh)	3433	8361	7731	9000
System load factor (per cent)	55.3	52.4	56.0	56.5
Sales (GWh)	2399	6354	4705	5700
System loss (per cent)	30.1	24.0	39.2	36.6
Avr. revenue/kWh (taka)	1.28	na	2.14	2.20
Consumer category				
Residential (per cent)	18.5	na	25.4	27.0
Industrial (per cent)	67.4	na	54.1	52.0
Commercial (per cent)	9.8	na	13.2	14.5
Irrigation (per cent)	1.6	na	2.3	2.5
Rural Electricity Board (per cent)	2.7	na	na	na
Other (per cent)	0.0	na	5.0	4.0

*Installed nominal capacity usually exceeds available capacity by a substantial margin (see text).

Sources: BPDB, Annual Reports; Asian Development Bank; World Bank; author estimates.

Bangladesh had an installed generation capacity of 908 MW, with 616 MW provided east of the Jamuna river and 292 MW west of the river. These historically separate sectors were connected by a 230 KV transmission line in 1982. In the east, thermal plants based on natural gas (from eastern Bangladesh) provided 486 MW of capacity and hydro generation supplied 130 MW. In the west, oil- and diesel-fired thermal plants provided the total capacity. However, of the total plant capacity nearly 10 per cent was non-operational.

In 1984 the BPDB, assisted by the Asian Development Bank, drew up a 20-year master plan for the power system. The plan forecast that system demand would increase by 13.5 per cent per annum and peak demand by 14.5 per cent per annum in the 1980s. In the following five years to 1989–90, the BPDB commissioned 1200 MW of new generating capacity, all based on gas fuel. This more than doubled existing capacity, although it was only about 80 per cent of the forecast capacity requirements. The strategy was to add large natural-gas-fuelled power stations in the east, to transfer surplus energy to the west so as to minimise fuel costs, and to phase out old generating units. In 1984–5, natural gas fuelled 64 per cent of electricity generation; in 1989–90 it fuelled 86 per cent. Also, the BPDB increased transmission capacity by 50 per cent and strengthened and expanded the distribution networks in the main urban centres.

Between 1984–5 and 1989–90, electricity consumption rose only slightly slower than forecast and it has continued to rise at double-digit rates. On the other hand, due to breakdowns effective generation capacity averaged only 2040 MW in 1989–90, compared with installed capacity of 2352 MW. No new generating capacity came on-stream between 1989–90 and late 1992 and further breakdowns (as well as a critical water shortage for the hydro plant) occurred. The World Bank and most major donors refused to fund new generating plants while system losses remained at 35–40 per cent. The BPDB estimates that 12.5 per cent of this was due to technical losses and the rest to theft (illegal connections and by-passing, tampering with or misreading meters). At the end of 1992 the generating system was again under strain and load shedding and outages were frequent events.

Electricity Transmission and Distribution in Dhaka

Dhaka is the largest load centre in Bangladesh, accounting for 40 per cent of BPDB's peak demand and 25 per cent of BPDB's sales. Drawing on consultant work, the BPDB forecast that the demand for electricity would increase by 11 per cent per annum in Dhaka in the 1980s. This increase in demand would require more infeed capacity to Dhaka, additional

Table 6.4 Greater Dhaka electricity statistics

	1983	*1988*
Transformer capacity (MVA)		
132/33 kV	589	1 060
33/11 kV	610	974
11/0.4 kV	350	476
Line lengths (km)		
132 KV	230	330
33 kV	680	760
11 kV	1 730	2 130
0.4 kV	2 270	2 720
Consumer numbers		
11 kV	602	791
0.4 kV	207 630	329 000
Demand/energy		
33 kV peak demand (MVA)	278	479
Energy (GWh)	645	1475

Sources: ODA and Asian Development Bank reports.

transmission capacity around Dhaka, more substations and a strengthening and extension of the distribution system with the city. Table 6.4 summarises the planned increases between 1983 and 1988.

After completing this five-year improvement programme, the BPDB, supported by the ODA and the Asian Development Bank, continued to upgrade the distribution system in Dhaka. In mid-1992 peak demand in Dhaka was about 650 MW. DESA has 390 000 customers. Industry accounts for 60 per cent of sales, the domestic sector for 28 per cent and commercial customers for 9 per cent.

6.5 EVALUATION OF 1985–90 NATIONAL ELECTRICITY PROGRAMME

Evaluation of the National Programme: General Principles

In this section the economic benefits of the total investment in generation, transmission and distribution facilities commissioned in Bangladesh between 1984–5 and 1989–90 are estimated. In Bangladesh, as in many other countries, electricity generation, transmission and distribution are interdependent and geographical areas are interlinked. It is therefore appropriate to assess system changes as a whole. But it is also important to evaluate alternatives within the system. Section 6.7 examines the economic benefits of the investment in transmission and distribution facilities in Dhaka.

Even with the national programme we are concerned with the *incremental* costs and benefits of the investment programme. Therefore assumptions are required about how services would have been supplied without the programme. If the base system had been managed inefficiently and unplanned outages frequent, the incremental benefits of the programme would be high. On the other hand, if the base system had been operated efficiently and electricity allocated to those who needed it most, the incremental benefits would be lower. Analysts often fail to make explicit assumptions about how the base system would be managed in the absence of a planned investment. Estimated net benefits are usually based on crude estimates of the increase in consumption due to the expanded system and the prices that consumers would be willing to pay for the extra electricity. We follow this practice below but discuss the costs of outages in more detail in Section 6.7.

Ignoring discounting, the net social benefit (NSB) of system improvement can be expressed as:

$$\text{NSB} = \Delta E \cdot \text{WTP} - \text{I} - \Delta\text{OC} +/- \text{EXT} \qquad (6.1)$$

where ΔE is the increase in electricity consumption, WTP is the amount(s) that consumers are willing to pay for the extra electricity, I is capital investment, ΔOC is the change in operating costs, and EXT represents externalities. Let us briefly note some implications.

Firstly, the benefits are based on additional consumption, not on capacity. Secondly, WTP includes consumer surpluses. Because of the lack of convenient substitutes for electricity, the high costs of outages and the underpricing of electricity by some suppliers, many consumers are willing to pay more for electricity than the tariffs they actually pay (Desai, 1985; Webb and Pearce, 1985). As Barnett *et al.* (1994, vol. 2, p. 43) observe, 'Electricity facilitates so many aspects of urban life that it is difficult to conceive of a city the scale of Dhaka without electricity'.

Of course, when electricity is not available substitutes are often found. For example paraffin may be used for domestic lighting and diesel generation for industrial power. Because these are usually inefficient sources of electricity, costs per unit of energy are generally high.

Figure 6.1 illustrates how the estimated willingness to pay for electricity can be based on the price of substitutes. In this diagram, Q_s units of

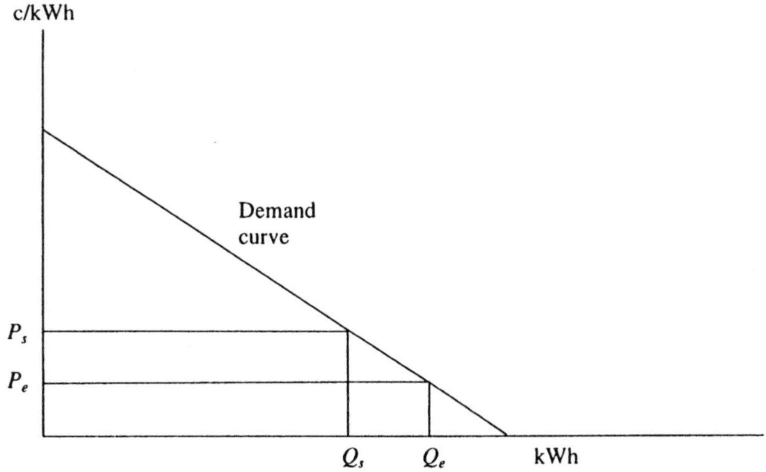

Figure 6.1 The demand for electricity and substitutes

substitutes are consumed initially at price P_s. When electricity is introduced, Q_e units of electricity are consumed at price P_e. The willingness to pay for electricity may be estimated by the formula $(Q_s \times P_s) + (Q_e - Q_s) + P_e + 0.5(Q_e - Q_s)(P_s - P_e)$. This presumes that there is little difference between a kwh of electricity and its substitutes and that the demand curve for power is linear. If P_s is much higher than P_e, the demand curve may be non-linear and the product of the quantity and price changes should be multiplied by about 0.3 instead of 0.5 (Desai, 1985).

Of course the forecast increase in electricity consumption should be consistent with plausible assumptions about the price elasticity of demand. This usually varies by sector: industrial demand is generally less price elastic than residential demand. Desai (1985) suggests that in developing countries the overall elasticity of demand for electricity is usually about 0.5.

Thirdly, the main changes in operating costs relate to plant operating, maintenance and fuel costs. If large alterations in the electricity system are proposed, allowance should also be made for changes in variable overheads, for instance in sales and accounts. Total operating costs usually rise with large increases in system size. However capital investment can reduce operating costs, for example by saving fuel, reducing transmission losses and substituting new for old plant for base loads.

Finally, externalities may also be positive or negative. Potential positive externalities are indirect development benefits, improved law and order and a better home-learning environment. These are rarely valued in monetary terms. The main negative externalities are environmental costs. If these costs are not quantified, a judgement is still required as to whether they would offset any estimated net project benefits.

Evaluation of the National Programme: Assumptions and Results

For this evaluation all costs and benefits are in 1984–5 prices. Non-tradeables, including electricity, are estimated in local prices. Tradeables, including energy sources, are estimated at border prices. The new facilities are assumed to last until 2014–15, when they will be retired. A real discount rate of 10 per cent is assumed. For convenience, results are expressed in US dollars.

The estimated capital costs ($997 million in discounted real terms) are based on BPDB's cost estimates but exclude taxes and duties. A 50 per cent premium is applied to the foreign exchange component (55 per cent) of the capital costs. This premium is a weighted average of the 25 per cent premium generally applied in cost–benefit studies in Bangladesh in 1984–5 and the actual 60 per cent depreciation of the Bangladesh taka required since then to produce an equilibrium exchange rate. BPDB operating costs are 30 per cent of sale revenues. Given that the size of the whole electricity system more than doubled, operating costs are assumed to continue to equal 30 per cent of revenues.

Fuel costs are based on an estimated economic cost of $0.65 per 1000 cubic feet of gas in 1984–5 prices. This includes a depletion premium. The economic cost of gas in Bangladesh is the international price of alternative energy sources when the domestic gas supply is expected to run out (conservatively estimated as about year 2020) discounted by the real interest rate to the relevant operating year. (See Chapter 3 for further discussion of the depletion premium.) This estimated economic cost significantly exceeds the very low extraction cost for natural gas in Bangladesh. However, in the first few years of operation, the BPDB's total fuel costs fell in real terms as the substitution of gas for more costly fuels more than offset the increase in fuel consumption. On the other hand the depletion component of real fuel costs rose over time with the interest rate as resources became scarcer.

Turning to benefit estimation, the BPDB is assumed to continue to sell 60 per cent of its output, to lose 12.5 per cent of output in technical losses and to lose 27.5 per cent through theft. Users paying officially for electricity are assumed to be willing to pay 1.5 times the average tariff of $0.061 per kWh (in 1984–5 prices). The reasoning behind this assumption is that many new electricity users will be willing to pay the price for substitutes based on diesel fuel or paraffin, which cost over twice as much as electricity, while others will be willing to pay only the electricity tariff or a little more. The figure of 1.5 may be too low. Barnett *et al.* (1994) report that landlord charges for electric light bulbs and paraffin wicks are often three times the prices actually paid by their landlords. Drawing on detailed estimates of electricity substitutes used by each main category of user, the World Bank has used an average willingness-to-pay value of 1.75 times the average tariff in recent evaluations.

It is also assumed in this study that the net value of stolen electricity is equal to half the average tariff. Of course some users of stolen electricity would be willing to pay more than the legal tariff; others less than the tariff. In practice most consumers of stolen electricity make informal payments to BPDB employees. Little electricity can be stolen without the collusion of BPDB employees. Barnett *et al.* (1994, vol. 2, p. 48) suggest that 'the people providing illegal connections, repairs and other services are similarly able to charge a "market clearing rent" for their services above the prices charged by the utility'. However part of these payments to employees may be regarded as payment for work done and necessary extra payment to attract people to work for the BPDB. The net (economic) value of stolen electricity is the gross value of electricity to the users less the opportunity cost of the labour providing the illegal services.

The results of the evaluation are shown in Table 6.5. The estimated NPV of the 1985–90 Bangladesh power improvements is \$406 million, the benefit–cost ratio 1.4 and the economic internal rate of return 14 per cent. However, due to underpricing and theft the estimated financial NPV is –\$362 million. Because these results are based on observed costs and usage, they are more accurate than results based entirely on forecasts. However the results are sensitive to assumptions about consumer surpluses of legal users and the value of stolen electricity.

6.6 ENVIRONMENTAL ISSUES IN NATIONAL ELECTRICITY GENERATION

Introduction

The environmental impacts of the national electricity programme include the effects of gas production, electricity generation and resource usage. For the potentially significant impacts (air pollution and global warming), a rough costing is made and the effect on the programme's viability is indicated.

Table 6.5 Bangladesh power sector improvements, 1985–90: economic evaluation

	Additional system costs ($m)				*Additional power (GWh)*				*Benefits ($m)*			*Net benefits ($m)*
	Capital[1]	*O & M*	*Fuel*	*Total*	*Generated*	*Lost*	*Sold*	*Stolen*	*Sales*	*Thefts*[2]	*Total*	
1985	478	0	0	478	0	0	0	0	0	0	0	–478
1986	319	0	0	319	270	34	162	74	15	2	17	–302
1987	255	12	0	267	1058	132	635	291	58	9	67	–200
1988	128	22	0	150	2013	252	1208	554	110	17	127	–23
1989	32	28	0	60	2586	323	1552	711	142	22	163	103
1990	–	35	10	45	3203	400	1922	881	175	27	202	157
1991	–	47	28	75	4323	540	2594	1189	237	36	273	197
1992	–	57	34	92	5250	656	3150	1444	287	44	331	240
1993	–	57	36	94	5250	656	3150	1444	287	44	331	238
1994	–	57	38	96	5250	656	3150	1444	287	44	331	236
1995	–	57	40	97	5250	656	3150	1444	287	44	331	234
1996	–	57	42	100	5250	656	3150	1444	287	44	331	232
1997	–	57	44	102	5250	656	3150	1444	287	44	331	230
1998	–	57	46	104	5250	656	3150	1444	287	44	331	228
1999	–	57	48	106	5250	656	3150	1444	287	44	331	226
2000	–	55	49	103	5000	625	3000	1375	274	42	315	212
2001	–	55	52	106	5000	625	3000	1375	274	42	315	209
2002	–	55	55	109	5000	625	3000	1375	274	42	315	206
2003	–	55	58	112	5000	625	3000	1375	274	42	315	203
2004	–	55	61	115	5000	625	3000	1375	274	42	315	200
2005	–	55	64	118	5000	625	3000	1375	274	42	315	197
2006	–	55	67	121	5000	625	3000	1375	274	42	315	194
2007	–	55	70	124	5000	625	3000	1375	274	42	315	191
2008	–	55	74	128	5000	625	3000	1375	274	42	315	187
2009	–	55	78	132	5000	625	3000	1375	274	42	315	183
2010	–	55	82	136	5000	625	3000	1375	274	42	315	179
2011	–	55	87	141	5000	625	3000	1375	274	42	315	174
2012	–	55	92	146	5000	625	3000	1375	274	42	315	169
2013	–	55	98	152	5000	625	3000	1375	274	42	315	163
2014	–	55	105	159	5000	625	3000	1375	274	42	315	156
2015	–	55	113	167	5000	625	3000	1375	274	42	315	148
NPV at 10%	997	345	256	1597	–	–	–	8735	1738	266	2004	406

NPV (Econ) at 10% ($m)	406
NPV (Fin) at 10% ($m)	–362
BC Ratio[3]	1.41
IRR	0.14

Notes:

1. Based on 80% of ADB generation costs and 90% ADB transmission/distribution costs; and 50% foreign exchange premium on 55% foreign component costs.
2. Estimated user benefits of thefts less payments to BPDB employees (see text).
3. Equal to (benefits – O & M costs – fuel cost)/capital costs.

More detailed impacts relating to transmission and distribution in Dhaka are discussed in Section 6.8.

As usual, the assessment of impacts depends on the alternatives considered. The new generating plants along with improved transmission facilities led to the decommissioning of several old, air polluting, oil and diesel-fired plants in West Bangladesh. They reduced the need for diesel-fired in-house generating plants. They also led to some substitution of gas-based electricity for fuelwood-based energy in the rural areas. The World Bank (1991) noted that, to meet rural demands for energy, 5 per cent of the standing volume of trees are harvested annually. In all these cases the substitution of gas-fired plants for other energy sources provided significant, unquantified, environmental benefits.

Gas Production

The production of gas can create local pollution problems due to poor wastewater treatment and potentially explosive leaks. Operational safety issues, for example protection from electrical systems and safety distances, are also important and it appears that these may be neglected in some gas fields. However the on-shore gas producing installations in Bangladesh are small-scale developments and have little environmental impact (Mahtab *et al.*, 1991). The gas transmission lines are generally buried underground and run mostly through countryside. Estimates of gas leakages over the whole system vary from a range of 2–5 per cent (Bangladesh Oil, Gas and Minerals Corporation) to 8–10 per cent (unofficial estimates). However most of these losses are on the low-pressure distribution network. Losses on the main high-pressure gas grid supplying power stations are minimal.

Electricity Generation: Air and Water Pollution

As noted above, gas-fired power stations produce few air pollutants other than carbon dioxide. Bangladesh gas is high quality with little contamination from hydrogen sulphide, nitrogen or carbon dioxide. The studies quoted in Section 6.3 indicate that the air pollution costs from new gas-fired plants are about c 0.25 per kWh and the costs from old plants about c 0.40 per kWh (in 1989–90 prices). However these are based mainly on abatement costs, which are generally higher than damage costs. Moreover, because of lower output and wages damage costs would be lower in Bangladesh than in Western economies even allowing for the greater population densities. If air pollution damage costs from the 1985–90 gas-fired plants in Bangladesh were say c 0.10 per kWh (in 1984–5 prices), they would be about 1.5 per cent of the electricity price and 1.0 per cent of estimated user benefit per kWh. Including these costs in the evaluation would have negligible impact on the results.

There is some concern that the heat discharged into receiving waters may cause thermal pollution. For example, Mahtab *et al.* (1991) suggest that water returned from the power plants at Ghorasal and Siddhirganj may markedly raise the temperature in the Sitalakhya river, although probably not by enough to harm fish. However operators of the Ashuganj plant believe that the water returned at 40° C to the Dhaleswari river would have negligible impact on the spacious waterbody, whose ambient temperature is usually about 33° C. The ODA concluded in an unpublished energy sector review that, because the power stations are sited on banks of large rivers with perennial flows, they should not create significant thermal pollution.

Lubricating oils are washed away into local water bodies at most power plants when parts are stripped out and cleaned. However the amounts discharged are small and are not likely to cause damage.

Electricity Generation: Global Warming

Drawing on Section 6.3, estimated global warming costs from gas-fired generating plants (based on abatement costs) are about c 1.0–1.5 per kWh in 1989–90 prices. However global damage costs per kWh are probably less than half of abatement costs. Allowing damage costs of say c 0.6 per kWh in 1984–5 prices, global warming costs amounted to about 9 per cent of the electricity price in Bangladesh and to 6 per cent of the estimated user benefit per kWH. Reducing the estimated benefits by 6 per cent would lower the estimated NPV for the national electricity programme by $120 million (and the estimated NPV for the Dhaka improvements estimated below by $32 million). Although significant costs, in neither case would they affect the basic viability of the programmes.

Nevertheless a global warming cost of c 0.6 per kWh could affect the results of a marginal project and a few further comments on the applicability of such costs in evaluation work are in order. On efficiency grounds, global warming costs per kWh hour of electricity produced from natural gas or other sources should apply in Bangladesh as elsewhere. Indeed Bangladesh has special cause for concern because it is highly vulnerable to flooding as a result of global warming. Mahtab *et al.* (1991) estimate that if the sea level were to rise by one metre by the end of the next century, as is possible, Bangladesh would lose output valued at 13 per cent of GDP and assets worth US$14 billion in 1984–5 prices.

Nevertheless there are compelling equity arguments why Bangladesh should not include a global warming cost in its cost–benefit calculus for electricity projects (unless other countries compensate Bangladesh for the loss of electricity). Globally, Bangladesh's contribution to greenhouse gas emissions is minimal because total energy consumption is so small (0.3 per cent of energy consumption in the US) and because Bangladesh does not use coal to generate power. Any reduction in CO_2 emissions in Bangladesh would have a negligible benefit in Bangladesh itself. In 1985 the industrialised countries emitted 3.1 tonnes of carbon per capita; the countries of South and East Asia emitted only 0.2 tonnes per capita (IPCC, 1991). On equity grounds, reductions in carbon emissions should take place overwhelmingly in the industrialised countries.

Resource Use and Energy Efficiency

The limited known reserves of natural gas (about 17 trillion cubic feet of recoverable reserves) are a more pressing problem for Bangladesh. At current growth rates in consumption, 80 per cent of proven gas reserves will be used by the year 2010 and other energy sources will be required for new users. Some analysts predict that, unless gas production is increased, there will be excess demand for gas in the mid-1990s. Of course new reserves may be found – indeed geological data suggest they will. But alternative fuels are high cost and more polluting than natural gas and biomass is in short supply. Efficient energy production and use is therefore important for economic growth and environmental quality.

In order to achieve efficient exploitation of natural gas, the price of gas should correspond to the marginal opportunity cost of supply, including a depletion premium (if required). With a 10 per cent discount rate the depletion premium is negligible if reserves are sufficient for 40 or more years, but the premium increases as the life of the reserves falls. Consultants (for example Coopers and Lybrand, 1987) and the World Bank have conducted several studies of energy prices. These show that the low price received by gas producers has discouraged investment in gas exploration and production; that the gas price to the BPDB was well below long-run marginal opportunity costs including an appropriate depletion premium; that customer tariffs did not reflect real economic cost; and that the tariffs resulted in cross-subsidisation. In the early 1990s the Bank recommended a 25 per cent increase in the gas price to the BPDB.

Electricity prices have also been low, with losses running at about 33 per cent of operating revenue (in 1989–90 operating revenue was $400 million and losses $135 million). Moreover prices do not reflect peak load costs.

Energy consumption per unit of industrial output is significantly higher in Bangladesh than for similar processes under similar conditions elsewhere. However numerous attempts to reform the BPDB's management and pricing structures have been unsuccessful (Barnett *et al.*, 1994).

Concluding Comments

The main environmental concerns in Bangladesh are the long-term shortage of gas supplies, inefficient use of gas and electricity, and global warming. The 1985–90 national electricity programme had significant positive environmental impacts as gas-fired electricity was substituted for oil and diesel-fired electricity and fuelwood-based energy. It also contributed to global warming and some minor air pollution associated with the increase in electricity generation. The evaluation included a depreciation premium to account for the use of scarce natural gas. Rough monetisation of the global warming and negative air pollution impacts indicated that they did not offset the benefits of the 1985–90 programme.

6.7 EVALUATION OF THE 1985–90 DHAKA TRANSMISSION AND DISTRIBUTION PROGRAMME

Evaluation of the Dhaka Programme: General Principles

This section evaluates the investment in transmission and distribution facilities commissioned in Dhaka between 1984–5 and 1989–90, based on estimated *incremental* costs and benefits. The costs include capital expenditures on the distribution system, additional purchases of power by DESA from the national generating and transmission system, and changes in operating costs within the Dhaka distribution system. The most controversial issue is the real cost of purchases from the generating grid. Three possibilities can be identified. Firstly, if there is over-capacity in generation, the real purchase costs are the short-run marginal energy costs. Secondly, if there is currently equilibrium in generation, and capacity increases with demand, the real purchase costs are the long-run marginal costs of increasing the electricity supply. For the long run, the equilibrium assumption is usually appropriate. But, thirdly, if there is a shortage of capacity the real costs of purchases are the prices that other users would pay for the electricity.

The benefits from strengthening and extending the distribution include improved reliability of supply as well as increased usage. What are the benefits of improved reliability (less outages)? Consistent with the discussion of valuation in Section 6.5, the benefits of extra electricity consumption should be based on WTP values, which may include consumer surplus.

There is a risk, however, that this approach may underestimate the benefits of avoiding outage. Outage costs are generally based on either estimated losses of industrial value added or the cost of back-up power required to avoid lost output. Drawing on studies of outage costs in 12 developing countries, London Economics (1992) estimated that the average cost of lost electricity to industry was $1.50 per kWh in 1987 dollars. This was usually eight to ten times the price of electricity in those countries. Estimated outage costs to households were typically about $0.50 per kWh. In the study most relevant to Bangladesh, Pasha *et al.* (1989) estimated that the cost of planned outage to industry in Pakistan ranged from $0.26 to $1.77 per KWh and the cost of unplanned outage ranged from $0.36 to $2.54 per Kwh. For evaluation purposes it is important that WTP values for additional electricity allow adequately for the benefits of reduced outage, but that double counting is avoided.

Evaluation of the Dhaka Programme: Assumptions and Results

As for the national programme, all costs and benefits are expressed in 1984–5 prices in US dollars; the facilities operate to 2014–15 and a real discount rate of 10 per cent per annum is assumed.

The capital costs are based on BPDB estimates of internationally competitive prices. These were significantly lower than the prices of UK firms supplying plant under ODA grant aid conditions. The real costs ($94 million in discounted terms) exclude indirect taxes and duties but include a 50 per cent foreign exchange premium applied to the foreign exchange component (66 per cent). Estimated operating costs of Dhaka distribution are $0.006 per KWh. Costs of electricity purchases are based on the writer's estimate of the long-run marginal costs ($0.042 per kWh) for new generating and transmission capacity plus operating and fuel costs.

Turning to benefits, this study assumes that the investment made possible 80 per cent of the increases in electricity consumption in Dhaka between 1984–5 and the early 1990s. This allows for some increase in distribution even under the stretched distribution system of the mid-1980s. Similar system losses and user benefits, including consumer surpluses, are attributed to Dhaka as to Bangladesh. However a slightly higher average tariff of $0.0648 per kWh applied in Dhaka. In the absence of any estimates of reduced outages due to the improved distribution, no benefits are included specifically for reduced outages. Of course it would be double counting to

Table 6.6 Dhaka electricity distribution improvements, 1985–90: economic evaluation

	Additional system costs ($m)				*Additional power (GWh)*				*Benefits ($m)*			*Net benefits ($m)*
	Purchases	*Capital*[1]	*O & M*	*Total*	*Bought*	*Lost*	*Sold*	*Stolen*	*Sales*	*Thefts*[2]	*Total*	
1985	0	17	0	17	0	0	0	0	0	0	0	–17
1986	2	39	0	41	47	2	32	13	3	0	4	–37
1987	8	37	1	46	185	9	125	51	12	2	14	–32
1988	15	26	1	42	352	18	238	97	23	3	26	–16
1989	19	1	2	22	453	23	305	124	30	4	34	12
1990	24	–	2	26	561	28	378	154	37	5	42	16
1991	32	–	3	35	757	38	511	208	50	7	56	22
1992	39	–	4	42	919	46	620	253	60	8	68	26
1993	48	–	5	53	1148	57	775	316	75	10	86	33
1994	48	–	5	53	1148	57	775	316	75	10	86	33
1995	48	–	5	53	1148	57	775	316	75	10	86	33
1996	48	–	5	53	1148	57	775	316	75	10	86	33
1997	48	–	5	53	1148	57	775	316	75	10	86	33
1998	48	–	5	53	1148	57	775	316	75	10	86	33
1999	48	–	5	53	1148	57	775	316	75	10	86	33
2000	46	–	4	50	1094	55	738	301	72	10	82	31
2001	46	–	4	50	1094	55	738	301	72	10	82	31
2002	46	–	4	50	1094	55	738	301	72	10	82	31
2003	46	–	4	50	1094	55	738	301	72	10	82	31
2004	46	–	4	50	1094	55	738	301	72	10	82	31
2005	46	–	4	50	1094	55	738	301	72	10	82	31
2006	46	–	4	50	1094	55	738	301	72	10	82	31
2007	46	–	4	50	1094	55	738	301	72	10	82	31
2008	46	–	4	50	1094	55	738	301	72	10	82	31
2009	46	–	4	50	1094	55	738	301	72	10	82	31
2010	46	–	4	50	1094	55	738	301	72	10	82	31
2011	46	–	4	50	1094	55	738	301	72	10	82	31
2012	46	–	4	50	1094	55	738	301	72	10	82	31
2013	46	–	4	50	1094	55	738	301	72	10	82	31
2014	46	–	4	50	1094	55	738	301	72	10	82	31
2015	46	–	4	50	1094	55	738	301	72	10	82	31
NPV at 10%	273	94	26	393	–	–	–	1785	426	58	484	91

NPV (Econ) at 10% ($m)	91	BC Ratio[3]	1.33
NPV (Fin) at 10% ($m)	–102	IRR	0.18

Notes:
1. At internationally competitive prices.
2. Estimated user benefits of thefts less payments to BPDB employees (see text).
3. Equal to (benefits – O & M costs – fuel cost)/capital costs.

include both the full value of the electricity consumed with the project and the costs of outages avoided.

The results are shown in Table 6.6. The estimated NPV of the 1985–90 Dhaka power distribution improvements is $91 million, the benefit–cost ratio 1.3 and the economic internal rate of return 18 per cent. Due to underpricing and theft, the estimated financial NPV is –$102 million. Like the national results, the economic results are sensitive to changes in assumptions about consumer surpluses and the value of stolen electricity. However the conclusions are robust against realistic variations in assumptions. If allowance were made for the benefits of reduced outages, the real economic returns would be probably higher than estimated. On the other hand, as Barnett *et al.* point out (1994, vol. 2, p. 52), although the project was beneficial to the Bangladesh economy, the project would not be financially viable under any realistic set of assumptions.

6.8 ENVIRONMENTAL IMPACTS OF TRANSMISSION AND DISTRIBUTION IN DHAKA

Possible Adverse Impacts

Possible adverse impacts of additional transmission and distribution of electricity in Dhaka are land acquisition and resettlement, increased areas subjected to electromagnetic radiation, visual disamenities, access facilities for substations and adverse impacts on land use locations. However none of these can be considered a major cost.

Firstly, land requirements for substations and related facilities and transmission lines were modest (only 2–3 ha) compared with those for large infrastructure projects. Many acquired plots were located in areas with few inhabitants or on vacant land. When constructed, the high-voltage transmission ring around Dhaka was located outside the built-up area. Although the BPDB has resumption powers, it generally paid market prices for land. Also, the board compensates farmers for land loss when transmission lines are constructed. Most communities welcomed the extension of electricity supply and did not object to expansion of the system. Only 10–13 families were displaced under the ODA project(s).

However land acquisition has not been without difficulties and various costs have been incurred to mitigate impacts. Vacant urban land has become more difficult to find and more valuable in crowded Dhaka. One substation (Wagda) is in a congested commercial centre; another substation (Shabag) is located next to a hospital. In the most crowded areas the BPDB has started to use underground cabling, despite the considerable costs. Also, the board changed some proposed substation locations rather than confront land-owners who would not agree compensation terms and incurred extra construction costs on sites that no one else wanted. In Dhaka's volatile political climate a tactical withdrawal is sometimes necessary to ensure the safety of utility personnel.

Secondly, many people live close to electrical distribution facilities and even under transmission lines. Whether this is dangerous to health is not yet known.

Thirdly, the electrical distribution system, including substations, is unsightly in many places. Large steel towers and bulk power transmission lines have been constructed around Dhaka, often across extensive wetlands. With hindsight, the location of some transmission facilities further from the city would have enhanced the environment. However many other features of urban life in Dhaka, notably waste strewn over the streets, are far worse visual disamenities. The present visual impacts of electricity supply are of minimal concern to most Dhaka households.

Fourthly, access to substations may also require valuable land and intrude on local settlements. However land requirements for access have been generally planned well in advance and social costs have not been substantial.

Finally, concern is sometimes expressed that extension of electricity supply may cause development to occur in unwanted areas, especially in a city with few effective zoning regulations. Because many factors influence industry location it is difficult to establish the effect of electricity supply. In one area (Dhanmondi) dramatic developments followed extension of electricity supply, but in another two areas (Ramna and Kawranbazar) substations are operating well within their installed capacity. Dhaka planners argued to the writer that they do not believe that the distribution of electricity within the city has influenced the pattern of development, although it may have affected the pace of development in some areas. Some believe that the relative availability of electricity in Dhaka encourages industry to locate in the capital rather than elsewhere and that this has social costs. However such ideas are speculative. And it should be noted that, insofar as power supply can influence land-use development, it may also be used to promote socially beneficial development patterns.

Environmental Benefits

On the other hand the improved distribution system has had some significant environmental benefits. It has saved energy costs (most of which benefits show up as user benefits), reduced the pollution associated with displaced energy sources and reduced the incidence of industrial accidents.

The main energy sources displaced in Dhaka were diesel used in generators by industry and paraffin used by households for lighting. Most households use gas for cooking, but some substitution of electricity for biomass in household cooking may have occurred. These displacements improved outdoor and indoor air quality. But the extent of these improvements has not been measured.

The safety of Power Board employees and the general public is a major issue. Members of the ODA evaluation team were given many graphic accounts of fires, explosions and electrocutions, especially in slum areas. The upgrading of the distribution system has undoubtedly improved safety. Before the upgrading the low-voltage system was so overloaded that transformer fires and explosions were commonplace. Since the upgrading there have been fewer explosions in substations, better insulated CV conductors, less system overload and fewer equipment failures. On the other hand some accidents will have been associated with the installation of plant and equipment.

National statistics from the BPDB and the Independent Office of the Electrical Inspector indicate that accidents associated with electricity supply fell in most years from 1984–5 to 1991–2. However these two data sets do not tally. There appears to have been considerable under-reporting of accidents (the statistics contain a disproportionately high number of fatalities). Also, the data for Dhaka are seriously incomplete. In the time available to the ODA evaluation team it was not possible to make accurate estimates of the safety gains from the improved distribution of electricity in Dhaka.

Concluding Comments

The main environmental cost associated with the extension of electricity in Dhaka is land acquisition. However much of this cost is included in BPDB expenses, either in the market-plus prices paid to landowners or in moving to less preferred sites with higher construction or operating costs. The main environmental benefit is improved safety. This could be substantial but cannot be valued reliably from existing data. Overall, although the analysis of environmental impacts is qualitative, it is clear that the net effects do not offset the efficiency benefits estimated in the previous section.

6.9 CONCLUSIONS

In Bangladesh there are far more complaints about the lack of electricity than there are about the environmental impacts of electricity supply. Local citizens usually welcome the construction of substations as a sign that electricity is coming. They stone them when power shedding occurs. Barnett *et al.* (1994) document the dramatic improvements in employment prospects and the quality of home life due to electricity.

Using cost–benefit criteria, the investments in electricity supply in Bangladesh and in Dhaka between 1985 and 1990 were well justified. However the estimated rates of return are significantly lower than those forecast by the Asian Development Bank and ODA before the projects started. The main reasons for the fall in return are the slower than forecast increase in consumption, higher operating costs and higher system losses.

In order to estimate costs and benefits, some substantial adjustments to market prices were made. These included a 50 per cent premium for foreign exchange costs, estimates of the real costs of natural gas including a depletion premium, a 50 per cent premium for consumer surplus from electricity sales and estimates of the real net benefits of stolen electricity.

Environmental impacts were not included formally within the cost–benefit estimates. However on any plausible estimates of their net costs they would not offset the estimated efficiency benefits. This is partly because gas-fired generating plants produce relatively little air or water pollution. Also, in any evaluation it is the changes from some alternative that matter. In Bangladesh the gas-fired plants reduced the use of the more polluting oil- and diesel-fired plants in urban areas and biomass use in rural areas.

The main environmental impacts associated with electricity generation in Bangladesh are excessive energy resource use, air pollution and greenhouse impacts. Under-pricing natural gas discourages investment in gas exploration and over-use of gas. Under-pricing electricity causes excess consumption of electricity and excessive air pollution and CO_2 emissions. The appropriate technical solutions to conserve energy, including appropriate prices, are well-known, but there is a local institutional reluctance to adopt efficient prices. Stolen electricity and bureaucratic corruption are chronic problems. Although (or perhaps because) the electricity authorities control potentially huge revenues in excess of half a billion dollars annually, Barnett *et al.* (1994, vol. 2) conclude that the authorities are incapable of running the systems at a profit and therefore of providing an inherently sustainable electricity system.

The problems associated with air pollution are more technical. Monitoring and measuring air pollution from power plants have proved difficult tasks in developed countries, and even in these countries limited reliance can be placed on the damage cost estimates produced to date. It is not realistic to expect to cost air pollution from power plants in developing countries without a substantial research effort (see also the study of transport impacts in Lagos in Chapter 8). In this study we were obliged to modify estimates of air pollution costs in developed countries to obtain estimates of local air pollution costs. A similar procedure would be required in most developing countries.

Because global warming costs are not country specific, the same global warming costs for CO_2 emissions from power stations can (and from an efficiency perspective should) be applied in Bangladesh as in developed countries. However most estimates of global warming costs are based on inappropriate abatement cost estimates and there is no consensus yet on appropriate damage cost estimates. Further to this, however, it is absurd to expect a poor country such as Bangladesh to curtail its supply of electricity for the purpose of reducing CO_2 emissions when the per capita emissions of CO_2 in industrialised countries are 20 times the per capita emissions in Bangladesh, unless the less developed country receives international compensation.

Turning to the transmission and distribution of electricity, the main environmental impacts were land acquisition and safety. In both cases valuation procedures are well-known (see earlier chapters). In fact many land costs were included in BPDB expenditures in the cost–benefit analysis. But it was not possible to quantify the apparently substantial reduction in accidents due to the improved distribution system. Nor was it possible to estimate the relationship (if any) between electricity and land use developments or to cost the impacts (if any) of electromagnetic transmission effects. Other local impacts, such as visual or access effects, were considered negligible.

7 Valuing Urban Slum Improvements in Visakhapatnam, India

7.1 INTRODUCTION

In India nearly 40 million people live in officially designated slums in cities with over a million residents. Although slum environments vary, they share some basic characteristics: very poor households, mostly living below official poverty lines; poor quality shelter, often temporary in structure; exceptional population densities and overcrowding; inadequate water supply; insanitary conditions; a high incidence of sickness; and short life expectancies. Many slum dwellers are illegal squatters living on the margin of society, without security of tenure, receiving few public services and vulnerable to the strongest members of the slum.

This chapter evaluates strategies to deal with slums, taking Visakhapatnam as a case-study. Visakhapatnam lies on the east coast of India, midway between Calcutta and Madras. Between 1971 and 1991 its population trebled from 360 000 to 1.05 million. This rapid increase reflected the city's industrial growth as a major naval base and manufacturing centre, the poverty of the surrounding rural areas from which many migrate, and the high natural birth rate. However there is an acute shortage of land in the city, which is bounded by hills and sea. Population density is high, with 30 000 persons per square kilometre over much of the city. Despite some industrial prosperity over 200 000 people (40 000 households) live in nearly 200 officially designated slums with an average annual household income of 13 000 rupees (£260). Half the adults in the slums are illiterate. Few slum households have private tap water and only half the slums have public tap water. Under one in five slum houses has a toilet and 60 per cent of slum dwellers defecate in the open. Not surprisingly, health problems are rife.

In 1988 the Municipal Corporation of Visakhapatnam, supported by the UK Overseas Development Administration (ODA), started a major programme to improve 170 slums (subsequently expanded to cover 200). This programme included physical infrastructure improvements (roads, drainage, paths, street lighting), improved water supply, public toilets, community centres, primary health care services, and educational and training services. Concurrently the Municipal Corporation provided subsidised housing loans to 25 per cent of slum residents to improve their dwellings. The costs and benefits of the slum improvement programme are estimated below.

This chapter starts with an overview of the general characteristics and consequences of slums and policies towards slums that draws on the World Bank Environment Department (1991, pp. 153–67). The next three sections describe the Visakhapatnam slum improvement programme, its costs and main impacts. Section 7.6 discusses approaches to benefit valuation. The following three sections evaluate the net benefits of the whole Visakhapatnam programme; the net benefits of the programme in a sample of 19 slums; and the returns to investment in education, vocational training and health services. The final two sections discuss policy issues and summarise the study's conclusions.

7.2 THE NATURE OF SLUMS AND POSSIBLE POLICIES

Major Characteristics of Slums

As noted, slums are generally characterised by extreme population density, household poverty, poor housing, often on unsuitable land, and a highly degraded environment. Water is almost invariably in short supply. Slum residents often have to walk long distances to obtain safe drinking water. Human excrement is a major concern. Few slums are connected to sewer systems. Household waste is usually a problem and frequently ends up in the drainage system, causing blockages and flooding or water quality deterioration. Or it is left in open dumps where it harbours hosts to parasites and causes toxic air pollutants when burned off. Indoor air pollution is common, due to indoor combustion of highly polluting traditional fuels for cooking and heating in the absence of adequate ventilation.

Notwithstanding these common features, low-income urban settlements are differentiated and not equally degraded and hopeless. Inner city slums have the highest densities, but they may offer good access to jobs and income. Peripheral slum settlements have the fewest urban services and offer poorer access to income opportunities. Tenurial status is often crucial, as occupation rights, or better still land ownership, offer prospects for betterment. Also, within slums it is not uncommon to find some relatively solid dwellings cheek-by-jowl with shanties.

Causes of Slums

The main causes of urban slums are high rates of growth of urban populations, an impoverished urban underclass and a shortage of urban land suitable for housing. Paradoxically, the worst slums may occur in prosperous cities as these encourage most migration from rural areas and tend to be densely populated. The quality of life at the urban margin also reflects the poverty of the rural alternative. In cities poor households usually occupy the least desirable housing land. This is often marginal urban land barely suitable for housing: for example it may be prone to flooding, landslides or erosion. Slum development frequently occurs illegally, haphazardly, and without planning or controls.

Poor urban management encourages slum development. Governments frequently exacerbate natural land shortages by inefficient regulation of land and building developments and poor management of public land. Poorly defined or administered property rights weaken the functioning of property markets. Abuse of common property is a common cause of urban degradation. Inadequate pricing policies cause resources to be wasted (water is a prime example); stifle enterprise and restrict supply (rent control is a major example); and cause shortages of public funds and services.

Once created, slum environments tend to deteriorate. Many writers claim that slum households are unaware of the importance of a clean environment for personal health and are slow to adopt clean practices. However slum dwellers often lack incentives to improve their environment. Polluting activities typically damage the community more than the polluter, while individual actions to improve slums are ineffectual and unrewarded.

Consequences of Slums

Slums impact on health, productivity and amenity. Slum dwellers are more vulnerable to disease than are other urban residents. In slums the incidence of acute gastroenteritic and respiratory disorders is high; more infants suffer low birthweights and malnutrition; slum inhabitants have a greater risk of contracting chronic and degenerative diseases, as well as being subjet to traumas and psycho-social problems due to environmental stress.

Slums are usually low productivity areas. They provide a poor educational learning and training environment and, generally, poor income opportunities. Poor health also reduces productivity. Moreover unsuitable housing land and inadequate urban infrastructure in slums impose high recurrent costs on slum residents and public authorities. Slum housing is especially vulnerable to accidents, damage and collapse and there is a high risk of fire and flood.

Household amenity is greatly diminished by highly congested living conditions, poor housing, lack of open spaces and a polluted, insanitary environment. Slum environments are conducive to adverse social impacts, a high incidence of family breakdown, alcohol and drug abuse, informal violence and psychological stress with little hope for improved living standards.

Although slums principally affect their inhabitants, they also affect neighbouring areas and sometimes the whole urban community. Improper disposal of waste can degrade water and air quality over a wide area. Diseases spread into neighbouring areas and, in epidemics, across the whole city.

Strategies for Slum Improvements

In the long term, lower rates of population growth, improved conditions in rural areas and increased incomes in urban areas are needed to reduce the demand for slum housing in cities. Without changes in demand there will always be slums. Nevertheless the immediate plight of slum households cannot be ignored. To eliminate or at least improve slums, three distinct but complementary strategies can be adopted.

One strategy is to improve the overall efficiency of urban land and housing development. This means ensuring that potential urban land is available for development; land is put to its best possible use; planning rules for housing are flexible and reflect low-income housing needs as well as middle-class environmental standards; urban infrastructure services are provided efficiently and at marginal cost; all industries have equal access to resources and all households have equal access to services; and that polluters pay for damages. This 'efficiency' strategy should maximise the total housing services available to the community. Through the market filtering process, each section of the community moves over time into improved housing. Slum dwellers move into vacated lower-income housing outside slums areas and slums are knocked down and redeveloped. Unfortunately this 'trickle-down' approach has two defects. Benefits take a long time to trickle down to slum dwellers. And unless slum incomes rise or house prices fall, slum dwellers cannot afford to move to higher quality housing.

A second strategy is to develop new, low-cost, site-and-service land, with or without low-cost housing, and make this available to low-income households. However, low-income households, especially slum households, can rarely afford the cost of new housing or land so that large subsidies are required. Also, the strategy often requires households to relocate away from their established communities and sources of income.

Another strategy is to improve the slum areas themselves. Such improvements need to be comprehensive. They should include improved housing as well as a wide range of infrastructure improvements, for example improved drains, roads, footpaths, waste disposal, water supply and sanitation facilities. Households should be aware of the importance of environmental health and family planning techniques. There should be improvements in income earning capacities in the slums and financial provision for infrastructure maintenance. Moreover slum improvements may not be appropriate on unsuitable housing land, for example on steep hillsides, land prone to flooding, land close to hazardous industry and land with a high opportunity cost in the centre of cities.

In conclusion, some policies (for example changes in planning regulations or pricing policies) are usually low cost and should be part of any slum improvement programme. But such policy changes alone are rarely sufficient. Likewise, by themselves slum improvements may encourage poor families to migrate into these improved slums, resulting in minor overall improvements in urban housing conditions. The best approach usually includes elements of each strategy plus an income-enhancement policy. Of course priorities must be determined. In order to develop rational priorities based on cost-beneficial criteria, data on household needs, environmental conditions and production costs are required. Often such data are scarce.

7.3 URBAN SLUM IMPROVEMENT IN VISAKHAPATNAM

The government of India has adopted various strategies towards slums. It initially attempted to prevent the growth of slum areas. In the mid-1950s the government introduced slum clearance schemes designed to rehouse slum families in tenements and developed low-cost housing in green-field sites. However only the more affluent half of the community could afford this 'low-cost' housing (Lipton and Toye, 1990). Likewise the development of site and service plots, again in green-field sites, attracted higher income households. In the early 1970s the government provided funds to municipal corporations for environmental improvements within slums. Subsequently the Housing and Urban Development Corporation provided funds to local housing corporations to lend to households for housing improvements in slums. Households were initially expected to upgrade and occupy their own houses, but recently houseowners have been permitted to hire labour and to rent out parts of their houses. Throughout, the government has separately provided other social programmes, such as health care and education.

Slum improvement programmes in Visakhapatnam date from 1979, when the Visakhapatnam Urban Community Development Department (UCDD) was established with special responsibility for slum improvements. But the scope to carry out improvements was constrained at first by lack of finance.

In the mid-1980s the Municipal Council of Visakhapatnam (MCV) and the ODA developed a comprehensive programme in Visakhapatnam to improve the living conditions, health and incomes of 190 000 people living in 36 500 houses in 170 slums over 10 years old. Of these slums, 110 were on public lands, 37 on private landlord property and 23 largely in private individual land ownership. At that time, one in five dwellings were pucca houses with stabilised block walls and permanent roofs; one in ten were semi-pucca houses with mud walls and tiled roofs; seven in ten were kutcha houses with thatched roofs and various wall materials, including many pyramid-shaped houses constructed entirely of thatching materials. A local household survey in 1984–5 showed that most slum households were earning under R500 (£10) per month; four out of five slum dwellers were illiterate; the incidence of gastro-intestinal and respiratory diseases was high; and one in five children were suffering from malnutrition. The MCV/ODA programme included civic infrastructure improvements and health and education services, to be provided by the UCDD; land ownership reform, to be implemented by MCV; and housing improvements, to be funded through the city's Housing Corporation.

The ODA-Funded Slum Improvement Programme

The *main physical achievements* of the programme are shown in Table 7.1. Roads, paths, storm drains and multi-purpose community halls were the main elements. The city's main drainage channels were also improved where they affected conditions in the slums. Water, sanitation services and dustbins for garbage collection were much smaller elements. Government targets of a public tap for each 20 households and a public toilet for each 10 households have not been met. The ODA/MCV view is that community latrines are difficult to maintain, unpopular and a poor investment if space permits individual latrines.

The *health services* concentrate on primary health care, provided six days a week from 46 centres each serving about 5000 people. The services include health education, family planning, nutrition supplementation for preschool children, immunisation programmes, the training of traditional birth attendants, treatment of minor ailments and provision of basic drugs. *Socio-economic services* include preschool activities (three hours a day), non-formal education for school drop-outs (two hours daily), adult literacy courses (one hour daily) and vocational training, usually in local training institutions, for example craft training, sewing, welding, training in repair services and various other trades. These ODA-funded services have been complemented by the national adult mass literacy programme and the government's Nehru Rozgar Yogana programme, under which subsidised bank loans are provided to low-income households to start a business.

Land Reform and Housing Improvements

The land reforms were designed to give slum inhabitants security of tenure and a stake in the slum improvements, and to provide an organised layout for each slum. The MCV purchased land in about 20 slums then in private

Table 7.1 Main physical achievements

Civic infrastructure (to September 1992)	
Roads/paths (bitumen) (m^2)	98 915
Roads/paths (concrete) (m^2)	95 815
Dustbins (large and small) (no.)	129
Slum drains (all sizes) (l.m.)	107 871
Gedda (town drain) improvements (l.m.)	25 905
Culverts (no.)	92
Community halls (large and small) (no.)	139
Street lights (no.)	955
Water pipelines (l.m.)	4 999
Water fountains (no.)	99
Bore wells (no.)	267
Pilot water project (l.m.)	1 375
Public latrines (no.)	37
Public bathrooms (no.)	7
Health programmes (to March 1992) (no.)	
Primary health centres	46
Trained delivery nurses	356
Clean hut competitions	119
Food and nutrition camps	94
Socioeconomic programmes (to March 1992) (no.)	
Pre-school education centres	106
Non-formal education centres	142
Adult education centres	142
Reading rooms/libraries	162
Short-term vocational courses	27
Nos trained on vocational courses	1 008
Sewing centres	162

Sources: ODA and Visakhapatnam UCDD.

ownership, planned the 170 slums, allowing 60 square yards per plot, and provided legal tenures (pattas) to the plots. The layouts were planned to minimise the loss of established pucca houses. However the 60 square yard lot criterion sometimes reduced the number of dwellings in a slum.

Pattas are usually permanent (free) land leases. Households are generally not allowed to sell pattas when they are used as security for Housing Corporation loans or for the first five years of the grant. The granting of pattas combined with lot size restrictions created considerable excess demand for lots in many slums (with owners, tenants and family members all demanding pattas). This placed considerable power and some black market funds in the hands of the slum neighbourhood committees, who determined lot allocations (Prasada Rao and Rajesh Patnaik, 1992).

Between early 1990 and late 1992 the Housing Corporation provided subsidised loans for pucca house construction to about 12 000 households in 71 slums. In 1992 the normal loan was R11 700 and a grant of R1000 was also provided. Because construction of even a modest pucca house cost about R23 000, households had to find another R10 000 or so. By late 1992 about 6000 houses had been completed. The Housing Corporation also supplied subsidised loans of R4000 for house improvements to 3000 households.

Programme Maintenance

Maintenance of infrastructure is shared between the MCV and the slum communities. The MCV is responsible for replacing worn-out asphalt roads, waste collection and maintaining drains. The slum communities are responsible for cleaning drains and sewers, patching roads, replacing inspection chambers and manhole covers, repairing leakages in pipelines and maintaining community centres. The state (Andhra Pradesh) is expected to take over responsibility for providing health care in the slums and will integrate the established PHC centres into the city health care system. The MCV will probably take over responsibility for providing socioeconomic services to the slums.

7.4 PROGRAMME COSTS

ODA Expenditures

The ODA provided £9.0 million for the programme. Of this, 71 per cent had been expended by September 1992 (when this study was done). However the rupee devaluation from R23.0 = £1.0 when the project was approved in 1987 to R48.5 = £1.0 in 1992 enabled the MCV to complete most of the proposed programme by September 1992 and plan some extra work within the original pound sterling budget.

Table 7.2 shows expenditure by major activity category in 1991–2 rupees. Engineering accounted for two thirds of expenditure by September 1992 and will account for 75 per cent when the projects are complete. Relatively small parts of the budget were allocated to health and education services. In addition, the ODA has provided £100 000 per annum in off-budget management and advisory services to the project.

Housing Expenditures

Data on housing expenditure in the slums from 1988 to 1992 are not readily available. However, allowing for full completion of 6000 houses, half completion of another 1500 houses and improvements to a further 3000 houses, total housing expenditure in the slums to September 1992 would have been about R185 million. This was only slightly less than total programme expenditure.

Maintenance Expenditure

Annual civil engineering maintenance expenditure is usually 5–10 per cent of capital expenditure. The higher percentage would probably be required to maintain the slum assets close to their original condition. Some roads and drains constructed early in the programme already require rehabilitation. One third of the bore wells were reported out of order within one year. Also, water supplies to some public latrines failed. The lower expenditure percentage (5 per cent) would probably lead to major asset deterioration in 10–15 years.

Resource Costs

In order to evaluate the programme, it is necessary to consider whether the financial expenditure adequately reflects resource costs. The main resource omitted is land. This is reasonable because with or without the programme most land in the slums would be devoted to housing. The compulsory purchase of some slum land from private landlords is a transfer of ownership, not a use of resources.

Table 7.2 Direct ODA funded expenditures (1991–2 rupees)[1]

	1988 to Sept. 1992 (*Rs mn*)	(*%*)	*After Sept. 1992* (*Rs mn*)
Engineering	136.9	67.6	82.4
Health services	17.6	8.7	2.5
Socio-economic[2]	5.5	2.7	2.0
Education[3]	9.7	4.8	3.1
Establishment[4]	17.9	8.8	0.9
Office costs[5]	8.4	4.1	0.0
Training/eval./computers[6]	3.9	1.9	2.7
Machinery[7]	2.7	1.3	1.8
Total	202.6	99.9	95.4

Notes:
1. Based on annual inflation rate of 6 per cent advised by the Visakhapatnam Institute for Development and Planning Studies.
2. Income generating and cultural activities, including vocational training, revolving loans and so on.
3. Nursery schools, non-formal education and adult literacy.
4. Staff overheads/permanent employees of UCDD, including engineers and community development officers.
5. Office overheads in Visakhapatnam.
6. Includes staff training.
7. Includes JCBs to clear drains.

Source: ODA.

Of course land costs should be included when the land has a valuable alternative use, for example inner city commercial land. Then, the value forgone is an implicit cost of the programme. Also, when land shortage combined with the lot size rule causes the MCV to relocate households to other areas, the replacement costs should be added to project costs. However these cases are exceptional and are not included below.

Nor has any adjustment been made for possible differences between financial and resource costs. The differences were considered minor. Most expenditure was on local Indian goods and services; imports were minimal. The prices of some materials, for example cement prices, were controlled and did not fully represent the value of the materials to the Indian economy. Also, no adjustment has been made for possible discrepancies between wages and the opportunity costs of labour.

7.5 PROGRAMME SERVICES AND IMPACTS

Approach to Measurement of Impacts

Outputs of social programmes are rarely easy to value. In national income accounting these outputs are often measured by the inputs, for example of health or education services. This approach would be self-defeating in an evaluation study because, by definition, benefits (outputs) would equal costs (inputs). Fortunately various ODA-commissioned studies of the Visakhapatnam programme provide valuable output data.

The main study was a household survey (in 1988 and 1991) by the Visakhapatnam Institute for Development and Planning Studies (IDPS) (Sarveswara Rao and Ramachandrudu, 1992a). The IDPS selected 800 households (one third of all households) from 10 of the 45 slums improved in 1988–9. One slum was omitted from the 1991 survey because the development programmes had not been completed. Allowing also for emigrating households, 612 households were interviewed in both 1988 and 1991. The sample of nine slums is fairly representative of the slums in the city. It may be noted, however, that six of these slums also had housing schemes whereas, overall, only 25 per cent of slum households were involved in housing schemes. The survey provides useful data on changes in housing conditions and health and education status.

In addition the IDPS carried out a nutrition and morbidity survey of 80 households in 1988 and 1991 (Swarajyalakshmi *et al.*, 1992); analysed the households moving in and out of the slums (Sarveswara Rao and Ramachandrudu, 1992b); and conducted a detailed review of the impacts of the programme on the lives of 35 households in four slums (Prasada Rao and Rajesh Patnaik, 1992). Also the UCDD studied the impacts of the vocational training programme (Patrudu, 1992).

Most of the surveys described slum households before and after the provision of programme services. Such observations must be interpreted carefully. Some observed changes (for example rising incomes) may be due to causes other than programme services. On the other hand some impacts (for example improved health) may not be observable within a three year period. The surveys did not include control slum areas without programmes because there were no strictly comparable slums outside the programme.

The following subsections summarise the impacts on housing and the environment, health care and status, education and income, and other impacts. They show some substantial improvements in living standards.

Housing and Environment

As shown in Table 7.3, many more slum households had secure land tenure in 1991 than in 1988. There were more pucca houses, and house size and electricity supply increased significantly. Waste disposal practices improved, with greater use of dustbins for solid waste and drains (instead of roads or paths) for wastewater. The risk of flood and fire was reduced.

However some important elements of environmental quality improved little. Households with access to protected (tap) drinking water increased only marginally. Nearly half the households still depend on well water, which tends to be saline, may be polluted and is often inconvenient to obtain. Few households have their own latrines – even in pucca houses under one third had separate latrines in 1991. Moreover communal latrines were not properly maintained (Hodgson, 1992). Two-thirds of all households continue to use traditional, polluting, fuels (firewood, dung cakes and charcoal) for cooking, although there has been some substitution of firewood for dung cakes.

Health Care and Status

The programme's health care services have been well utilised. In 1990–1 there were 172 000 attendances at the 46 PHC centres, equivalent to about one attendance per slum resident. The proportion of fully immunised

Table 7.3 Housing and environment

	1988		*1991*		*Change*
Households	*No.*	*%*	*No.*	*%*	*(%)*
Owning house	533	87.1	542	88.6	1.5
With land tenure	186	30.4	449	73.4	43.0
With pucca houses	182	29.7	339	55.4	25.6
Less than 100 sq. ft	–	34.8	–	19.8	–15.0
More than 200 sq. ft	–	17.3	–	34.1	16.8
Average area sq. ft	144	–	171	–	18.8
With electricity	211	34.5	381	62.3	27.8
With separate latrine	72	11.8	133	21.7	9.9
With tap water	325	53.1	345	56.4	3.3
Using dustbins	108	17.7	282	46.1	28.4
Using drains	368	60.1	529	86.4	26.3
Using traditional fuel	405	66.2	414	67.6	–1.4

Source: Household Surveys, Sarveswara Rao and Ramachandrudu, 1992a.

children (aged one to three years) rose from 25 per cent to 83 per cent. More women adopted permanent family planning methods. Pregnant women registered more quickly and institutional deliveries increased from 42 per cent to 72 per cent.

Nevertheless there was little immediate evidence of an overall improvement in health status. In 1991–2 there were 42 stillbirths and seven maternal deaths during 2628 deliveries in the 170 project slums. The increase in institutional delivery did not reduce the probability (14 per cent) of problems during delivery. There have been fewer post-natal problems, but whether this is due to the changed delivery process is not known.

Between 1988 and 1991 reported diseases actually increased in the slums (Table 7.4). Among general diseases, malaria, typhoid, respiratory disorders and skin diseases increased significantly and gastroenteric disorders also rose. Among chronic diseases, cases of strokes, high blood pressure and diabetes all rose. On the other hand, unlike in 1988 there were no reported cases in 1991 of whooping cough or diphtheria, both of which are preventable by immunisation.

The increased morbidity incidence almost certainly reflected a city-wide trend, for example for malaria. It may also have reflected an increased tendency to report diseases. However the incidence of malaria is 3–4 times higher in the slums than elsewhere (Hodgson, 1992). Moreover several morbidities, such as respiratory infections and skin diseases, can be attributed to the ongoing poor slum environments – the poor water supply, inadequate sanitation, indoor air pollution, the lack of personal hygiene and still inadequate nutrition.

In 1991 nearly all surveyed adults suffered vitamin and iron deficiencies, two thirds suffered calorie deficiencies and one-third suffered protein deficiencies. There had been no significant improvement since 1988 (Swarajyalakshmi *et al.*, 1992). On the other hand the nutritional well-being of children under five improved. The proportion of under-fives weighing less than 80 per cent of the relevant ICMR standard weight fell from fell from 47 per cent to 32 per cent in three years, and no under-twos were less than 80 per cent of the relevant weight in 1991.

Education, Vocational Training and Incomes

Education and training courses were also well-attended. Eighty per cent of slum children (3–6 years) attended preschool in 1991; two thirds attended ODA-funded pre-schools. Of the 8000 school dropouts in the slums, 3500 enrolled for non-formal education (about half of those enrolled attend);

Table 7.4 Health care and status

Category[1]	*1988*[1] *No.*	*%*	*1991* *No.*	*%*	*1988–91 Change (%)*
Tubectomies[2]	193	64.1	262	67.2	3.1
Vasectomies[2]	106	35.2	106	27.2	–8.0
No delivery problems[3]	52	86.7	40	85.1	1.6
Post-natal consultations[3]	32	53.3	8	17.0	–36.3
Fully immunised (1–3 age)	56	24.7	92	82.9	58.2
Persons sick, last 14 days[4]	43	1.5	130	4.5	3.0
Persons chronically ill[4]	39	1.4	92	3.2	1.8
Households under-caloried[5]	55	68.8	53	66.3	–2.5
Children 20% + underweight[6]	60	46.7	41	31.7	–15.0

Notes:
1. The first 8 rows are based on 612 households; the last 2 rows are based on 80 households.
2. Percentages in couples.
3. Percentages of deliveries.
4. Percentages of all population.
5. Percentages of households.
6. Percentages of children from 0 to 5 years.

Sources: Household surveys; Sarveswara Rao and Ramachandrudu, 1992a; Swarajyalakshmi *et al.*, 1992.

21 000 illiterates enrolled for adult literacy classes (about one third of these attend). In the three years to the end of 1991, 746 people received vocational training in one of 15 trades and 3422 completed sewing courses.

There are some positive output measures. For example literacy rates improved (see Table 7.5). Also vocational courses improved employment and income prospects. Of a sample of 129 trainees, 26 per cent were employed before training and 59 per cent after training, and average (nominal) wages rose by 37 per cent (Patrudu, 1992). Adult female employment increased from 21 per cent to 25 per cent, but male employment did not increase. Nearly half of all workers were employed in unskilled occupations in 1988 and 1991 and there was no evidence of vertical mobility from unskilled to skilled labour.

Between 1988 and 1991, the income and wealth of slum households rose considerably. Average reported real household income rose by 15 per cent; real household expenditure (excluding debt repayment) increased by 33 per cent; and the real value of gross household assets rose by 82 per cent. These data must be interpreted cautiously. Sarveswara Rao and Ramachandrudu (1992a) suggest that respondents are likely to understate income by more than they overstate expenditure and that expenditure figures are therefore more reliable. However reported income comfortably exceeded expenditure (see Table 7.5). This may be explained by the omission of spending on consumer durables and debt repayments from expenditure. The relatively high rise in expenditure may have been influenced by increased access to grants and loans.

Table 7.5 Education, employment, income and assets

Category	*1988** *No.*	*%*	*1991* *No.*	*%*	*1988–91 Change (%)*
Children at pre-school	68	29.4	117	57.1	27.6
Adult literacy	769	44.5	948	51.5	7.0
Overall literacy	1 508	53.7	1 818	62.9	9.2
Adults employed	897	51.9	967	52.5	0.6
Household income/month (Rs)	1 163	–	1 348	–	15.2
Male income/month (Rs)	854	–	926	–	8.4
Female income/month (Rs)	381	–	380	–	–0.3
Household expend./month (Rs)	816	–	1 087	–	33.2
Household assets	17 113	–	31 132	–	81.9
Household debt	5 723	–	9 840	–	71.9

*All rupee figures in 1991 prices: the nominal 1988 values are inflated by the consumer price index for Visakhapatnam.

Source: Household surveys; Sarveswara Rao and Ramachandrudu, 1992a.

Other Impacts

Slum improvement programmes also affect households who move into or out of improved slums. In-movers usually gain from such programmes. Out-movers may be either gainers who take advantage of increased wealth or losers who are pushed out by higher rents or new land arrangements. It appears that most households move for positive rather than for negative reasons (Sarveswara Rao and Ramachandrudu, 1992b). Neighbourhood leaders claim that half the out-movers sell or rent out their slum houses. On the other hand the out-movers sampled stated that improved access to work and education and housing allocations in other areas were the main reasons for moving. In-movers gave employment and lower rent as the main reasons.

The net population impacts vary. On the one hand slum improvements and housing schemes encourage immigration into the slums, in part to gain access to a housing plot. A UCDD officer put it this way to the writer: 'after improvement plans are announced, the slum community expands like a sponge absorbing water as households move into the area. People subdivide single room huts into small rooms and claim a new house for each room'. On the other hand the lot size provisions tend to reduce densities. In a sample of 21 slums improved in 1988–89, population increased by more than 10 per cent in seven slums, remained within 10 per cent of the original number in six slums and fell by more than 10 per cent in eight slums.

Adjacent neighbourhoods also benefited from the improved slums. In some adjacent areas improvements followed directly after the slum upgrading. However there is no record of these indirect effects.

Impacts by Beneficiaries

IDPS studies show that, in 1991 compared with 1988, about 50 per cent of slum households had a significantly higher income, 30 per cent a slightly lower income and 20 per cent a much lower income. However the studies do not attempt to assess the effects of the improvement programme on incomes.

Apart from households who lost tenure, most slum households gained from one or other aspect of the programme. But it appears that the most powerful, well-established and better-off households gained more than others. Between 1988 and 1991 income differentials in the slums widened; landlords gained significant real rent increases; male earnings rose more than female earnings; employed persons' earnings rose more than the earnings of self-employed persons; and the relative position of the scheduled castes deteriorated. The anthropological case-studies confirmed that the more powerful families gained more land rights. On the other hand, less well-off households probably benefited more from the health care services and the nursery schools.

7.6 GENERAL BENEFIT VALUATION ISSUES

Few evaluations of socially oriented projects estimate economic rates of return. As Lipton and Toye (1990) point out, the evaluations tend rather to resemble laundry lists in which objectives are ticked off as they are (more or less) achieved. Consequently the effectiveness of resources used by projects cannot be assessed.

It may be argued that the benefits of poverty-focused projects should not be measured by conventional economic criteria, that is, by the amounts that the beneficiaries on very low cash incomes are willing to pay for them. As the Director of the IDPS, Dr Sarveswara Rao, commented to the writer: 'If you are dealing with the poorest members of society, you cannot avoid some element of continuing social support'.

However economic rigour and social subsidy can coexist. Consistent assessment of the relative rates of return in different projects is desirable, although not necessarily easy. If the returns on poverty-oriented projects are lower than the returns on other projects, government can then determine the appropriate level of subsidy (if any).

When slum improvements are formally evaluated, benefits are almost always based on estimated increases in land values or rents. For example World Bank studies forecast that increased land values or rents would produce real rates of return of 15–19 per cent for slum improvement programmes in Madhya Pradesh, Uttar Pradesh and Calcutta, and estimated an *ex post* 23 per cent rate of return for slum improvements in Madras. The studies did not estimate other measures of benefit, for example access to health care or water. Likewise the ODA's slum improvement project in Hyderabad was justified by forecast land value increases as proxies for project benefits.

This approach can be criticised from theoretical and data perspectives. In imperfect markets, land values may not accurately reflect household preferences. On empirical grounds Clarke *et al.* (1989) strongly criticised the use of land values in Hyderabad because the land value data were extremely unreliable. Lacking adequate data, planners may simply assume *ex ante* that, because their planned improvements are desirable, land values will rise to reflect these expenditures. But this process is circular and does not provide independent justification of proposed expenditure.

To adopt the land value approach, three questions must be answered. What benefits do land values reflect? Are land value data adequate? Are there alternative valuation methods that would measure the benefits more precisely or draw on more reliable data? Before answering these questions it may be helpful to outline the complex relationships between the major

Table 7.6 Summary of project inputs, outputs and benefit measures

Project inputs	*Main project outputs*
Civic infrastructure	Health; amenity; productivity;* reduced flood damage.
Housing improvements	Amenity; health; reduced fire damage.
Health/nutrition	Health; life expectancy; reduced health expenditures.
Education	Productivity.
Vocational training	Productivity.
Community centres	Amenity; health; productivity; reduced public facility expenditures elsewhere.
Project outputs	*Benefit measures*
Improved health	Increased incomes (due to increased productivity); reduced health care expenditures; quality and value of life measures; increased property values.
Improved amenity	Property values/rents; user payments and taxes.
Improved productivity	Increased incomes; property values/rents.
Improved assets	Property values/rents; reduced public expenditures; participation rates.

*Minor effect related to more useable road spaces and street lighting.

improvement programme inputs and outputs and the variety of possible benefit measures (Table 7.6).

The Use of Property Values or Rents

Under certain conditions, nearly all private benefits (including health, productivity and amenity benefits) will be reflected in increased land prices, rents and house prices in the slums. These conditions are:

- All private benefits accrue only to residents of the slum area.
- All improvement programme benefits (including health benefits, reduced flood and fire damages and so on) are fully perceived by potential buyers.

- Slum property prices are not controlled; slum residents can sell or rent their properties to outsiders as well as to other slum residents.
- Property transactions are costless.

Even under these conditions, there are usually some residual householder (consumer) surpluses. For example it is unlikely that the full benefits of training programmes or health care are precisely capitalised in property values.

Moreover several conditions are unlikely to hold fully. In Visakhapatnam some benefits accrue to non-slum residents, health benefits may not be fully appreciated, there are some official restrictions on the sale of slum properties (which are often bypassed) and there are transaction costs. If the above conditions are not met fully, changes in slum property values do not reflect all the private benefits of such programmes. There may also be public benefits, for example savings in expenditure on asset restoration and replacement and on emergencies caused by floods, fires and health epidemics, and increased revenues from user payments or taxes.

Turning to the second question, if property values are nevertheless considered to provide an approximate measure of most private programme benefits to slum households, are adequate property data available? The answer to this (empirical) question depends on the circumstances. However a few general observations may be made here.

There are two basic data issues. First, even when property sale prices are registered with public bodies and officially available, the price data are often recorded manually and are difficult to access. Data collection and interpretation generally requires a special research exercise. Property valuations, usually made for taxation purposes, are generally imprecise and sometimes unreliable. The second issue relates to the analysis. In time-series analysis, changes in property prices in improved slums may be compared with changes in unimproved slums or non-slum areas. But there is a major presumption that any differential change is attributable to the programmes and not to other factors such as changes in access to employment. If this presumption does not hold, the data and analysis requirements are much greater. In cross-section comparisons there must again be a presumption that observed price differentials are due to the programmes and not, say, to access differentials. Generally controls, and data, for other important independent variables are required. At the very least, the price data must be interpreted very carefully.

Other Valuation Methods

The main alternative valuation method would be *contingent valuation*: asking slum and non-slum households what they would be willing to pay for an improvement programme. It has been shown that low-income households can usefully be asked what they would be willing to pay for specified improvements, for example a water supply (Whittington *et al.*, 1990; Whittington *et al.*, 1991). Likewise slum households would probably give useful answers to questions dealing with the allocation of a given total programme budget.

However households may be unable or unwilling for various reasons to say what they would be prepared to pay. First, many people would find it difficult to state accurately the total amount that they would be willing to pay for such a complex package of disparate services as distinct from what they would pay for particular components. Secondly, care is required to obtain accurate answers, even if the respondent wishes to cooperate. For example community development officers in Visakhapatnam considered that stated willingness to pay monthly contributions for public toilet use would be less than the equivalent daily amounts (that is the daily rate times 30). Thirdly, if households believe that they are entitled to the urban services in any case, or if they know that the services are provided under foreign aid, they may not cooperate wholeheartedly in a willingness to pay survey.

Real changes in household incomes may measure some slum improvement benefits associated with education and training. Also, some health improvements and infrastructure benefits, such as improved open spaces for trading, may enhance productivity and incomes. However amenity improvements, some health benefits and some collective asset improvements, for example those due to reduced flood and fire risk, are not reflected in incomes.

Travel cost analysis can be used to infer the value of services when there are significant differentials in both access costs and usage. Examples are water supply and health care services. However this requires a special study of service use and travel costs.

When none of these benefit valuation methods can be used, the *switching value method* may be used. If total service costs and participation rates are known or forecast, unit service costs can be computed. A judgement whether unit value would exceed unit costs may then be made.

Alternatively, slum improvements are sometimes justified using a '*cost-effectiveness*' criterion. A proposed programme is said to be cost-effective if expenditure per household is in line with, or lower than, the norm in other such programmes. This approach presumes that outputs are similar and that expenditure variations reflect differences in unit costs. However Clarke *et al.* (1989) conclude that the cost variations within the Hyderabad programme reflect political pressures to improve the quality of facilities. When output quantity or quality varies, an assessment of benefits is needed: cost-effectiveness is not an adequate criterion.

Conclusions

The total benefits (TB) of a slum improvement programme can be expressed as:

$$TB = \Delta LV + \Delta HS + PNSB + GB \qquad (7.1)$$

where ΔLV are changes in land values in the slums, ΔHS are changes in householder surpluses of slum households that are not capitalised in land values, PNSB are private non-slum benefits, and GB are government benefits (increased user fees and taxes and expenditure savings).

In unregulated property markets, land values (or house prices) can provide a measure of most improvement programme benefits to slum residents. But property price data are not always readily available and analysis of the determinants of land or house prices requires care. Also, some benefits (for example, health and education benefits) may not be fully reflected in property values. In these cases other valuation methods, such as willingness-to-pay surveys, may provide supplementary information on benefits apparently excluded from property values. Most benefits to non-slum households are likewise reflected in (non-slum) land prices, but these are difficult to measure.

Of course some non-slum households within and without India may be willing to contribute altruistically to such programmes. To discover what they would be prepared to contribute, a survey of Indian and other households would be needed.

Finally, assessments of the costs, benefits and rates of return to major components of public programmes are generally desirable. But due to complementarities in the programme, the return to the whole programme may be greater than the sum of the returns to the individual parts.

7.7 EVALUATION OF THE TOTAL VISAKHAPATNAM SLUM IMPROVEMENT PROGRAMME

Project Costs

The estimated project costs are shown in Table 7.7. Total capital expenditure on the programme, including ODA overheads, was about

Table 7.7 Summary of project costs (million 1992 rupees)

	1988 to Sept. 1992	*After Sept. 1992*	*Total*
Slum improvement programme			
Engineering	137	82	219
Education	10	3	13
Socio-economic	6	2	8
Health	18	3	21
Other	32	5	37
Total	203	95	298
ODA overheads[1]	12	5	17
Infrastructure maintenance[2] (p.a.)	–	–	22
Housing improvements[3]	185	91	276

Notes
1. £100 000 p.a. converted at current exchange rates and into 1992 rupees.
2. Assumes that annual infrastructure maintenance is 10 per cent of the cost of engineering works, but this may not be affordable.
3. Assumes that total improvements will be equivalent to 12 000 new houses at R23 000 per house.

Source: ODA.

R315 million in 1992 rupees. Also, infrastructure maintenance could cost up to an additional R22 million per annum: with a 10 per cent discount rate, the capital equivalent would be R220 million. Estimated housing expenditure amount to another R276 million.

Projects Benefits

The evaluation below is based on benefits to slum households measured through property value changes, although we also consider income changes. In addition, indicative figures for benefits to government and non-slum households are given. However detailed quantification is not possible from available data. There are no records of public spending in the slum areas. Moreover, valuing external benefits in one area due to improvements in another is extremely difficult and rarely attempted. Special analyses of possible public savings and non-slum area benefits would be required.

Property Value Analysis

This subsection estimates the city-wide benefits of the programme based on increases in land values, house prices and rents. Visakhapatnam has an active housing market. Records of the Land Registration Department indicate that between 1.5 and 2.0 per cent of the housing stock is sold each year. Recorded sales in the slums are lower due to restrictions on sales. But there are many unofficial ('benami') sales where prices are known locally. Of course houses sold under restrictions sell at a discount. Also, there are fewer land than house sales. Therefore land values must be inferred from house prices or based on valuation data.

For this study, UCDD officers collected official land valuation data for typical properties in 24 slum areas that were improved in 1988 or 1989 and valued (to the nearest R50 per square yard) in 1987 and 1990. In the three years to 1990 mean land values in the sample slums increased from R256 to R441 per square yard. Elsewhere in Visakhapatnam land values rose by an estimated average 20 per cent except in commercial development areas, where land values rose by another 10–20 per cent. Allowing for an overall increase in land values in Visakhapatnam of 25 per cent, average slum land values would have risen to R320 without the programme: the difference between R441 and R320 is attributable to the programme. Applying a benefit of R121 per square yard to 36 500 houses with an average 50 square yards per house produces a total increase in land values of R221 million in 1990 rupees or about R254 million in 1992 rupees.

UCDD officers also estimated the prices of pucca, semi-pucca and kutcha houses in 19 improved slums in 1992 with and without the programme. The without programme estimates were based on prices in comparable slums that had not been improved. The programme increased the average price of pucca houses by an estimated R11 400, semi-pucca houses by R7800 and kutcha houses by R4250 (see Table 7.9 for some details). In 1991, 42.2 per cent of houses in these 19 slums were pucca, 15.4 per cent were semi-pucca and 42.4 per cent were kutcha. Applying the increases in house prices to the 36 500 houses in the 170 slums (using constant sample percentages for house type) produces a total increase in house prices due to the programme of R285 million in 1992 rupees. (note this does not include value increments due to upgrading kutcha and semi-pucca houses to pucca houses). The estimated benefits from the land value and house price approaches are reassuringly close. The UCDD researchers did not know how their figures would be used and could not massage the figures to produce these close results.

Alternatively, in competitive markets increased rents could be a measure of improved living conditions. Between 1988 and 1991 the average rent of Visakapatnam slum tenants increased from R114 per month to R145 per month in 1992 prices (Sarveswara Rao and Ramachandrudu, 1992a). Applying a notional annual rent increase of R372 to 36 500 slum house-holds, total rent increases would be R13.6 million per annum. With a 10 per cent discount rate, the capital equivalent would be R136 million. This figure is well below the estimated increase in land values or house prices and cannot be considered relevant to the evaluation of the programme. The relatively low rate of return can be explained partly by the unrepresentative nature of the rental market: only 13 per cent of households are tenants and they mostly rent in the lower to middle end of the slum housing market. Moreover restrictions on tenant evictions substantially reduce market rents.

Income Analysis

As seen above, real slum household incomes rose by 15 per cent between 1988 and 1991. This reflected a rise in adult female employment from 22 per cent to 28 per cent. Also, the average real income of males rose by 8.4 per cent whereas the average real income of females remained constant.

However the impact of the programme on slum incomes cannot be estimated because there are no comparable data on income changes in other parts of Visakhapatnam and numerous extraneous factors affect income changes in other cities. Within Visakhapatnam, 1988–91 was a period of high economic activity, including much construction and a new steel plant. The ODA programme itself increased employment opportunities. Furthermore, according to the IDPS, real wages increased as labour became more organised and obtained a larger share of output. Therefore no general estimate of the total value of the programme can be derived from income changes in the slums.

Evaluation Summary

Table 7.8 summarises total improvement programme costs and benefits. Annual maintenance expenditure is assumed here to be 5 per cent of civil engineering capital expenditure and capitalised using a 10 per cent discount rate. This maintenance expenditure would not maintain the assets adequately, but it is realistic. Moreover it may be considered consistent with household expectations, which in turn determine the capital value of land and housing.

Table 7.8 Summary of slum improvement programme costs and benefits (million 1992 rupees)

Slum improvement programme costs	
Expenditure 1988–93	298
ODA overhead expenditure	17
Maintenance expenditure capitalised[1]	110
Total costs	425
Slum improvement programme benefits	
Increased slum property values	270
Slum household surpluses[2]	27
Private benefits to non-slum households[2]	27
Government benefits[2]	27
Total benefits	351
Social surplus or subsidy	
Including only programme expenditure	53
Including ODA and maintenance expenditure	–74

Notes
1. Based on likely maintenance expenditure (see text).
2. Assumed to be equal to 10 per cent of increased slum land values.

The increase in slum property values shown is the mean of the land value and house price estimates (for constant house types). Importantly, it is assumed that slum household surpluses (benefits not capitalised into property values), private benefits to non-slum households and government benefits would each be equal to 10 per cent of increased slum property values. These judgements appear plausible, but lack empirical support.

As shown, estimated total benefits to slum households (including household surpluses) approximately equal capital expenditure. Including assumed private benefits to non-slum households and government savings, there would be a surplus of R53 million over capital expenditure. Note that, because the benefits are capitalised in property prices, a precise discounting exercise is not made. On the other hand, including ODA overheads and capitalised maintenance expenditure, there would be a total social deficit of R74 million. Maintenance costs critically affect this result.

To gain perspective, improvement programme expenditure per slum household can be compared with household income. Expenditure per slum household is R8300 without slum maintenance and R11 600 with it, compared with an average slum household income of R16 000. Therefore in order to pay for the capital *and* recurrent costs of the programme, slum households would have to make a one-off payment of about three quarters of their annual income. If this is more than they would be willing to pay, the difference must be made up by benefits to non-slum households and government, or by social subsidy.

7.8 EVALUATION OF INDIVIDUAL SLUM IMPROVEMENTS

The benefits of improvements in the 19 sample slums, for which detailed engineering expenditure and property price data were available, are estimated below. The main workings and results are presented in Table 7.9.

The following procedural points may be noted. Estimated total expenditure (in 1992 rupees) in each slum includes estimates for health, education and other expenditure as well as engineering, but not ODA overheads or slum maintenance expenditure. Increases in land values and house prices (both in 1992 rupees) were based on Land Registration data and UCDD estimates. In order to estimate the total land improved in each slum, 60 square yards were allowed per pucca house, 50 square yards per semi-pucca house and 40 square yards per kutcha house.

Drawing on the land valuations, the mean benefit–cost ratio (BCR) is 1.18. The improvements have a BCR above 1.0 in 10 slums and below 1.0 in nine slums. The house price results indicate a mean BCR of 1.86. In this case 13 slums show a BCR above one and six slums a BCR below one.

These results suggest that the net benefits of slum projects vary considerably. Importantly, there are significant economies of scale. As shown in Equation 7.2, the net benefit in each slum (NB_h, based on increased house prices less expenditure) is positively related to the number of houses (H) in each slum:

$$NB_h = -625\,000 + 5174H\ (4.8) \quad R^2 = 0.58 \qquad (7.2)$$

The figure in parenthesis is the t-statistic. It would be useful to know more about what determines the net benefits, but this would need more investigation.

Unlike the aggregate results in the last section, the average return for the individual slums suggests that increases in land values slightly exceed programme expenditure and that increases in house prices are much higher than programme expenditure. Sampling could explain the small difference between the aggregate and individual slum results if the programmes in the excluded slums produced less benefits. The differences between the land value and house price results for the individual slums suggest that the land value increases were underestimated or house price rises overestimated, but these possibilities also require more investigation.

Table 7.9 Economic analysis of slum improvements

Slum	Year[1]	Engineer expend[1] (Rs)	Est. total expend[2] (Rs)	Dwellings[3] Pucca (No.)	Dwellings[3] S-pucca (No.)	Dwellings[3] Kutcha (No.)	Increased land value ($Rs/yard^2$)	Increase in house prices Pucca (Rs)	Increase in house prices S-pucca (Rs)	Increase in house prices Kutcha (Rs)	Total increases Land (Rs)	Total increases Houses (Rs)	B–C Ratio Land[4]	B–C Ratio Houses	Rate of Return Land (%)	Rate of Return Houses (%)	Net Present Value Land (Rs)	Net Present Value Houses (Rs)
1	1988	702647	1193507	156	0	43	29	10000	5000	2500	318550	1667500	0.27	1.40	2.67	13.97	–874957	473993
2	1988	769487	1307040	11	346	261	43	10000	7500	5000	1224750	4010000	0.94	3.07	9.37	30.68	–82290	2702960
3	1988	707040	1200969	44	94	177	101	15000	5000	4000	1451013	1838000	1.21	1.53	12.08	15.30	250044	637031
4	1988	748793	1271890	159	0	0	316	10000	10000	2500	3017025	1590000	2.37	1.25	23.72	12.50	1745135	318110
5	1990	792050	1210829	91	2	3	316	10000	10000	2500	1796300	937500	1.48	0.77	14.84	7.74	585471	–273329
6	1988	512954	871297	106	1	44	216	10000	10000	3000	1761656	1202000	2.02	1.38	20.22	13.80	890360	330703
7	1988	641385	1089448	361	22	585	43	10000	5000	4000	1990650	6060000	1.83	5.56	18.27	55.62	901202	4970552
8	1988	491888	835514	43	0	9	216	10000	10000	5000	633938	475000	0.76	0.57	7.59	5.69	–201577	–360514
9	1988	1702229	2891383	73	11	61	101	10000	5000	4500	741606	1059500	0.26	0.37	2.56	3.66	–2149777	–1831883
10	1989	1115566	1803931	136	21	27	158	15000	10000	6000	1627106	2412000	0.90	1.34	9.02	13.37	–176825	608069
11	1988	344270	584772	63	23	44	173	10000	8000	5000	1154025	1034000	1.97	1.77	19.73	17.68	569253	449228
12	1988	501942	852592	87	0	0	101	15000	10000	6000	525263	1305000	0.62	1.53	6.16	15.31	–327329	452408
13	1988	1408663	2392736	80	56	255	115	5000	3000	2000	2047000	1078000	0.86	0.45	8.56	4.51	–345736	–1314736
14	1988	656936	1115863	206	2	103	101	15000	10000	6000	1668363	3728000	1.50	3.34	14.95	33.41	552500	2612137
15	1989	145511	235299	80	30	20	43	15000	10000	5000	306188	1600000	1.30	6.80	13.01	68.00	70888	1364701
16	1990	423180	646927	58	12	20	158	10000	10000	4500	771650	790000	1.19	1.22	11.93	12.21	124723	143073
17	1988	1081763	1837468	150	20	2	158	10000	8000	5000	1593900	1670000	0.87	0.91	8.67	9.09	–243568	–167468
18	1987	569152	989956	82	1	20	216	15000	10000	4500	1244156	1330000	1.26	1.34	12.57	13.43	254200	340044
19	1988	941663	1599496	120	0	30	158	10000	8000	3000	1328250	1290000	0.83	0.81	8.30	8.07	–271246	–309496
Average													1.18	1.86	11.8	18.63	66867	586610

Notes
1. Engineering expenditure in year of project.
2. Includes all programme expenditures, but no maintenance expenditures, in 1992 Rs.
3. At time fo engineering work.
4. Assumes a real annual return of 10% on capitalised benefits.

Sources: UCDD, Land Registration Department, author's estimates.

7.9 EVALUATION OF EDUCATION AND HEALTH INVESTMENTS

Evaluation of Training

By mid-1992 the MCV had spent nearly R1.0 million on training courses. Patrudu (1992) reported detailed costs and results of the courses for a sample of 129 trainees, and these data form the basis of the evaluation below.

Per capita costs and returns to 11 training courses in 1991 rupees are summarised in Table 7.10. The costs include the direct training costs of the courses paid by the MCV, a 50 per cent mark-up to allow for MCV overhead costs, and the opportunity costs of trainees. The last cost was based on the numbers in employment before the courses and their pretraining earnings. Also, the unemployed were assumed to forgo informal earnings of R150 per month.

Per capita returns are a weighted average of the increased income due to each course. Of the 129 trainees, 34 were employed before and after training. Following training, an extra 30 were employed in the trade for which they had trained, another 12 were employed in other occupations and 53 remained unemployed (though usually in informal income earning activities). For the evaluation it is assumed conservatively that those who gained employment would lose their informal earnings and that the increased earnings of trainees employed in occupations for which they had not trained were not attributable to the training.

Despite these conservative assumptions there were high rates of return to training in eight of the 11 courses. The returns to training in welding and fabrication, by far the most expensive course, were marginal. However there were zero returns to the craft courses in cane weaving and knitting. Most of these results are strong ones that would not be sensitive to changes in assumptions. However for the smaller samples, including welding and fabrication, the results could change with a larger sample. Also, it should be noted that the results are time and place specific and that the high returns were made possible by the buoyant state of the Visakhapatnam economy.

Evaluation of Education

By mid-1992 the MCV had spent R8.9 million on education services (nursery schools, non-formal adult education and adult literacy classes). In the absence of detailed costs and outcomes for these services, only broad unit costs and willingness to pay measures can be considered.

Table 7.10 Evaluation of training courses

Trade	Number persons in survey	*Average trainee costs (1991 Rs)* MCV	Opp. costs	Overhead and other	Total	Persons employed before	Persons employed after[1]	*Increased earnings due to training (1991Rs)* Weighted monthly average[2]	Weighted annual average[2]	Per cent rate of return	Payback period (years)
Printing, binding	20	410	532	205	1147	112	295	120	1441	126	0.8
Cane weaving	5	375	338	188	900	0	0	0	0	0	na
Food processing	16	400	0	200	600	111	261	128	1537	256	0.4
Motor rewinding	4	1000	300	500	1800	188	388	241	2892	161	1.6
Electrician, wiring	14	650	589	325	1564	240	402	126	1512	97	1.1
Embroidery	13	400	612	200	1212	71	211	60	717	59	1.7
Welding, fabrication	10	4675	1320	1000	6995	170	345	51	612	9	11.4
Motor servicing	16	400	614	200	1214	141	335	212	2539	209	0.5
Motor driving	5	1000	765	500	2265	153	553	313	3756	166	0.6
Radio/TV servicing	19	680	1042	340	2062	38	263	73	879	43	2.3
Wool knitting	7	450	45	225	720	0	0	0	0	0	na

Notes:
1. Assume earning R150/month informally before
2. This allows for those who are not employed before or after the training course and for those employed in other trades who were assumed not to gain from the training.

Source: Patrudu, 1992.

From 1988–9 to 1991–2 the MCV spent an average of R2.25 million per annum on the three educational services. UDDC officers indicated that there were about 1.0 million nursery school attendances (of three hours) per annum, 0.5 million attendances (two hours) at non-formal education classes per annum and 1.0 million attendances (one hour) at adult literacy classes per annum. The average cost for these 2.5 million education services was therefore slightly under R1 per attendance or R20 for a month of attendances. This represented about 1.5 per cent of average household incomes. It is a matter for judgement whether these courses represented value for money as there is no evidence (one way or the other) on productivity changes due to the courses or on what the slum households would have been willing to pay for the courses. However the anthropological studies suggested that the nursery school sessions were popular.

Evaluation of Health Care

Improvements in the physical environment and health services in the slums would be expected significantly to improve the health of slum residents and reduce infectious diseases generally. However apart from some improvements in the weight and health of young children, there was little evidence of improved health status by 1992 (possibly because this was too soon to observe any measurable improvement, for example from immunisation services). Without physical measures of improved health status there can of course be no meaningful evaluation of health improvements. Nor can conclusions be drawn about changes in productivity because slum residents were not asked about their attendance at work.

Lacking measures of health outputs, we can consider how much slum residents would be willing to pay for the specially provided health care services. In an attempt to use travel cost analysis to estimate willingness to pay, the writer asked the UCDD for data on health care visitation rates and distances from the centre of each slum to the nearest health care centre. However there are few data on visitation rates from individual slums. In any case, health care access differences between slums are probably too small to cause significant differences in attendance.

Turning to the unit cost approach, annual recurrent expenditure on health care services was about R6.0 million, of which perhaps R4.0 million was spent on services from primary health care centres, including the provision of drugs (this does not include any opportunity cost for volunteer health care officers or rent for community halls). With an annual utilisation rate of 170 000 attendances, the average cost per attendance was R24. Of this, medicines accounted for R13 and labour for R11.

IDPS surveys suggest that the primary health care services are popular because they are convenient and free. However the unit cost of R24 is well above the normal price (R5–10) for a consultation with a doctor, which deters many slum residents from visiting doctors. Also, several respondents expressed disappointment that the quality of the services was not higher. Overall it is doubtful whether slum residents would be willing to pay for more than a small part of the cost of the health services provided. This does not mean that the service should not be provided as subsidies are widely provided for health care services, especially for poor households. However it appears that the health care services provided in the slums may not be cost-effective. Further analysis of the service benefits and, possibly, some service rationalisation seem appropriate.

7.10 OTHER POLICY CONSIDERATIONS

As described in Section 7.2, urban management policies can complement slum improvement programmes. In Visakhapatnam the following policies could improve shelter and urban infrastructure for poorer households.

- State industries, the railway and port authorities and the armed forces, control much land in Visakhapatnam that is underutilised and does not contribute to municipal revenues. Release of some of this land for housing would relieve the acute shortage of housing land in the city
- The director of the Urban Development Authority indicated in a discussion with the writer that he favoured more intensive (more vertical) development of urban land. This would not directly assist slum households, who could not afford conventional apartments, but could relieve land pressure.
- Visakhapatnam residents currently receive an average of 13 gallons of water per person per day compared with the government recommendation of 40 gallons. A combined pricing and administrative water policy could conserve the scarce water and allocate it more fairly to slum households, who receive little or no water.
- The housing market in slum areas could be deregulated to encourage developments by allowing households to capitalise more freely on improvements. This should be conditional on proper servicing of subsidised housing loans, many of which are not repaid.
- Maintenance of engineering standards and service levels in the slums will be difficult. Disrepair and neglect are already evident. Estimated maintenance costs of R11–22 million per annum are substantial compared with the MCV's current expenditure of R50 million on public

sanitation and routine maintenance. Presently, half of the corporation's total budget of R500 million is financed by grants and capital receipts, which makes it vulnerable to changes outside its control. Slum households pay only a nominal R4 per annum in property tax. Given the public good nature of urban infrastructure and the social frictions within many slum communities, it is unrealistic to expect slum communities to cooperate in a sustained way to maintain the infrastructure. The main burden of maintenance will fall on the MCV. Adequate slum maintenance is likely to depend on some reform and extension of the local property tax system.

7.11 CONCLUSIONS

The Municipal Corporation of Visakhapatnam has spent about R300 million on improving 170 slums. An additional R10 million or more per annum will be required to maintain the physical improvements. These expenditure will bring benefits to slum and non-slum households and savings to the government.

Most slum household benefits are reflected in increased land and house prices, although some benefits may not be fully capitalised into property prices. The slum improvement programmes increased total land values in the 170 slums by an estimated R254 million and house prices by R285 million. Given a perfect market and accurate data, these two increases would be the same. In addition, benefits associated with slum householder surpluses, private non-slum benefits and government savings may be conservatively expected to equal to at least one quarter of the programme's costs. Therefore the total value of social benefits will exceed capital expenditure. However, once maintenance expenditure and ODA overheads are taken into account, the estimated social deficit is about R70 million.

These results are not surprising. It is not, after all, surprising that low-income slum households and adjacent communities may not be willing (or able) to pay for all improvement programme and maintenance expenditure. But this is not a good reason for abandoning willingness to pay as the basis for the evaluation, nor for abandoning explicit estimates of the social subsidy component. If a subsidy is required, decision makers must decide whether, given the poverty focus of the project, such a subsidy is reasonable. Of course they could ask the wider community what it is prepared to contribute to such a programme, but they rarely do.

The study also evaluated the programmes in 19 separate slums by comparing increases in local land and house prices with estimated local programme expenditure, excluding maintenance. The estimated rates of return varied considerably, with about two thirds of the sample slums showing a benefit–cost ratio of above one, the rest having a ratio of below one. Economies of scale were significant, with much higher returns in the larger slums.

The Visakhapatnam programme is a comprehensive approach to slum improvements, which includes educational, training and health care services. Notwithstanding the holistic nature of the programme, we would like to know which parts produce the best, or worst, results. The analysis showed that there have been high returns to most training courses and that slum households might be willing to pay for most of the educational services, which have a low unit cost.

On the other hand the health care services and improved slum infrastructure had made little impact on the health status of slum residents by 1992 and it is doubtful whether slum households would be willing to pay the direct health care costs. It may be too early to observe health improvements. However the project concentrated on readily achievable roads and drains. There was little improvement in slum water supply (partly because of a chronic city wide water shortage) or in sanitary facilities (partly because public facilities were considered less effective than private ones).

By itself, a slum improvement programme is unlikely to bring an end to slums. Indeed it may encourage immigration into slum areas. In Visakhaptnam the land reform in the slums probably contributed significantly to the positive results. However the programme should be complemented by other urban policies, notably the efficient use of all urban land, including public land, the efficient and fair use of scarce key resources such as water, and fiscal reform that ensures the urban infrastructure can be maintained.

Finally, it should be noted that although there are many more data on the impacts of the Visakhapatnam programme than is usual, gaps in the data remain. For example there is little information on maintenance expenditure. Land valuation data are crude. Estimated house prices in the no-programme scenario could not be based on clearly established control cases. Also, we were obliged to speculate on the extent to which benefits are capitalised in property prices, the benefits to non-slum households, and the savings to government. All of these basic topics could usefully be the subject of more research in Visakhapatnam or elsewhere.

8 Valuing Mass Transit and the Environment in Lagos, Nigeria

8.1 INTRODUCTION

Motor vehicles are a prime cause of air pollution, noise and accidents in cities and a heavy consumer of energy resources. Roads divide communities and encourage urban sprawl. Moreover they often fail to provide an efficient service – heavy congestion characterises most cities.

Rail services, on the other hand, are widely perceived to provide a solution to urban pollution and congestion. For example Lowe (1993, p. 121) argues that 'many transport problems of the twentieth century can be addressed by creating a diverse system in which rail plays a major role'. Rail is safer than road, creates less air pollution, uses less fuel and can move more people along a crowded traffic corridor. Unfortunately railways usually require buckets of public subsidies. Moreover rail is not always clean, quiet and environmentally advantageous. Traditionally, the construction of railways cut swathes through existing cities, destroyed thousands of homes and severed many communities. Rail construction in crowded cities can cause similar disruption today.

This chapter analyses these issues in the context of a proposed major railway development for Lagos, the commercial capital of Nigeria. Since 1970 the city population has soared from one and a half million to six million. Nevertheless poverty is widespread and average annual household income in Lagos is only US$600. Because of topographical constraints on development, three quarters of Lagos residents live and work on the north–south axis through the city. Urban density is high: over 20 000 persons per square kilometre. Congestion is chronic, the speed of buses averaging under 20 kilometres per hour. A derelict railway corridor, occupying prime land down the centre of the north–south axis, carries an occasional train. Increasingly other land uses (especially informal markets) have taken over the railway corridor.

In 1991 the Nigerian Department of Transport and Communications and the World Bank commissioned consultants Dar Al-Handasah (DAH) to develop a scheme that, if successful, would greatly reduce the city's horrendous congestion. The writer contributed an economic assessment of the social and environmental impacts of the proposed scheme. The evaluation in this chapter draws on the detailed work by DAH (1992a, 1992b), but the estimates and interpretation below represent the writer's views.

The chapter starts with an overview of environmental issues of urban transport. The next sections outline the transport problems in Lagos, the proposed rail solution and other options. There follow descriptions of the method of evaluation, rail and bus costs, demand forecasts and user benefits. The last three sections discuss the social and environmental benefits and costs, give the full cost–benefit results and financial analysis, and summarise the main conclusions.

8.2 URBAN TRANSPORT AND ENVIRONMENT: GENERAL ISSUES

The demand for urban transport everywhere is high and growing. Households typically spend one tenth of their consumption expenditure on transport services. Between 1970 and 1985 the number of private cars in OECD countries rose from 174 million to 298 million; in other countries, cars quadrupled from 20 million to 80 million (OECD, 1988). Urban road networks have not increased at anything like the same rate. In Third World cities most passenger trips are made in buses. The World Bank (1986) predicts that bus passenger trips will double from 600 million in 1980 to 1200 million by the year 2000. Also, freight transport rises steadily with GDP.

On the other hand transport activities impact on congestion, land use, accidents, air pollution, noise, visual blight and energy consumption. The costs associated with accidents, air pollution and noise alone are estimated to equal 2.5 per cent of GDP in OECD countries (Quinet, 1990).

Total accident costs include loss of life, the pain and suffering of victims and their friends, damages to vehicles and other property, and medical, police and other accident-related costs. Estimates of these costs range from 1.5 per cent of GDP for the UK and the Netherlands to between 2.0 per cent and 2.5 per cent of GDP for the US, France and Germany (Quinet, 1990).

The main air pollutants from transport activities are carbon monoxide (CO), nitrogen oxide (NO_x), hydrocarbons (HCs) or more correctly volatile organic compounds (VOCs), sulphur dioxide (SO_2), lead and particulates. In cities, motor vehicles usually account for virtually all CO and lead levels, 60 per cent of NO_x and HC levels, 50 per cent of particulates and 10 per cent of SO_2 (OECD, 1988). Also, transport sources lead to secondary forms of air pollution. HCs with NO_x, oxygen and sunlight cause photochemical oxidants (smog), which includes ozone. SO_2 and NO_x combine to form acids and acid salts and return to earth as acid deposition. These air pollutants damage buildings, reduce soil and water productivity, cause ill health (especially respiratory disorders) and reduce the quality of the environment with odours and loss of visibility. Also, fossil fuel combustion increases the carbon dioxide (CO_2) content of the atmosphere and contributes to global warming.

Various studies have estimated the costs of air pollution in OECD countries, based on damage costs, what people would be willing to pay for improved air quality, or abatement expenditures. Estimated total air pollution costs are typically around 1.0 per cent of GDP. The costs attributable to transport, mainly motor vehicles, average 0.3 per cent to 0.4 per cent of GDP (Quinet, 1990).

Transport is a major source of unwanted noise. The OECD (1988) estimates that 110 million people in OECD countries are exposed to 'unacceptable' levels of noise due to road transport. Unacceptable is defined as a daytime L_{eq} above 65 dB(A), where L_{eq} is average noise energy over the measurement period. Noise affects health, productivity and general well-being. Exposure to high levels of traffic noise can accelerate hearing loss caused by ageing, reduce sleep and induce stress that contributes to high blood pressure and disorders of the cardiovascular and digestive systems. Productivity losses occur because of communication difficulties and lost sleep. Also, many surveys have shown that people are highly annoyed by traffic noise.

Quinet (1990) reviews studies of the costs of noise due to land transport in seven OECD countries and concludes that the costs are about 0.1 per cent of GDP. About 90 per cent of these costs are attributable to road transport and the rest to rail. The estimates are based on property price depreciation – with prices typically falling by 0.5 per cent per dB(A) increase in the L_{eq} index above 50 dB(A) (Nelson, 1982) – and the costs of protecting properties from noise. These measures may not capture all health and productivity impacts. Uncertainties in measurements may partly explain why the estimated costs range from 0.02 per cent to 0.10 per cent of GDP in the Netherlands up to 1.0 per cent of GDP in Germany.

Improving the Transport Environment

The basic principle of environmental planning for transport is to separate traffic from other land uses. This reduces accidents and pollution impacts. However in cities, major new engineering solutions are constrained by social and financial costs. Surface solutions often cause huge social disruption; underground or overhead solutions are hugely expensive. The main alternatives to major engineering are incremental improvements to the transport infrastructure, such as road widening and noise barriers, and better management of transport facilities, for example by improved traffic signalling.

Policies to control pollution fall into two main categories: actions relating to vehicles and those relating to vehicle use. For any abatement strategy, emission controls are the highest priority. Of course controls are rarely costless. For example catalytic converters may cost over 10 per cent of the capital cost of a car. But old vehicles are a greater problem than new ones. Old vehicles were built to lower standards and emissions usually increase with vehicle age. Consequently enforcement of emission standards and the maintenance of vehicles are critical elements of pollution control. But enforcement is often inadequate. Measures related to vehicle use include regulation of heavy vehicles, bus lanes, incentives for high vehicle occupancy and pricing vehicle use instead of ownership.

Public Transport as a Solution

Another potential solution to congestion and pollution is substitution of private cars by public transport (rail or bus). Unfortunately many car owners are reluctant to use public transport. Numerous studies have shown that automobile and public transport usage are price inelastic; typical own price elasticities for both are –0.3 to –0.4 (Goodwin, 1992; Oum *et al.*, 1992).

More importantly, the average cross price elasticity of public transport demand with respect to petrol prices is only +0.3 (Goodwin, 1992). After reviewing the performance of 13 metros in developing countries, Allport and Thompson (1990, p. 32) conclude that, although relief of traffic congestion was everywhere a major reason for building the metro, 'nowhere has this been a notable result. Consequently there has been little positive impact on either the environment or energy consumption'.

This does not mean that metros (or buses) are necessarily failures. They may provide substantial user benefits. Also, when traffic is heavy even small time savings on the road network can have large benefits. Fouracre *et al.* (1990) calculate that seven out of these 13 metros have a total social return above 12 per cent and another three a return of between 10 per cent and 12 per cent. About 60 per cent of the benefits are travel time savings. But, as Gakenheimer (1990) points out, rail systems are usually hugely expensive and the returns are uncertain. Expenditure on nearly all systems overruns, often heavily. Only three of the 13 metros surveyed show a clear financial surplus. Several do not cover operating costs. Therefore, to achieve such environmental and other benefits as public transport can provide, governments may have to make substantial financial commitments.

8.3 LAGOS TRANSPORT: AN OVERVIEW

Transport Overview

A large part of the working population of Lagos is immobilised daily in traffic jams as residents attempt to make nearly six million passenger trips in motor vehicles across a grossly inadequate road network. On some links traffic volumes are as high as 80 000 vehicles per day (Barrett, 1988). Congestion is worst in the central north–south corridor, which caters for over half of all passenger movements. Moreover traffic volumes stay high over most of the day, with the morning peak hour accounting for only 8 per cent of daily traffic movements.

Nearly half of all passenger trips are made in medium or large diesel-fuelled buses. A third of all trips are made in private cars and the rest in minibuses and taxis. City rail services have virtually ceased. On the other hand, private cars account for three quarters of all vehicle trips. Usage is encouraged by very low domestic gasoline prices. In 1990 Nigerian crude oil sold locally for only $3 per barrel. Buses and taxis each account for about 10 per cent and other vehicles for 5 per cent of vehicle trips.

Transport in Lagos is administered by all three tiers of government. The national government in Abuja controls primary intercity roads. The federally owned National Railways Corporation (NRC) is responsible for rail transport in Lagos. The Lagos state government controls all other primary roads and determines traffic management policies. Local governments organise some road maintenance and administer traffic management. The three tiers do not always cooperate. Unlike its predecessors, the current Lagos state government favours bus transport and has not supported the national government's attempts to improve the railway.

Roads

The road network in Lagos is very limited, generally poorly designed with inadequate drainage, and under-maintained. Lagos has only 0.47 kilometres of main road per thousand population (compared with Harare, 0.54; Accra, 0.65; Nairobi, 1.24). Moreover the city relies heavily on a few primary roads. In 1992 four roads carried over 470 000 passengers and 13 roads carried over 200 000 passengers per day. There are few effective secondary and access roads.

Lagos traffic is also poorly managed. There are only 40 signal-controlled intersections in the city, and at any point in time many of these are out of operation. A city of the size of Lagos would usually have 200 to 250 sets of traffic signals. Few traffic management measures have been implemented. Parking charges are low. There are no road or bridge tolls. Traffic regulations are widely disregarded, with a reported 50 per cent of drivers ignoring stop signs. There is, moreover, a general failure to segregate traffic from people. Many busy roads are *de facto* markets.

Bus and Taxi Services

Bus and taxi services are highly competitive, mainly privately operated and, in effect, unregulated. The large private buses typically carry 500 000 passengers a year, minibuses carry 350 000 annually and taxis carry 110 000. Buses are frequently 30–40 per cent overloaded. Despite these loads, profits are very low (see Section 8.6).

Publicly owned bus services are run inefficiently by the Lagos State Transport Corporation. In 1991 the corporation's buses averaged only 100 kilometres per day, the mean age of the fleet was over seven years old, usually only half of the buses were available and the corporation employed 9.6 staff per available bus.

Rail Services

An upgraded rail service for Lagos has been a major political objective for nearly 30 years (DAH, 1989). A French consortium started construction of a metroline in 1982, but the project was cancelled in 1985. In the late 1980s the federal government invested $2 million in tracks, terminals, coaches and locomotives in an attempt to revive the decaying suburban system. Services peaked in 1989 with 26 daily suburban services to 18 stations, carrying an average daily load of 7600 passengers (0.13 per cent of the daily passenger market). But by early 1992 there were only six services. In mid-1992 non-payment of wages caused a three-month strike and the infrastructure continued to deteriorate.

The chronic failure of the Lagos rail system has many technical and institutional causes. Technical problems include poor bus interchanges, train speeds of less than 20 kilometres per hour due to the poor state of the tracks, wrong rolling stock (converted from long-distance coaches with no standing room) and poor rolling stock maintenance (several new locomotives are not working). These technical problems are in turn caused by poor financial returns and the inability of the NRC to improve operating efficiency.

Environmental Issues

There are five main environmental concerns with traffic, of which four are discussed in detail in Section 8.9. These concerns are vehicle emissions, traffic noise, the discharge of sump oil into drainage systems, traffic accidents and energy use. Air pollution is widely considered a serious problem in Lagos, although data on air quality are virtually non-existent. In many places traffic noise is high by international standards. The dumping of sump oil into the drainage system is a cause of high oil content in the surface waters of Lagos Lagoon. Traffic accidents, including fatalities, are very high in Lagos (Barrett, 1988). And, as observed above, subsidised fuel encourages excessive energy use.

Summary of Issues

The growth of the Lagos population over two decades has outstripped the institutional capacity to plan and manage land use and transport development. Congestion in Lagos is chronic, vehicle operating costs are high and there are huge numbers of traffic accidents. The road network cannot cope with traffic levels and is under-maintained. The traffic system is poorly managed, price signals encourage excessive motor vehicle use and many traffic regulations are routinely ignored. Old, poorly maintained vehicles cause high air pollution. There is little segregation of vehicular and pedestrian movements. Buses provide most passenger trips, but most buses are old and poorly maintained. The railway is delapidated and city rail services virtually non-existent.

8.4 THE PROPOSED RAILWAY AND OTHER OPTIONS

The right-of-way (RoW) owned by the NRC represents a major opportunity for improving the transport infrastructure in the congested north–south spine of Lagos. Any major transport development outside the RoW would be very expensive and socially disruptive. And traffic management alone would not provide adequate system capacity.

Within the RoW the main options are rail development or a dual two-lane road alongside the existing rail tracks. Such a road could serve all motor vehicles or be reserved for busways. More radically, the whole corridor within the city could be turned over to road space. Unfortunately these road-based options were not formally evaluated because of the perception that the NRC would effectively veto any conversion of the RoW to road space.

The proposed railway will run for 26 km from Iddo Terminus, just off Lagos Island (the main employment centre in Lagos), to Agbado in the north (see Figure 8.1). Buses will take passengers from Iddo over Carter Bridge to Lagos Island. The rail will be a new dual track system parallel to the existing tracks, which will be retained for long distance rail traffic. The scheme will require new facilities over the whole length, including 10 new stations and the redevelopment of Iddo Terminus. Services will be automated, train doors will be automatic with a guard override and entry to the stations will be by automatic coin ticketing. The service is designed to operate with six-minute headways and to have a one-way capacity of 37 500 passengers per hour. Maximum speed between stations will be 90 kilometres per hour and the planned average stopping time at stations will be one minute. Average trip speed, including stops, will be 37 kilometres per hour.

To protect the railway and minimise train/pedestrian conflicts and accidents, the plan includes a two-metre-high block wall topped with anti-intruder spikes on both sides of the facility for most of its length – a total 47 km of block wall. Lighter fencing materials are considered theft-prone and ineffective. To ensure patronage and an efficient public transport service, each station will be served by a bus interchange.

In addition, the plan includes 31 new footbridges about 800 metres apart (and removal of seven existing footbridges). Seven new road flyovers will replace existing level crossings, which will be closed. To meet flyover elevations, roads adjacent to the RoW will be raised in four places, and parts of the north–south route close to the RoW will be realigned. Major road construction will be required to facilitate bus movements from the Iddo terminus to Carter Bridge.

DAH (1992a) recommends two staging options. One, that the proposed rail be completed initially from Iddo to Agege, and extended to Agbado when required. Two, that the system be operated at a lower capacity level with 12 minute headways for up to five years. The cost savings in both cases are estimated to exceed the temporary loss of user benefits.

DAH (ibid) does not discuss how the railway will be built, managed and funded. These are critical issues. On its record, the NRC will be an inefficient project manager and rail operator. Possibly an independent statutory authority could lease the land from the NRC and build the rail facility and a separate private company could operate the service. But such arrangements are difficult to establish in the insecure administrative environment of Lagos.

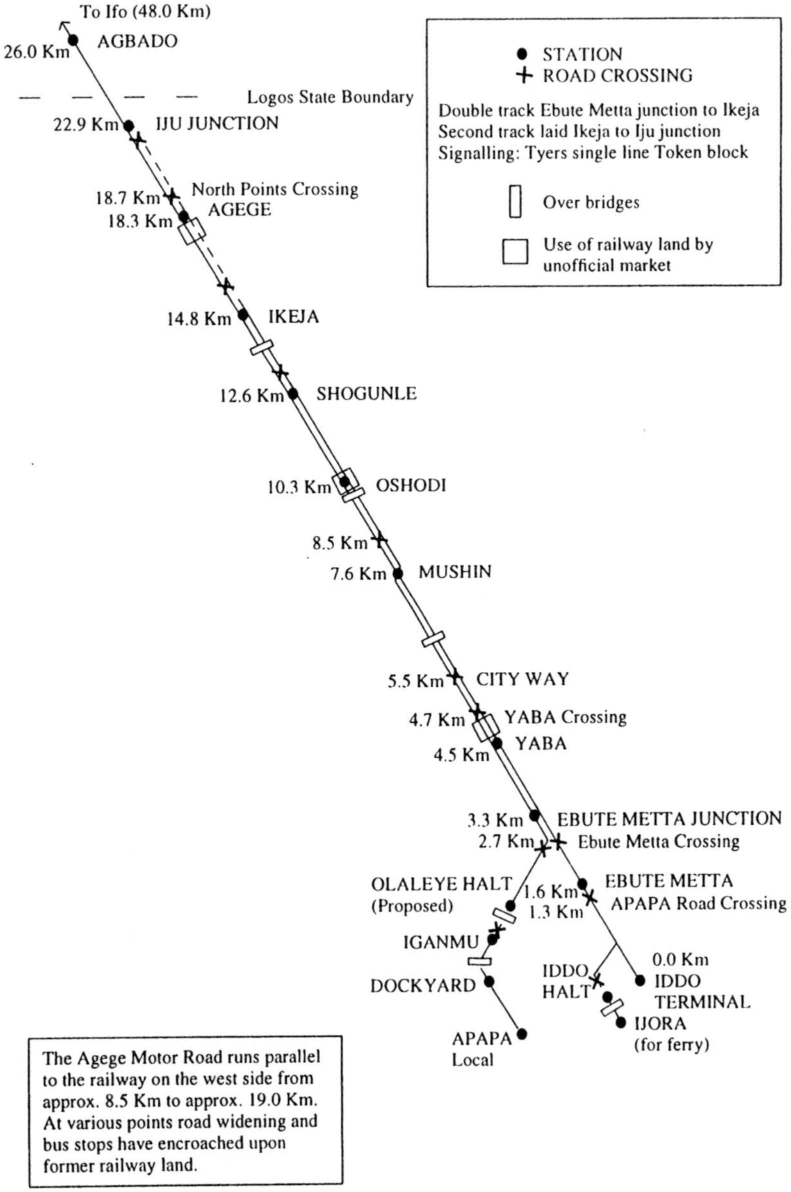

Source: Dar-al-Handasah, 1992a.

Figure 8.1 The existing NRC railway

In any complex system there are many options. Three are highlighted here. An upgrade of the existing dual track NRC rail would be a low-cost alternative. DAH (1992a) considered this based on 15–20 minute headways, automatically controlled level crossings and a lightweight security fence. However DAH concludes that this will produce unacceptable road and rail traffic delays. Another cost-saving option would be to locate the southern terminus at Ebute Metta Junction instead of Iddo. This would save substantial capital expenditure, provide bus access to all three bridges to Lagos Island, release valuable land between Ebute Metta and Iddo, and maximise the potential of land around Ebutte Metta. Despite these advantages, this option has received little attention, apparently because of likely NRC opposition. Conversely, the third option would be to extend the rail from Iddo Terminus across the bay into Lagos Island itself. However there is no convenient land for a rail terminus on Lagos Island and the costs of the bay crossing are prohibitive.

DAH (1989) examined light and rapid rail options. 'Light rail transit' (LRT) covers a range of electrical rail systems from traditional trams to scaled-down versions of rapid rail systems. LRT capacity varies greatly with the system but can be as high as 36 000 passengers per hour per track. Rapid rail systems are electrically operated high capacity systems (up to 70 000 passengers per hour in one direction) offering high speeds and reduced headways. They require a fully segregated facility, sophisticated signalling and high-level supporting infrastructure (for instance modern stations with wide platforms level with trains to minimise waiting times). Of the rail systems, LRT is usually most cost-effective for low traffic loads, conventional rail for medium loads and rapid rail for high loads. For the predicted load in Lagos, DAH found that the capital and operating costs of both an LRT and an electrically operated rapid rail system would be 40–50 per cent higher than the corresponding costs for the proposed diesel rail and recommended that they be ruled out.

Also, various busway schemes could be constructed in the NRC corridor. The main proposal considered (but not formally evaluated) was a dual two-lane busway, grade separated and fenced for its whole length like the railway. It would provide a line haul service from Iddo to Agbado, with exits at special points such as Agege, Ijeka and Oshodi. To reduce spacing between stops, 14 bus stopping points (four more than for rail) would be provided. A bus lane can carry 20 000 passengers per hour.

8.5 METHOD OF EVALUATION

This evaluation of the proposed Lagos rail is based on standard cost–benefit analysis principles. As far as possible, impacts on transport users and producers and third parties are valued in monetary terms, based on willingness-to-pay valuations. The quantified costs and benefits are discounted and net present values estimated. All impacts are estimated relative to a no-metro base case. For this case it is assumed that extensive traffic management improvements will be introduced, but that there will be no major road developments in central Lagos. It is assumed that metro construction will take five years and that the service will run for 25 years, which is the expected lifetime of the major operating plant and equipment. All costs and benefits are estimated in local 1992 prices. For convenience, these are expressed mainly in equivalent US dollars. Because some prices, notably fuel and foreign exchange, are regulated, shadow prices are used as appropriate (see Section 8.6).

Benefit estimates depend crucially on traffic forecasts. Three important assumptions (based on DAH's forecasts below) should be noted here. The first is that the metro will not affect total trips in Lagos or their origin and destination. It would be preferable to estimate the benefits of generated traffic (for example by allowing for them at half the rate of normal traffic – Abelson, 1982), but this is rarely done. Possible land use and development impacts of the metro are discussed in Section 8.8. Secondly, it is assumed that all rail users will transfer from buses. (Actually, DAH estimated that 95 per cent will switch from buses and 5 per cent from taxis). Because of the differences in service characteristics, the net benefits of transfers from taxis and cars to rail will be slightly different from the net benefits of transfers from buses. Ideally, the demand for travel by each mode should be estimated independently (from market behaviour or stated preference methods) and the consumer surpluses of diverted traffic should be derived from the estimated demand curves (see Neuburger, 1971; Jones, 1977). However, given the small numbers likely to transfer from taxis and cars to rail, little is lost by this second assumption. Thirdly, metro fares are assumed to equal bus fares. Given constant producer revenues, the net transport benefits over the network will equal the sum of all changes in user surpluses and producer costs. Because DAH's forecasts of rail users are not price sensitive, the constant fare assumption does not affect estimated net benefits. Fare differences will redistribute the surpluses but will not change the net benefits over the network.

User surpluses will accrue to both rail and other travellers. Rail users may be willing to pay more for the metro than for bus services because it will provide higher quality services, for example extra comfort, as well as travel time savings. Other travellers, including those who continue to take buses, and car drivers and occupants, may save travel time and road accidents due to reduced road congestion. Fouracre *et al.* (1990) estimated that, in the first years of 13 new metro systems, over 40 per cent of all benefits accrued to existing bus passengers and 14 per cent to car drivers and passengers due to reduced congestion on the roads.

Turning to the real resource costs incurred by producers, the metro producer will of course incur capital and operating costs. On the other hand bus operators will save capital and operating costs, mainly because fewer bus services are required and to a minor extent because of lower road congestion. Private motorists may also save vehicle operating costs.

In sum, the main transport benefits will be the travel time savings and comfort of rail passengers, the travel time savings of those who stay in buses or cars, savings in accidents, savings in bus capital and operating costs, and possibly some savings in private car operating costs. The project's direct costs will be rail capital and operating and land costs.

Many other, third party, impacts are assessed below. The main quantified benefits are improved air quality, flood mitigation and indirect traffic benefits due to the flyovers. The main costs are the social costs of relocating people and businesses, severance costs and traffic delays during project construction. Other impacts considered include noise, visual impacts, toxic waste disposal, land use changes and energy consumption.

8.6 RAIL AND BUS COSTS

Table 8.1 shows rail costs in 1992 local prices, expressed in dollars. To allow for trade distortions, the World Bank recommends that the prices of domestic goods and services be discounted by 11.3 per cent (the standard conversion factor is 0.886). To evaluate the metro, an equivalent foreign exchange premium of 12.9 per cent is applied to the estimated costs of imports, equivalent to one third of the construction expenditures and two thirds of the rolling stock costs. Estimated total economic costs are $225 million compared with financial costs of $212 million. Economic operating costs also exceed financial costs because in 1992 the real prices of diesel fuel and electricity were 6.0 and 3.5 times their respective nominal prices.

Table 8.2 shows estimated bus costs, including depreciation and the cost of busways. Bus operating costs per passenger kilometre are highly sensitive to assumptions about annual mileage and the interest rates charged for bus

Table 8.1 Estimated rail capital and operating costs (million dollars 1992 prices)

Basic construction costs	
Earthworks and causeway widening	2.1
Track	17.7
Signalling	8.6
Telecommunications	1.5
Depot facilities	17.9
Eleven stations	5.4
Grade separation	18.8
Fencing	6.2
Sub-total	78.2
Additional costs	
Training and start-up costs	5.0
Bus interchanges and road access	12.6
Footbridges over rail	4.2
Remove and reconstruct running shed	1.3
Diversion of NRC track around stations	0.8
Utilities	1.6
Sub-total	25.5
Contingencies over above costs	6.0
Rolling stock	2.7
Total capital costs	12.4
Operating costs*	
Fixed annual operating costs	2.86 million
Economic operating costs/passenger km	\$0.00342 = N0.062
Financial operating costs/passenger km	\$0.00134 = N0.024

*Excluding depreciation of rolling stock.

Source: Dar al-Handasah, 1992a.

Table 8.2 Costs of buses and busways (1992 prices)

Bus operating costs (including depreciation)	
Economic operating costs/passenger km	\$0.00831 = N0.150
Financial operating costs/passenger km	\$0.01050 = N0.189
Average bus revenues per passenger km	\$0.01017 = N0.183
Construction costs of dual-two busways	\$69.5 million

Source: Dar al-Handasah, 1992a.

purchase. On plausible assumptions, for example 90 bus kilometres per day, an average of 42 passengers and a 30 per cent borrowing rate, average bus financial costs slightly exceed average revenues. Economic operating costs are below financial costs because the real risk-free rate of interest (10 per cent) is far lower than the nominal rate and this more than offsets the impact of the diesel fuel subsidy.

A dual-lane busway would be far cheaper to construct than a metro. Busways would also reduce unit bus operating costs because they would increase mileages. However bus operating costs would still be higher than rail operating costs (assuming high patronage rates). Also, busways have a much lower capacity than a metro.

8.7 METRO DEMAND FORECASTS

This section outlines how DAH (1992a) forecast rail passengers and then comments briefly on them.

1. In 1992 there were an estimated 5.8 million daily passenger trips in Lagos, of which 4.0 million were by public transport, including taxis. DAH forecast that very few car passengers will divert to rail and therefore ignored them.
2. DAH assigned these trips from 44 zones to major road links and calibrated the model on actual 1992 trips.
3. DAH assume that the Lagos population will increase by 5 per cent annually and distributed the forecast increase in population to the 44 zones on the basis of spare zone capacity.
4. Public transport trips are assumed to increase pro rata with population. DAH assume that the metro will not increase public transport trips or significantly change the forecast distribution of population and employment.
5. A manual route assignment model was used to assign the forecast public transport trips to road routes in 1996, 2001, 2011 and 2015. The model allowed for no significant road improvements in Lagos over this period. When the model assigned grossly excessive trips to links, DAH reallocated the trips iteratively to alternative potential destinations and re-ran the assignment model until it produced realistic link volumes.
6. For each OD pair, DAH forecast the percentage likely to use each rail link, assuming a minimum rail journey of five km. The consultants forecast that there will be zero diversion to rail for three quarters of the OD trips, rising to 80 per cent diversion for a few OD pairs close to the rail.

Table 8.3 Consultant forecasts of metro passenger trips

All Public Transport		*Rail Forecasts*				
	Trips/day (mn)	*Trips/day*	*Trips/year (mn)*	*Av. trip length (km)*	*% of PT trips in corridor*	*% of all PT trips*
1992	3.97	–	–	–	–	–
1996	4.54	533 000	178.5	11.7	25–38	11.50
2001	5.72	660 000	221.1	11.5	25–38	11.80
2011	7.66	859 000	287.8	11.2	25–38	12.26
2015	9.17	977 000	327.3	10.7	25–38	12.26

Source: Dar al-Handassah, 1992a.

DAH forecast that daily rail passenger trips will rise from 533 000 in 1996 (the assumed opening year) to 977 000 trips in 2015 (see Table 8.3). Annual trips will rise from 179 million to 327 million over the same period, an implicit annual growth rate of 3.8 per cent. The metro is forecast to capture up to 38 per cent of public transport trips close to the rail and 11 per cent of all public transport trips in Lagos. However, because buses are only 10 per cent of all vehicle trips, total vehicle trips will fall by only 3 per cent close to the rail and by 1 per cent overall in Lagos.

As Fouracre *et al.* (1990) point out, most rail passenger forecasts are too high. If the proposed Lagos metro does proceed, will DAH's forecasts be met? Much depends upon the congestion in Lagos. If this becomes as extreme as many fear, the forecasts will be fulfilled. Nevertheless, for several reasons the consultant's forecasts appear to be too high.

- The forecast that total public transport trips in Lagos will increase by 5 per cent annually over 30 years implies both a high annual rate of growth of total trips and an ongoing high share by public transport. The forecast also presumes that the ongoing transfer of central government activities to the new capital at Abuja will not impact significantly on population growth.
- Rail passengers to or from the major destination, Lagos City, are expected to travel by bus between the Iddo Terminus and the City. However Fouracre *et al.* (1990, p. 6) note that the failure of the metro in Porto Alegre was due critically to the termination of the line 'too far from the city centre to meet effectively the travel needs of central area

commuters. This is the result of trying to exploit an old railway line compounded by a parallel high capacity road which buses use'.

- The DAH forecasts presume that the planned high-frequency rail service will be achieved.
- The forecasts are based on a capacity constraint of about one million passenger trips a day. This appears too high. The forecast peak one-way capacity is 37 500 passengers per hour. Allowing 60 000 passengers in both directions per peak hour (as peak directional flows are not even) and 8 per cent of trips in the peak hour, effective daily capacity will be 750 000 passenger trips. This daily figure implies 250 million trips per annum and 8.9 million trips per route kilometre per annum. These figures are high by international standards (see Fouracre *et al.*, 1990). Even higher figures for Lagos appear implausible.

In the evaluation below, the metro is constructed over five years and opens with 400 000 passenger trips in 1999, which is considered a more realistic opening year figure than the DAH forecast. Patronage rises to 660 000 passengers (the DAH forecast) in 2001. Capacity of 750 000 daily trips and 250 million annual trips will be reached in 2006, after which time usage will level off.

8.8 TRAFFIC USER BENEFITS FOR RAIL PASSENGERS AND OTHERS

Direct Consumer Surpluses

The value of travel time savings per rail passenger trip depends on the 'door-to-door' travel time saved (not just time saved on the rail section) and the value of the total time saved. It is estimated that rail passengers will save an average of 16 minutes per rail trip, even including a time penalty (eight minutes) for rail users to allow for bus/rail changes and circuitous routing. The estimated average value of travel time savings of \$0.11 per hour is based on the assumption that rail passengers will have an average income of \$0.22 per hour; that 75 per cent of travellers will gain leisure time (Banjo, 1978) and be willing to pay one third of their hourly income to save an hour of travel time (a standard empirical finding in developed countries); and that the other 25 per cent of travellers (or their employers) will be willing to pay their wage rate to gain working time. The estimated average value of travel time savings is \$0.03 per rail trip. This represents a consumer surplus equivalent to 25 per cent of the average metro fare.

In addition, many studies have found that, other things being equal, most public transport users prefer rail to bus because of its greater comfort. In order to model this choice accurately, a penalty of 4–6 minutes must often be attached to bus travel to reflect the relative discomfort of buses (see Fouracre *et al.*, 1990, p. 19). Because the Lagos metro will be less crowded than the overloaded buses, this study adopts the monetary equivalent of a five-minute saving ($0.009) per rail trip to proxy for a comfort premium. This premium is 7.7 per cent of the average rail fare. Together with travel time benefits, the estimated average surplus of rail passengers is one third of the average rail fare.

For other travellers, drawing on data from DAH, this study assumes that passenger diversion to rail will increase travel speeds for one third of Lagos trips by road; average bus speeds will increase from 16.5 kilometres per hour to 18 kilometres per hour; bus and car passengers will obtain similar time savings and will value them at the same rate as rail passengers (this is conservative because car passengers have higher incomes); and annual congestion relief benefits will level off when rail and road rail capacity is reached in 2006. Arguably, congestion relief will actually fall after 2006 as the road network becomes increasingly congested. However, even in this case the metro should enable some people to use the roads who would not do so otherwise. Post-2006 annual traffic benefits should be at least equal to year 2006 congestion-relief benefits or traffic management should restrict the excess traffic.

Also, increased speeds on the road network could marginally reduce the operating costs of private cars by reducing fuel consumption. However this benefit is likely to be small and is not estimated.

Other Network Impacts

Construction impacts: traffic delay costs

The major construction impacts will be associated with the seven flyovers. These constructions will temporarily close several major roads and severely disrupt traffic. An estimated 150 000 vehicle trips per day cross the seven affected level-crossings with an average passenger load of six persons. Allowing nine months for construction of one flyover and an average vehicle delay time of 10 minutes, total delay cost will be $4.2 million spread over five years. This allows car and bus passengers the same travel time values and assumes no indirect congestion impacts on other vehicles not using the level crossings. Other construction impacts have not been quantified.

Congestion relief due to flyovers

On the other hand, the dual two-carriageway flyovers will significantly increase traffic speeds over four of the seven crossings, which are presently congested, poorly surfaced single carriageways. Allowing that average speed will increase from 20 kilometres per hour to 40 kilometres per hour over 400 metres, average time savings will be 0.6 of a minute per vehicle (for 60 000 vehicles per day). Adopting previous passenger/vehicle and time value parameters, the annual benefits will be $0.13 million, which will increase with traffic growth.

Reductions in Vehicle Accidents

The transfer of 200 million or more passengers annually from buses to rail will significantly reduce road accidents. But to estimate the cost savings we have to draw on scant data and make some important assumptions (especially about the value of life). We estimate, first, the total bus-related accident costs on the north–south corridor in Lagos (Table 8.4) and, second, the savings due to transfers from bus to rail.

Police records show that on the four main north–south roads close to the NRC corridor (Ikorodu Road, Agege Motor Road, Western Avenue Road and Herbert Macaulay Road) there were 944 traffic accidents in the first half of 1992, including 195 deaths, 326 serious accidents and 423 minor accidents. Drawing on research (for example Owasina, 1981) it is assumed that 10 per cent of deaths from road accidents, 25 per cent of serious road accidents and 90 per cent of minor accidents were not reported. Buses were involved in 32 per cent of all reported accidents. Costs per accident are based on average 1992 OECD values ($900 000 for a fatality, $75 000 for a serious

Table 8.4 Accident costs in the north–south Lagos corridor

Accidents	*Jan–June 1992 (no.)*	*Assumed unreported (%)*	*All 1992 (no.)*	*Bus-related (no.)*	*Cost of accident ($)*	*Bus acc. costs ($000)*
Fatal	195	10	433	139	22 500	3128
Serious	326	25	869	278	1 875	521
Minor	423	90	8460	2707	150	406
Total	944	–	9762	3124	–	4055

Source: Police Department, Lagos; author's research.

accident and $6000 for a minor accident) divided by 40 to allow for the differences in household incomes (as proxies for differences in willingness to pay) between OECD countries and Nigeria. Estimated bus-related accident costs in the north–south Lagos corridor in 1992 totalled $4.1 million. Finally, it is assumed that the transfer of one third of the corridor's bus passengers to the metro will reduce bus-related accident costs by one third, that is, by $1.35 million per annum at 1992 traffic levels. Also, there will be lower accident costs on other roads from which bus passengers divert to rail. On the other hand there will be some rail accidents, especially in the start-up period. These latter two sets of costs are assumed to balance out.

8.9 OTHER COSTS AND BENEFITS

Other Quantified Costs

Land take: inside the NRC right of way

The metro will require 33 hectares in the NRC RoW. At a conservative residential market price of $0.3 million per hectare the land can be valued at $9.9 million. However this presumes unrealistically that land use conversion in the RoW will be permitted.

Nevertheless the RoW land is valuable to thousands of stallholders and pedestrians who use it daily. Its value is what users will be willing to pay for it, or its replacement cost, whichever is lower. Of course, as trespassers RoW users will not be entitled to compensation. But this does not mean the RoW land has no value. Moreover, in the absence of compensation the social costs of moving people out of the RoW will be high (see disturbance costs below).

Drawing on survey data, DAH (1992b) estimates that the metro will remove at least 10 000 stalls from the RoW and that traders will be willing to pay an average annual rent of $40 per stall. The total annual value of the RoW to traders is therefore $400 000. In addition there will be an unquantified loss of surplus for shoppers who lose easy access to markets.

The RoW is also a valuable, heavily used, north–south pedestrian route. It saves time because it is straight and relatively uncongested (because of its width) and it is safe and dry compared with walking on or beside adjacent roads. In many places there are no off-road pathways. Based on DAH surveys, at least 150 000 daily pedestrian trips are made along the RoW between Agbado and Iddo. These trips save an estimated 7.5 minutes of travel time at the low rate of $0.055 per hour of time saved, which is half the value of travel time savings of public transport users. This works out at $0.007 per pedestrian trip (which is two thirds of the one kilometre bus fare). These assumptions produce a RoW value to north–south pedestrians of $350 000 per annum. Capitalised at 10 per cent, the value would be $3.5 million. This is slightly higher than the replacement land cost for a metre-wide path for 26 kilometres at a marginal commercial rate of $55 per square metre, which would cost $3.0 million excluding construction cost.

Land take: outside the right of way

The estimated land take outside the RoW is 25.5 hectares. This includes land for bus interchanges, rail depot, flyovers, the Iddo interchange and rail stations. However the bus interchanges include four hectares for relocation of markets from the RoW and land required for the flyovers, which is already costed. Therefore, for our valuation purposes, the net land requirement is 21.5 hectares. Three quarters of this requirement will be met from undeveloped land (or land with worthless structures). Assuming a mixed commercial/residential opportunity cost, the average opportunity cost of undeveloped land will be $0.42 million per hectare. The average cost of developed land is $1.68 million per hectare. Total land opportunity costs add up to $15.7 million.

Social disturbance costs

Construction of the metro along with the six flyovers will cause substantial relocation of businesses and households. At the three busiest new flyovers, 137 commercial buildings, 50 mixed commercial and residential properties, 49 residential buildings and several public facilities will be removed. Evidence in developed countries indicates that property owners require an average premium of 30 per cent of market value to compensate for involuntary sale and relocation (Abelson, 1986). Planners in Lagos suggest that a similar or higher premium will apply there because most businesses and households are strongly attached to their local area and move infrequently. In this evaluation a 30 per cent disturbance and relocation premium is allowed.

In addition about 20 000 stall holders inside and outside the RoW will be deprived of their livelihood until they find alternative locations, which will not be easy. Whatever their legal rights, or lack thereof, the traders will bitterly oppose any move without meaningful consultation and compensation. One DAH surveyor observed: 'Eighty per cent of traders would die rather than be relocated. Blood will be shed'. As a measure of their disturbance costs, stall traders are assumed to be willing to pay 15 per cent of actual or estimated land values (half the premium assumed for legal land owners) to avoid loss of *de facto* use rights and relocation. The amount they would be willing to accept as compensation would doubtless be much higher.

Severance costs

Currently the households on either side of the RoW mix freely and regularly and enjoy continuous visual contact. There are 49 well-used crossing points and another seven conveniently located pedestrian bridges. Surveys indicate at least 500 000 daily pedestrian crossings of the RoW. The proposed two-metre security wall will cause major severance. This could be mitigated by the 31 pedestrian bridges, one every 0.8 of a kilometre, and two underpasses. Nevertheless many people will have to walk half a kilometre or more to see people they could previously greet across the RoW or walk to meet in less than a minute. Nor are bridges convenient for people carrying loads, as many do in Lagos. For the evaluation we allow an average time penalty of 5 minutes per trip at the pedestrian rate of $0.055 per hour. This translates to a cost of $0.0046 per trip and to $0.77 million per annum.

Other Quantified Benefits

Flood mitigation benefits

The rail RoW, as presently designed, severely limits cross-drainage. It acts as a dam wall that causes flooding over 123 hectares to the east of the RoW for an average of 15 days a year. Flood costs include road and utilities damages, property damages, health hazards, vehicle delays, pedestrian inconvenience and land sterilisation. The drainage incorporated into the new rail design will prevent this flooding. DAH estimate that the cost of other drainage works to prevent the flooding will be $4.3 million and that the flood mitigation benefits will be significantly higher than these defensive expenditures. For this evaluation, the savings in defensive expenditures are attributed to the metro project.

Improved air quality

Akerdolu (1989) notes that suspended particulates are the most evident form of air pollution in Lagos, that the air often has an unpleasant odour and that a greyish haze often obscures the skyline till mid-morning. Thirty per cent of heavy trucks and 13 per cent of cars are reported to emit dark smoke continuously, as do many buses. However there are no detailed measurements of air quality in Lagos.

Drawing on international research on vehicle emissions, DAH (1992a) estimates that the transfer of 200–300 million passengers annually from diesel buses to diesel trains will substantially reduce emissions of carbon monoxide, nitrogen oxides, hydrocarbons and particulates (see Table 8.5). However, because the metro will reduce bus travel in Lagos only by one tenth, the relative decline in emissions will be slight. Also, the metro will not affect carbon dioxide or lead emissions because few passengers are expected to divert from petrol driven vehicles.

Air pollution in cities is of concern mainly because of its likely impact on health. The World Bank (1992) considers suspended particulate matter (SPM) to be a major cause of ill-health. In some cities excess SPM is reckoned to be responsible for between 2 per cent and 5 per cent of deaths and to cause chronic coughing in children and permanent respiratory damage. The Bank estimates that excess SPM causes between 0.6 and 2.1 work loss days per working adult per annum. Ostro (1983) estimates that restricted activity days (which include work loss days) are double work loss days. The World Health Organisation also views polyaromatic hydrocarbons associated with diesel exhaust as probable carcinogens. Nitrogen oxides are a respiratory irritant and cause bronchitis and oedema of lungs. Low levels of exposure to ozone cause eye irritation, coughs, chest discomfort, headaches, respiratory illness and asthma (UN, 1989).

On the other hand Ball *et al.* (1990, p. 17) conclude that 'the link between air pollution and public health is a tenuous one.... Only a small fraction of the variance in mortality and morbidity seems statistically attributable to air pollution'. Watkins (1991) shares this scepticism, pointing out that the black

Table 8.5 Forecast emission levels over project life (tonnes)

Pollutants	*Buses* *No metro*	*With metro*	*Metro*	*Net savings due to metro*
Carbon monoxide	107 720	96 948	2478	8 294
Nitrogen oxide	196 980	177 282	3158	16 540
Hydrocarbons	23 080	20 772	168	2 140
Particulates	18 470	16 623	na	1 847*

* Gross savings from reduced bus operations.

Source: Dar al-Handasah, 1992a, based on emission data from Warren Springs Laboratory, UK.

smoke from diesels is almost pure carbon with no specific toxic properties, although it does act as a nucleus to carry other products of partial combustion such as polyaromatic hydrocarbons, which may stimulate carcinogenic activity. Hine (1991) summarises impacts of vehicle pollution on mortality in the UK as one cancer death per five million people (which is close to the Lagos population) per annum, and the total toxicological impact of air pollutants as five deaths per five million, although he recognises that the real figure could be anywhere between one and 50 deaths. But it will still be very low compared with 1000 deaths from vehicle accidents per five million people in the UK.

People generally object to the disamenity of fumes from diesel vehicles and the associated malodours and loss of visibility. Hydrocarbons and nitrogen oxides have a less obvious effect but people suffer breathing discomfort and dislike the smell. These disamenities are striking in Lagos, but difficult to cost. Surveys, for example Strand (1985), have found that disamenity contributes to the total that people are willing to pay for improved air quality but it is difficult to identify its precise contribution. Moreover some surveys have found that people object to fumes mainly because of their supposed impact on health rather than because of the fumes themselves (Ball *et al.*, 1990).

This evaluation assumes, loosely following the World Bank, that all forms of air pollution from buses cause adults in the labour force to lose an average of 1.5 working days per annum and that transfers to the metro will reduce these losses proportionately by 10 per cent. These health benefits will total $0.67 million per annum (that is, an average benefit of 0.15 work days per annum for three million workers at $1.5 per day). This is increased by 50 per cent (to $1.01 million per annum) to allow for savings in health care expenditure, improved health in children, and improved amenity for a million residents who live close to the major north–south transport corridor. This benefit estimate implies that each affected household (about 400 000 households) will be willing to pay $2.5 per annum (0.4 per cent of household income) for the forecast improvements in air quality. However it is assumed that these improvements will not be sufficient to save lives.

Other Unquantified Impacts

Traffic noise

Noise levels around busy roads in central Lagos are high. The average noise level is generally about 75 dB (A) and L_{10} measures (the mean sound exceeded for 10 per cent of the time) are usually over 80 dB(A). However the metro will not reduce noise annoyance by much for three main reasons. Firstly, a small reduction in vehicles on busy roads (with over 1200 vehicles per hour) will cause a negligible reduction in the noise level (see Table 8.6). Secondly, in admittedly casual discussion, several Lagos residents insisted to the writer that local residents like noise and that even traffic noise is not an exception! Thirdly, the metro itself will be noisy. The noise level from diesel locomotives at 50 feet is typically around 90 dB(A). On the other hand the two-metre block wall may give significant protection from noise. Also, noise from rail is generally tolerated more than noise from other sources (Nelson, 1987).

Visual impacts

Assessment of the visual impacts of the metro has not been attempted. A 26 kilometre long, two-metre high block wall topped with anti-intruder spikes will be a visual eyesore and reduce the view of many households. On the other hand much of the railway line is currently strewn with garbage and is visually degraded.

Toxic wastes

Toxic wastes occur as a byproduct of rail depot operations. Acid baths and toxic disinfectants are required for coach cleaning. These chemicals and oil waste from fuel spillages and maintenance activities are washed off concrete stands into holding tanks and then carted away. With careful depot design and appropriate mitigating measures there should be no residual pollution of local waterways.

Land use changes

The metro will encourage more intensive development around the RoW. It will facilitate employment in the commercial centre on Lagos Island; encourage development of underutilised land, for example around Ebutte Metta; and generate more residential development at the northern end of the line around Aggege and Agbado. The beneficial development effects will be largely reflected in increased local land values. Such changes in land values usually in turn reflect the user surpluses of generated traffic on the new transport mode (unless there are economies of scale in production, in which case the increases in local land values will exceed the user surpluses). On the other hand the intensive development may increase local congestion and pollution. But as we have seen, generated traffic benefits and land use

Table 8.6 Noise levels in Lagos and some UK research results

Location	L_{10}	L_{eq}	*Hourly traffic*	*Heavy vehicles (%)*
Murtala Muhamed/Commercial St	85.0	79.5	2710	8.5
Murtala Muhamed/Hughes Ave.	82.7	67.0	2210	10.0
Murtala Muhamed/Petgrave St	81.5	76.8	1810	10.0
Herbert Macaulay/Harvey Rd	80.8	75.5	2140	6.0
Herbert Macaulay/Club St	79.1	74.6	2670	7.0
University Rd	76.6	73.3	840	2.0
Moshalashi crossing	86.0			6.5
Yaba crossing	79.0			2.4
Herbert Macauley	84.0			5.4
Western Avenue	82.0			11.0
Agege Motor Road	80.0			10.0
Estimated relationships between noise levels and traffic volumes	69.0		400	0–16
	74.0		800	0–16
	76.0		1200	0–16
	77.0		1600	0–16
	77.0		2000	0–16
	78.0		2500	0–16
	78.0		3000	0–16

Sources: Yakasi, 1992; Wilbur Smith, 1976; UK Ministry of Transport, quoted in Dar al-Handasah, 1992a.

changes are rarely valued. These are topics on which more research is needed in Lagos and elsewhere.

Energy consumption

The metro will increase energy consumption. It will require substantial energy inputs for construction and consume twice as much diesel fuel each year as buses. The proposed two-locomotive diesel train will require an estimated 10.25 litres of fuel per train kilometre compared with 0.235 litres per bus kilometre. This will not be offset by the much higher occupancy rates of trains (average 800) than buses (42). Also, the metro will use more electricity than will buses. However these resources are accounted for by shadow prices in the economic evaluation and should not be counted twice.

8.10 EVALUATION OF THE PROPOSED RAILWAY

Economic Evaluation

Table 8.7 summarises the results of the economic evaluation. Tables 8.8 and 8.9 show details based on the now historic assumption that the project would start in 1994. The estimated internal rate of return (IRR) for the railway is 8.7 per cent. Adopting the 10 per cent discount rate used by the World Bank in Nigeria (which presumably reflects the social opportunity cost of capital), the estimated net present value (NPV) is –\$19 million. On the basis of the quantified costs and benefits, the proposed railway is therefore highly marginal.

To what extent is the result sensitive to project design and phasing or to other project assumptions? There are many options. In this evaluation the metro is assumed to operate from the outset from Iddo to Agbado, but some staging of rolling stock purchase and a two-year build up of traffic is allowed. The rate of return could be improved by terminating the rail at Ebutte Metta Junction, but this possibility has not been developed for evaluation. It might also be increased marginally by delaying construction

Table 8.7 Summary of economic evaluation

	*NPVs \$m**	*%*		*NPVs \$m**	*%*
Metro costs:			*Metro benefits*:		
Construction	85.6	36.8	Rail user time	34.4	16.1
Rolling stock	53.9	23.2	Rail user comfort	10.6	5.0
Operating costs	62.0	26.7	Other time savings	36.7	17.2
Land in RoW	6.4	2.8	Bus cost savings	115.1	53.9
Other land	12.4	5.3	Accident savings	9.0	4.2
Disturbance	3.1	1.3	Air quality	4.2	2.0
Severance	6.3	2.7	Flyover benefits	0.9	0.4
Traffic delay	2.9	1.2	Flood mitigation	2.8	1.3
Total	232.6	100.0	Total	213.7	100.0
Total NPV (\$m)	–19.0				
Total IRR	8.7				

*Discount rate 10 per cent

Source: Details in Tables 8.8 and 8.9.

Table 8.8 Proposed Lagos railway: summary economic spreadsheet (1992 $USm)[1]

	Capital Costs				Main direct travel benefits									
	Rail[2]	*Rolling stock*	*Operating costs*	*Total costs*	*Rail pass. time*	*Rail pass. comfort*	*Other pass. time*	*Savings in bus op. costs*	*Main travel benefits*	*Net other benefits*[3]	*Net project benefits*	*Rail fin. costs*	*Rail fares*	*Net rail revenues*
	(1)	*(2)*	*(3)*	*(4) (1+2+3)*	*(5)*	*(6)*	*(7)*	*(8)*	*(9) (5+6+7+8)*	*(10)*	*(11) 9–(4+10)*	*(12)*	*(13)*	*(14)*
1993	0.00	0.00	0.00	0.00	0.00	0.00	0.00	0.00	0.00	0	0.00	0.00	0.00	0.00
1994	24.85	0.00	0.00	24.85	0.00	0.00	0.00	0.00	0.00	–11.76	–36.61	24.00	0.00	–24.00
1995	24.85	0.00	0.00	24.85	0.00	0.00	0.00	0.00	0.00	–11.15	–36.00	24.00	0.00	–24.00
1996	24.84	0.00	0.00	24.84	0.00	0.00	0.00	0.00	0.00	–1.26	–26.10	24.00	0.00	–24.00
1997	24.85	0.00	0.00	24.85	0.00	0.00	0.00	0.00	0.00	–1.26	–26.11	24.00	0.00	–24.00
1998	24.85	66.00	0.00	90.85	0.00	0.00	0.00	0.00	0.00	–1.26	–92.11	84.00	0.00	–84.00
1999	–	17.00	8.33	25.33	3.97	1.23	6.24	13.28	24.72	1.34	0.73	21.05	16.25	–4.80
2000	–	17.00	10.10	27.10	5.26	1.63	6.35	17.60	30.84	1.40	5.13	22.48	21.53	–0.95
2001	–	–	11.88	11.88	6.55	2.02	6.47	21.92	36.96	1.47	26.55	8.27	26.81	18.54
2002	–	–	12.15	12.15	6.75	2.09	6.70	22.58	38.12	1.54	27.50	9.37	27.63	18.26
2003	–	–	12.43	12.43	6.95	2.15	6.94	23.24	39.28	1.61	28.46	10.51	28.44	17.93
2004	–	–	12.70	12.70	7.15	2.21	7.18	23.91	40.45	1.68	29.43	11.72	29.25	17.53
2005	–	–	12.97	12.97	7.35	2.27	7.44	24.57	41.63	1.76	30.42	12.97	30.06	17.09
2006	–	–	13.11	13.11	7.44	2.30	7.72	24.91	42.37	1.84	31.10	13.11	30.47	17.36
2007	–	–	13.11	13.11	7.44	2.30	7.72	24.91	42.37	1.85	31.11	13.11	30.47	17.36
2008	–	–	13.11	13.11	7.44	2.30	7.72	24.91	42.37	1.85	31.11	13.11	30.47	17.36
2009	–	–	13.11	13.11	7.44	2.30	7.72	24.91	42.37	1.86	31.12	13.11	30.47	17.36
2010	–	–	13.11	13.11	7.44	2.30	7.72	24.91	42.37	1.86	31.12	13.11	30.47	17.36
2011	–	–	13.11	13.11	7.44	2.30	7.72	24.91	42.37	1.87	31.13	13.11	30.47	17.36
2012	–	–	13.11	13.11	7.44	2.30	7.72	24.91	42.37	1.87	31.13	13.11	30.47	17.36
2013	–	–	13.11	13.11	7.44	2.30	7.72	24.91	42.37	1.88	31.14	13.11	30.47	17.36
2014	–	–	13.11	13.11	7.44	2.30	7.72	24.91	42.37	1.88	31.14	13.11	30.47	17.36
2015	–	–	13.11	13.11	7.44	2.30	7.72	24.91	42.37	1.89	31.15	13.11	30.47	17.36
2016	–	–	13.11	13.11	7.44	2.30	7.72	24.91	42.37	1.90	31.16	13.11	30.47	17.36
2017	–	–	13.11	13.11	7.44	2.30	7.72	24.91	42.37	1.91	31.17	13.11	30.47	17.36
2018	–	–	13.11	13.11	7.44	2.30	7.72	24.91	42.37	1.91	31.17	13.11	30.47	17.36
2019	–	–	13.11	13.11	7.44	2.30	7.72	24.91	42.37	1.92	31.18	13.11	30.47	17.36
2020	–	–	13.11	13.11	7.44	2.30	7.72	24.91	42.37	1.92	31.18	13.11	30.47	17.36
2021	–	–	13.11	13.11	7.44	2.30	7.72	24.91	42.37	1.93	31.19	13.11	30.47	17.36
2022	–	–	13.11	13.11	7.44	2.30	7.72	24.91	42.37	1.94	31.20	13.11	30.47	17.36
2023	–	–	13.11	13.11	7.44	2.30	7.72	24.91	42.37	1.94	31.20	13.11	30.47	17.36
NPV 10%	85.63	53.91	62.01	201.55	34.40	10.63	36.70	115.08	196.80	–11.83	–16.58	187.30	140.79	–46.52
IRR											0.089			0.056

Notes
1. Does not include generated traffic or land development benefits.
2. Includes all costs necessary to make rail work, e.g. flyovers, utility relocation etc. but not land costs.
3. See Table 8.9.

Table 8.9 Proposed Lagos railway: other costs and benefits (1992, $USm)

	Other costs						*Other benefits*					
	Land costs											
	RoW land costs (1)	*Other land costs (2)*	*Disturbance costs (3)*	*Severance costs (4)*	*Traffic delay costs[1] (5)*	*Total other costs (6) (1 to 5)*	*Traffic flyover benefits[2] (7)*	*Savings flood costs (8)*	*Savings accident costs (9)*	*Air quality benefits (10)*	*Total other benefits (11) (7 to 10)*	*Net other benefits (12) (11–6)*
1993	0	0	0	0	0	0	0	0	0	0	0	0
1994	0.75	7.85	1.94	0.38	0.84	11.76	0	0	0	0	0	–11.76
1995	0.75	7.85	1.94	0.77	0.84	12.15	0	1	0	0	1	–11.15
1996	0.75	0	0	0.77	0.84	2.36	0	1.1	0	0	1.1	–1.26
1997	0.75	0	0	0.77	0.84	2.36	0	1.1	0	0	1.1	–1.26
1998	0.75	0	0	0.77	0.84	2.36	0	1.1	0	0	1.1	–1.26
1999	0.75	0	0	0.77	0	1.52	0.13	0	1.72	1.01	2.86	1.34
2000	0.75	0	0	0.77	0	1.52	0.13	0	1.78	1.01	2.92	1.40
2001	0.75	0	0	0.77	0	1.52	0.14	0	1.84	1.01	2.99	1.47
2002	0.75	0	0	0.77	0	1.52	0.14	0	1.90	1.01	3.06	1.54
2003	0.75	0	0	0.77	0	1.52	0.15	0	1.97	1.01	3.13	1.61
2004	0.75	0	0	0.77	0	1.52	0.15	0	2.04	1.01	3.20	1.68
2005	0.75	0	0	0.77	0	1.52	0.16	0	2.11	1.01	3.28	1.76
2006	0.75	0	0	0.77	0	1.52	0.16	0	2.19	1.01	3.36	1.84
2007	0.75	0	0	0.77	0	1.52	0.17	0	2.19	1.01	3.37	1.85
2008	0.75	0	0	0.77	0	1.52	0.17	0	2.19	1.01	3.37	1.85
2009	0.75	0	0	0.77	0	1.52	0.18	0	2.19	1.01	3.38	1.86
2010	0.75	0	0	0.77	0	1.52	0.18	0	2.19	1.01	3.38	1.86
2011	0.75	0	0	0.77	0	1.52	0.19	0	2.19	1.01	3.39	1.87
2012	0.75	0	0	0.77	0	1.52	0.19	0	2.19	1.01	3.39	1.87
2013	0.75	0	0	0.77	0	1.52	0.20	0	2.19	1.01	3.40	1.88
2014	0.75	0	0	0.77	0	1.52	0.20	0	2.19	1.01	3.40	1.88
2015	0.75	0	0	0.77	0	1.52	0.21	0	2.19	1.01	3.41	1.89
2016	0.75	0	0	0.77	0	1.52	0.22	0	2.19	1.01	3.42	1.90
2017	0.75	0	0	0.77	0	1.52	0.23	0	2.19	1.01	3.43	1.91
2018	0.75	0	0	0.77	0	1.52	0.23	0	2.19	1.01	3.43	1.91
2019	0.75	0	0	0.77	0	1.52	0.24	0	2.19	1.01	3.44	1.92
2020	0.75	0	0	0.77	0	1.52	0.24	0	2.19	1.01	3.44	1.92
2021	0.75	0	0	0.77	0	1.52	0.25	0	2.19	1.01	3.45	1.93
2022	0.75	0	0	0.77	0	1.52	0.26	0	2.19	1.01	3.46	1.94
2023	0.75	0	0	0.77	0	1.52	0.26	0	2.19	1.01	3.46	1.94
NPV 10%	6.43	12.39	3.06	6.28	2.89	31.05	0.85	2.81	10.37	5.19	19.22	–11.83

Notes
1. During construction.
2. Benefits due to improved intersection arrangements.

of the Agege–Agbado section. More generally, the more that Lagos traffic increases over time without a solution, the higher will be the return to rail investment.

It is clear from Table 8.7 that the most important determinants of the results are rail construction and operating costs, benefits to rail users and benefits to other users of the transport network (in terms of time savings and reduced bus operating costs). Both rail construction and operation assume efficient procedures and cost overruns are much more likely than surpluses. Passenger forecasts are crucial to both user and network benefits. Fulfilment of the forecasts depends heavily on achievement of projected service levels. As discussed above, the forecasts are more likely to be too high than too low. On the other hand, generated traffic benefits and network benefits to private vehicle users may have been underestimated.

The results are not very sensitive to environmental costs and benefits. Defining environmental costs narrowly as social disturbance and severance, estimated environmental costs make up only 4.0 per cent of total costs. Land costs make up another 8.1 per cent. Defining environmental benefits as accident savings, air quality and flood mitigation, environmental benefits constitute 8.5 per cent of total benefits.

Financial Analysis

In order to estimate financial returns to the metro, someone must decide the costs to be borne by the metro agency. This is an arbitrary business. For example, should the metro bear the costs of land take outside the RoW, the bus interchanges, the footbridges and the flyovers? In this evaluation it is assumed that the metro will bear all the capital expenditures shown in Table 8.1, but no land costs. Also, the metro is assumed to receive decreasing subsidies for fuel and electricity, which will be phased out by 2005. On these assumptions, the NPV of the financial returns to the metro will be –$47 million and the IRR will be 5.6 per cent. Assuming an (upward) fare price elasticity of –0.5, in order to achieve break-even point fares will have to rise by about 75 per cent. However it will not be economically efficient to raise prices so far above short run marginal costs.

Project Feasibility and Risk

The viability of the railway depends crucially on the efficient construction and operation of the metro. The proposed metro is a capital intensive, high tech solution for which there is no precedent in the Nigerian transport sector. On the contrary, rail management in Lagos has a history of failure. In other countries, railway cost overruns, construction delays and underfulfilled forecasts are common. It is doubtful whether the Nigerian government could provide adequate guarantees of financial returns and employee safety (robbery with violence is common in Lagos) to induce private foreign companies to undertake so large a venture.

The government's ability to handle the social impacts of the metro will be critical to its success or failure. The thousands of households who will be affected by the metro will be bitter if they are not consulted or treated fairly; violence and sabotage might result. However senior members of the government have no doubt that the government will be able to construct the metro without social upheaval. In the words of the chairman of the Oshodi Municipality to the writer: 'In this part of the world, government is Alpha and Omega'. In that same week, on 22 September 1992, a leading article in the Nigerian newspaper, *The Guardian*, noted that 'Oshodi mocks all levels of government.... Oshodi symbolises everything to do with the failure of municipal government in this country'.

8.10 CONCLUSIONS

Traffic congestion, accidents and air quality are serious problems in Lagos. Traffic noise is substantial but appears to be a minor concern. Emission controls on motor vehicles, efficient pricing policies and traffic management are the most cost-effective instruments for reducing congestion and pollution. However they will not provide a complete solution. The NRC corridor is the only major opportunity for improving the transport infrastructure.

The estimated internal rate of return for the proposed railway is 8.6 per cent. The majority of benefits are relief of congestion and reduced travel time. There will be significant savings in accident costs and air quality benefits, but other environmental benefits will be minor. On the other hand, construction of the metro will impact severely on the thousands of households who will be relocated and cut off from established businesses and ways of life. Severance is also a problem. These social impacts could jeopardise timely construction of the metro even though construction itself presents few technical problems on the flat Lagos terrain. Also, the estimated rate of return presumes high standards of technical operating efficiency and maintenance. These standards could be jeopardised by poor financial returns.

In the writer's view the risk of a lower than forecast return, due to cost overruns and underfulfilled forecasts, is significant. On the other hand, the generated traffic, network and development benefits may have been underestimated. Overall it is concluded that it will be sensible to proceed with the railway only if it is believed that the relevant Nigerian governments and the rail authority are able to deliver the planned project and that there are no viable alternatives.

The several alternatives include constructing the metro to Ebutte Metta Junction instead of Iddo, or to Agege instead of Agbado; light rail; a dual two-lane busway instead of the metro; an upgraded rail service on the existing line along with a busway or road in the other half of the NRC corridor. Some of these merit more attention. Armstrong-Wright (1986) points out that dedicated bus lanes have been effective in Bangkok and Porto Alegre and that insufficient attention was given to bus and other alternatives to the metro in Caracas. It should also be noted that although traffic management is not a complete alternative in Lagos, it would be a complementary policy. But consideration of traffic management was not part of the consultants' terms of reference.

Finally, the study may offer some lessons for evaluation procedures. It shows that many social and environmental costs and benefits can and should be included in a cost–benefit analysis: this brings out the critical elements in policy decisions within a coherent and consistent framework. True, many assumptions have been required. But the assumptions about the environment are generally no more heroic than those about transport, even though more thorough evaluation procedures have been developed for transport than for most other sectors. Plausible and coherent results have been achieved despite the extreme difficulty of obtaining data in Lagos, which one consultant described to the writer as a 'data-less city'. It has been possible to collect survey data on land uses both quickly and cheaply. It has also been possible to draw on international data in order to make plausible estimates of some social and environmental costs and benefits. On the other hand the evaluation would have benefited from further study of network impacts and local and regional land use impacts, and from a social impact assessment analysis.

9 Valuing Tropical Forest in Kenya

9.1 INTRODUCTION

> Forest management is a critical policy interest in the 1990s.... In some countries the rate of deforestation exceeds three per cent. Globally, deforestation occurs at an annual rate approaching 0.7 per cent and it annually disturbs land cover on an area the size of Great Britain. The exploitation of global, and especially tropical forests threatens the earth's long-term climate patterns, its reserves of genetic resources, and the more immediate life support of dependent local human communities (Hyde and Newman, 1991, p. 1).

This chapter discusses two tropical forest case-studies: the Kakamega and Arabuko-Sokoke forests in Kenya. Kakamega is the only lowland forest remaining in western Kenya. Covering about 24 000 hectares, it lies between the lowland forest of the Congo and the afro-montane forest of the western Rift Valley and produces a unique mixture of species from these two areas. The Arabuko-Sokoke forest covers nearly 42 000 hectares close to the Indian Ocean between Kilifi and Malindi. It is the last large remnant of the forest that once dominated Kenya's coastal areas.

In 1992 the UK Overseas Development Administration (ODA) funded a consultant team to produce pilot conservation plans for both forests, along with cost–benefit justifications for each plan. These plans, modified by the ODA review missions, were supported initially by the ODA under the Kenya Indigenous Forests Conservation Project (KIFCON). In June 1994 the ODA closed down KIFCON and terminated support for the Kakamega and Arabuko-Sokoke forests, apparently because of lack of domestic support for the projects.

This chapter draws heavily on the KIFCON studies and the unpublished reports of the ODA review missions. While in Kenya for a separate biodiversity study the writer discussed the conservation plans with KIFCON and visited part of the Arabuko-Sokoke forest as a tourist. However it was not possible to do field work specifically for this study. Accordingly this chapter focuses more on general evaluation issues than on the validity or otherwise of specific numbers or results.

The chapter starts with an outline of the general causes and consequences of deforestation. The next three sections describe the two Kenyan forests, the services they presently provide, and the main options and conservation costs for each forest. Section 9.5 outlines an approach to evaluating these options. Sections 9.6 to 9.8 discuss the valuation of direct and indirect forest benefits and existence values. Section 9.9 summarises the main results and management issues for each forest. There is a brief concluding section.

9.2 DEFORESTATION: GENERAL ISSUES

Deforestation: Extent and Causes

Pearce (1990) estimates that planet Earth has 800 million hectares of 'closed' tropical forests and loses 15 million hectares (nearly 2 per cent) each year. Closed forests are dense forests in which grass cover is limited or non-existent due to low light penetration through the forest canopy. Sixty per cent of these deforested areas are in Latin or Central America, a quarter in Asia and the rest in Africa and Oceania.

The prime direct causes of deforestation are timber exploitation and conversion of forests to grazing land and agriculture. These causes are related because the construction of forest access roads and the loss of timber increase the incentive to convert forest to grazing land and agriculture. Although properly managed logging need not destroy forests, long-term timber yields from mixed tropical moist forests are low and economically less attractive than yields from tropical conifer plantations (Dalfelt, 1991).

Deforestation has accelerated in recent years in developing countries where the population explosion, unequal land holdings, widespread poverty and the lack of alternative forms of income have led to intensive exploitation of forest products and extensive encroachment on forests for grazing or cropping purposes. Livelihoods often depend on exploiting forests at a non-sustainable rate. Some traditional land uses, such as shifting agriculture, are not sustainable because of population pressure and declining yields. Low yields on existing agricultural land encourage frontier expansion (Southgate, 1991).

Market failures take two main forms and both are conducive to deforestation. Firstly, many forest services (such as catchment protection and carbon store) are public goods that are of little or no value to private landowners. Secondly, property rights in forests are often unclear or disputed. In these circumstances each social group or household has an incentive to exploit the forest (and establish *de facto* property rights) and little reason to limit its forest utilisation to sustainable levels. When statutory rights are imposed in conflict with customary rights or interests, they are likely to be ignored and unenforceable.

Also, to gain income and foreign exchange, governments may encourage exploitation of forests for timber or conversion of forests to agriculture. Other policies may lead indirectly to deforestation. Hyde and Newman (1991) estimate that half the forest destruction in Brazil's Amazonia has been caused by subsidies for livestock production and agricultural settlement. On the other hand, even when they oppose forest exploitation, governments are often too weak or corrupt to prevent illegal exploitation.

Forest Values

Following Pearce (1990), it is convenient to identify four main sets of forest values: direct and indirect forest use values, and option and existence values. The main *direct use values* are:

- Timber products, including commercial timber and subsistence fuel-woods, charcoal and construction materials.
- Other forest-related products, including fruit, oil seeds, nuts, game, medicines, fibres, and fodder for livestock.
- Human habitat: forests provide land, shelter and traditional location as well as subsistence livelihood.
- Wildlife habitat: forests are the essential habitat for many forms of wildlife and the source of much irreplaceable genetic material for medicine, industry and agriculture.
- Recreation and tourism: forests attract many visitors, not only to see wildlife, but also for nature appreciation and adventure.

The main *indirect use values* of forests are:

- Soil productivity and protection: forests are semi-closed ecological systems that encourage nutrient recycling of soils. Deforestation reduces litterfall, which is critical to nutrient cycling. It also reduces overhead protection and leads to a breakup of fragile soils, which in turn reduces soil structure and fertility and causes an outflow of nutrients.
- Protection of watersheds: without the stabilising effect of roots and vegetation, run off usually increases and causes greater variation in stream flow, flooding and siltation (although the impact depends on the land uses that follow deforestation). Also, infiltration and groundwater recharge are reduced.
- Carbon store: growing forests absorb carbon dioxide and give off oxygen. When mature, forests release approximately as much carbon into

the atmosphere as they absorb. Forest destruction releases substantial CO_2 into the atmosphere, without an offsetting credit, and contributes to global warming.

- Climate stability: in some areas of the world, notably the Amazon, rainfall occurs from water recycled into the atmosphere through evapotranspiration. Extensive deforestation may reduce the amount or location of rainfall and lower stream flows in dry seasons.

The *option value* of a forest is the amount that people are willing to pay to ensure that it is conserved for future uses over and above the amount that they are willing to pay for their expected uses of it. As discussed in Chapter 2, option value is essentially an insurance policy. Option values are more likely to apply to uncertain indirect forest uses, which cannot be easily replicated, than to direct product uses for which there are usually substitutes.

The *existence value* of a forest is the amount that people are willing to pay to conserve the forest, or the biodiversity within the forest, for its own sake independently of what they are willing to pay for forest uses or the option of conserving the use potential.

Policies

How should forest land be used? Should the forest ecosystem be conserved or should the land be developed for other uses? Broadly conceived, conservation and development strategies may contain several options. Conservation options may include complete protection of the forest from human use other than for some very limited purposes (for example scientific research), indigenous settlement and sustainable extraction of subsistence forest products, controlled selective logging, tourism, and even shifting cultivation with full regeneration of forest between cultivation periods. Of course there is a risk that each of these options, except perhaps the first, could lead to an unplanned irreversible change in the ecosystem. For example Anderson (1989) questions whether hardwood timber production is sustainable. Development options include the use of the land for commercial plantations, agriculture, livestock or mining. These options usually damage the soils and prevent forest regeneration, but this is not inevitable.

The optimum strategy may be a mixed one that changes over time. Destruction of some tree cover is often unavoidable as populations grow and settlements and agriculture expand. On the other hand some afforestation may be viable, especially in social forestry projects (World Bank, 1991, p. 72). Trade-offs between forest services and the other uses of forest land are invariably needed. The choices and decisions vary with circumstances. For example protection of watersheds is usually more important on slopes than in lowland forests.

The specification of project objectives and outputs is particularly important for development of forest policies. In his review of ODA forest projects, Flint (1992) contends that the major causes of failure have been unclear objectives, overemphasis on simple physical measures of project achievement and underemphasis on the end-uses and beneficiaries of forests. Also, identification of domestic and international interests is crucial. Forest policies cannot work without domestic support.

Institutional issues matter because of the intensive nature of forest management. Also, the process of decision making is important; local people must be consulted and committed to the forest management plan. Ryan (1992, p. 17) points out that the viability of protected areas depends on the support of local people rather than on 'fences, fines and armed forces'. In order to reduce the pressure for forest exploitation, the poverty of communities near forests has to be alleviated by, for example, buffer zones on forest fringes where limited exploitation is permitted; support for local development efforts in crop growing, tourism and wildlife ranching; and provision of local services such as water supplies and health care. But, Ryan continues 'the difficulty of this approach should not be underestimated. Many villagers are rightly suspicious of parks departments which in their view have stolen resources from them often not for protective purposes but for wealthier bureaucrats to exploit. Park managers typically find calls for more participatory management a threat to their authority'.

Finally, complementary policies may be required to support forest land use decisions. Some damage can be mitigated by adoption of good forestry practices. For example good logging practices should include the use of low impact harvesting equipment, reduced logging in the rainy season and the restoration of disturbed areas. Financial incentives, for instance performance bonds for selective loggers, should be designed to give the right signals to households and developers (unlike the pro-deforestation fiscal policies in Brazil). And, if the developed world is serious about reducing logging in tropical forests, it could impose environmental taxes on the use of tropical timbers (Roselle and Katelman, 1990).

9.3 THE KENYAN FORESTS

KIFCON (1992a) report that in 1981, the latest year for which an inventory of forest resources is available, forests covered 1.4 million hectares in Kenya, about 2.5 per cent of the country's land area. The forest areas are in four biogeographical units, with distinct flora and fauna and utilisation patterns. These units are coastal, east Rift mountains, west Rift mountains, and Guineo-Congolan uplands, with several dry forest and riverine outliers. Most of Kenya's forested area is indigenous, but 170 000 hectares are plantations and degraded bushland. It is generally believed that indigenous forests have declined significantly since 1981, but the extent of the decline is not known.

Forests provide substantial economic benefits. They regulate and assist the distribution and flow of water, protect soils and provide habitats for wildlife, the basis for the large tourist industry. They also provide building materials, fuelwood, charcoal and many other materials such as fodder and fruit. Over 90 per cent of all Kenyan households use woodfuel and other biomass fuels for their domestic needs.

However Kenya has high population densities, with 230 persons per square kilometre of agricultural land. Four fifths of the population and the forests are located in one fifth of the total land area. Moreover the population is growing at 3.5 per cent per annum. Crop production and livestock compete with forestry for high and medium potential land.

The two government agencies responsible for most forest and wildlife management are the Forestry Department (FD) and the Kenya Wildlife Service (KWS). The FD has been a weak line agency receiving limited political support. Its budget has been static and forest infrastructure assets have fallen into disrepair. Traditionally the FD has been more concerned with plantations than with indigenous forests, with 80 per cent of its budget devoted to industrial forestry. The FD has attempted to protect the forests using a policing approach with guard houses and armed guards to prevent illegal utilisation. However the 'poor bloody infantry' approach (lots of underpaid and frightened guards in isolated guard posts) has failed to prevent widespread, illegal exploitation of the forests. The FD and the KWS have now agreed to share management of selected forests, including Kakamega. The KWS is responsible for developing forest-based tourism and will assist the FD in wildlife management.

Kakamega

Kakamega forest (KF) is a small, undulating area at the base of the Nandi escarpment in western Kenya (see Figure 9.1). The forest consists of two parts. The larger part, nearly 20 000 hectares, is the Kakamega Forest Reserve. This is trust land: ownership is vested in the people of the area and land administration is the responsibility of the county council, but forest management is the responsibility of the FD. The smaller part, 4500 hectares,

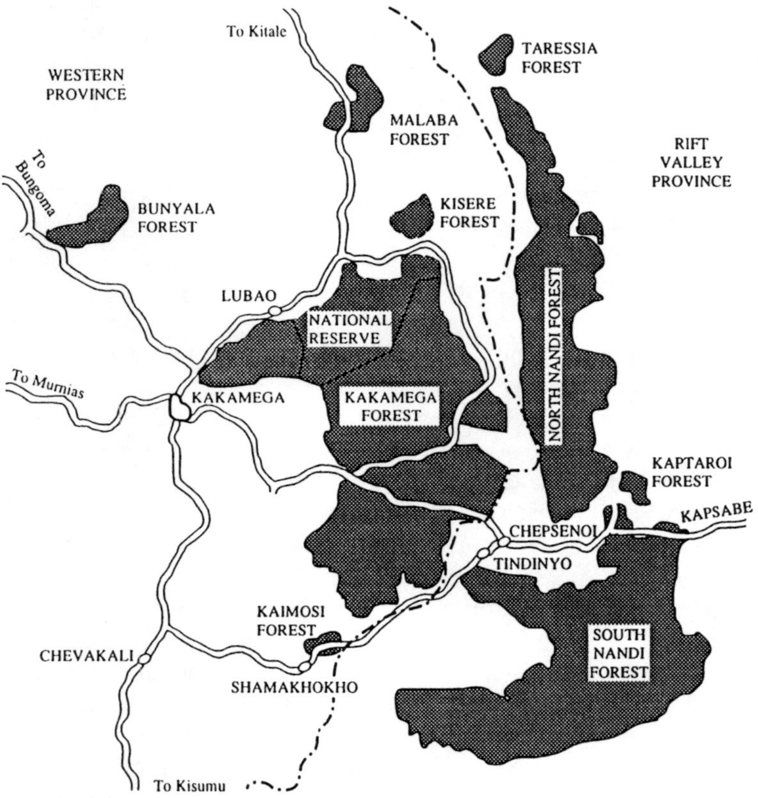

Source: KIFKON, 1992a.

Figure 9.1 Location of Kakamega forest

is the Kakamega National Reserve, which is owned by the state and managed by the KWS. Of the total forest area, approximately 14 000 hectares are covered by indigenous forest and the rest by non-indigenous forest, including plantations and grassland. Two main roads and numerous access tracks run through the forests. (See Figure 9.2.)

KF is regarded as an 'extremely valuable fauna reserve' (KIFCON, 1992a). The forest contains many forest primates, various snakes and birds that occur nowhere else in Kenya, and nearly half the butterflies recorded in Kenya. Also, the mixture of lowland and highland plant species is rare. In 1990 an estimated 2000 tourists visited KF.

The densely populated area around KF draws heavily on the forest's products. In 1991, 155 000 persons lived in 220 square kilometres adjacent

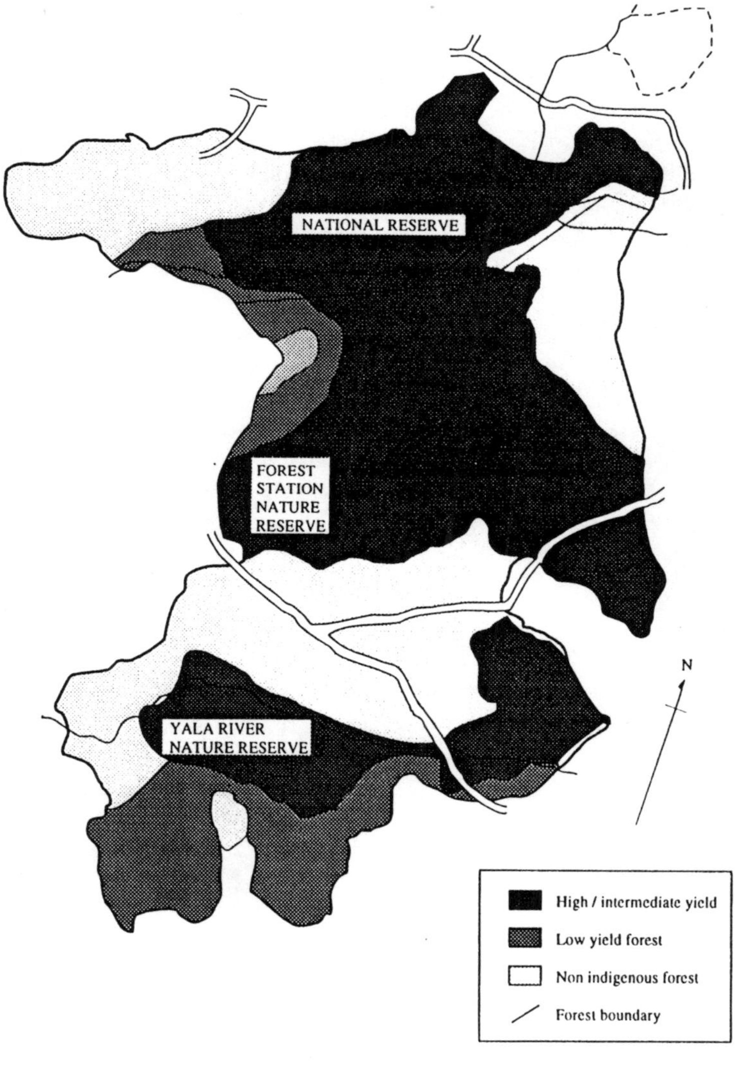

Source: KIFCON, 1992a.

Figure 9.2 Kakamega – forest type

to the forest. This represents just over 15 000 households with an average household size of 10, and an average population density of over 700 per square kilometres. Virtually all these households obtain at least one essential need, usually fuelwood or grazing, from the forest. KIFCON (1992b) estimates that the average net income of adjacent households was about Ksh 40 000 at that time (US$1 200), made up of forest products valued at $720, crop production ($400) and livestock ($80) outside the forest.

The estimated total value of products from the forest in 1991 was $11.6 million (Table 9.1). The main products were wood products ($3.8 million), grazing ($3.8 million), charcoal ($3.1 million) and gold ($0.8 million). Some 85 per cent of all product value, including much timber and all grazing and charcoal, was extracted illegally. Other illegal activities included collecting seedlings and plant materials for ropes, baskets and medicinal uses, and gold extraction. KIFCON describes the illegal removal of forest produce as widespread, frequently with the collusion of forest guards, and subject to minimal deterrence. About 15 per cent of forest product represented legal utilisation, mainly of fuelwood. Less than 1 per cent of the value of forest production accrued to the FD.

However Kakamega forest is under extreme threat. Between 1965 and 1991 the volume of timber in the forest fell from 3.1 million cubic metres to 1.5 million cubic metres. This reflects a 13 per cent reduction in forest area

Table 9.1 Estimated product value of Kakamega forest in 1991 ($ million)

	Local households	*Commercial interests*	*Total income*
Legal activities			
Fuelwood	1.67	neg.	1.67
Plantation timber	–	0.05	0.05
Total	1.67	0.05	1.72
Illegal activities			
Forest timber	0.73	0.31	1.04
Plantation timber	–	0.79	0.79
Polewood	0.24	–	0.24
Grazing	3.83	–	3.83
Charcoal	3.05	0.03	3.08
Gold	0.80	–	0.80
Other*	0.13	–	0.13
Total	8.78	1.13	9.91
All activities	10.45	1.18	11.63

*Thatch and seedlings.

Source: KIFCON, 1992b (allowing 33 ksh = $1.0).

and a 42 per cent fall in volume per hectare. KIFCON (1992a) estimates that 105 000 cubic metres of fuelwood and 8000 cubic metres of timber were being extracted annually from the forest, which far exceeded estimated sustainable extraction rates of 20 000 cubic metres and 4300 cubic metres respectively. KIFCON also notes that the forest has become fragmented and vegetation damaged by widespread cattle grazing. One fifth is grassland or scrub. On the other hand three fifths of the forest have modest agricultural potential for vegetables or tea or coffee.

Arabuko Sokoke

The Arabuko Sokoke (AS) forest contains mainly indigenous forest and woodland (see Figures 9.3 and 9.4). Many tracks run through the forest.

Unlike Kakamega, AS is not subject to heavy population pressure. In 1990 an estimated 84 000 people lived in villages around the forest. This represents about 7300 households with an average household size of nearly 12. Although the local population is increasing by 3.5 per cent a year, population density is only about 50 persons per square kilometre.

However, like Kakamega, AS is an 'extremely valuable fauna reserve' (KIFCON, 1992c). The International Council for Bird Preservation considers AS the second most important forest for birds in Africa. AS contains 10 per cent of Kenya's bird species and 30 per cent of its butterfly species. It is also home to 50–100 elephants, which damage crops and plantations at an estimated annual cost of $45 000. Despite the fauna and the large numbers of tourists on the Kenyan coast, only a few hundred visitors are recorded annually at the main (Gede) forest station. This partly reflects the poor tourist facilities in AS. But as a reviewer of this chapter observed, it also reflects the fact that the forest is 'boring to most tourists'.

In 1991 local households and commercial interests extracted 5000 cubic metres of fuelwood, 2500 cubic metres of carving wood and 360 cubic metres of timber from AS (KIFCON, 1992d). Most of the carving wood and one third of the fuelwood and timber were extracted illegally. Local households also engaged in illegal subsistence hunting, the collection of medicinal plants and the collection of water from seasonal ponds.

In 1991 the estimated value of products taken from AS was only $460 000 (Table 9.2). The main products were various wood products ($340 000) and hunting ($90 000). Four fifths of total product value was extracted illegally.

Based on a survey of 31 forest-adjacent households, mean cash household income was $525 in 1991, with the main contributions from wage employment, tree crops and tree-crop products, and forest derived

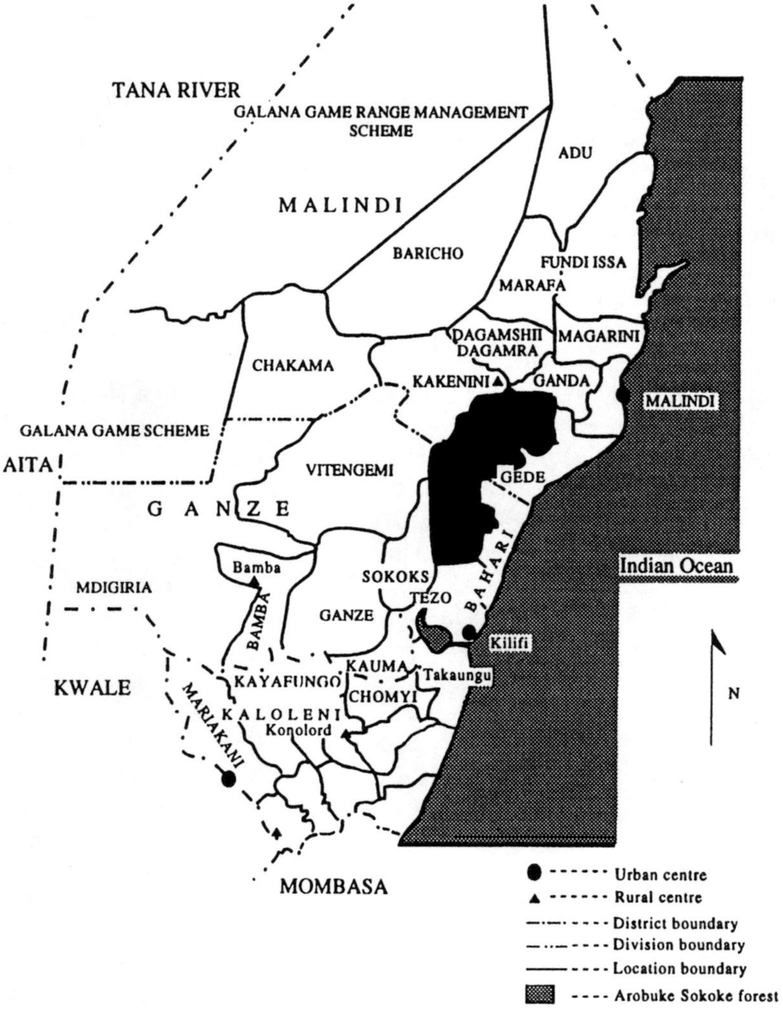

Source: KIFCON, 1992c.

Figure 9.3 Location of Arabuko–Sokoke forest reserve in Kilifi district

products. Also, these households typically saved \$160 per annum by extracting forest products such as fuelwood, meat and polewood from AS.

Overall, unlike Kakamega, AS is under only moderate threat from the local population or developers. KIFCON (1992c) estimates that the

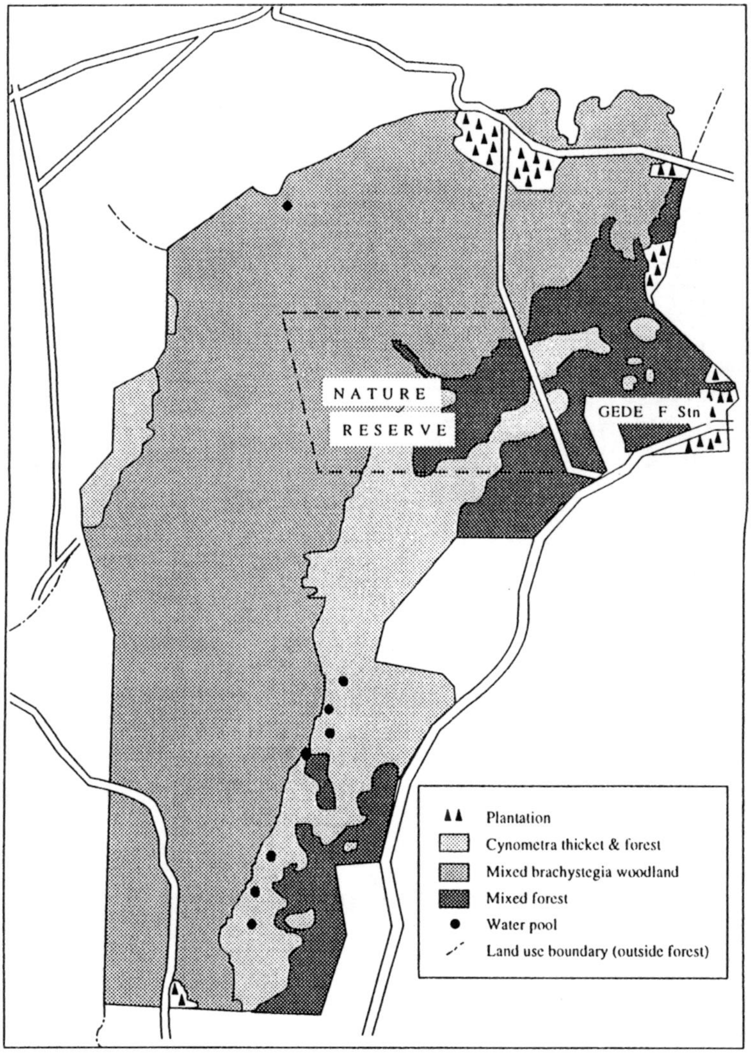

Source: KIFCON, 1992c.

Figure 9.4 Arabuko–Sokoke forest–nature reserve and vegetation

sustainable yield of AS is 21 800 cubic metres of fuelwood, 270 cubic metres of logs and, 189 cubic metres of wood for carving. The present extraction rate for carving wood is not sustainable and timber extraction is probably

Table 9.2 Estimated product value of Arabuko Sokoke forest in 1991 ($ thousand)

	Local households	*Commercial interests*	*Total income*
Legal activities			
Fuelwood	21	9	30
Plantation timber	–	18	18
Carving wood	–	45	45
Total	21	72	93
Illegal activities			
Fuelwood	18	–	18
Other woods	6	224	230
Hunting	87	–	87
Other*	6	30	36
Total	117	254	371
All activities	139	326	464

*Medicines, herbs, honey, water and utility items.

Source: KIFCON, 1992d.

probably also unsustainable. Following past heavy logging, there are no significant stands of commercial species. AS also contains slightly less than 500 hectares of low-productivity plantations. Some extraction (Brachylaena) is unsustainable. However the level of regeneration is generally excellent and exploitation does not presently threaten important species.

9.4 PROPOSED FOREST MANAGEMENT STRATEGIES, COSTS AND ALTERNATIVES

KIFCON considered three main strategies for each forest. One was the *continuation* of present land uses and policies; this was expected to lead to increased forest degradation and loss, especially in KF.

The second strategy was forest *conservation*, designed to maximise sustainable output from the forest, prevent further species extinction and assist rural development around the forest. The rural development components were an important part of a comprehensive approach: they were designed to improve farm productivity and incomes, compensate forest users for the loss of forest products and reduce their need to exploit the forest. The conservation strategy also contained components for institutional and regulatory reform, tourism and visitor development, environmental education, training and plantation development.

The third strategy was *agricultural development*. In this case, existing forest was to be rapidly cleared and replaced by agriculture. This strategy shows the opportunity cost of conservation but was not developed in detail.

Kakamega Strategies

KIFCON (1992a) forecast that under existing use and management practices, Kakamega forest resources would be depleted and forest output would decline rapidly by 10 per cent per annum. The value of forest products was forecast to fall to $5.2 million by the year 2001 and to $1.8 million by 2011.

The proposed *conservation strategy* for Kakamega combined a land use plan with capital investment and annual protection costs. The land uses included:

- Protection zones: these would permit tourism, education and research but prohibit all other activities. Some areas would be rehabilitated with enrichment planting.
- Three forms of 'utilisation' zones: next to the protection zones there would be some subsistence use zones, from which forest-adjacent households would be licensed to collect traditional forest products (for example food, fuelwood and medicinal plants). Limited forest exploitation, though not mechanised extraction of timber, would be permitted in commercial use zones on the forest fringes. Also, some community use zones would be established on the degraded forest periphery for the supply of community owned woodlots and cattle grazing.
- Some plantation zones would be established on the west and south flanks of the forest.

Figure 9.5 shows the conservation plan drawn up by KIFCON. The ODA review mission proposed a modified conservation programme at an incremental cost of $3.8 million (in 1992 prices) over five years compared with present expenditures. One third of this would be for indigenous forest management (housing, plant and equipment, operating costs and so on), one quarter for project management and one quarter for assistance for rural development (including assistance for community-based forest management in the forest and crop development and stock improvement outside). Other programme components included visitor programme development, environmental education and wildlife conservation. The ODA proposed to fund 90 per cent of the programme.

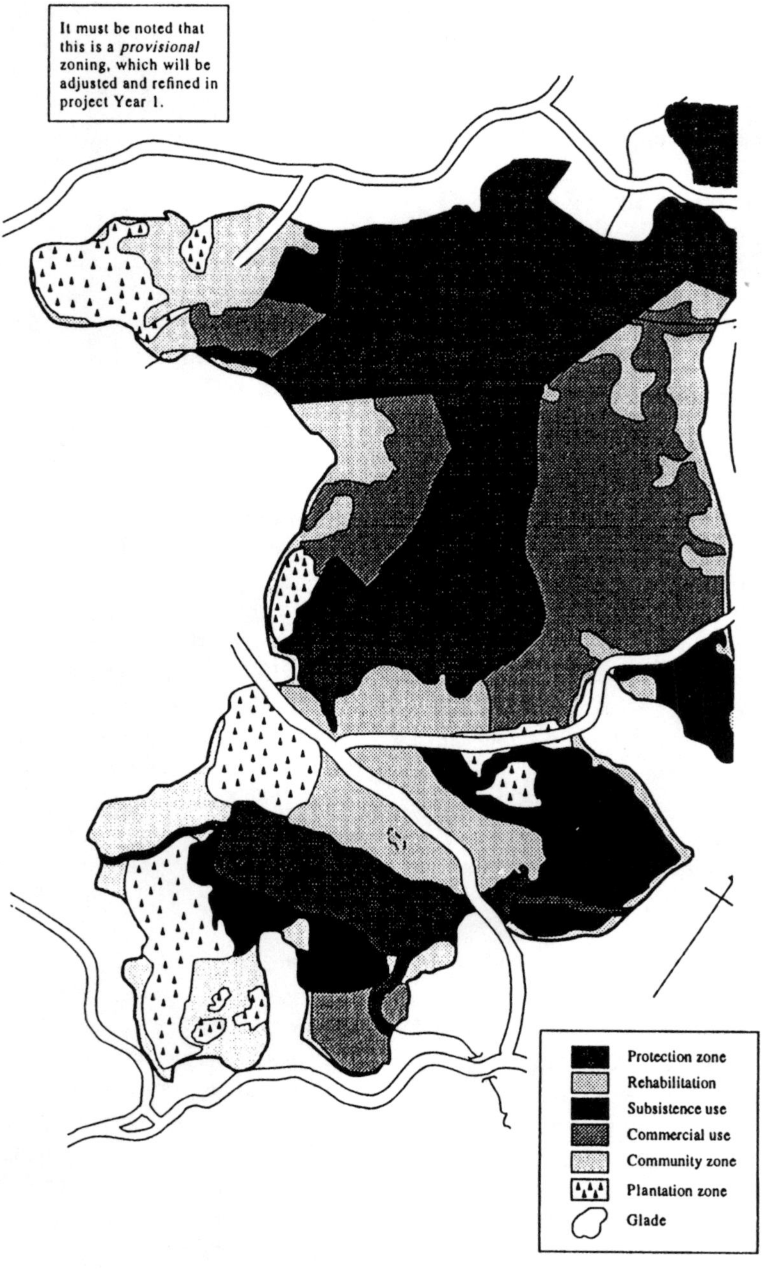

Source: KIFCON, 1992a.

Under the *development strategy*, Kakamega would be deforested in about five years and converted to agricultural use.

Arabuko-Sokoke Strategies

KIFCON (1992c) forecast that under existing use and management practices, AS forest output would decline marginally by 2 per cent per annum. The proposed *conservation plan* for AS, like that for KF, defined areas for protection, subsistence and commercial use, and plantations. A license would be required for any exploitative purposes.

The conservation plan, as developed by the ODA review mission, was costed at an incremental $1.8 million (in 1992 prices) over the first five years, compared with current expenditure. Forest and project management accounted for nearly 70 per cent of costs. The plan included expenditure on rural development (mainly outside AS), conservation education, visitor development and wildlife conservation. The rural development consisted of water development, on-farm tree planting, citrus production and wood conservation. The budget also allowed for elephant control and the development of visitor facilities.

Under the *development strategy*, AS would be deforested in about eight years and converted to agriculture.

9.5 APPROACH TO EVALUATION

General Principles

The evaluation below, based on the KIFCON studies, estimates the present value of the net benefits of each forest strategy (no policy change, conservation and development). The net benefits are the estimated direct use benefits less the capital and recurrent costs incurred. Indirect use benefits and existence values were taken into account, but not quantified. Although evaluation procedures for forests are similar to those for other assets, four special problems arise. These are the variety of forest uses, related valuation issues (which are discussed in the next sections), the allocation of overhead costs, and the choice of discount rate.

The variety of forest uses complicates the evaluation because each strategy provides multiple services. For example, significant benefits of KIFCON's conservation strategies accrued from investment in rural development adjacent to the forest, such as on-farm planting of polewood and fuelwood. Under the development strategies, forest products would be obtained before the land had been cultivated. But the timing and value of output would vary under each strategy. With regard to timing, the forecast rate of depletion of forest values under 'do-nothing' policies is often critical. Once forests are heavily degraded they may be converted to other uses. Therefore the difference between do-nothing and development strategies may be small.

There are substantial overhead costs in forest management. In Kenya, overheads include administration by the FD and KWS as well as inputs from other departments, notably the police and legal agencies. Allocating these overheads to particular forests requires information not readily available from government accounts.

Benefits from forests are generated by natural resources and financial capital as well as by labour. If resources produce consumption goods that cannot be converted readily into financial capital, the flow of goods attributable to the resource should be discounted by the social time preference rate for consumption. In this case the value of forest output should be discounted by a synthetic rate (*sr*) described in Equation 2.17.

$$sr = (w \times \text{SOC}) + (1 - w)\text{STPR} \qquad (9.1)$$

where w is the proportion of the capital employed in the project that could be employed elsewhere and $(1 - w)$ is the proportion that reflects consumption forgone, SOC is the social opportunity cost of capital and STPR is the social time preference rate. As noted in Chapter 2, the social time preference rate may be only 2–4 per cent compared with a social opportunity cost of 7–10 per cent.

In practice, few evaluations adopt a synthetic rate. Both KIFCON and the ODA appraisal missions used a 10 per cent discount rate on the ground that the return to capital invested in the forests should at least equal the returns from alternative projects. This overlooks the fact that much of the forest output is attributable to natural capital (which produces non-marketed consumption goods) rather than to financial capital.

Some Economic Parameters in the Kenyan Evaluations

The ODA review missions adopted the following economic parameters for their evaluations.

- Traded goods were valued at 1992 international prices less transport and distribution costs. Forest-edge or village prices were used to value non-traded inputs and outputs.

- To allow for trade price distortions, the prices of non-traded goods and services were discounted by 8 per cent (based on the World Bank's standard conversion factor of 0.92 for Kenya).
- A constant exchange rate was applied, that is, the rate prevailing at the start of 1992 (UK£1.0 = Ksh.51, US$1.0 = Ksh.33).
- To allow for unemployment and underemployment, a shadow wage rate factor of 0.7 was applied to unskilled labour time
- Forests were evaluated over a 25 year period, but included a residual value.

9.6 VALUING DIRECT USER BENEFITS OF FORESTS AND ADJACENT AREAS

In this and the next two sections a number of valuation topics are briefly discussed. For each topic some key valuation principles are outlined, followed by a description of the procedures adopted in the Kenyan case-studies.

Timber and Other Forest Products

Marketed forest products are usually valued at their forest edge prices. To estimate the net benefits, resource costs (including imputed opportunity costs of unpaid labour) should be deducted from gross values. Unmarketed forest products may be valued at the prices of the closest substitutes. For example, woodfuels may be valued at the price of the closest energy substitutes. However this is a maximum value and overstates the value of woodfuel if the substitute is too expensive to purchase. Again, to estimate net value, resource costs should be deducted. Alternatively the travel cost valuation method may be adopted. Amacher *et al.* (1991) used this approach to estimate what households would be willing to pay for firewood in Nepal.

The KIFCON studies valued all forest products extracted respectively by licensed users, forest-adjacent dwellers and illegal commercial users using forest-edge prices or close surrogates. Indigenous timber prices were assumed to increase by 3 per cent per annum in real terms. It was also estimated that, without a conservation programme, extraction for most products would increase by 3 per cent per annum. With extraction five times the sustainable yield in Kakamega, the forest would be depleted by year 17. In AS, where extraction had been below sustainable levels for most products, forest biomass would increase although carving wood would decline. The conservation project would reduce illegal commercial extraction in both forests, charcoal-making in KF and licensed timber extraction in AS. But most uses by forest-adjacent dwellers would be little changed. The studies allowed no resource costs for collection, thus assuming implicitly that labour opportunity costs for extracting forest products were zero.

Agricultural and Pasture Benefits

If there is a competitive market for farm land, agricultural land values of forests can be inferred from prices or rents for similarly productive and accessible land. If there is no such market, forest land values are the estimated present value of potential revenues less production costs. Likewise, if livestock graze in forests, the grazing value is the charge for an equivalent grazing area elsewhere or the increased value of the livestock less any increase in operating costs, for example for livestock supervision.

The KIFCON studies used comparable land values to estimate the agricultural value of forest land. Estimates of returns from complementary investment in rural development around the forests were more problematic. The KIFCON studies indicated a range of potentially profitable investments. The ODA review missions allowed for a high (40 per cent) rate of return for on-farm tree planting but assumed conservatively that the benefits of the rural development component of the programme (discounted at 10 per cent) would match the costs.

Settlement Benefits

Forest settlements are often valued on a replacement basis. This is the most practical valuation method and acceptable when forest settlers are willing to accept resettlement. However forest settlers are often strongly opposed to resettlement. In such cases, patience as well as generous compensation is required.

Resettlement was not an issue in the Kakamega or AS forests. However, it is critical elsewhere in Kenya, for example in the Mau forest.

Recreation Benefits

Producers of recreational services, including park management, guides and suppliers of board and lodging and transport services, may earn profits from visitors to forests. There may also be secondary benefits if tourist expenditures lead to the employment of otherwise unemployed resources. In addition visitors may obtain user surpluses. These surpluses are the amounts that visitors are willing to pay for access to forests over and above what they actually pay, and can be estimated by the travel cost method or by surveys (Dixon and Sherman, 1990).

KIFCON (1992b, 1992d) equated recreational benefits with average daily tourist expenditures inclusive of air fares in and out of Kenya. This amounted to $380 per day for foreign tourists, $15 per day for non-citizen Kenyan residents, and $8 per day for Kenyan citizens. There are two problems with this approach. Firstly, it erred in treating travel expenditures and visitor surpluses as identical. Given the large number of recreational substitutes available in Kenya, very few people would be willing to pay $380 a day to visit the Kakamega or AS forest. Secondly, it ignored producer surpluses.

The ODA review missions estimated recreational benefits as the sum of forecast gate fees and tourist benefits of $67 per day. The latter assumption was based on previous ODA estimates of the contribution of tourism to the Kenya economy. This approach also had two significant weaknessess. It presumed unrealistically that the conservation projects would cause visitors to spend extra time in Kenya rather than divert from another local experience. Secondly, it did not allow for visitor surpluses.

9.7 VALUING INDIRECT USER BENEFITS OF FORESTS AND ADJACENT AREAS

Protection of Soils

Deforestation affects soils in various ways. It may lead to soil erosion on- or off-site with consequential loss of agricultural productivity, silting up of downstream dams and reservoirs, and increased flooding. Deforestation also disturbs the nutrient cycle. The nutrient outflow reduces the productive capacity of forest land and can lead to downstream pollution of river and coastal ecosystems.

KIFCON considered that the conservation projects in Kakamega and Arabuko Sokoke would not produce significant soil productivity benefits compared with the do-nothing strategies. However KIFCON debited the development strategy in AS with the costs of containing soil erosion. It may also be noted that deforestation in another Kenyan forest (the Mau) could cause significant soil erosion.

Protection of Water Catchments

Deforestation can affect water regulation and alter water quantity and quality downstream due to increased runoff. The potential effects include changes in soil productivity and the quantity and quality of water available for irrigation, flooding, treatment costs for industrial users, and the pollution of rivers and other waterways, with associated impacts on human health and amenity and on marine and plant life. Identification of the ecological impacts is critical. If this can be done, the productivity, health and amenity impacts can be valued, as discussed in Chapter 4. Ruitenbeek (1989) estimates that loss of the Korup rainforest in the Cameroons will reduce watershed protection and cause damage of over $7.5 million annually in flooding and loss of fish production. However Aylward and Barbier (1992) note that the ecological basis for these estimates is slim.

The ODA review missions judged that, due to the size and topography of the forests, the watershed values of Kakamega and Arabuko Sokoke were slight. Again, this may not be the case in the Mau forest.

Biodiversity Use Values

Plants and animals have various uses in addition to ecotourism, including meat and skin products, genetic material that can be bred into a distant member of the same species (this process has greatly increased yields from rice, millet, corn and wheat), and other properties that can be replicated or synthesised (for example plants are a major source of pharmaceuticals).

Of course valuation of biodiversity loss requires estimates of species loss. According to island biogeography (which deals with the relationship between species and land area), the number of species within clusters of islands increases approximately as the fourth root of the area of the island (Wilson and Peters, 1988). This means that when an area loses one quarter of its land the population falls by about 7 per cent; when it loses half its land the population falls by 16 per cent; and when it loses 90 per cent of its land the population falls by nearly half.

Valuing the loss of genetic material and information is also problematic. There is no market for tropical plants and animals as genetic materials. There are no data on what drug companies would be willing to pay for plant material, nor on the consumer surplus from new plant-based drugs. Ruitenbeek (1989) has attempted to value the genetic material in the Korup Rainforest, Cameroons, using estimated values of patents ($7500 per patent based on Schankerman and Pakes, 1986) and the likely number of research discoveries in the forest. However patent values usually embody high research cost as well as plant value and the discovery rate is speculative.

The respective ODA review missions called AS 'a global biological asset' due mainly to its birdlife, and described KF as 'species rich and a productive forest ecosystem'. However the missions did not quantify biodiversity benefits other than tourist benefits, presumably because this was regarded as too difficult. Without more research on the use benefits of biodiversity (other than direct forest products and tourism), there is little choice but to treat such benefits as intangibles.

Climate: Deforestation and Global Warming

Deforestation releases carbon (and some methane) into the atmosphere when the biomass is burned or left to rot. This accumulation of CO_2 gases in the atmosphere causes global warming and results in various economic costs. In order to estimate the costs, we require estimates of the tonnes of carbon released into the atmosphere per hectare and the cost per tonne of CO_2 released.

The carbon released into the atmosphere depends on the biomass per hectare, the carbon content of the biomass and the proportion of locked-up carbon that is released. Tropical closed forests have more biomass than subtropical open forests. The burning of timber causes total release of carbon. On the other hand long-lived timber products lead to little release of carbon. Also, actively growing crops and secondary forests contribute to a decrease in atmospheric carbon. Table 9.3 shows some research findings on carbon release and sequestration. The average net carbon release due to deforestation is 90–100 tonnes per hectare.

Table 9.3 Carbon release due to deforestation (tonnes/hectre)

Biomass	150–382
Carbon content of biomass	75–191
Carbon release due to deforestation	80–120
Carbon sequestered by crops	1–5
Carbon sequestered by afforestation	6–10

Sources: Makundi, Sathaye and Cerutti, 1992; Houghton, 1990; Fearnside, 1992; Pearce, 1990; Sedjo, 1989; Myers, 1989.

The cost per tonne of CO_2 released depends on the rate of global warming and the damages. To put the matter into perspective, there are currently 700 billion tonnes of carbon in the atmosphere and a further 7.5 billion tonnes are emitted annually into the atmosphere, of which half is absorbed by the oceans. A tonne of carbon emitted anywhere on earth has the same effect as a tonne emitted anywhere else and it lasts for over 100 years. Climate models suggest that a doubling of CO_2 in the atmosphere will lead to an average increase in global surface warming of between 1.5° C and 4.50° C, which is a wide margin. The Intergovernmental Panel on Climate Change (1991) forecast that global warming will occur at a mean rate of 0.30° C per decade, equivalent to about 2.5° C in 80 years, when atmospheric carbon is expected to double.

Damages due to global warming are controversial and sensitive to discount rates. Nordhaus (1991a, 1991b) argues that falling agricultural productivity and rising sea levels will account for most of the damage and that other economic activities will be not much affected. Agriculture and forestry account for less than 3 per cent of world GDP and some plants and crops will benefit from increased photosynthesis due to the increase in CO_2. A one-twentieth decline in agriculture would cause world GDP to fall by only 0.15 per cent. Construction and transport could benefit. Nordhaus (ibid.) estimates that a doubling of atmospheric CO_2 could reduce GDP in the US by 0.26 per cent and observes that, although damages elsewhere may be higher, there is no strong presumption of substantial net economic damages. On the other hand Cline (1992) estimates that a doubling of CO_2 will cause losses of at least 1 per cent of US GDP and that the longer-term effects could be several times greater. Cline forecast major additional electricity and water supply requirements, higher mortality rates, disruption to winter leisure activities, air pollution costs, hurricane costs and increased migration. While some of these costs could doubtless occur, Nordhaus's estimates of net costs appear to this writer to be more plausible.

Table 9.4 shows the present value of damage costs per tonne of CO_2, estimated by Nordhaus (1991a). As shown, the estimated present values are highly sensitive to both the estimates of damage as a percentage of GDP and the difference between the real interest rate and the growth rate of the economy. Of course these are average costs per tonne of carbon emitted. They are not estimates of *marginal* greenhouse warming costs attributable to deforestation, given the greenhouse warming that is likely to occur in any case.

Given the great uncertainties surrounding climate forecasts and damage estimates, Hyde and Newman (1991) conclude that there are no defendable

Table 9.4 Present value of damages per tonne of CO_2[1] (1989 $ per tonne)

	Greenhouse costs: damages as per cent of World GDP		
$(r - h)^2$	2	1	0.25
0	65.9	33.0	8.2
1	14.6	7.3	1.8
4	2.4	1.2	0.3

Notes:
1. Carbon weight equivalent
2. The difference between the real interest rate on goods (r) and the growth rate (h).

Source: Nordhaus, 1991a.

benefit estimates for increased carbon storage. If a figure must be chosen, this writer inclines to the lower end of the damage scale of around $2–3 per tonne of CO_2 emitted. This would reflect greenhouse warming costs in the order of 0.5 per cent of GDP and a value for $r - h$, the difference between the real interest rates on goods and the growth rate, of about 2 per cent. A cost of $2.50 per tonne of CO_2 would imply a cost of about $250 per hectare of deforestation in Kenya.

In order to value carbon store, KIFCON (1992b, 1992d) adopted Pearce's (1990) estimates that, on average, deforestation of one hectare of tropical forest releases 100 tonnes of carbon into the atmosphere at $13 per tonne damage (that is $1300 per hectare of forest lost), with no offsets for any regrowth. On the other hand the ODA review missions considered that the areas were too small to be of any global significance as carbon sinks.

Climate: Deforestation and Rainfall

There is concern that deforestation could reduce rainfall where precipitation results from water recycling into the atmosphere through evapotranspiration. Unfortunately this is another topic about which little is known. Hamilton and King (1983) surveyed the evidence and concluded that rainfall is unlikely to reduce, except possibly after large-scale and permanent deforestation in the Amazon. The ODA review missions described the influence of the Kenyan forests on regional climate as 'probably slight' and did not quantify the impact.

9.8 OPTION AND EXISTENCE VALUES

Option Values

It was shown in Chapter 2 that households may be prepared to pay a premium (an option value) to avoid the possible loss of a valued asset for which demand is certain. However, if demand and supply are uncertain, option values may be positive or negative. Therefore, for most practical purposes, option values should be assumed to be zero. In his survey of the economics of tropical forests, Pearce (1990) does not argue for estimating option values, nor does he produce any examples where such values have been estimated.

Most likely, some households would be willing to pay a premium over expected use values to preserve access to the extraordinary biodiversity of the Kenyan forests. However there is no survey or other indication of the size of this premium, if any. Also, it is doubtful whether households would be willing to pay a premium over expected use values to retain other forest services for which substitutes are generally available. Neither KIFCON nor the ODA review missions estimated option values.

Existence Values

Various studies (for example Samples, Gowen and Dixon, 1986) have used contingent valuation surveys to estimate existence values for selected animal species and natural amenities. These studies indicate that American households are prepared to pay \$6–8 a year to preserve well-known and valued endangered local species such as the blue whale and the Northern elephant seal, with preservation values ranging from \$1 a year for the whooping crane to \$15 a year for the grizzly bear.

Kakamega forest contains several endangered or rare animal species and an unusual mixture of lowland and highland plant species. The forest contains 12 rare butterflies, including two that exist only in KF. It also contains an endemic snake and an endemic bird, as well as seven snake species, three amphibians and 48 bird species that occur in no other Kenyan forests. The forest primates include the nocturnal potto and the rare de Brazza monkey. Several of these endemic fauna are likely to disappear from Kenya unless a conservation strategy is adopted in KF. Also, if the forest were to disappear, significant cultural and heritage values could be lost.

The AS forest contains 15 rare or endemic bird species (including the Sokoke Scops Owl and Clarks's Weaver, found only in AS), six species of butterfly endemic to the forest or coastal area, and three endemic but endangered mammals (the Golden Rump Elephant Shrew, Aders Duiker and the Bushy Tailed Mongoose). However, given the mild threat from existing land use practices in AS, these would be threatened only in the unlikely event of widespread deforestation (the 'development' option).

No valuation studies have been done for endangered species in the Kakamega or AS forest. American values for local US species cannot be readily transplanted to quite different endangered species in the Kenyan forests, most of which are known to only a few people outside Kenya.

The KIFCON studies did not attempt to estimate existence values. Instead they considered whether possible existence values would justify the proposed conservation projects, which were not justified by the quantified cost–benefit estimates (see below).

9.9 SUMMARY OF RESULTS FOR KENYAN FORESTS

Cost–Benefit Results and Unquantified Factors

Table 9.5 shows the estimated net present values (NPVs) of the two forests under the no-change, conservation and development strategies. The NPVs in the no-change cases are estimated by the author, drawing on KIFCON work. The NPVs of conservation and development are based on the net benefits of these strategies compared with the no-change cases estimated by the ODA review missions.

Under a no-policy change strategy, Kakamega has an estimated NPV of $40 million and AS a NPV of $3 million. The proposed conservation plans would have resulted in a small fall in these estimated NPVs. On the other hand the development options would have provided significant net benefits.

However these quantified figures are based only on estimated direct user benefits. The ODA review missions argued that when unquantified indirect benefits, especially existence values, were taken into account, the proposed conservation programmes for both forests would be justified. To understand these results and conclusions, we consider how the ODA review missions estimated the net benefits of the conservation programmes compared with the no-change strategies, and how they justified the conservation programmes.

The estimated incremental effects of the conservation programmes compared with the no-change cases are summarised in Table 9.6. The following main observations can be made.

- KIFCON planned that local households would continue to benefit (legally) from forest products and from investment in on-farm tree-

Table 9.5 Estimated forest values (NPVs in $ million 10 per cent discount rates)

Strategy	*Kakamega*	*Arabuko-Sokoke*
Total forest values		
No policy change	40.0	3.0
Conservation programme	38.8	0.8
Agricultural development	56.1	18.7
Net benefits		
Conservation programme	–1.2	–2.2
Agricultural development	16.1	15.7

Sources: Author's estimates and ODA review missions.

planting and rural development under the conservation programmes. Nevertheless these programmes would have disadvantaged many local households.

- The conservation programme would also have required substantial changes in forest management practices and social organisation.
- Estimated visitor benefits are relatively unimportant because of the small number of visitors.
- The sensitivity of the results to the discount rate was not reported. Most likely, the results would have been only slightly sensitive to a different discount rate as many costs, as well as benefits, occur over a long period.

To justify conservation rather than development, the unquantified benefits of conservation should be worth at least $17.3 million in Kakamega and $17.9 million in AS. The main unquantified factors in both forests are carbon store benefits, biodiversity, existence values, and conceivably some option values. Apparently no significant soil or water catchment benefits or local climatic benefits are associated with the two forests.

This writer, like the ODA review missions, is cautious about ascribing carbon store values to small forests as the marginal impact of deforestation on global warming would be negligible. However assuming that, under development strategies, three quarters of the total areas of Kakamega and AS would lose forest cover and that the cost of carbon loss is $250 per hectare (see Section 9.7), the greenhouse warming costs of deforestation would be $4.5 million for Kakamega and $7.85 million for Arabuko Sokoke.

Table 9.6 Impacts of conservation programmes compared with no-change strategies (NPVs in $ million 10 per cent discount rates)

	Kakamega	*Arabuko-Sokoke*
Benefits		
Licensed users	7.2	0.0
Visitor value	1.2	0.9
On-farm tree planting	2.7	0.8
Rural development	0.9	0.0
Forest residual value	1.9	0.2
Total	13.9	1.9
Costs		
Direct project costs*	–3.9	–2.4
Adjacent dwellers	–1.8	0.0
Licensed users	0.0	–0.3
Illegal commercial users	–9.4	–1.3
Total	–15.1	–4.1
Net benefits	–1.2	–2.2

*NPV of incremental capital and recurrent costs over 25 years.

Source: ODA review missions.

Given that the estimated agricultural development values of the forests are significantly higher than these carbon credits, conservation must also be justified by biodiversity and existence values. The ODA review missions did not distinguish clearly between the use and non-use (existence) values of biodiversity. However the Kakamega mission supported the conservation programme in Kakamega because the forest has biodiversity of 'national, if not international significance' and has 'local, national and international existence value', and because without the conservation programme the forest would be lost as a result of natural economic processes. The AS mission supported the conservation programme in AS because, although the forest is not under present threat, the biodiversity value is 'much higher than that of Kakamega'.

Policy and Management

Proposed conservation programmes were based on complex zoning and policing arrangements, multiple investments in and around the forests, and major changes in the established practices of local households. Before these changes were effected, three issues would have to be resolved.

Firstly, although the Kenyan Forestry Department has attempted to protect local forests by supplying additional control resources, including extra forest guards, the forest guards are usually too poorly resourced to protect the forests. In any case it is doubtful whether the existing regulatory framework can successfully protect forests. In order to achieve conservation, local communities must have some incentive to safeguard local resources. It is doubtful whether the Kenyan programmes provide for sufficient local incentives for effective forest protection, especially for Kakamega, where significant sections of the community would lose income as a result of conservation.

Secondly, as Flint (1992) observes in a survey of ODA forest schemes, 'the most obvious shortcoming (of four ODA forest appraisals) was the absence of a detailed appraisal of the effect of the project on government recurrent expenditure. This had major implications for sustainability'. The projected recurrent costs of the conservation programmes for Kakamega and AS exceeded projected revenues by 15 per cent and 50 per cent respectively. Additional capital expenditures would also have been required periodically.

Thirdly, many benefits of Kenyan forests are valued principally by households outside Kenya. To preserve these benefits, non-Kenyans will have to contribute significantly to the conservation programmes on a continuing basis.

9.10 CONCLUSIONS

Forest management problems are most acute when the benefits of both exploitation and conservation are high. Kakamega forest is under acute threat because of the high local population densities and the value of forest products to the local population. The Arabuko Sokoke forest is not under immediate threat. Both forests are rich biodiversity resources.

Management problems are possibly even more acute in the Mau forest in Kenya, which was also studied by KIKCON. Many households live permanently in the Mau forest and would probably have to be resettled under an effective conservation plan, Also, there are significant ecological issues related to soil conservation and water catchment that do not arise in the Kakamega or AS forests.

A conservation (sustainable use) forest programme differs in several ways from a conventional development project. Firstly, a large part of the costs of conservation are borne by local households who are denied customary access to the forest resource. Taxpayers' contribution to conservation may be relatively small. As the KIFCON studies showed, valuation of these household costs is both possible and a prerequisite for development of a realistic conservation policy. Secondly, if a conservation programme is to succeed it must be an ongoing and cooperative project. Policing forests can temporarily prevent excessive local exploitation. In the long run forests can be conserved only if there are sufficient local incentives to encourage conservation. Forest management depends crucially on resolution of social conflicts.

Much has been written about valuation of the indirect benefits of forests, such as soil retention, water catchment protection, carbon store values, climate (rainfall) stability, and biodiversity use and existence values. Few studies have succeeded in measuring these benefits, and the KIFCON studies of Kakamega and AS were no exception. This was not due to lack of effort as KIFCON devoted considerable resources to examining these issues. In the Kakamega and AS forests it turned out that there were no significant soil or water catchment benefits, deforestation would have a minor impact on global warming and probably none on rainfall, and there were few visitors and low tourism values.

Nevertheless, by valuing forest outputs where possible, the KIFCON studies usefully clarified the trade-offs involved in conservation of the Kakamega and Arabuko Sokoke forests. In essence, it was proposed that the forests should be conserved mainly for their biodiversity use and existence values. Because these values are especially precious to non-Kenyans, a substantial part of the resources required to make conservation possible would have to come from the international community. But international resources alone cannot ensure conservation if the local will to conserve is lacking.

10 Valuing Soils in the Tropical Lowlands of Eastern Bolivia

with Penny Davies

10.1 INTRODUCTION

There has long been concern that farmers use soil resources extractively without regard for their long-run value. Over 30 years ago FAO staff warned that 'Shifting cultivation in the humid tropical countries is the greatest obstacle not only to the immediate increase of agricultural production, but also to the conservation of production potential of the future, in the form of soils and forests' (FAO, 1957).

This chapter examines the sustainability of land productivity and farm incomes, along with deforestation and off-site impacts, in the Santa Cruz region in the tropical lowlands of eastern Bolivia. This is a generally fertile area of 37 million hectares, similar in size to Spain. But it is sparsely populated with only 1.4 million people, half of whom live in the city of Santa Cruz. About 500 000 hectares are under cultivation and produce one third of Bolivia's agricultural output. The region also contains over a million cattle on five million hectares, including one million degraded hectares that were formerly under cultivation. Seventy per cent of the region is mainly under primary forest, most of which lies within Amazonia.

Pressure to develop uncleared land in the Santa Cruz region is considerable. Bolivia is one of the poorest countries in Latin America, with an official annual income of US$630 per capita (Instituto Nacional de Estadisticas, 1992). Nearly 70 per cent of Bolivians live on or around the Altiplano and Andean valleys at altitudes of 2000–4000 metres above sea level. Since the 1950s land scarcity, drought and mine closures have driven highlanders to migrate towards the agricultural frontier in the lowlands, encouraged by the government's transmigration programme of colonisation. Also, from the east, Brazilians have crossed the border and occupied land. Traditionally, high transport costs have limited access to domestic and export markets. As these costs have fallen, the incentive to develop land in

Santa Crùz has risen. This process has been accelerated by the availability of cocaine capital. Currently 40 000 hectares are being cleared annually, about half the deforestation rate in the Brazilian Amazon (CUMAT, 1992).

Specifically, this study examines farming systems in two agroecological areas around Santa Cruz (see Figure 10.1). These are:

- Peasant colonist, slash and burn farming on relatively infertile and acid soils in the Yapacani area, about 150 kilometres north-west of Santa Cruz city.
- Large-scale, commercial, fully-mechanised annual cropping in the new 'expansion zone' to the east of the River Grande on fertile soils, about 100 kilometres from Santa Cruz.

In each case the study estimates the economic rate of return of the adopted farming system, assesses its sustainability and considers whether, taking all factors into account, the farming system is justified.

The study draws heavily on the valuable work on soil productivity and farming systems by the British Tropical Agricultural Mission (BTAM), a team providing technical assistance over many years to the Centro de Investigacion Agricola Tropical (the local agricultural research institute in Santa Cruz). However data on deforestation and off-site impacts in Bolivia, such as river sedimentation downstream, are scarce. Conclusions on the merit of converting forests into farming land are therefore heavily qualified.

The chapter starts with a brief general discussion of tropical land development, focusing on soil productivity. Section 10.3 describes the development of land in the Bolivian lowlands and the main environmental issues. Section 10.4 outlines the two case-studies. The next three sections describe the evaluation method and estimated farming returns for each case-study. Sections 10.8 and 10.9 describe deforestation and off-site costs respectively. Section 10.10 briefly discusses policy issues for land use. Finally, the main conclusions are summarised.

10.2 TROPICAL AGRICULTURE: GENERAL ISSUES

Problems

ICRAF *et al.* (1992) estimate that shifting, slash and burn cultivation is responsible for 70 per cent of the deforestation in Africa, 50 per cent in Asia and 30 per cent in Latin America. Moreover they argue that deforestation is a major contributor to global warming, loss of plant and animal diversity,

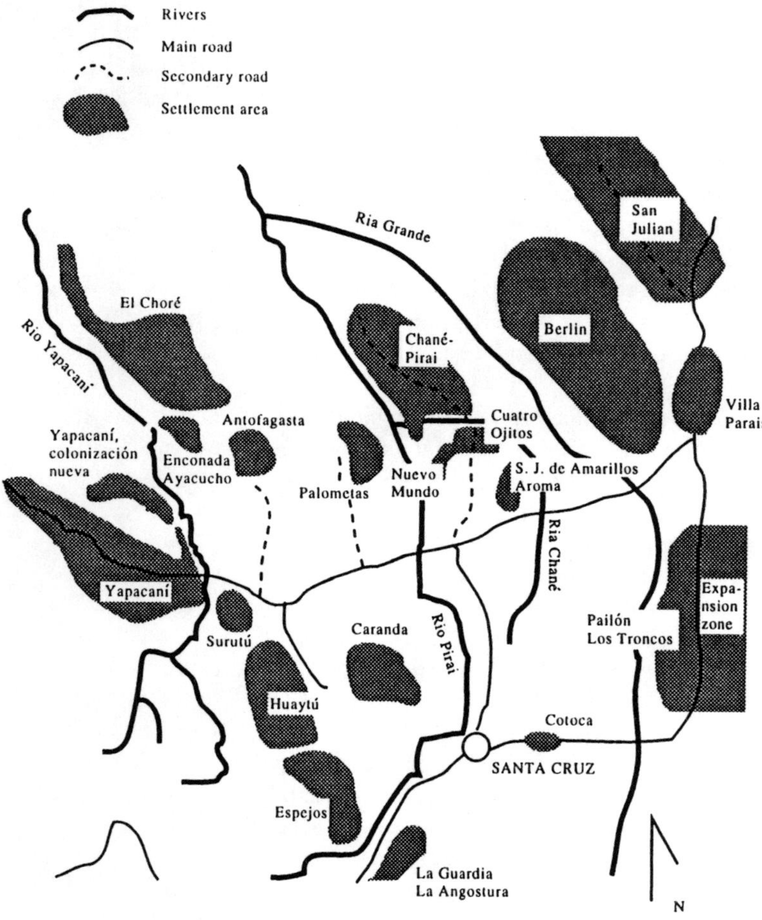

Source: Thiele, 1990.

Figure 10.1 Location of national colonisation areas in Santa Cruz

and instability of watersheds; that slash and burn farming is frequently unsustainable; and that voiding the land of soil cover can lead to major erosion and siltation of rivers.

Traditional slash and burn food-crop systems in the tropics depend largely on the nutrient values and restorative properties of woody species. Initially, a farmer clears a small area of forest and burns the biomass to release nutrients for agriculture. He sows mainly annual crops and some perennials. After a year or two, crop yields decline due to depletion of soil fertility, increased weed infestation and in some cases soil erosion and increased incidence of pests and disease. Typically the peasant farmer then leaves the plot to return to secondary forest fallow. This regenerates soil productivity as the natural soil reconstructs and weeds are suppressed. Meanwhile the farmer slashes and burns a new plot. Where land is abundant and reasonably fertile, slash and burn systems with adequate fallow periods result in stable low-productivity production systems. As the World Bank (Africa Region, 1991) notes: 'Shifting cultivation and pastoralism are the appropriate responses to abundant land (and) limited capital'.

However population growth and the demand for higher living standards have destabilised traditional systems. When land is in short supply, traditional shifting cultivation practices can cause soil degradation and lead to a decline in agricultural output. The same World Bank report estimates that up to 80 per cent of Sub-Saharan Africa's pasture and range areas show signs of degradation. Timber harvesting, fuelwood gathering and deforestation are increasing. When fallow periods shorten or a dense bush cover is not established, nutrients do not build up sufficiently and weeds carry over into the next cultivation cycle. Soil erosion exacerbates land degradation, especially on land with inadequate vegetative cover in rainy or windy seasons. Finally, the degraded land is often abandoned to poor quality scrubby grasslands (Uhl *et al.*, 1991).

High input commercial agriculture can also severely degrade land. Mechanised felling and windrowing, followed by the burning of deforested land, can damage a fragile soil structure. The uprooting of large trees causes a loss of soil organic matter. Use of heavy tractors and disc ploughs for land preparation on wet ground may compact soils, compound drainage problems, and restrict root access to soil humidity. Agricultural ecosystems, especially those based on only a few plant species, tend to be less stable than forests. Such ecosystems are less efficient at performing protective functions such as soil conservation, nutrient recycling and population regulation. They also depend on continued human intervention with chemical inputs, mechanisation and irrigation.

In the Amazon, settlers frequently exploit timber as the first step in a process of land clearance, agriculture and the establishment of pasture. Critics view this as a process whereby each land use system is replaced by another of fewer species and lower productivity. In some cases the trend may be effectively irreversible as the technology to rehabilitate the land to a more productive system either is not accessible to farmers or is too costly. The situation is aggravated by indiscriminate use of fire.

Although it is generally acknowledged that most agricultural systems cause some land degradation, views differ widely on the severity of the problem and the long-term sustainability of Amazonian soils for cultivation. Some commentators (for example Young and Wright, 1980) conclude that continuous soil degradation is virtually unavoidable under agriculture in the tropics. In their view, in the long run food crop production will require the use of inputs at an uneconomic level.

Other experts believe that agricultural productivity can be maintained, or even increased, despite soil degradation (for example ICRAF *et al.*, 1992). In fact crop yields per unit of land have remained steady, or risen, in many countries, though total yield has not always kept pace with population growth. However views differ on the means. One school of thought (for example Hecht, 1982) emphasises adaptation of traditional indigenous technologies. These include minimising disturbance to topsoil, agroforestry, multiple cropping and the use of legumes and other nitrogen fixers. Others argue for highly domesticated agroecosystems that depend on external inputs under which, it is claimed, both soil and off-site impacts can be controlled. The mechanised farming in our second Santa Cruz case-study, which is supported by the World Bank, is an example.

Policies

As a general principle, intensity of land use should match the quality of soil resources. Thus fertile robust soils may be used for intensive horticulture. Slightly less fertile soils may be suitable for annual cropping systems. Ecosystems that have a protective as well as a productive function, such as some livestock or treecrop systems, may be suited for more fragile soils. Sometimes preservation of forest or wilderness management would be more appropriate. On hilly slopes susceptible to erosion, systems that include tree crops or forests are likely to be appropriate.

However optimal land use also depends on other physical factors such as watersheds, social factors such as traditional land settlement, and access to markets. Land close to cities or well served by transport should be developed more intensively. On the other hand, land use and prices should reflect the full opportunity costs of the land and off-site costs. Raw land prices should encourage farmers to intensify production rather than clear new land. Moreover optimal land use is dynamic and changes as soil quality and technology change.

Farm management critically affects long-run output. Tropical soils may require chemical soil amendments as well as biological and organic nutrient sources. Keeping the soil surface covered at all times is essential to sustainability in the tropics, (ICRAF *et al.*, 1992). Practices that protect agroecosystems include:

- Zero or minimum tillage to prevent disturbance of the topsoil.
- Agroforestry and silvipastoral systems, such as alley farming and multi-storey tree gardens, that fix atmospheric nitrogen, recycle nutrients through leaf drop and encourage root turnover of soil.
- Multiple and sequential cropping that maximises soil cover, minimises erosion and water run-off, and controls pests and weeds.
- The use of legumes and other nitrogen-fixers, such as lichens and algae.

Farmers adopt such practices only when they make commercial sense. For example alley cropping sacrifices 20 per cent of annual crop planting area and reduces understorey access to light. Also, some winter crops are not viable because of a lack of markets. More profitable alternatives may encourage farmers to exploit their land more intensively in the short run and to move on to the agricultural frontier, leaving behind degraded, low-quality land use systems.

Concluding Points

Land use plans are required to protect the environment (ICRAF *et al.*, 1992). They should be based on land capability assessments and should identify areas to be protected, farmed, reserved for logging, multiple uses and so forth. If logging in intact tropical forests is permitted, it should be regulated and properly priced.

However a prescriptive, top-down approach to agricultural development may not work. It is more likely to be successful in homogeneous, high-potential regions such as South Asia than in areas of high variability, as found in Bolivia. In such cases, land use options and local needs must be assessed carefully. Despite widespread concern about soil degradation in Bolivia, there has been little work on the costs and benefits of maintaining soil quality, or on acceptable rates of soil loss or quality decline.

Finally, the government must have the capacity to implement its land use policies. Regulations are rarely sufficient. Local community participation is essential. Most importantly, land and usufruct rights, as well as prices and fiscal policies, need to provide farmers with appropriate incentives to manage their land sustainably.

10.3 AGRICULTURAL DEVELOPMENT IN THE SANTA CRUZ REGION

General Agricultural Development

Extensive development has traditionally accounted for most of the increase in agricultural output in Bolivia. In the 1950s and 1960s, 80 per cent of the increase in agricultural output was due to land settlement, mainly in the lowlands (Nelson, 1973). In the 1980s total farm land in Bolivia increased by 1.6 per cent per annum while the value of agricultural output rose by only 1.4 per cent per annum.

In the Santa Cruz region, agricultural development started close to the city of Santa Cruz, where soils were fertile and the market assured. Development moved outwards as soil productivity fell. Various groups were involved in the process. Logging companies usually opened up the forested areas with roads. Individual colonists or organised community groups, such as the Menonites, Japanese and Crucenos, followed. In the 1950s and 1960s governments encouraged small farmers to migrate from the highlands by giving them plots ranging from 10–50 hectares. Since then migration has been spontaneous, encouraged by improved roads between La Paz and Santa Cruz. Also, concessionary credit for large farmers encouraged farming around Santa Cruz. In the 1980s the main commercial crops were soya beans, rice, maize, wheat and sugar cane.

In the traditional sector, settlers typically cut down two hectares of forest per year and cultivate rice for one or two years, along with some maize, cassava or bananas. The degraded land is then often turned over to pasture. Sometimes bushy weed growth takes over and secondary forest grows up. Farmers then leave land idle to regrowth for four to eight years and exploit other primary forest. When no more primary forest land is available locally, they go through the cycle again, cropping in cleared secondary forest. But low fertility and weed growth produce lower crop yields than before. The decline in yields is known as the 'barbecho' crisis. In the worst cases the land is abandoned. Ways out of the crisis include better soil management, which lengthens the cropping period, improved pasture control, agroforestry practices, mechanisation of rice cropping or establishment of other annual crops. These often require substantial capital investment, which the high value cash crop coca leaf can sometimes provide. Despite the loss of fertility, unlike in Brazil most peasant settlement has persisted, although the present population has changed (Thiele, 1992).

Farm sizes and technologies in the higher input, more commercial sector vary greatly. Menonite farms are usually between 50 hectares and 100 hectares, are developed by a mixture of slash and burn and mechanised processes, and have mixed crop and livestock outputs. Some other farms are over 1000 hectares and use highly mechanised, mono or duo crop systems. In the 1970s cotton was sown intensively around Santa Cruz. But despite heavy use of agro-chemicals – running to eight to ten sprays a year – yields fell and extensive degraded lands were turned over to pasture. Some people fear that the current soya bean boom will suffer a similar fate.

Summary of Current Issues

Expansion of the agricultural frontier in the eastern lowlands has long been used to relieve acute poverty in Bolivia. However this strategy has several costs:

- *Deforestation.* Although the rate of deforestation is low compared with some tropical countries and little is known about local damages, the potential costs of deforestation are considerable. Short-term forest concessions have encouraged rapid exploitation. The government exercises little control over deforestation.
- *Land degradation.* Hecht (1992) estimates that over two million hectares in the Santa Cruz region are degraded pasture, secondary growth or abandoned land. This is several times the amount of cultivated land. The main problems are poor soil structure, soil compaction and wind erosion, rather than unfavourable chemical qualities. Average regional yields have been maintained only by clearing and exploiting new land. This can not be sustained indefinitely.
- *Poor land management.* Farming land is often poorly managed because of lack of technical know-how and the availability of new land. The latter has made conservation unnecessary. Land titling is chaotic. Public land is often allocated administratively, not sold. Moreover the cost of reversing mistaken management is high. It is generally more profitable to clear primary forest than to rehabilitate degraded land.
- *Off-site impacts.* Little is known about these impacts. However deforestation combined with poor farming practices has probably contributed to flooding and silting downstream.

10.4 INTRODUCTION TO THE TWO CASE STUDIES

Peasant Slash and Burn Farming in Yapacani South

Yapacani South is a hilly area with an altitude of 300–350 metres. Vegetation is mostly semi-deciduous, subtropical and tropical rain forest, which includes some mahogany-rich areas. Soils are acid and infertile, with a low content of potassium and sodium. Cochrane (1973), an acknowledged authority on land uses, recommends only tree crops or pasture in this area and only in well-drained soils. Barber (1987) argues that slash and burn rice (the most common crop) causes unacceptable erosion on hills with more than a 15 per cent slope.

Over the last 30–40 years Yapacani South has been colonised through migration. Farm systems range from slash and burn agriculture on the forest frontier to mechanised annual cropping systems and extensive cattle ranches on grassland. However, small 20 hectare family farms are the most common form of landholding.

This study models two typical peasant management systems for a 20 hectare farm. One is the traditional cut and burn peasant colonist who clears different plots and moves around his 20 hectares and does not diversify into cattle or coca. Such a farm typically enters the 'barbecho' crisis in about 18–20 years, depending upon the rate at which the farmer clears his primary and secondary forest.

Alternatively, the farmer diversifies into mixed crop and cattle production from the beginning in an attempt to escape from the expected 'barbecho' crisis. This turns out to be a more-or-less sustainable, low productivity system. However the farm may be over-grazed and encounter a low-productivity pasture crisis.

Commercial Farming in the Expansion Zones

The 'expansion zone' covers over one million hectares of mainly flat land to the east of the Rio Grande. The vegetation is deciduous forest. Most soils are highly fertile and are composed of recent alluvial deposits from the Rio Grande, 18–24 cm deep with high phosphorous, nitrogen and basic cation contents. Some soils are entisols (clay that dries into loose powder) where nitrogen and sulphur could be limiting factors in the future. Much of the area is susceptible to soil compaction, crusting and wind erosion. The area is also subject to flooding. In 1991–2 one quarter of the sown area was lost as a result of flooding, aggravated by poor internal drainage and intensive mechanical cultivation.

Cochrane (1973) considers that the area is suitable for short-cycle annual crops (such as cotton, soya and sunflower) and improved pastures for fattening or dairy. He also notes that annual cropping would be constrained by dry periods and that poorly drained and compacted soils should be avoided. Barber (1992) estimates that, with appropriate management techniques, continuous cultivation of the better soils will be possible for at least 60 years with only minimal inputs, for example some nitrogen fertiliser for maize.

About 200 000 hectares have been developed mainly as large-scale, commercial, fully mechanised farms with twice-yearly crops. Summer crops are soya or maize; winter crops are soya or wheat. In the late 1980s the World Bank authorised a $64 million loan for the Eastern Bolivia Lowlands project in this area. The main aim was to increase soya production based on assistance for roads, extension, research and credit. However most landowners had access to private capital and little official credit has been taken up. The evaluation below is based on a 2000 hectare farm principally producing soya, but with some seasonal maize and wheat rotations.

10.5 APPROACH TO THE EVALUATION

General Approach

The farm models for Yapacani and the expansion zone draw on data collected by BTAM in the late 1980s and early 1990s. Special attention is paid to the impact of soil quality changes on farm productivity. The models show estimated real net income, including subsistence farm output, obtained over 25 years from the farms. The basic features of the models are outlined here. More details are given in the next section and in Appendix Tables 10.A1 and 10.A2.

Land uses and yields. Detailed assumptions are made about the rate at which primary forest is cleared, the amount of land under various crops and livestock, fallow periods and other land uses (land under secondary forest and uncultivatable land). Also, estimates are made of crop and livestock yields over time.

Capital expenditure and work. The models include estimates of the initial price of land, public capital expenditure (for example on roads and bridges), private capital expenditure (for example on farm equipment and livestock) and on-farm capital work provided by family and non-family labour (including land clearing and crop establishment).

Operating expenditures. The models contain detailed estimates of operating inputs for crops and livestock. Crop inputs include family and non-family time spent sowing, weeding, spraying and harvesting crops, and amounts of agrochemical inputs. Livestock inputs include guarding and milking time, pasture maintenance and feed and veterinary costs.

Farm income includes estimated revenue from crops and livestock, the imputed value of non-market family consumption from these items, estimated net income from coca and off-farm income.

Outputs. The two main outputs are estimates of farm net cash flow and net surplus. The latter is a measure of land value. It excludes land price but includes public expenditure and the imputed value of non-market consumption and family labour costs.

General Economic Parameters

The following general economic parameters are adopted:

- All costs and revenues are valued in 1992 prices.
- Farm commodities are valued at farm-gate prices.
- Net revenues are discounted using real discount rates of 10 per cent and 5 per cent per annum.
- Relative prices of all traded and non-traded goods are assumed to remain constant.
- Non-family labour is costed at \$3.50 per day. The estimated opportunity cost of family labour is also \$3.50 per day for crop work and \$2.00 per day for livestock work.

10.6 CASE-STUDY: PEASANT FARMING IN YAPACANI SOUTH

Main Assumptions about Inputs and Yields

We describe below the diversified small-farm model. This consists of rice produced under the slash and burn system and includes cattle, which provide significant market and non-market income. The undiversified farm model is similar except that all cattle are excluded. Of course even 'undiversified' farms may have one or two cows. However this element of consumption and the associated labour cost are assumed to be negligible in the undiversified case.

Land uses. Cleared primary forest land is used to produce rice and maize for two years before being turned over to secondary forest or sown pasture.

Some secondary forest is also cleared and used for crops for one year. The model assumes that in year 25 the farm will have a maximum of five hectares of sown pasture and five hectares of natural pasture, along with two hectares on recently cleared secondary forest with less than five years fallow.

Inputs. Only simple farm plant and equipment is used. Four fifths of labour days for crops and all labour days for livestock are provided by the farm family, leaving only a small hired labour requirement. The farm uses small amounts of herbicide and insecticide and no fertiliser.

Yields. Rice yields fall from three tonnes per hectare in the first year of cleared primary forest land to two tonnes per hectare in the second year, down to 1.3 tonnes per hectare on cleared secondary forest land with six or more years fallow, and to 0.9 tonnes per hectare on similar land with under six years fallow. The yield from maize, which is intercropped every five metres with rice, averages 0.4 tonnes per hectare. The milk yield is 820 litres per cow per annum on fair pasture and in year 17 drops to 420 litres per cow per annum on poor pasture. The calving interval is also affected by poor quality grazing and increases slightly. Cattle are sold at a live weight of 300 kilos per head, of which 50 per cent can be consumed as meat.

Land price. For estimating cash flows to the farm family, a land price of \$50 per hectare (or \$1000 per farm) is assumed.

Income sources. The farm derives cash income mainly from rice and cattle, plus a little from wood products. The family may also derive significant income from coca leaf sales and off-farm work. The results are shown with and without coca income, but do not include off-farm income. Farm families also obtain subsistence income from maize and various livestock (sheep, pigs and hens) as well as from rice and cattle.

Peasant Farm Results

The estimated farm returns for five five-year periods and in total are summarised in Table 10.1. More detailed results are given in the Appendix.

Without diversification into livestock, farm net cash flows decline substantially over the 25-year period. Indeed by the fourth five-year period, farm income is insufficient to offset even the modest opportunity cost of farm labour and the farm is not viable (net farm surplus is substantially negative) unless there is a large coca income. This result is consistent with the common observation that many traditional farms fall into the 'barbecho' crisis in about 20 years.

Nevertheless the undiversified farm is profitable overall. The farm generates a net cash flow with a present value of between \$5000 and \$8000, depending on the discount rate, after allowing for a land price of \$1000.

Table 10.1 Summary for slash and burn farm in Yapacani (average annual results, 1992 dollars)

	Years				
	1–5	*6–10*	*11–15*	*16–20*	*21–25*
Income					
Annual crops	855	753	831	372	207
All livestock	121	233	417	520	679
Trees/tree crops	40	40	40	40	40
Coca[1]	210	300	300	300	300
Total	1226	1326	1588	1234	1226
Costs[2]					
Capital[3]	87	60	360	60	60
Annual crops	88	81	87	77	47
All livestock	9	43	114	113	178
Total	184	184	561	250	285
Farm net cash flow[4]					
With cattle	832	842	727	682	641
Without cattle	720	652	424	275	140
Farm consumption	262	284	351	321	343
Family labour[5]	610	854	714	661	754
Farm Surplus[6]					
With cattle	484	272	364	342	230
Without cattle[7]	352	244	–152	–296	–548

Estimated net present values:	*At 5 per cent*	*At 10 per cent*
Diversified farm with cattle		
Farm net cash flow (exc. coca)[8]	9 770	6135
Farm net cash flow (with coca)[8]	13 576	8461
Farm surplus (exc. coca)	4 971	3365
Farm surplus (with coca)	8 778	5691
Traditional farm without cattle		
Farm net cash flow (exc. coca)[8]	8 091	5377
Farm net cash flow (with coca)[8]	11 897	7703
Farm surplus (exc. coca)	441	1088
Farm surplus (with coca)	3 414	4248

Notes:
1. Net coca income after costs.
2. Excluding family labour inputs.
3. Excluding land purchase price and public expenditure. Includes fencing in years 11–15.
4. Excluding coca income.
5. Based on \$3.50/day for crops and \$2.0/day for livestock.
6. Includes imputed values for family consumption and labour and excludes coca income and land price.
7. Excludes commercial and subsistence cattle (see text).
8. Assumes land price of \$50/ha, equal to \$1000 for 20 ha farm.

Also, the farm generates a net present surplus of between $400 and $1100 after allowing for imputed family labour costs but excluding the land price. Because farm returns in later years are negative, the surplus is higher with a 10 per cent discount rate than with a five per cent discount rate.

Farm cash flows also decline in the livestock diversification model. However cash flows are sufficient in this case to continue to pay for imputed family labour costs. The net farm surplus remains positive, and is likely to continue to be positive after year 25. Although agricultural practices reduce land productivity, diversified farming is economically sustainable even without coca and off-farm income over the 25 year period.

The diversified farm generates a net cash flow with a present value of between $6000 and $10 000, depending on the discount rate, after allowing for a land price of $1000. The incremental value compared with the undiversified farm is low because the main benefits are obtained after year 15. Excluding the land price, the diversified farm generates a net present surplus (after allowing for family labour) of between $3000 and $5000, without including coca or off-farm income.

10.7 CASE-STUDY: COMMERCIAL FARMING EAST OF RIO GRANDE

Inputs and Yields of Commercial Farms

Farm system. The model of a 2000 hectare commercial farm in the expansion zone is based on farms starting in the mid-1980s.

Land uses. Primary forest is cleared in one major operation over a few months. In summer the farms grow soya, except in the first three years when maize is grown. In winter farms rotate between soya, maize and wheat.

Inputs. Heavy imported equipment is used for land clearing, preparation and harvesting, and for aerial spraying. All agrochemicals are imported and use is high. Summer soya requires 60 kilos per hectare of seed, three litres per hectare of herbicide, one litre per hectare of insecticide and one kilo per hectare of innoculant, but no fertiliser. Winter soya requires more seed and innoculant and less herbicide. All labour is hired.

Yields. Summer soya yields are expected to fall from 3.5 tonnes per hectare in the early years down to 2.5 tonnes per hectare in years 18–25. Winter soya yields fall from 2.0 tonnes per hectare to 1.5 tonnes per hectare over the 25 years. The maize yield falls from 4.6 tonnes per hectare to 2.0 tonnes per hectare. The winter wheat yield is constant at 1.5 tonnes per hectare.

The combined effects of wind erosion and soil compaction could increase the forecast rate of yield decline. However some farmers are adopting windbreaks and vertical tillage, which will hold back the decline in yields.

As the area is located in an ecological transition between the Amazon (humid) and Chaco (dry), the farms are threatened periodically with severe drought. To allow for this, farm output is reduced in the model by 70 per cent each fifth year. This factor could improve if farmers were to adopt better soil cover and machinery that does not compact the soil.

Prices. Soya prices are volatile. The results reported below are based on conservative farm-gate prices of $140 per tonne for soya, $50 per tonne for maize and $165 per tonne for wheat. The wheat price represents the protected Bolivian price rather than the lower internationally competitive price for Argentinian wheat.

Commercial Farm Results

Estimated farm returns are summarised in Table 10.2. This includes public infrastructure inputs but excludes land price. More details are shown in Appendix 10.A2.

There are two main findings. Firstly, the model farm is highly profitable. On quite conservative assumptions – for example for yields, poor seasons

Table 10.2 Summary of results for expansion-zone large commercial farms (average annual results, 1992 '000 dollars)

	Years				
	1–5	*6–10*	*11–15*	*16–20*	*21–25*
Income					
Soya	512	928	800	701	670
Maize/wheat	288	253	226	195	184
Total	800	1181	1026	896	854
Costs					
Capital*	221	22	22	22	22
Operating	474	545	563	591	599
Total	695	567	585	613	621
Farm surplus	105	614	441	283	233
NPV at 5 per cent	$4.8 million				
NPV at 10 per cent	$3.0 million				

*Including government inputs but excluding land purchase price.

and prices, and a 10 per cent discount rate – the net present value of a 2000 hectare farm is $3.0 million. This represents a land price of $1500 per hectare, which is well above the price that most landowners paid for the land.

Secondly, net income falls substantially after about 10 years as yields decline and operating expenses rise. Although forecast operating margins are still healthy in years 20–25, there is a major question mark over yields and the maintenance of fertility in the long run. Despite improved soil cover and windbreaks, the harsh climate (wind and rain) is likely to cause increasing wind and water erosion, and some land may 'go down' to pasture.

10.8 FOREST RESOURCES FORGONE IN THE SANTA CRUZ REGION

This section briefly reviews the direct costs of forest loss in the Bolivian lowlands. General issues of deforestation were discussed in Chapter 9.

As an introduction, three points should be made. Firstly, forests are heterogeneous. The Bolivian Tropical Forestry Action Plan nominated the humid rain forest areas of the north-east lowlands (which are outside the two case-study areas), along with the Yungas mountain forests north of La Paz, as the main national conservation priorities. The dryer areas to the south and east of Santa Cruz city produce smaller, less valuable trees. Secondly, the impacts of deforestation depend on what replaces primary forest. As Nye and Greenland (1960) point out, a mature secondary forest with more than 20 years growth is often 'scarcely distinguishable from the original' forest. Thirdly, there are few data on the value of forests in Bolivia.

Timber Values

Selective logging of the most valuable species, notably mahogany, usually precedes forest clearing. Clearing then prevents exploitation of less valuable species and precludes the possibility of sustained timber management.

The sustainable extraction rate is theoretically the annual increment in standing volume of forests. In Eastern Bolivia this varies from 0.5 cubic metre to 10 cubic metres per hectare. In well forested areas a sustainable average yield of 2–3 cubic metres per hectare per annum can typically be achieved.

However this yield is not being achieved and is not likely to be. After the best timbers have been cleared, the remaining timbers have low market or household value. Current farm-gate timber prices do not justify sustained small-scale timber extraction. Although woodfuels are a staple source of household energy in rural Bolivia, at present they are readily available to most rural households in the colonisation zones.

Also, ongoing commercial logging operations face numerous constraints. These include high transport costs to markets, the heterogeneous nature of the forests (there is no proven way of managing tropical forests sustainably with over 100 species), the low volume of marketable trees per unit area, technical difficulties in milling or processing a wide range of hardwoods for lumber and particle board, and costly processes for pulp and paper manufacture from mixed tropical hardwoods. Neither large milling operations for export markets nor small-scale milling operations in new colonisation areas are justified with present farm-gate timber prices.

The conclusion is that, after mahogany is removed, the direct forest values forgone due to agriculture in Yapacani and the expansion zone are small. Yapacani can provide a fair amount of timber but transport costs are high. The price of logged but uncleared forest land is usually $20–30 per hectare. This price reflects the demand for agricultural land and generally exceeds the value of unmanaged timber resources to the farmer. Timber values in the expansion zone are also below the land price for agriculture.

Other Forest Products Forgone

Little is known about the values of non-timber forest products in Bolivia. Colonist farmers in Yapacani South report that it is increasingly difficult to catch game and that their protein sources and incomes are being affected (with the price of game exceeding the price of beef). Also, Hecht (1992) notes that three extractive products (cochinilla, palm heart and Brazil nuts) account for about 1.5 per cent of Santa Cruz exports. She suggests that there is a large potential for Cusi (Corbygnya spp), a palm whose nuts provide lauric acid, edible oils and charcoal, and points out that the palm-like perennial, jipi japa (Cardludovica palmata), which provides leaf fibre for making panama hats, can be easily cultivated.

Tourist attractions in Santa Cruz province include the city of Santa Cruz, some seventeenth and eighteenth century Jesuit settlements and the Amboro National Park, an area of global biodiversity importance that borders the Yapacani area. Deforestation to date in the two case-study areas appears to have had a minimal impact on tourism. However ecotourism in the Amboro Park may be affected by the decline in wildlife due to hunting by colonists and the fall in the availability of feed in Yapacani South.

Deforestation combined with local population growth has almost certainly reduced local biodiversity. The Conservation Data Centre in La Paz estimates that 17 bird species are endemic to Bolivia, including four that are endemic in the tropical forests. Eastern Bolivia is believed to have an exceptionally high level of biodiversity, but large parts of it have not been explored or documented. Continual colonisation close to the Amboro Park has probably affected the survival of some of the park's unique species (for example the Andean Spectacled Bear and the Southern Helmeted Currasow). Biodiversity studies in reserves around Santa Cruz estimated that the number of bird species fell by 30 per cent after selective logging (Taber, 1993). The number would have fallen further after the land had been cropped. However it is believed that virtually all the species that have disappeared locally still exist in the extensive forests remaining in the lowlands. This is consistent with Wilson and Peters' estimate that 30 per cent deforestation leads to the loss of some 3 per cent of species (Wilson and Peters, 1988).

Summary

Several opportunity costs are associated with the development of agriculture, especially in the Yapacani area. These include the loss of timber products, the loss of non-timber forest products including game and various nuts, a significant threat to biodiversity and a risk to ecotourism, especially in the Amboro National Park. The resource values forgone to date due to deforestation in the two case-study areas appear small. But cumulatively these opportunity costs could be substantial in the future, especially in connection with the Amboro National Park.

10.9 COSTING OFF-SITE IMPACTS OF DEFORESTATION AND AGRICULTURAL DEVELOPMENT

This section briefly discusses off-site impacts relating to soil erosion, hydrology and water catchment protection, and climate and greenhouse effects. Some of these problems (for instance soil erosion and water run-off) are related. Natural or chemical agricultural wastes are not discussed because there is no evidence of adverse downstream effects from the two case-study sites.

Estimation of off-site impacts is notoriously difficult. For example it is difficult to measure the difference between natural and accelerated erosion. Moreover soil shifts can increase productivity in the receiving area, rather than harm it. Barnes and Olivares (1988) find that off-site externalities are rarely dealt with in any depth in World Bank projects. Van Pelt (1991) notes that even qualitative assessment is problematic.

Soil Erosion

In Yapacani, some hills carry spectacular scars from deforestation, many farms are gullied and soil movement is common. Soil erosion in the inter-Andean foothills has helped to cause serious river siltation and flooding in colonised parts of the lowlands, and has affected roads, bridges and railway infrastructure. No costing is available.

In the expansion zone the farms are exposed to soil erosion from high winds. However windbreaks reduce soil deposition. Off-site impacts appear less severe than soil crusting on site.

Hydrology and Catchment Protection

The complex hydrology of the vast river systems of the Amazon and the Orinoco is not thoroughly understood. There are no official records of sedimentation, waterflows and water levels in the lowlands, where floods have always occurred. Data are passed on orally. Damage estimates are scarce and are usually unreliable. There has been no definitive analysis of the potential downstream effects of flooding and silting caused by accelerated run-off or erosion.

Deforestation in upstream areas in Yapacani has increased sedimentation in lower areas of the watershed, adding to the likelihood that rivers such as the Pirai will overflow. Indeed in 1977 and 1983 floods from the Pirai caused millions of dollars of losses to agricultural production and civil infrastructure. Roads, bridges and railways in the lowlands are often impassable. However, significantly accelerated run-off occurs only on the small part of slash and burn farms under annual crops.

On the floodplains to the north and east of Santa Cruz, run-off from freshly cleared, bare land is five times the rate from forests; run-off from pastures is about 2.5 times the rate from forests. The run-off from cleared farms is often exacerbated by farm design and practice. On some large commercial farms in the expansion zone, drainage is especially poor. Heavy machinery increases compaction. Also, absentee landlords often employ untrained tractor drivers who have no incentive to practice soil conservation. All these practices have increased natural run-off and flooding of downstream farms.

However the costs of downstream flooding attributable to land clearing and farming practices in the expansion zone appear small. Land clearance within 300 metres of rivers is forbidden. Future damages may be contained by improved on-site drainage and improved techniques to reduce compaction, such as vertical tillage and less use of disc tools.

Climate

Large areas of deforestation could reduce rainfall, which would in turn affect vegetation. Rainfall ultimately returns to the atmosphere through evapotranspiration. Estimates of the amount returned in this way vary from 30–60 per cent (Bunyard, 1985). Permanent agriculture could change the water cycle and decrease precipitation by 1–5 mm per day in the wet season and by less than 2 mm per day in the dry season. Changes in the rainfall pattern could also alter the frequency of rainfall, possibly increasing its intensity and potential to cause flooding.

Major natural shifts of climate have occurred in Bolivia. Also, climate variations within areas are large. But little is known about the effects of large forest areas on climate. Moreover a senior officer in the Officer of the President told the writers that 'climate data collected in Bolivia are lamentable'. They are inconsistent with satellite data and are not systematically recorded or analysed.

Unfortunately the probability of rainfall change and its economic consequences are quite unknown at this stage. It appears unlikely, however, that deforestation around Santa Cruz todate has been sufficient to affect rainfall.

Greenhouse Effect

As discussed in Chapter 9, the costs of greenhouse warming are the product of the net amount of carbon released into the atmosphere and the cost per tonne of carbon released. In a lightly wooded forest, burning off causes the release of about 70 tonnes of carbon per hectare. This is offset by the 5–10 tonnes of carbon that is sequestered in crop growth and secondary forest. Net carbon release is probably about 65 tonnes per hectare around Santa Cruz and 75 tonnes per hectare in Yapacani. Allowing $2.50 of damage per tonne of carbon loss (Section 9.7), the greenhouse cost would be about $160 per hectare in the expansion zone and $190 per hectare in Yapacani.

Off-site Impacts: Summary

The main quantified off-site impact is the greenhouse effect, which is costed at $160–190 per hectare in our case-studies. Soil erosion and water catchment costs due to development in Yapacani could be significant. These costs are probably small downstream of the expansion zone. In neither case can the costs be quantified. Rainfall consequences of deforestation are also unknown but appear to be small.

10.10 POLICY OBSERVATIONS

A national land use plan is required to allocate land between major competing uses (national parks, reserves, logging, mixed forest/farming activities, other farming activities and so forth). Evaluations of particular land use changes, such as those in this study, are inevitably partial assessments of marginal changes. However, in total, marginal changes can produce fundamental environmental changes, for example in climate. They should therefore be assessed within a national land use framework. This should be firm enough to ensure consistent decisions but flexible enough to allow for change as information and circumstances change.

An effective land use plan requires information and revenue. Much more location-specific information is needed about soil conditions, productivity under different technologies, the value of forest products, the off-site impacts of deforestation and agricultural development and so on. Agricultural research is poorly funded in Bolivia; funding, including aid, accounts for less than 0.5 per cent of the value of agricultural output. Royalties and charges for selective loggers are low. Rural taxes are low and widely evaded. Consequently the government has to draw on urban-based revenues to fund infrastructure and environmental protection in rural areas.

Confused and inefficient land ownership titling is a major problem in Bolivia. Under the Agrarian Reform Law, 1952, the state owns and allocates all land and issues private titles to those working the land or those who are willing to improve it, but it cannot sell the land. Also, rental contracts are prohibited and land distributed under the Reform Law cannot be sold without state authorisation. Therefore, even when smallholders have adequate title, their property rights are limited. Further, the government can acquire land at low prices, which discourages long-term investment. Those using land for three years can claim squatter's rights. If the land is not worked, the right is lost.

Land is often allocated administratively rather than sold by tender. This may be neither efficient nor equitable. More than one government agency gives land titles so that multiple titles can exist. On the other hand, in some cases no titles formally exist as the process for land titlement is bureaucratic and lengthy and may involve sizeable private payments. Land hoarding for speculative purposes is encouraged, as land provides economic rents and there is no capital gains tax. Most forest concessions are short term; many permits have to be renewed annually. Tenure insecurity and short-term concessions promote rapid and inefficient exploitation of forests before concessions are withdrawn. Moreover, despite the Agrarian Reform land is held unequally. Large land holdings lead to more pressure on the forest frontier.

In addition to a national land use policy, various other policies would enhance both economic development and environmental protection. These include the provision of public goods, especially roads, where development is considered desirable but not elsewhere; increased research into sustained forest management and intermediate farm technology; tightening up on logging policies, including the use of performance bonds to ensure rehabilitation requirements are met; investment in improved pasture management and seeds; surface protection with cover crops; more use of the chisel plough to reduce compaction; and promotion of agro-forestry schemes. To be effective, these policies need to be supported by economic incentives as well as by regulations.

10.11 CONCLUSIONS

There has been considerable concern that farming in the Santa Cruz region is not sustainable. Farmers have deforested, exhausted and abandoned to poor pasture or secondary growth over a million hectares in the region. In order to examine this phenomenon of land abandonment, this study developed models of two representative farming systems: peasant cut and burn farming on the hill slopes in Yapacani and large-scale commercial farming in the expansion zone to the east of Santa Cruz.

It was found that 20 hectare peasant farms in Yapacani with only conventional crops produce a modest income for a farming family for about 15 years but are not sustainable for much longer. However the farms continue to produce a viable annual income at least up to year 25 (the last year of the model) if they diversify into livestock or coca, or both. The diversified farm generates a net cash flow with an estimated present value of between \$6000 and \$10 000, depending on the discount rate, plus subsistence income.

Modern commercial farms east of Santa Cruz are highly profitable. At a conservative estimate, the net present value of a 2000 hectare soya-based farm is \$3.0 million. However net income falls substantially after the first 10 or so years as yields decline and operating costs rise. Although forecast operating margins are still healthy in years 20–25, some land may 'go down' to pasture and cattle in due course.

Several environmental costs are associated with agricultural development in the two case-study areas, especially in Yapacani. These include the loss of timber products, the loss of non-timber products including game and nuts, a significant threat to biodiversity and ecotourism, especially in the Amboro National Park, some greenhouse warming effects, and some soil and water catchment costs. Our judgement is that these associated costs are generally not so substantial as to warrant stopping the developments. However, as has been emphasised, there are very few data on these impacts.

Several other caveats should be made. Firstly, generalisations are risky. The model's results are based on representative farms. In practice, commercial and environmental results vary greatly. For example erosion depends on slope gradients. The expansion zone has high natural soil fertility and little need for fertilisers. But lack of soil cover and heavy tractor use can cause excessive compaction and desertification. Secondly, there is much scope for improved agricultural practices to prevent land degradation. Recommended practices include greater use of cover crops, more crop rotations, windbreaks and vertical tillage.

Thirdly, the short-term benefits of land development have not been shared equally. Land has not been available to all on equal terms. There has been more official Bolivian and World Bank support for the prosperous developments east of Santa Cruz than for the poor farmers in Yapacani. Fourthly, although individual small projects may not cause significant environmental damage, they may do so collectively, for example to catchments or to climate. To avoid this a national land use and environmental plan is required. This plan should provide the policy framework for individual land use decisions.

Our final observation is that hindsight is much easier than foresight. Uncertainty is a major feature of farming. In the words of a successful colonist farmer in the Santa Cruz region, 'life is a trial'. This explains why so many farmers and loggers are anxious to exploit potential short-term gains. But long-run environmental impacts are also uncertain. Public policy has to try to satisfy the immediate needs of farmers and ensure the long-term productivity of the environment. This study and the research work by BTAM suggest that this can be done.

Appendix 10A.1 Evaluation of peasant earning in South Yapacani, Santa Cruz

Development path: slash and burn into low input, traditional management, livestock.
Farm size : 20.0 hectares
Prices: US$ 1992

	Years 1	2	3	4	5	6	7	8	9	10	11	12	13	14	15	16	17	18	19	20	21	22	23	24	25
Land use assumptions (ha)																									
1st yr ann. crops into cleared primary forest	2	–	3	–	2	1	1	2	–	1	2	–	1	1	1	1	–	–	–	–	–	–	–	–	–
2nd yr ann. crops after clearing prim. forest	–	2	–	3	–	1	1	1	2	–	1	2	–	1	1	1	1	–	–	–	–	–	–	–	–
Ann. crops into sec. forest (fallow 6 yrs+)	–	–	–	–	–	–	–	–	–	2	–	2	1	1	–	–	1	1	1	1	1	–	–	–	–
Ann. crops into sec. forest (fallow 1–5 yrs)	–	–	–	–	–	–	–	–	–	–	–	–	–	–	–	–	–	1	1	1	1	2	2	2	2
Livestock: land under sown pasture	–	–	–	–	–	1	1	2	2	3	4	4	5	5	5	5	5	5	5	5	5	5	5	5	5
Livestock: land under natural pasture	–	–	–	–	–	–	–	–	–	–	–	–	–	–	–	–	–	–	–	–	1	2	3	4	5
Other: land remaining in primary forest	16	16	13	13	11	10	9	7	7	6	4	4	3	2	1	0	0	0	0	0	0	0	0	0	0
Other: land remaining in sec. forest			2	2	5	5	6	6	7	6	7	6	8	8	10	11	11	11	11	11	10	9	8	7	6
Other: uncultivated land, house, ponds etc.	2	2	2	2	2	2	2	2	2	2	2	2	2	2	2	2	2	2	2	2	2	2	2	2	2
Total land in farm	20	20	20	20	20	20	20	20	20	20	20	20	20	20	20	20	20	20	20	20	20	20	20	20	20
Main yields/outputs																									
Rice yields (t/ha)	3.0	2.0	3.0	2.0	3.0	2.5	2.5	2.7	2.0	1.9	2.7	1.7	2.2	2.1	2.5	2.5	1.7	1.1	1.1	1.1	1.1	0.9	0.9	0.9	0.9
Rice output total (t)	6.0	4.0	9.0	6.0	6.0	5.0	5.0	8.0	4.0	5.6	8.0	6.6	4.3	6.3	5.0	5.0	3.3	2.2	2.2	2.2	2.2	1.8	1.8	1.8	1.8
Maize yield (t/ha)	0.4	0.4	0.4	0.4	0.4	0.4	0.4	0.4	0.4	0.4	0.4	0.4	0.4	0.4	0.4	0.4	0.4	0.3	0.3	0.3	0.3	0.3	0.3	0.3	0.3
Maize total (t)	0.8	0.7	1.2	1.1	0.8	0.8	0.8	1.2	0.7	1.1	1.2	1.4	0.8	1.1	0.8	0.8	0.7	0.6	0.6	0.6	0.6	0.5	0.5	0.5	0.5
Cow female 3+ yrs (No)	–	1.0	1.0	1.0	1.5	1.5	2.0	2.0	2.8	2.8	3.8	3.8	5.1	5.1	7.0	7.0	9.6	9.6	9.6	13.1	13.1	13.1	17.8	17.8	17.8
Calves female 1–2 yrs (No)	–	–	0.5	–	0.5	–	0.8	–	1.0	–	1.4	–	1.9	–	2.6	–	3.5	–	–	4.8	–	–	6.5	–	–
Calves male 1–2 yrs (No)	–	–	0.5	–	0.5	–	0.8	–	1.0	–	1.4	–	1.9	–	2.6	–	3.5	–	–	4.8	–	–	6.5	–	–
Cattle – milk (1/year)	–	820	820	820	1230	1230	1640	1640	2255	2255	2921	2768	3572	3362	4305	4018	3921	3921	3921	5356	5356	5356	7316	7316	7316
Cattle – beef (1wt.kg/year)	–	–	0	0	150	0	150	0	225	0	300	0	413	0	563	0	769	0	0	1050	0	0	1434	0	0
Public Capital Expenditure ($)	20	–	–	–	–	–	–	–	–	–	–	–	–	–	–	–	–	–	–	–	–	–	–	–	
Farm capital works (family labour)																									
Land clearing (days)	60	6	90	9	60	33	33	63	6	70	63	46	50	53	33	33	23	35	35	35	35	30	30	30	30
Pasture establishment (days)	0	0	0	0	0	3	0	3	0	3	3	0	3	0	0	0	0	0	0	0	0	0	0	0	0
Constuctions (days)	–	15	2	2	2	2	2	2	2	2	15	2	2	2	2	2	2	2	2	2	2	2	2	2	2
Other (road maint. etc.) (days)	24	24	24	24	24	24	24	24	24	24	24	24	24	24	24	24	24	24	24	24	24	24	24	24	24
Total labour days	84	45	116	35	86	62	59	92	32	99	105	72	79	79	59	59	49	61	61	61	61	56	56	56	56
Total costs ($)	294	158	406	123	301	217	207	322	112	347	368	252	277	277	207	207	172	214	214	214	214	196	196	196	196
Farm capital expenditure ($)																									
Land price	1000	–	–	–	–	–	–	–	–	–	–	–	–	–	–	–	–	–	–	–	–	–	–	–	–
Farm equipment	100	50	50	50	50	100	50	50	50	50	100	50	50	50	50	100	50	50	50	50	100	50	50	50	50
Fencing	–	–	–	–	–	–	–	–	–	–	375	375	375	375	–	–	–	–	–	–	–	–	–	–	–
Livestock purchase	160	–	–	–	–	–	–	–	–	–	–	–	–	–	–	–	–	–	–	–	–	–	–	–	–
Total expenditures	1260	50	50	50	50	100	50	50	50	50	475	425	425	425	50	100	50	50	50	50	100	50	50	50	50

Operating inputs for annual crops																									
Sowing (days)	8	8	12	12	8	8	8	12	8	12	12	16	8	12	8	8	8	8	8	8	8	8	8	8	8
Weeding (days)	8	26	9	36	8	17	17	18	26	27	18	46	17	27	17	17	26	36	36	36	36	46	46	46	46
Spraying (days)	3	3	4	4	3	3	3	4	3	4	4	5	3	4	3	3	3	4	4	4	4	5	5	5	5
Harvest/post harvest (days)	3	3	3	3	3	3	3	3	3	3	3	3	3	3	3	3	3	2	2	2	2	2	2	2	2
Total labour (days)	22	40	28	55	22	31	31	37	40	46	37	70	31	46	31	31	40	50	50	50	50	61	61	61	61
Family labour (days)	21	38	27	53	21	30	30	36	38	44	36	68	30	44	30	30	38	49	49	49	49	60	60	60	60
Non-family (days)	2	1	2	1	2	2	2	2	1	1	2	1	2	1	2	2	1	1	1	1	1	1	1	1	1
Herbicide use (l)	2	2	3	3	2	2	2	3	2	1	3	2	1	2	2	2	1	6	6	6	6	0	0	0	0
Insecticide use (l)	2	2	3	3	2	2	2	3	2	1	3	2	1	2	2	2	1	1	1	1	1	0	0	0	0
Operating cost for annual crops ($)																									
Family labour costs	72	134	93	187	72	103	103	124	134	156	124	239	103	156	103	103	134	172	172	172	172	210	210	210	210
Non-family labour costs	6	5	6	5	6	5	5	5	5	5	5	5	5	5	5	5	5	4	4	4	4	4	4	4	4
Seed inputs	33	33	50	50	33	33	33	50	33	50	50	66	33	50	33	33	33	33	33	33	33	33	33	33	33
Chemical inputs	36	36	54	54	36	36	36	54	36	18	54	36	18	36	36	36	18	48	48	48	48	0	0	0	0
Total non-family costs	75	74	109	108	75	74	74	109	74	73	109	107	56	91	74	74	56	85	85	85	85	37	37	37	37
Total ann. crop op. costs	147	208	202	295	147	178	178	233	208	228	233	346	160	246	178	178	190	257	257	257	257	247	247	247	247
Operating inputs for livestock																									
Grazing/guarding (days)	0	100	120	140	160	180	200	220	240	240	100	100	100	100	100	100	100	100	100	100	100	100	100	100	100
Milking etc. (days)	0	8	8	8	12	12	16	16	23	23	29	28	36	34	43	40	39	39	39	54	54	54	73	73	73
Family labour (days)	0	108	128	148	172	192	216	236	263	263	129	128	136	134	143	140	139	139	139	154	154	154	173	173	173
Operating costs for livestock ($)																									
Family labour costs	0	216	256	296	345	385	433	473	525	525	258	255	271	267	286	280	278	278	278	307	307	307	346	346	346
Veterinary costs	0	4	7	7	9	9	12	12	17	17	23	23	31	31	42	42	58	58	58	79	79	79	108	91	91
Pasture maintenance	0	0	0	0	0	18	18	35	35	53	70	70	88	88	88	88	88	88	88	88	88	88	88	88	88
Total livestock op. costs	0	220	263	303	353	411	463	520	577	594	351	348	390	386	416	410	424	424	424	474	474	474	542	525	525
Operating costs for tree crops ($)																									
Family labour (days)	6	6	6	6	6	6	6	6	6	6	6	6	6	6	6	6	6	6	6	6	6	6	6	6	6
Family labour costs	21	21	21	21	21	21	21	21	21	21	21	21	21	21	21	21	21	21	21	21	21	21	21	21	21
Income for annual crops ($)																									
Rice	825	525	1275	825	825	675	675	1125	525	765	1125	915	570	870	675	675	420	255	255	255	255	195	195	195	195
Income from livestock ($)																									
Cattle (milk)	0	66	66	66	98	98	131	131	180	180	234	221	286	269	344	321	314	314	314	428	428	428	585	585	585
Cattle (beef)	0	0	0	0	48	0	48	0	72	0	96	0	132	0	180	0	246	0	0	336	0	0	459	0	0
Other (sheep, pigs, hens etc.)	0	65	65	65	65	65	65	65	65	65	65	65	65	65	65	65	65	65	65	65	65	65	65	65	65
Total livestock income	0	131	131	131	211	163	244	196	317	245	395	286	483	334	589	386	625	379	379	829	493	493	1109	650	650
Income from tree crops ($)																									
Timber	20	20	20	20	20	20	20	20	20	20	20	20	20	20	20	20	20	20	20	20	20	20	20	20	20
Other (poles, firewood, seeds etc.)	20	20	20	20	20	20	20	20	20	20	20	20	20	20	20	20	20	20	20	20	20	20	20	20	20
Total tree-crop income	40	40	40	40	40	40	40	40	40	40	40	40	40	40	40	40	40	40	40	40	40	40	40	40	40
Other income																									
Net coca income	0	150	300	300	300	300	300	300	300	300	300	300	300	300	300	300	300	300	300	300	300	300	300	300	300
Off-farm income	100	200	300	300	300	300	300	300	300	300	300	300	300	300	300	300	300	300	300	300	300	300	300	300	300
Value own consumption ($)																									
Annual crops	189	175	247	225	189	182	282	239	175	232	239	275	182	232	182	182	175	161	161	161	161	147	147	147	147
Cattle (milk)	0	16	16	16	25	25	33	33	45	45	85	55	71	67	86	80	78	78	78	107	107	107	146	146	146
Cattle (meat)	0	0	0	0	12	0	12	0	18	0	24	0	33	0	45	0	62	0	0	84	0	0	115	0	0
Livestock (other)	40	40	40	40	40	40	40	40	40	40	40	40	40	40	40	40	40	40	40	40	40	40	40	40	40
Total	229	232	303	282	266	247	267	312	278	317	362	371	327	340	353	303	355	279	279	392	308	294	448	333	333

Summary of results: with livestock deversification

Farm cash flows ($)																									
Total expenditure (inc. land price)	1335	127	166	165	133	201	154	206	176	192	677	625	600	634	254	304	251	281	281	302	352	253	282	265	265
Total revenues (exc. coca and off-farm income)	865	696	1446	996	1076	878	959	1361	882	1050	1560	1241	1093	1244	1304	1101	1085	674	674	1124	788	728	1344	885	885
Net cash flow (exc. coca and off-farm income)	-470	568	1280	830	943	678	805	1155	707	859	883	617	493	610	1050	797	833	393	393	823	437	475	1062	620	620
Net cash flow (inc. coca)	-470	718	1580	1130	1243	978	1105	1455	1007	1159	1183	917	793	910	1350	1097	1133	693	693	1123	737	775	1362	920	920
Net cash flow (inc. coca and off-farm income)	-370	918	1880	1430	1543	1278	1405	1755	1307	1459	1483	1217	1093	1210	1650	1397	1433	993	993	1423	1037	1075	1662	1220	1220
Imputed Farm (Land) Returns ($)																									
Total farm costs [1]	742	657	943	792	872	926	918	1146	968	1240	1448	1392	1272	1355	871	915	857	966	900	1016	1066	987	1055	1039	1039
Total farm income (exc. coca)[2]	1094	927	1749	1277	1342	1125	1226	1673	1161	1368	1922	1612	1419	1584	1658	1404	1440	953	953	1516	1096	1022	1792	1218	1218
Net farm surplus (exc. coca)	353	270	806	485	470	199	309	527	193	128	474	220	147	229	787	489	583	-13	-13	501	31	35	736	179	179
Net farm surplus (inc. coca)	353	420	1106	785	770	499	609	827	493	428	774	520	447	529	1087	789	883	287	287	801	331	335	1036	479	479

Summary of results: without livestock

Farm cash flows ($)																									
Total expenditure (inc. land price)	1175	124	159	158	125	174	124	159	124	123	209	157	106	141	124	174	106	135	135	135	185	86	87	86	86
Total revenue (exc. coca and off-farm income)	865	630	1380	930	930	780	780	1230	630	870	1230	1020	675	975	780	780	525	360	360	360	360	300	300	300	300
Net cash flow (exc. coca and off-farm income)	-310	506	1221	772	805	606	656	1071	506	747	1021	863	569	834	656	606	419	225	225	225	175	214	213	214	214
Net cash flow (inc. coca)	-310	656	1521	1072	1105	906	956	1371	806	1047	1321	1163	869	1134	956	906	719	525	525	525	475	514	514	514	514
Net cash flow (inc. coca and off-farm income)	-210	856	1821	1372	1405	1206	1256	1671	1106	1347	1621	1463	1169	1434	1256	1206	1019	825	825	825	775	814	814	814	814
Imputed farm (land) returns ($)																									
Total farm cost[1]	742	440	686	496	527	542	485	674	443	715	1189	1137	1001	1087	585	635	578	687	687	709	759	680	709	692	692
Total farm income (exc. coca)[2]	865	614	1364	914	893	755	735	1197	567	825	1148	965	571	908	649	700	385	282	282	169	253	193	39	154	154
Net farm surplus (exc. coca)	123	173	677	418	366	214	250	524	124	110	-42	-172	-430	-180	64	65	-193	-406	-406	-540	-506	-487	-670	-539	-539
Net farm surplus (inc. coca)	123	323	977	718	666	514	550	824	424	410	258	128	-130	120	364	365	107	-106	-106	-240	-206	-187	-370	-239	-239

Notes:
1. Includes imputed family labour costs, but excludes land price.
2. Includes value of family own compsumption, but not off-farm income.

Appendix 10A.2 Evaluation of commercial farms in the expansion zones east of Santa Cruz

Farm size: 2000 hectares
Prices: US$ 1992

Years	1	2	3	4	5	6	7	8	9	10	11	12	13
Land Use Assumptions (ha)													
Crops: Destumped land	650	1300	1950	1950	1950	1950	1950	1950	1950	1950	1950	1950	1950
Of which: Summer Soya		650	1300	1950	1950	1950	1950	1950	1950	1950	1950	1950	1950
Of which: Winter Soya		650	650	650	650	650	650	650	650	650	650	650	650
Of which: Maize	650	650	650	-	-	-	-	-	300	300	300	300	300
Of which: Wheat	650	650	1300	1300	1300	1300	1300	1300	1000	1000	1000	1000	1000
Other: Left in primary forest	1300	650	0	0	0	0	0	0	0	0	0	0	0
Other: Uncultivated (roads, etc.)	50	50	50	50	50	50	50	50	50	50	50	50	50
Total land in farm	2000	2000	2000	2000	2000	2000	2000	2000	2000	2000	2000	2000	2000
Yields/Outputs (inc. bad years)													
Summer soya (t/ha)	3.5	3.5	3.5	3.5	1.05	3.5	3.5	3.5	3	0.9	3	3	3
Winter soya (t/ha)	2	2	2	0.6	2	2	2	2	1.75	0.525	1.75	1.75	1.75
Maize yield (t/ha)	4.6	4.6	4.6	4.6	1.38	4.6	4.6	4.6	2	0.6	2	2	2
Wheat yield (t/ha)	1.5	1.5	1.5	1.5	0.45	1.5	1.5	1.5	1.5	0.45	1.5	1.5	1.5
Summer soya output (t/pa)	0	2275	4550	6825	614.25	6825	6825	6825	5850	526.5	5850	5850	5850
Winter soya output (t/pa)	0	1300	1300	1300	117	1300	1300	1300	1138	102	1138	1138	1138
Maize output (t/pa)	2990	2990	2990	0	0	0	0	0	600	54	600	600	600
Wheat output yield (t/pa)	975	975	1950	1950	175.5	1950	1950	1950	1500	135	1500	1500	1500
Public Capital Expenditure ($s)(1)	13200	-	-	-	-	-	-	-	-	-	-	-	-
Farm Capital Expenditures ($s)													
Land price	240000	-	-	-	-	-	-	-	-	-	-	-	-
Access	6600	-	-	-	-	-	-	-	-	-	-	-	-
Farm machinery	145000	65000	21000	21000	21000	21000	21000	21000	21000	21000	21000	21000	21000
Farm tools	550	55	55	55	55	55	55	55	55	55	55	55	55
Land clearing	260000	260000	260000	0	0	0	-	-	-	-	-	-	-
Constructions	25000	1250	1250	1250	1250	1250	1250	1250	1250	1250	1250	1250	1250
Total expenditures	677150	326305	282305	22305	22305	22305	22305	22305	22305	22305	22305	22305	22305
Operating Inputs for Crops													
SS – seed (kg)	0	39000	78000	117000	117000	117000	117000	117000	117000	117000	117000	117000	117000
SS – herbicide (l)	0	1950	3900	5850	5850	5850	5850	5850	5850	5850	5850	5850	5850
SS – insecticide (l)	0	650	1300	1950	1950	1950	1950	1950	1950	1950	1950	1950	1950
SS – innoculant (kg)	0	650	1300	1950	1950	1950	1950	1950	1950	1950	1950	1950	1950
WS – seed (kg)	0	52000	52000	52000	52000	52000	52000	52000	52000	52000	52000	52000	52000
WS – herbicide (l)	0	1300	1300	1300	1300	1300	1300	1300	1300	1300	1300	1300	1300
WS – insecticide (l)	0	650	650	650	650	650	650	650	650	650	650	650	650
WS –innoculant (kg)	0	1300	1300	1300	1300	1300	1300	1300	1300	1300	1300	1300	1300
M – seed (kg)	19500	19500	19500	0	0	0	0	0	9000	9000	9000	9000	9000
M – herbicide (l)	1300	1300	1300	0	0	0	0	0	600	600	600	600	600
M – insecticide (l)	650	650	650	0	0	0	0	0	300	300	300	300	300
W – seed (kg)	61750	61750	123500	123500	123500	123500	123500	123500	95000	95000	95000	95000	95000
W – herbicide (l)	1300	1300	2600	2600	2600	2600	2600	2600	2000	2000	2000	2000	2000
W – insecticide (l)	1300	1300	2600	2600	2600	2600	2600	2600	2000	2000	2000	2000	2000
W – fungicide (l)	975	975	1950	1950	1950	1950	1950	1950	1500	1500	1500	1500	1500
Operating Costs for Crops ($s)													
Labour costs on farm	13500	13500	13500	13500	13500	13500	13500	13500	13500	13500	13500	13500	13500
Labour administration	5000	5000	5000	5000	5000	5000	5000	5000	5000	5000	5000	5000	5000
Labour professional	4000	4000	4000	4000	4000	4000	4000	4000	4000	4000	4000	4000	4000
Total labour costs	22500	22500	22500	22500	22500	22500	22500	22500	22500	22500	22500	22500	22500

Years	14	15	16	17	18	19	20	21	22	23	24	25
Land Use Assumptions (ha)												
Crops: Destumped land	1950	1950	1950	1950	1950	1950	1950	1950	1950	1950	1950	1950
Of which: Summer Soya	1950	1950	1950	1950	1950	1950	1950	1950	1950	1950	1950	1950
Of which: Winter Soya	650	650	650	650	650	650	650	650	650	650	650	650
Of which: Maize	300	300	300	650	650	650	650	650	650	650	650	650
Of which: Wheat	1000	1000	1000	650	650	650	650	650	650	650	650	650
Other: Left in primary forest	0	0	0	0	0	0	0	0	0	0	0	0
Other: Uncultivated (roads, etc.)	50	50	50	50	50	50	50	50	50	50	50	50
Total land in farm	2000	2000	2000	2000	2000	2000	2000	2000	2000	2000	2000	2000
Yields/Outputs (inc. bad years)												
Summer soya (t/ha)	3	0.9	3	2.5	2.5	2.5	0.75	2.5	2.5	2.5	2.5	0.75
Winter soya (t/ha)	1.75	0.525	1.75	1.5	1.5	1.5	0.45	1.5	1.5	1.5	1.5	0.45
Maize yield (t/ha)	2	0.6	2	2	2	2	0.6	2	2	2	2	0.6
Wheat yield (t/ha)	1.5	0.45	1.5	1.5	1.5	1.5	0.45	1.5	1.5	1.5	1.5	0.45
Summer soya output (t/pa)	5850	526.5	5850	4875	4875	4875	438.75	4875	4875	4875	4875	438.75
Winter soya output (t/pa)	1138	102	1138	975	975	975	88	975	975	975	975	88
Maize output (t/pa)	600	54	600	1300	1300	1300	117	1300	1300	1300	1300	117
Wheat output yield (t/pa)	1500	135	1500	975	975	975	87.75	975	975	975	975	87.75
Public Capital Expenditure ($s)(1)	-	-	-	-	-	-	-	-	-	-	-	-
Farm Capital Expenditures ($s)												
Land price	-	-	-	-	-	-	-	-	-	-	-	-
Access	-	-	-	-	-	-	-	-	-	-	-	-
Farm machinery	21000	21000	21000	21000	21000	21000	21000	21000	21000	21000	21000	21000
Farm tools	55	55	55	55	55	55	55	55	55	55	55	55
Land clearing	-	-	-	-	-	-	-	-	-	-	-	-
Constructions	1250	1250	1250	1250	1250	1250	1250	1250	1250	1250	1250	1250
Total expenditures	22305	22305	22305	22305	22305	22305	22305	22305	22305	22305	22305	22305
Operating Inputs for Crops												
SS – seed (kg)	117000	117000	117000	117000	117000	117000	117000	117000	117000	117000	117000	117000
SS – herbicide (l)	5850	5850	5850	5850	5850	5850	5850	5850	5850	5850	5850	5850
SS – insecticide (l)	1950	1950	1950	1950	1950	1950	1950	1950	1950	1950	1950	1950
SS – innoculant (kg)	1950	1950	1950	1950	1950	1950	1950	1950	1950	1950	1950	1950
WS – seed (kg)	52000	52000	52000	52000	52000	52000	52000	52000	52000	52000	52000	52000
WS – herbicide (l)	1300	1300	1300	1300	1300	1300	1300	1300	1300	1300	1300	1300
WS – insecticide (l)	650	650	650	650	650	650	650	650	650	650	650	650
WS –innoculant (kg)	1300	1300	1300	1300	1300	1300	1300	1300	1300	1300	1300	1300
M – seed (kg)	9000	9000	9000	19500	19500	19500	19500	19500	19500	19500	19500	19500
M – herbicide (l)	600	600	600	1300	1300	1300	1300	1300	1300	1300	1300	1300
M – insecticide (l)	300	300	300	650	650	650	650	650	650	650	650	650
W – seed (kg)	95000	95000	95000	61750	61750	61750	61750	61750	61750	61750	61750	61750
W – herbicide (l)	2000	2000	2000	1300	1300	1300	1300	1300	1300	1300	1300	1300
W – insecticide (l)	2000	2000	2000	1300	1300	1300	1300	1300	1300	1300	1300	1300
W – fungicide (l)	1500	1500	1500	975	975	975	975	975	975	975	975	975
Operating Costs for Crops ($s)												
Labour costs on farm	13500	13500	13500	13500	13500	13500	13500	13500	13500	13500	13500	13500
Labour administration	5000	5000	5000	5000	5000	5000	5000	5000	5000	5000	5000	5000
Labour professional	4000	4000	4000	4000	4000	4000	4000	4000	4000	4000	4000	4000
Total labour costs	22500	22500	22500	22500	22500	22500	22500	22500	22500	22500	22500	22500

(continued)																									
SS – hired mach.(2)	0	7800	15600	23400	23400	23400	23400	23400	23400	23400	23400	23400	23400	23400	23400	23400	23400	23400	23400	23400	23400	23400	23400	23400	23400
SS – own mach.(2)	0	37050	74100	111150	111150	111150	111150	111150	111150	111150	111150	111150	111150	111150	111150	111150	111150	111150	111150	111150	111150	111150	111150	111150	111150
SS – seed	0	13650	27300	40950	40950	40950	40950	40950	40950	40950	40950	40950	40950	40950	40950	40950	40950	40950	40950	40950	40950	40950	40950	40950	40950
SS – herbicide	0	11700	23400	35100	35100	35100	35100	35100	35100	35100	35100	35100	35100	35100	35100	35100	35100	35100	35100	35100	35100	35100	35100	35100	35100
SS – insecticide	0	6500	13000	19500	19500	19500	19500	19500	19500	19500	19500	19500	19500	19500	19500	19500	19500	19500	19500	19500	19500	19500	19500	19500	19500
SS – innoculant	0	5850	11700	17550	17550	17550	17550	17550	17550	17550	17550	17550	17550	17550	17550	17550	17550	17550	17550	17550	17550	17550	17550	17550	17550
SS – total op. costs	0	82550	165100	247650	247650	247650	247650	247650	247650	247650	247650	247650	247650	247650	247650	247650	247650	247650	247650	247650	247650	247650	247650	247650	247650
WS – hired mach.(2)	0	3900	3900	3900	3900	3900	3900	3900	3900	3900	3900	3900	3900	3900	3900	3900	3900	3900	3900	3900	3900	3900	3900	3900	3900
WS – own mach.(2)	0	32500	32500	32500	32500	32500	32500	32500	32500	32500	32500	32500	32500	32500	32500	32500	32500	32500	32500	32500	32500	32500	32500	32500	32500
WS – seed	0	18200	18200	18200	18200	18200	18200	18200	18200	18200	18200	18200	18200	18200	18200	18200	18200	18200	18200	18200	18200	18200	18200	18200	18200
WS – herbicide	0	7800	7800	7800	7800	7800	7800	7800	7800	7800	7800	7800	7800	7800	7800	7800	7800	7800	7800	7800	7800	7800	7800	7800	7800
WS – insecticide	0	6500	6500	6500	6500	6500	6500	6500	6500	6500	6500	6500	6500	6500	6500	6500	6500	6500	6500	6500	6500	6500	6500	6500	6500
WS –innoculant	0	11700	11700	11700	11700	11700	11700	11700	11700	11700	11700	11700	11700	11700	11700	11700	11700	11700	11700	11700	11700	11700	11700	11700	11700
WS – total op. costs	0	80600	80600	80600	80600	80600	80600	80600	80600	80600	80600	80600	80600	80600	80600	80600	80600	80600	80600	80600	80600	80600	80600	80600	80600
M – hired mach.(2)	7800	7800	7800	0	0	0	0	0	3600	3600	3600	3600	3600	3600	3600	3600	7800	7800	7800	7800	7800	7800	7800	7800	7800
M – own mach.(2)	32500	32500	32500	0	0	0	0	0	15000	15000	15000	15000	15000	15000	15000	15000	32500	32500	32500	32500	32500	32500	32500	32500	32500
M – seed	97500	97500	97500	0	0	0	0	0	45000	45000	45000	45000	45000	45000	45000	45000	97500	97500	97500	97500	97500	97500	97500	97500	97500
M – herbicide	7800	7800	7800	0	0	0	0	0	3600	3600	3600	3600	3600	3600	3600	3600	7800	7800	7800	7800	7800	7800	7800	7800	7800
M – insecticide	7800	7800	7800	0	0	0	0	0	3600	3600	3600	3600	3600	3600	3600	3600	7800	7800	7800	7800	7800	7800	7800	7800	7800
M – total op. costs	153400	153400	153400	0	0	0	0	0	70800	70800	70800	70800	70800	70800	70800	70800	153400	153400	153400	153400	153400	153400	153400	153400	153400
W – hired mach.(2)	3900	3900	7800	7800	7800	7800	7800	7800	6000	6000	6000	6000	6000	6000	6000	6000	3900	3900	3900	3900	3900	3900	3900	3900	3900
W – own mach.(2)	31200	31200	62400	62400	62400	62400	62400	62400	48000	48000	48000	48000	48000	48000	48000	48000	31200	31200	31200	31200	31200	31200	31200	31200	31200
W – seed	30875	30875	61750	61750	61750	61750	61750	61750	47500	47500	47500	47500	47500	47500	47500	47500	30875	30875	30875	30875	30875	30875	30875	30875	30875
W – herbicide	7800	7800	15600	15600	15600	15600	15600	15600	12000	12000	12000	12000	12000	12000	12000	12000	7800	7800	7800	7800	7800	7800	7800	7800	7800
W – insecticide	9880	9880	19760	19760	19760	19760	19760	19760	15200	15200	15200	15200	15200	15200	15200	15200	9880	9880	9880	9880	9880	9880	9880	9880	9880
W – fungicide	1463	1463	2925	2925	2925	2925	2925	2925	2250	2250	2250	2250	2250	2250	2250	2250	1463	1463	1463	1463	1463	1463	1463	1463	1463
W – total op. costs	85118	85118	170235	170235	170235	170235	170235	170235	130950	130950	130950	130950	130950	130950	130950	130950	85118	85118	85118	85118	85118	85118	85118	85118	85118
Other farm admin. costs																									
Office expenses	2000	2000	2000	2000	2000	2000	2000	2000	2000	2000	2000	2000	2000	2000	2000	2000	2000	2000	2000	2000	2000	2000	2000	2000	2000
Vehicles	8000	8000	8000	8000	8000	8000	8000	8000	8000	8000	8000	8000	8000	8000	8000	8000	8000	8000	8000	8000	8000	8000	8000	8000	8000
Total operating costs	271018	434168	601835	530985	530985	530985	530985	530985	562500	562500	562500	562500	562500	562500	562500	562500	599268	599268	599268	599268	599268	599268	599268	599268	599268
Total Revenue (inc. bad years) ($s)																									
Summer soya	0	318500	637000	955500	85995	955500	955500	955500	819000	73710	819000	819000	819000	819000	73710	819000	682500	682500	682500	61425	682500	682500	682500	682500	61425
Winter soya	0	182000	182000	182000	16380	182000	182000	182000	159250	143332.5	159250	159250	159250	159250	14333	159250	136500	136500	136500	12285	136500	136500	136500	136500	12285
Maize	149500	149500	149500	0	0	0	0	0	30000	2700	30000	30000	30000	30000	2700	30000	65000	65000	65000	5850	65000	65000	65000	65000	5850
Wheat	160875	160875	321750	321750	28957	321750	321750	321750	247500	22275	247500	247500	247500	247500	22275	247500	160875	160875	160875	14479	160875	160875	160875	160875	14479
Total revenue	310375	810875	1290250	1459250	131333	1459250	1459250	1459250	1255750	113017	1255750	1255750	1255750	1255750	113017	1255750	1044875	1044875	1044875	94039	1044875	1044875	1044875	1044875	94039
SUMMARY OF RESULTS																									
Farm Surpluses ($s) (3)																									
Total expenditures	721368	760473	884140	553290	553290	553290	553290	553290	584805	584805	584805	584805	584805	584805	584805	584805	621573	621573	621573	621573	621573	621573	621573	621573	621573
Total revenue	310375	810875	1290250	1459250	131333	1459250	1459250	1459250	1255750	113017	1255750	1255750	1255750	1255750	113017	1255750	1044875	1044875	1044875	94039	1044875	1044875	1044875	1044875	94039
Net revenue	-410993	50403	406110	905960	-421958	905960	905960	905960	670945	-471788	670945	670945	670945	670945	-471788	670945	423303	423303	423303	-527534	423303	423303	423303	423303	-527534

Notes: (1) Public expenditure on road and bridges per farm.
(2) 'mach.' stands for machinery.
(3) Includes public expenditures but excludes land prices.

11 Valuing the Environment: Main Conclusions

11.1 INTRODUCTION

This final chapter addresses two main related questions. Firstly, to what extent can environmental impacts in developing countries be valued? Secondly, can methods for valuing the environment, that originated in developed market economies, be used in less developed economies?

The answers draw mainly on the six case-studies discussed above but also on two other studies in which I was involved, namely a World Bank Mission to develop, with the Egyptian Environmental Agency, an Environmental Plan for Egypt and a study of biodiversity conservation needs in Kenya for the UN Environmental Programme (UNEP). It should be stressed that all these studies were designed primarily to guide investment or policy decisions and that they drew mostly on established data and research material. The studies were not designed or resourced to do primary research.

The following section summarises the extent to which we were able to value various environmental impacts, including changes in water and air quality, slum improvements, safety, resettlement, deforestation, soil quality, loss of biodiversity and global warming. Section 11.3 discusses the usefulness of the main valuation methods. In the final section some conclusions are drawn on the relationship between environmental valuation and project appraisal, the valuation of productivity, health and amenity impacts, benefit transfers and environmental sustainability.

11.2 VALUING ENVIRONMENTAL IMPACTS

Table 11.1 provides a selective list of the main environmental impacts found, and valuation methods employed, in the case-studies.

Starting with water, several benefits of planned improvements in *water quality* in Wuxi were forecast and valued (see Chapter 5). These benefits included savings in the water treatment costs of the municipal water supply company and other manufacturers using water from the extensive canal system or Lake Tai, productivity benefits to fisheries (increased output and

Table 11.1 Selected environmental impacts and valuations

Environment/place	*Main impacts*	*Valued*	*Valuation method*
Water quality:			
Wuxi	Industry	Yes	Industrial cost savings
	Fisheries	Yes	Productivity benefits
	Health	Yes	Various[1]
	Visual/odour	Yes	Property prices
	Recreation	Yes	Proxy wtp prices
Egypt	Various	No	na
Air quality:			
Lagos	Health	Yes	Output benefits (World Bank)
Bangladesh	Various	Yes	Averting expenditures (US)
Egypt	Various	No	na
Noise:			
Lagos	Amenity	No	na
Slum improvements:[2]			
Visakhapatnam	Amenity	Yes	Property prices
	Training	Yes	Income changes
	Health	Yes	Proxy wtp prices
Egypt (garbage)	Various	Yes	Proxy wtp prices
Safety:			
Lagos	Health	Yes	Transfer values (OECD)[3]
Bangladesh	Health	No	na
Resettlement/disturbance:			
Lagos	Output	Yes	Rents and lost surplus
Bangladesh	Housing	Yes	Property prices
Deforestation:			
Kenya	Forest products	Yes	Proxy prices
Santa Cruz	Forest products	No	na
Soil quality:			
S. Cruz	Output	Yes	Productivity benefits
Other ecological impacts:			
Kenya[4]	Negligible	No	na
S. Cruz[4]	Unknown	No	na
Egypt (coast)	Unknown	No	na
Biodiversity:			
Kenya	Eco-tourism	Yes	Travel expenditures
	Existence	No	na
Santa Cruz	Various	No	na
Global warming:			
Bangladesh (Electricity)	Output	Yes	Averting expenditure in US
Kenya (forests)	Output	Yes	Change in output (CDP)

Notes:
1. Including productivity benefits and savings on expenditure to avert and correct ill-health.
2. Slum improvements in Visakhapatnam included improvements to slum drains and footways, water supply, sanitation, garbage disposal and general urban amenity, preschool classes, vocational training and health care programmes.
3. Based on value of life plus savings in health expenditure.
4. For example, impacts of soil erosion on off-site soil quality and water catchments and the effect of deforestation on rainfall.

lower costs), benefits of reduced water-borne diseases, improved residential conditions (reduced odours and improved visibility) and improved recreational (swimming and boating) conditions for Chinese and foreigners. Estimated benefits to industry were especially important, but in the absence of detailed engineering and accounting study of production methods the accuracy of these critical estimates was questionable. On the other hand, health benefits were found to be small as virtually all households in Wuxi receive piped treated water and there was little evidence of any serious waterborne-based disease. Minor savings in health care expenditures and in work-loss days were allowed. The value of improved residential conditions was based on imputed property rental values. Recreational benefits were based on observed prices for boat trips and entrance fees for public baths. Overall, the estimated benefits of improved water quality in the city were plausible.

Air quality proved much more difficult to value in the three case-studies (Lagos transit, Bangladesh power and the Egyptian environmental masterplan) where it was important. In these places, monitoring of air quality was virtually non-existent, although some measures of air quality have been taken in Cairo. For the Lagos study, modified World Bank (1992) estimates of the productivity benefits (fewer work-loss days) of improved health were used. For Bangladesh, US data (Koomey, 1990) on the costs of averting SO_2 and NO_x were employed. Of course possible defensive expenditures, as distinct from actual expenditures, may bear little relationship to damage costs even in the US (and even less in Bangladesh). However, assuming that possible averting costs represent an upper limit on the cost of air pollution, the total benefits of electricity generation were shown to exceed the costs (Chapter 6).

Noise was not a significant issue in any of the studies, even in the worst case of the Lagos transport study. Apart from the fact that Lagos residents appear to like noise, even traffic noise, it turned out that the proposed metro would not reduce noise significantly.

The *slum improvements* in 170 Visakhapatnam slums included improvements to drains, footways, water supply, sanitation, garbage disposal and general urban amenity, as well as preschool classes, vocational training and health care programmes. A key issue was whether these improvements should be valued collectively or separately. In this case-study (Chapter 8) a property price study was used to estimate the benefits of most of the improvements in a sample of 24 slums and to compare these benefits with the programme costs. An analysis of wage changes showed that most of the training courses (except traditional craft courses) were productive. On the other hand the unit costs of services under the health care programme were shown to be higher than the prices charged by private doctors, and not necessarily more effective.

Safety is an important issue in Lagos traffic, where there are a huge number of road accidents, and in power supply in Bangladesh, where fires and other industrial accidents are common partly because of the high level of unauthorised electricity connections. In order to value safety improvements in Lagos it was necessary to draw on some sketchy local research to estimate the numbers of unreported accidents and to draw on OECD estimates of benefits per type of accident saved, which were factored down to allow for differences between OECD and Nigerian incomes. On the other hand no attempt was made to value the safety benefits of improved electricity distribution in Bangladesh as records of the volumes of accidents were highly deficient (and it was not necessary to value these to justify the investment in improved electricity distribution).

Resettlement is another important issue in many engineering and natural resource projects. Construction of the proposed Lagos metro will displace thousands of traders and many households from their existing locations and cause bitter social dispute, notwithstanding the fact that many traders are located illegally. For the evaluation, the costs of resettlement were based on rental or property values of land given up, based on observed prices and survey information on the rents that traders would be willing to pay, plus a percentage allowance for disturbance costs based on Australian and UK data (Abelson, 1986). Proposed forest conservation also involves resettlement of traditional communities in some Kenyan forests, for example the Mau and Tana reserves, but not in the Kakamega and Arabuko Sokoke. Resettlement is sometimes costed on the basis of new housing and related infrastructure costs, but this does not allow for welfare changes (usually losses) associated with resettlement.

Deforestation has numerous impacts (Chapter 9). A major impact is the loss of forest products, many of which are used for subsistence living. In Kenya, the Kenya Indigenous Forest Conservation group (KIFCON, 1992a, 1992b) made detailed estimates of the value of forest products from conservation based on several months of fieldwork and market or proxy prices for output. No remotely comparable data were available in Bolivia.

However it was possible to measure and value the output effects of on-farm changes in *soil quality* in Santa Cruz province, Bolivia, where the British Tropical Agricultural Mission had been based for some 15 years (Chapter 10).

Not surprisingly it proved impossible to value a large number of *other ecological impacts*. For example there are almost no data on the impacts of soil erosion off-farm or on water catchments in Santa Cruz, where these impacts are probably significant. There was no evidence of these impacts in the Kakamega and Arabuko Sokoke forests. There is also great uncertainty about the impact of deforestation on rainfall (Hamilton and King, 1983). In Egypt, tourism development is likely to have a major impact on the ecology of the Red Sea, but this could not be valued during the development of the Egyptian environmental plan.

The main use values of *biodiversity*, apart from meat and skin products, are genetic values and tourism. No attempt was made to value the contribution of flora and fauna to genetic production in either the Kenya biodiversity study or the forestry conservation studies. It is difficult to value the natural resource contribution to pharmaceutical and other production and the future genetic benefits of particular habitats, which usually contain unknown species. To value tourism benefits of forest conservation, KIFCON (1992a) adopted a travel cost approach, which (if correctly used) should show the benefits to tourists, but ignored possible benefits to local producers. On the other hand the ODA review missions estimated the benefits of tourist expenditures to the Kenyan economy but disregarded possible consumer surpluses.

Global warming is, as the name implies, a global rather than a local issue. The cost of a tonne of carbon emission is the same in Kenya or Bangladesh as anywhere else. There is much controversy about this cost (see Chapter 9). The ODA review missions in Kenya questioned the costs of small marginal quantities of emissions due to losses of small forests. There is less disagreement about the amount of carbon emitted by power stations or saved by conserving forests.

Existence (or non-use) values were not estimated in any study. Existence values were probably relevant only in the Kakamega and Arabuko Sokoke forests but there was no basis for estimating existence values for the many unusual species under threat or for transferring values from other studies (for example, Samples, Dixon and Gowen, 1986). However the ODA review missions argued that the high flora and fauna values justified pilot conservation schemes in each forest, despite the negative NPVs of the schemes based on detailed estimates of use values. This implied significant existence values for the threatened species.

11.3 THE USE OF VALUATION METHODS

Table 11.2 reproduces the classification of valuation methods used in this book. In this taxonomy, market-based methods are defined widely to include labour and property markets, as well as product markets, and to

Table 11.2 A taxonomy of valuation methods

Market-based[1]	*Other revealed preference*	*Stated preference*
Explicit markets	Defensive expenditures[2]	Contingent valuation
Implicit markets	Travel cost method	Other survey methods[3]
Proxy prices		
Production costs		

Notes:
1. Including product, labour and property markets.
2. Including averting and corrective expenditure.
3. Including contingent ranking and constructed markets where money actually changes hands.

include implicit prices, proxy prices and production costs, although the latter may not reflect market conditions, especially in public sector activities. Also, there may be a close relationship between public production costs and defensive expenditures.

In our case-studies *market-based methods* of valuation were the dominant mode of valuation. This partly reflected the importance of productivity impacts in *product markets*, including production cost savings as well as productivity improvements, for example in the water and soil quality case-studies. However valuation was often made difficult by the lack of technical information. For instance only crude estimates could be made of production cost savings in water treatment and of productivity improvements in fish farms in Wuxi. Also, off-site productivity changes could not be valued in Bolivia or Egypt, where they were probably important.

Labour market data were used in several studies. For example they were used to estimate the benefits of training programmes in Indian slums and the value of work days saved because of possible improvements in health due to improved water quality in Wuxi and air quality in Lagos.

Property market data were used to estimate the cost of land and property that would be forgone for the proposed metro in Lagos, the household benefits of slum improvements in Visakhapatnam and the commercial and household (amenity) benefits of better water quality in Wuxi. In each benefit valuation exercise a simple form of hedonic pricing was used. That is, an estimation of the property price change associated with the change in one particular variable (or one group of variables in Visakhapatnam).

The property price method of benefit valuation (usually based on estimated land values) has been employed in many World Bank studies of slum improvement schemes in India and water quality schemes in China (and doubtless elsewhere). Unfortunately, estimated land value changes have often been applied crudely as an aggregate measure of household benefits and have been based on speculative forecasts of changes in property prices rather than on observed price data. Naturally such exercises can be readily criticised. A lesson of the Wuxi study is that, where possible, it is preferable to identify and value separately the main household benefits, for example benefits from improved health and recreational opportunities, rather than rely on an all-encompassing benefit valuation based only on land prices. However the case-studies show that property price data are often available and can be used as a measure of carefully specified environmental improvements.

Proxy prices are also generally available and useful. Proxy prices were used to value forest products in Kenya and recreational (boating and swimming) benefits in Wuxi. Also, in Visakhaptnam proxy (private doctor) prices were used to show that the public health care services provided in the slums were not cost-effective.

Defensive expenditures, of one or other kind, were also a commonly used benefit valuation technique in the case-studies. The Bangladesh study drew on US costs of averting air pollution. The Wuxi study included, as benefits, forecast reductions in household expenditure on water purifiers and mosquito repellents. The Lagos metro study included, as a benefit, the savings in corrective expenditure that would otherwise be required to mitigate flooding caused by the existing railway. Resettlement costs are generally based on housing and community replacement costs. Also, the benefits of improved health routinely include savings in health care expenditure, which is a form of corrective expenditure.

Like any valuation technique, the defensive expenditure method can be misused. Defensive expenditure may not reflect actual or likely damages, especially in non-competitive situations. For example the cost of soil replenishment is sometimes used to indicate the cost of soil erosion (Convery, 1991). This may be a significant overestimation of the real cost of soil loss.

Estimated travel cost savings were a critical input to the Lagos study and were used to estimate both the loss of a major pedestrian thoroughfare and significant community severance, which may be regarded as environmental impacts. However the travel cost valuation method (TCM) for inferring household surpluses for non-market goods (see Bockstael *et al.*, 1991) was of little use in the case-studies. TCM might be used to infer the value of tourist trips to forests. KIFCON (1992a, 1992b) attempted to do so but misused the technique by equating visitors surpluses with gross travel expenditure. I attempted to use TCM to estimate the benefits of free local health care services to Visakhapatnam households but was stymied by insufficient differentiation in travel costs to the various health care centres. In Wuxi, proxy prices provided much more accessible measures of recreational benefits than could be obtained from TCM.

Likewise, the contingent valuation method (CVM) was not found to be useful in any of the case-studies. This was partly because the time and resources required for a successful CVM were beyond the scope of the consultant studies. As Whittington *et al.* (1990) and others have shown, CV studies are possible in developing countries. However even advocates of CVM (such as Carson, 1991) stress that such studies need careful preparation and much time. In Lagos the traffic consultants (Dar al-Handassah) attempted a simple survey-based study of the value of travel time savings but obtained implausible and unusable results.

I have a more general reservation about the use of CV studies in any context where there is substantial (and often bitter) dispute about income distribution or property rights. For example it is doubtful whether slum households in India would be prepared to state willingness to pay values for slum improvements to which they believe that they are entitled. Likewise it would be very difficult to determine from a survey what Kenyan forest dwellers would be willing to accept as compensation for being resettled or what Lagos stallholders on public roads or the railroad itself would be willing to accept as compensation for relocation. Such situations are common in developing countries, and not uncommon in developed ones. My colleague, Jim Winpenny, quickly backed off doing a CV survey of willingness to pay values for access to a public beach in Barbados when he realised the revolutionary implications!

However two further related observations about surveys should be made. Firstly, data collection surveys are generally cheap in developing countries. In Lagos, a notoriously inefficient working environment, consultants Dar al-Handassah quickly and cheaply obtained a great deal of information about traffic and pedestrian movements and the numbers and locations of stallholders on and around the existing railroad. Secondly, although complex CV studies may often be impractical, simpler more qualitative surveys and workshops may help to elicit popular attitudes and values. Where possible, official local opinion and values from developed country studies should be supported or modified by information on popular local values.

11.4 MORE GENERAL OBSERVATIONS ON ENVIRONMENTAL VALUATION

The Nature of Environmental Problems

For the case-studies the environment was taken broadly to be 'the natural and social conditions surrounding all ... mankind, and including future generations' (World Bank, 1991, p. 2). The studies confirmed that it is usually not practical or necessary to attempt to distinguish between impacts on the natural and the man-made environment. In the end we are concerned mainly, though not exclusively, about the impacts on human health, productivity and amenity. It would be inconsistent to worry about the health impacts of air pollution from industry without also being concerned about injuries and fatalities in industrial processes. As observed in Chapter 1, it is often in the social environment, in work places and slums particularly, that people experience the most degraded conditions.

Many environmental problems are inextricably linked to social problems. Deforestation in Bolivia is driven by poverty on the Altiplano and unequal landholdings in the lowlands. Deforestation in Kenya is driven by high population densities and the shortage of viable agricultural land. In Lagos the relocation of numerous traders and households to make way for the proposed metro will have more impact on household welfare than the minor relief of air pollution and noise. In the Tana reserve in Kenya the World Bank agreed to fund a resettlement programme for households in the forest in order to preserve a threatened species of monkey. However, when a World Bank official demurred at the prospect of a rapid resettlement programme until the local people had been adequately consulted, a then very senior official of the Kenya Wildlife Service is reputed to have replied: 'But, I don't want any of your World Bank sociologists in my reserves!'

General Evaluation Approach

To ensure a consistent evaluation procedure, all costs and benefits in the case-studies, including environmental impacts, were valued within a standard cost–benefit framework. That is, individual preferences were respected and willingness to pay values were estimated. In none of the studies was any attempt made to estimate willingness to accept values.

A cost–benefit framework is generally preferable to less comprehensive evaluation methods, such as cost-effectiveness. In Wuxi the engineering consultants designed the most cost-effective wastewater scheme to meet the water quality objectives of the Chinese government. This presumes that the water quality standards are justified. The case-study found that there were substantial net benefits in meeting water quality standards in the densely populated urban area. But the net benefits of meeting water quality standards downstream in a sparsely populated area, by treating large amounts of wastewater before discharging it, were probably negative. On the other hand a cost-effectiveness study did show up the cost of the public health programme in Visakhapatnam compared with the private alternative.

The Wuxi study also showed the importance of breaking up projects into separate components and the need for incremental analysis. Likewise, in Wuxi and elsewhere the valuation process was more transparent and easier to check when the main benefits were valued separately rather than as a whole. However if the components of a project have a synergistic effect, as for example in slum improvement programmes, more holistic measures of benefit (for example property value measures) may be required to supplement evaluation of each component.

Also, cost–benefit studies of marginal projects and impacts may not capture cumulative effects. For instance a small amount of deforestation may have a negligible impact on species loss and global warming. But many small deforestation projects combined could have a significant impact. Ideally, project evaluation would be made within the framework of an environmental and land use plan for each country, so that the nature of the marginal changes would be clear. In the absence of such macro plans it is generally prudent to assume that marginal impacts would equal average impacts.

As noted, cost–benefit analysis implies that people's preferences matter and that these preferences will determine the relative importance of environmental impacts. Thus it was evident in Bangladesh that household demand for electricity far exceeded the demand for environmental quality. On the other hand slum households in India were prepared to pay a significant premium for access to an improved slum.

Valuing environmental preferences was often hampered by poor data on physical impacts, for example on the relationship between industrial and transport emissions and air quality. In these circumstances it is important not to accept estimates without question. The engineering consultants in Wuxi initially accepted estimates by officers of the Finance Bureau that 20 per cent of serious disease in the city was caused by waterborne pollution. When I questioned this estimate I was referred to officers of the Department of Health, who insisted that no one in Wuxi suffered serious water-related illness because 99.9 per cent of city households receive treated tap water from the municipal water company! It should be noted, however, that uncertainty about environmental values was not necessarily greater than the uncertainty about the value of some conventional commodities such as electricity and travel time savings. Generally, the estimates of environmental values helped to provide a fuller and more useful picture than would have been available without them.

Valuing Environmental Effects on People

As we have seen, environmental impacts have three main effects on people. These are productivity, health, and amenity or quality of life effects. In all the case-studies, except the slum improvements in India, the productivity effects were the most important ones. They were also the effects that could most readily be valued, although off-site ecological impacts were not valued in any case-study.

Valuing health effects was generally difficult because of lack of data on the relationship between health and environment. In Egypt, for example, there is a study of the effect of air pollution from the cement industry in Cairo on the health of local residents, and another study of the incidence of cholera in the Mediterranean off Alexandria. But it was impossible to estimate the overall impact of air or water pollution on health in Cairo or elsewhere. Although the World Bank (1992) argues that pollution is a major killer and cause of disease, it was difficult to substantiate this in the case-studies, except in the Indian slums where morbidity had been closely monitored.

Most households in the case-studies were far more concerned with basic living standards, with access to food, housing and electricity, than with a peaceful environment or with access to recreation. Consequently valuing amenity (along the lines discussed in the environmental economics literature) was generally of minor importance. However, even in poor communities households do not want to live in garbage-strewn streets. Nor do they want to be involuntarily relocated. Property prices were used as a guide to residential and amenity values in several case-studies. In Egypt, private garbage charges provided an indication of willingness to pay values for garbage removal.

Valuation Methods

There is a common presumption in the economics literature that, because many environmental effects are externalities, markets and prices contribute little to the valuation of environmental impacts and that innovative valuation methods, based on studies of non-market behaviour and surveys, are required to value the environment. In our case-studies this presumption was found to be misplaced. Considerable valuation information could be obtained from a variety of markets, including labour and property markets, and from proxy prices, as well as from standard product market prices.

Nevertheless there are many impacts (especially some amenity impacts and existence values) that cannot be valued using market-based methods. In our studies, defensive (averting or corrective) expenditures provided useful valuation information. However the other two main non-market valuation methods, the travel cost and contingent valuation survey methods, were not useful. A major reason was that the consultant studies were too short to allow for the study time usually required to implement these methods. Moreover in all the case-studies (except for the Kenyan forests) the attempt to value environmental impacts was conducted at a late stage in the overall study process. Unfortunately economists have still not persuaded all administrators and engineers that they should be introduced to project planning and appraisal at the start of the process rather than at the end to append a project justification.

Benefit Transfers

In any event it is often impractical to do a substantive research exercise as part of a project appraisal process. Analysts frequently have to import values found in research studies in different environments, often in different countries. For example in the Lagos study the values of life and of travel time savings were adopted from OECD research (Quinet, 1990). Given the wide range of research results in valuation studies (see Pearce and Markandya, 1989), considerable care is required to ensure that the most relevant values are adopted.

There has been much discussion of benefit transfers in recent literature (for example McConnell, 1992; Smith, 1992; Krupnick, 1993). Broadly speaking there are three ways of estimating benefits for transfer purposes: by selecting the average unit value for an environmental good, by selecting a unit value from a comparable situation (one with similar demand and supply features) or by transferring a whole demand function estimated at a study site to the policy site. The first method is a crude one and the third method generally impractical. For most practical purposes it generally suffices to select unit values from comparable situations and to modify these to fit local conditions, for example to allow for income differentials. Where this is possible, it is generally preferable to make approximate (transferred) environmental valuations, including transfers from developed to less developed economies, than to make no attempt to quantify environmental impacts. However there are still very few good studies of existence values and I found none that could be applied to the Kenyan forests.

Environmental Valuation, Sustainability and Government

Generally, project appraisal and environmental valuation presuppose a democratic and open form of government. Specifically, it should be accepted that:

- individual preferences matter and the public should be consulted fully on their views,
- institutional financial accounts can and should be checked, and
- official data should be available freely or at reasonable cost to project analysts and other interested parties; they are not private property to be sold at the highest possible price.

It suffices to say here that these conditions were met in very varying degrees in the seven countries (including Egypt) discussed in this book. To be fair, it should be added that these conditions are not met fully in many developed economies.

Finally, sustainable environmental quality requires not only that major projects are evaluated well but also that they are managed efficiently. This usually requires efficient financial mechanisms. Regrettably, inefficient management was observed in all our case-studies. In Wuxi the sewerage treatment works was functioning far below capacity. In Lagos rail operations are chronically inefficient and it is highly doubtful whether the injection of huge capital funds into a high-tech solution will change this. In Kenya the Forestry Department has failed to protect local forests from major illegal incursions. In Bangladesh extensive theft of electricity has caused major financial losses and under-maintenance of the electricity system. In the Indian slums the lack of property tax or other financial mechanisms is a major reason why some of the environmental improvements are already breaking down. In Bolivia tenure insecurity and non-competitive short-term land concessions are a major cause of over-exploitation of land. Without competent administration, theoretically desirable projects have, at best, a short life.

References

Abelson, P. W. (1979) *Cost Benefit Analysis and Environmental Problems* (Aldershot: Gower).

Abelson, P. W. (1981) 'The Cost of Noise Nuisance from Aircraft', *International Journal of Environmental Studies*, vol. 17, pp. 225–32.

Abelson, P. W. (1982) 'Transport Economics and Urban Transport Planning', *Australian Economic Papers*, vol. 21, pp. 121–33.

Abelson, P. W. and A. Markandya (1985) 'The Interpetation of Capitalised Hedonic Prices in a Dynamic Environment', *Journal of Environmental Economics and Management*, vol. 12, pp. 195–206.

Abelson, P. W. (1986) *The Economic Evaluation of Roads in Australia* (Sydney: Australian Professional Publications).

Adams, J. (1992) 'Horse and Rabbit Stew', in A. Coker and C. Richards (eds) *Valuing the Environment, Economic Approaches to Environmental Evaluation* (London: Belhaven Press).

Akerdolu, F. (1989) 'Atmospheric Environment Problems in Nigeria – an Overview', *Atmospheric Environment*, vol. 23, no. 4, pp. 783–92.

Allport, R. J. and J. M. Thompson (1990) *Study of Mass Transit in Developing Countries*, Contractor Report 188 (Crowthorne, Berkshire: Transport and Road Research Laboratory).

Amacher, G., W. F. Hyde, and B. Joshee (1991) *Household Fuelwood Demand and Supply in Nepal's Hills* (Washington, DC: Economic Research Service).

Anderson, P. (1989) 'The Myth of Sustainable Logging: The Case for a Ban on Tropical Timber Imports', *The Ecologist*, vol. 19, no. 5, pp. 166–8.

Applied Economics (1995) Evaluation and Decision Making for Transport Infrastructure Investment in *Building for the Job*, Commissioned Work, vol. 2, Economic Studies, pp. 1–95, National Transport Planning Taskforce (Canberra: Australian Government Publishing Service).

Armstrong-Wright, A. (1986) *Urban Transit Systems, Guidelines for Examining Options*, Technical Paper no. 52, Urban Transport Services (Washington, DC: World Bank).

Arrow, K. J. and A. C. Fisher (1974) 'Environmental Preservation, Uncertainty, and Irreversibility', *Quarterly Journal of Economics*, vol. 88, pp. 312–19.

Arrow, K. J. and R. C. Lind (1979) 'Uncertainty and the Evaluation of Public Investment Decisions', *American Economic Review*, vol. 60, pp. 364–78.

Aylward, B. and E. B. Barbier (1992) 'Valuing Environmental Functions in Developing Countries', *Biodiversity and Conservation*, vol. 1, pp. 34–50.

Ball, D. J., P. Brimblecombe and F. M. Nicholas (1990) *Review of Air Quality Criteria for the Assessment of Near-Field Impacts of Road Transport*, Contractor Report 240 (Crowthorne, Berkshire: Transport and Road Research Laboratory).

Banjo, G. (1978) *The Value of Travel Time Savings in Nigeria*, PhD thesis, University of Liverpool.

Barber, R. G. (1987) *Report on the Progress of the BTAM II Soils Programme 1984–87 and Proposed Future Work*, mimeo (Santa Cruz: BTAM).

Barber, R. G. (1992) *Observations on the Nature of the Soils in the Expansion Zone of the World Bank Eastern Lowlands Project*, mimeo (Santa Cruz: BTAM).

Barnes D. F. and J. Olivares (1988) *Sustainable Resource Management in Agriculture and Rural Development Projects: A Review of Bank Policies, Procedures and Results*, Environment Working Paper no. 5 (Washington: Environment Department, World Bank).

Barnett, A., G. Armstrong and J. Munday (1990) *A Synthesis of Six Evaluations of ODA Aid to Six Large Power Generation Schemes* (London: Evaluation Department, Overseas Development Administration).

Barnett, A., D. Watson, J. Woodhouse, J. Tyson and S. Henderson (1994) *Evaluation Report EV 550, Greater Dhaka Power Transmission and Distribution Project Phases II and IIA*, vols i and ii (London: Evaluation Department, Overseas Development Administration).

Barrett, R. (1988) *Urban Transport in West Africa*, World Bank Technical Paper no. 81, Urban Transport Series (Washington: World Bank).

Bishop, R. C. (1982) 'Option Value: An Exposition and Extension', *Land Economics*, vol. 58, pp. 1–15.

Blomquist, G. (1979) 'Value of Life Savings: Implications of Consumption Activity', *Journal of Political Economy*, vol. 87, pp. 540–58.

Blomquist, G., M. Berger and J. Hoehn (1988) 'New Estimates of Quality of Life in Urban Areas', *American Economic Review*, vol. 78, pp. 89–107.

Bockstael, N. E., K. E. McConnell and I. E. Strand (1991) 'Recreation', in J. B. Braden and C. D. Kolstad (eds), *Measuring the Demand for Environmental Quality* (Amsterdam: North Holland).

Bohm, P. (1972) 'Estimating Demand for Public Goods: An Experiment', *European Economic Review*, vol. 3, pp. 773–6.

Braden, J. B. and C. D. Kolstad (eds) (1991) *Measuring the Demand for Environmental Quality* (Amsterdam: North-Holland).

Briscoe, J., P. Furtado de Castro, C. Griffin, J. North and O. Olsen (1990) 'Toward Equitable and Sustainable Rural Water Supplies: A Contingent Valuation Study in Brazil', *International Bank for Reconstruction and Development* (Washington, DC: World Bank).

Brookshire, D., L. Eubanks and A. Randall (1983) 'Estimating Option Prices and Existence Values for Wildlife Resources', *Land Economics*, vol. 59, no. 1.

Brown, L. *et al.* (eds) (1992) *State of the World 1992*, a Worldwatch Institute Report on the Progress Towards a Sustainable Society (London: Earthscan).

Brown, L. (1992) 'Launching the Environmental Revolution' in L. Brown *et al.* (eds), *State of the World 1992*, a Worldwatch Institute report on the progress towards a sustainable society (London: Earthscan).

Bunyard, P. (1985) 'World Climate and Tropical Forest Destruction', *The Ecologist*, vol. 15, no. 3, pp. 125–36.

Button, K. J. (1993) *Transport Economics*, 2nd edn (Aldershot: Edward Elgar).

Cameron, T. A. and M. D. James (1987) 'Efficient Estimation Methods for Close-Ended Contingent Valuation Surveys', *Review of Economics and Statistics*, vol. 69, pp. 269–76.

Carson, R. T. (1991) 'Constructed Markets', in J. B. Braden and C. D. Kolsted (eds) *Measuring the Demand for Environmental Quality* (Amsterdam: North-Holland).

CEC Staff, Energy Facility Siting and Environmental Protection Division (1989) *Valuing Emission Reductions for Electricity Report*, California Energy Commission, Staff Issue Paper no. 3R, California.

Centro de Investigaciones de la Capacidad de Uso Mayor de la Tierra (CUMAT) (1992) *Desbosque de la Amazonia Boliviana* (La Paz, Bolivia: CUMAT).

Chernick, P. and E. Caverhill (1989) *The Valuation of Externalities from Energy Production, Delivery and Use*, Fall 1989, update, a report by PLC Inc. to the Boston Gas Coy., Boston.

Clarke, J., S. Jones, J. Pickford, A. Higginbottom and C. Bennett (1989) *Evaluation Study of Hyderabad Slum Improvement Project, Evaluation Report EV475* (London: Evaluation Department, Overseas Development Administration).

Cline, W. R. (1992) *The Economics of Global Warming* (Washington, DC: Institute for International Economics).

Cochrane, T. T. (1973) *El Potencial Agriasha del Uso de la Tierra en Bolivia*, Un Mapa de Systemes de Tierra.

Commission of the European Communities, Directorate General for Transport (1994) *Cost–Benefit and Multi-Criteria Analysis for New Road Construction*, DOC EURET/385/94 (Brussels: CEC).

Convery, F. J. (1991) *Estimating the Gross Costs of Environmental Degradation in Ghana*, paper prepared for course in environmental economics for SIDA staff, Gothenberg School of Law and Economics, Sweden.

Coopers & Lybrand (1987) *Bangladesh Power Sector Tariff Study*, report to the UNDP and World Bank (Washington: IBRD).

Coursey, D. L., J. Hovis and D. W. Schulze (1986) 'The Disparity between Willingness to Accept and Willingness to Pay Measures of Value', *Quarterly Journal of Economics*, vol. 102, pp. 679–90.

Cropper, M. L. and A. M. Freeman III (1991) 'Environmental Health Effects', in J. B. Braden and C. D. Kolstad (eds), *Measuring the Demand for Environmental Quality* (Amsterdam: North Holland).

Cummings, R. G., D. S. Brookshire and W. D. Schulze (1986) *Valuing Environmental Goods, A State of the Arts Assessment of the Contingent Valuation Method* (New Jersey: Rowland and Allanheld).

Dalfelt, A. (1991) *Ecological Constraints to Sustainable Management of the Tropical Moist Forest*, World Environment Department, Divisional Working Paper no. 1991–25 (Washington DC: WED).

Dar-al-Handasah (DAH) (1989) *Lagos Mass Transit Options Study*, Nigeria: Federal Ministry of Works and Transport).

Dar-al-Handasah (DAH) (1992a) *Lagos Mass Transit Study* (Nigeria: Federal Ministry of Transport and Communications and Washington, DC: World Bank).

Dar-al-Handasah (DAH) (1992b) *Mass Transit and Transport Systems Management Programme for the Lagos Metropolitan Area, Environmental Issues*, Working Paper no. 6 (Nigeria: Federal Ministry of Transport and Communications and Washington, DC: World Bank)

Dardis, R. (1980) 'The Value of a Life: New Evidence from the Marketplace', *American Economic Review*, vol. 70, pp. 1077–82.

Dasgupta, P. and K.-G. Maler (1994) 'The Environment and Emerging Development Issues', in R. Layard and S. Glaister (eds), *Cost–Benefit Analysis* (Cambridge University Press).

Dasgupta, P., A. Sen. and S. Marglin (UNIDO) (1972) *Guidelines for Project Evaluation* (New York: United Nations).

Desai, N. (1985) *Economic Analysis of Power Projects*, Economic Staff Paper no. 24 (Manila: Asian Development Bank).

Desvouges, W. H., V. K. Smith and M. P. McGivney (1983) A *Comparison of Alternative Approaches for Estimation of Recreation and Related Benefits of Water Quality Improvements*, USEPA Report no. EPA-230-05-83-001 (Washington, DC: Environmental Protection Agency).

Dickens, W. T. (1984) 'Differences between Risk Premiums in Union and Nonunion Wages and the Case for Occupational Safety Regulation', *American Economic Review*, vol. 74, pp. 320–3.

Dickie, M. S., D. Gerking, D. Brookshire, D. Coursey, W. Schulze, A. Coulson and D. Tashkin (1987) 'Values of Symptoms of Ozone Exposure: An Application of the Averting Behaviour Method', in *Improving Accuracy and Reducing Costs of Environmental Benefit Assessments* (Washington, DC: Environmental Protection Agency).

Dixon, J. A. and M. M. Hufschmidt (1986) *Economic Valuation Techniques for the Environment: A Case Study Workbook* (Baltimore, Md: Johns Hopkins University Press).

Dixon, J. A. and P. B. Sherman (1990) *Economics of Protected Areas: A New Look at Benefits and Costs* (Washington, DC: Island Press).

Electric Power Research Institute (EPRI) (1987) *TAG-Technical Assessment Guide, Vol. 4, Fundamentals and Methods, End Use*, EPRI P-4463-SR, vol. 4 (August).

FAO Staff (1957) 'Shifting Cultivation', *Unasylva* vol. 11, no. 1, reprinted in *Tropical Agriculture Trin.*, vol. 34, pp. 159–64.

Fearnside, P. M. (1992) *Greenhouse Gas Emissions from Deforestation in the Brazilian Amazon*, review draft (Berkeley, California: Tropical Forestry Research Network, Lawrence Berkeley Laboratory).

Feenberg, D. and E. S. Mills (1980) *Measuring the Benefits of Water Pollution Abatement* (New York: Academic Press).

Fellner, W. J. (1967) 'Operational Utility: The Theoretical Background and a Measurement', in W. J. Fellner *et al.*, *Ten Economic Studies in the Tradition of Irving Fisher* (Chicester: John Wiley).

Ferguson, (1990) *Social Costs of Electricity Generation*, Working document, quoted by Lockwood, 1992.

Fisher, A. C. and W. M. Hanemann (1987) 'Quasi-option Value: Some Misconceptions Dispelled', *Journal of Environmental Economics and Management*, vol. 14, pp. 183–97.

Flint, M. (1992) *Forest Synthesis Evaluation Study*, Evaluation Report, EV541 (London: Overseas Development Administration).

Fouracre, P. R., R. J. Allport and J. M. Thompson (1990) *The Performance and Impact of Rail Mass Transit in Developing Countries*, Research Report 278 (Crowthorne, Berkshire: Transport and Road Research Laboratory).

Freeman, A. M. III (1979) *The Benefits of Environmental Improvement, Theory and Practice*, (Baltimore, Md: Johns Hopkins Press).

Freeman, A. M. III (1985) 'Supply Uncertainty, Option Price, and Option Value', *Land Economics*, vol. 61, pp. 176–81.

Freeman, A. M. III (1986) 'On Assessing the State of the Arts of the Contingent Valuation Method of Valuing Environmental Changes', in R. G. Cummings,

D. S. Brookshire and W. D. Schulze (eds), *Valuing Environmental Goods* (New Jersey: Rowman & Allanfield).

Gakenheimer, R. (1990) 'The Two Analytic Cultures of Rail Transit Planning', in *Rail Mass Transit for Developing Countries*, Proceedings of a conference organised by the Institute of Civil Engineers (Londo: Thomas Telford).

Gerking, S. and L. R. Stanley (1986) 'An Economic Analysis of Air Pollution and Health: The Case of St.Louis', *Review of Economics and Statistics*, vol. 68, pp. 115–21.

Gintis, H. (1972) 'Consumer Sovereignty and the Concept of Sovereignty, Explanations of Social Decay', *American Economic Review*, Papers and Proceedings, vol. 62, pp. 267–278.

Goodman, A. C. (1989), 'Topics in Empirical Housing Research', in R. Arnold (ed.), *The Economics of Housing Markets* (New York: Harwood).

Goodwin, P. B. (1992) 'A Review of New Demand Elasticities with Special Reference to Short and Long Term Effects of Price Changes', *Journal of Transport Economics and Policy*, vol. 24, no. 2, pp. 155–63.

Grandstaff, S. and J. A. Dixon (1986) 'Evaluation of Lumpinee Public Park in Bangkok, Thailand', in J. A. Dixon and M. M. Hufschmidt (eds), *Economic Valuation Techniques for the Environment* (Baltimore, Md: Johns Hopkins University Press).

Graves, P. E. (1991) 'Aesthetics', in J. B. Braden and C. D. Kolstad (eds), *Measuring the Demand for Environmental Quality* (Amsterdam: North Holland).

Graves, P. E., J. C. Murdoch, M. A. Thayer and D. Waldman (1988) 'The Robustness of Hedonic Price Estimation: Urban Air Quality', *Land Economics*, vol. 64, pp. 220–33.

Green, C. H. (1992) 'The Economic Issues Raised by Valuing Environmental Goods', in A. Coker and C. Richards (eds), *Valuing the Environment, Economic Approaches to Environmental Evaluation* (London: Belhaven Press).

Hamilton L. and P. King (1983) *Tropical Forested Watersheds: Hydrologic and Soils Response to Major Uses or Conversions* (Boulder, Co: Westview Press).

Hanemann, W. M. (1991) 'Willingness to Pay and Willingness to Accept: How much can they Differ?', *American Economic Review*, vol. 81, pp. 635–47.

Hanley, N. and C. L. Spash (1993) *Cost-benefit Analysis and the Environment* (Aldershot: Edward Elgar).

Harrington, W., A. J. Krupnick and W. O. Spofford, Jr (1989) 'The Economic Losses of a Waterborne Disease Outbreak', *Journal of Urban Economics*, vol. 25, pp. 116–27.

Heberlein, T. A. and R. Bishop (1986) 'Assessing the Validity of Contingent Valuation: Three Experiments', *Science of the Total Environment*, vol. 56, pp. 99–107.

Hecht, S. B. (1982) 'Agroforestry in the Amazon Basin: Practice, Theory and Limits of a Promising Land Use', in S. Hecht (ed.), *Amazonia: Agriculture and Land Use Research* (California: CIAT).

Hecht, S. B. (1992) *Reorienting the Bolivian Lowlands Project, Report to Cordecruz and KFW*, mimeo (Los Angeles: Graduate School of Planning, University of California).

Hine, J. (1991) *The Effects of Vehicle Pollution on the UK Death Rate*, TRRL Briefing Note TP3/91, Traffic Road and Research Laboratory, Berkshire, UK.

Hodgson, K. (1992) *Report on Environmental Health and Sanitation Visit to Visakhapatnam Slum Improvement Project* (Universities of the North of England Consortium for International Activities) Ref SIPVS 18, Overseas Development Administration, UK.

Hoehn, J. P. and A. Randall (1987) 'A Satisfactory Benefit Cost Indicator from Contingent Valuation', *Journal of Environmental Economics and Management*, vol. 17, pp. 213–29.

Hohmeyer, O. (1988) *Social Costs of Energy Consumption: External Effects of Electricity Generation in the Federal Republic of Germany* (Berlin: Springer-Verlag).

Houghton, R. (1990) 'Emissions of Greenouse Gases', in N. Myers, *Deforestation Rates in Tropical Forests and their Climatic Implications* (London: Friends of the Earth).

Hsu, G. J. Y. and Wen-Yao Liu (1990) 'Application of the Contingent Valuation Method to the Keelung River, Taipei', *Water Resources Development*, vol. 6, pp. 218–21.

Hufschmidt, M. M., D. E. James, A. D. Meister, B. T. Bower and J. A. Dixon (1983) *Environment, Natural Systems and Development: An Economic Valuation Guide* (Baltimore: Johns Hopkins University Press).

Hyde, W. F. and D. H. Newman (1991) *Forest Economics and Policy Analysis, An Overview*, World Bank Discussion Papers, no. 134 (Washington, DC: World Bank).

Imber D., G. Stevenson and L. Wilks (1991) *A Contingent Valuation Survey of the Kakadu Conservation Zone*, RAC Research Paper no. 3 (Canberra: RAC).

Instituto Nacional de Estadistianas (INE) (1992) *Censo de Publación y Vivianda* (La Paz, Bolivia: INE).

International Center for Research in Agroforestry (ICRAF), International Fertiliser Development Center, International Institute for Tropical Agriculture, International Rice Research Institute, Tropical Soil Biology and Fertility Programme, and Centro Internacional de Agricultura Tropical (1992) *Alternatives to Slash and Burn, A Global Strategy* (ICRAF, Nairobi, Kenya).

Intergovernmental Panel on Climate Change (IPCC) (1991) *Climate Change: The IPCC Response Strategies*, World Meteorological Organisation, United Nations Environment Program, Nairobi, Kenya.

Johansson, P.-O. (1987) *The Economic Theory and Measurement of Environmental Benefits* (Cambridge University Press).

Jones, I. S. (1977) *Urban Transport Appraisal* (London: Macmillan).

Kahnemann, D. and A. Tversky (1979) 'Prospect Theory: An Analysis of Decision Making under Risk', *Econometrica*, vol. 47, pp. 163–83.

Kahnemann, D. and J. L. Knetsch (1992) 'Valuing Public Goods, The Purchase of Moral Satisfaction', *Journal of Environmental Economics and Management*, vol. 22, pp. 57–70.

Kenya Indigenous Forest Conservation Project (KIFCON) (1992a) *Kakamega Forest Pilot Project*, vol. 1, Preparation Report (Nairobi: Forestry Department).

Kenya Indigenous Forest Conservation Project (KIFCON) (1992b) *Arabuko Sokoke Forest Pilot Project*, vol. 1, Preparation Report (Nairobi: Forestry Department).

Kenya Indigenous Forest Conservation Project (KIFCON) (1992c) *Arabuko Sokoke Forest Pilot Project, vol. 1, Preparation Report* (Nairobi: Forestry Department).

Kenya Indigenous Forest Conservation Project (KIFCON) (1992d) *Arabuko Sokoke*

Forest Pilot Project, Financial and Economic Analysis, Working Paper 9 (Nairobi: Forestry Department).

Kneese, A. V. (1974) 'The Application of Economic Analysis to the Management of Water Quality: Some Case Studies', in J. Rothenbrg and I. G. Heggie (eds), *The Management of Water Quality and the Environment* (London: Macmillan).

Kneese, A. V. (1984) *Measuring the Benefits of Clean Air and Water* (Washington, DC: Resources for the Future).

Knetsch, J. and J. Sinden (1984) 'Willingness to Pay and Compensation Demanded: Experimental Evidence of an Unexpected Disparity in Measures of Value', *Quarterly Journal of Economics*, vol. 99, pp. 507–21.

Koomey, J. (1990) *Comparative Analysis of Monetary Estimates of External Environmental Costs Associated with Combustion of Fossil Fuels*, Energy Analysis Program, Lawrence Berkeley Laboratory, LBL-28313 (Berkeley, California: University of California).

Krupnick, A. J. (1993) 'Benefit Transfers and Valuation of Environmental Improvements', *Resources* no. 110 (Winter), pp. 1–6.

Kruprick, A. and I. Sebastian (1990) *Issues in Air Pollution, A Review of the Beijing Case*, World Bank Working Paper, no. 31 (Washington, DC: World Bank).

Kula, E. (1984) 'Derivation of the Social Time Preference Rates for the United States and Canada', *Quarterly Journal of Economics*, vol. 99, pp. 873–82.

Kula, E. (1986) 'An Analysis of the Social Interest Rate in Trinidad and Tobago', mimeo (Belfast University of Ulster).

Layard, R. and S. Glaister (1994) 'Introduction', in R. Layard and S. Glaister (eds), *Cost–Benefit Analysis*, 2nd edn (Cambridge University Press).

Lindert, P. (1978) *Fertility and Scarcity in America* (Princeton, NJ: Princeton University Press).

Lipton, M. and J. Toye (1990) *Does Aid Work in India?* (London: Routledge).

Little, I. M. D. and J. A. Mirrlees (1969) *Manual of Industrial Project Analysis in Developing Countries: Volume II; Social Cost–Benefit Analysis* (Paris: Organisation for Economic Co-operation and Development).

Little, I. M. D. and J. A. Mirrlees (1974) *Project Appraisal and Planning for Developing Countries* (New York: Basic Books).

Little, I. M. D. and J. A. Mirrlees (1994) 'The Costs and Benefits of Analysis: Project Appraisal and Planning Twenty Yeasrs On', 199–231 in R. Layard and S. Glaister (eds) *Cost–Benefit Analysis* (Cambridge University Press).

Lockwood, B. (1992) *The Social Costs of Electricity Generation*, prepared for the UK Parliamentary Office of Science and Technology, Department of Economics, Birkbeck College, London.

London Economics (1992) *Study on the Costs of Unserved Electricity Supply*, Inception Report (London: Overseas Development Administration).

Lowe, M. (1993) 'Rediscovering Rail', 120–38 in L. Brown, L. Flavin and S. Postel (eds) *State of the World* (London: Earthscan).

Mahtab, F. U. *et al.* (1991) *Environment and Development, Report of the Task Forces on Bangladesh Development Strategies for the 1990s*, vol. 4, Environment Policy (Dhaka: University Press).

Makundi, W., J. Sathaye and O. M. Cerutti (1992) *Carbon Emissions and Sequestration in Forests: Case Studies from Seven Developing Countries*, draft (LBL-32119, University of California, Berkeley, California Energy and Environment Division, Lawrence Berkeley Laboratory).

Markandya, A. (1990) *Environmental Costs and Power Systems Planning*, Paper no. 90-02 (London: London Environmental Economic Centre).

McConnell, K. E. (1992) 'Model Building and Judgement: Implications for Benefit Transfers with Travel Cost Models', *Water Resources Research*, vol. 28, no. 3, pp. 695–700.

Meadows, D. H., D. L. Meadows, J. Randers and W. W. Behrens III (1972) *The Limits to Growth*, a report for the Club of Rome's project on the Predicament of Mankind (London: Pan).

Meyer, P. A. (1979) 'Publicly Vested Values for Fish and Wildlife: Criteria in Economic Welfare and Interface with the Law', *Land Economics*, vol. 63, pp. 153–6.

Mishan, E. J. (1971) 'Pollution, Economics and Liberalism', *Current Affairs Bulletin (April)*.

Mishan, E. J. (1982) *Cost–Benefit Analysis* (London: Allen & Unwin).

Mitchell, R. C. and R. T. Carson (1989) *Using Surveys to Value Public Goods* (Baltimore, Md: John Hopkins University Press).

Munasinghe, M. (1992) *Environmental Economics and Valuation in Development Decisionmaking*, Environment Working Paper, no. 51, Environment Department (Washington, DC: World Bank)

Myers, N. (1989) 'The Greenhouse Effect: A Tropical Forestry Response', *Biomass*, vol. 18.

Nelson, J. P. (1982) 'Highway Noise and Property Values', *Journal of Transport Economic and Policy*, vol. XVI, no. 2, pp. 117–38.

Nelson, J. P. (1987) *Transportation Noise, Reference Book* (London: Butterworths).

Nelson, M. (1973) *The Development of Tropical lands, Policy Issues in Latin America*, Resources for the Future (Baltimore, Md: Johns Hopkins University Press).

Neuberger, H. L. I. (1971) 'User Benefit in the Evaluation of Transport and Land Use Plans', *Journal of Transport Economic and Policy*, vol. 5, pp. 71–3.

Nordhaus, W. D. (1991a) 'To Slow or Not to Slow: The Economics of the Greeenhouse Effect', *Economic Journal*, vol. 101, pp. 920–37.

Nordhaus, W. D. (1991b) Economic Approaches to Greenhouse Warming, 33–66 in R. Dornbusch and J. M. Poterba (eds), *Global Warming: Economic Policy Response* (Cambridge, Mass: MIT Press)

Nye, P. H. and D. J. Greenland (1960) *The Soil Under Shifting Cultivation*, Technical Communication no. 51 (Farnham: Commonwealth Bureau of Soils,Commonwealth Agricultural Bureau).

Organisation for Economic Cooperation and Development (OECD) (1988) *Transport and the Environment* (Paris: OECD).

Organisation for Economic Co–operation and Development (OECD) (1991) *The State of the Environment* (Paris: OECD).

Organisation of American States and National Park Service (1988) *Inventory of Caribbean Marine and Coastal Protected Areas* (Washington, DC: US Department of Interior).

Ostro, B. D. (1983) 'The Effects of Air Pollution on Work Loss and Morbidity', *Journal of Environmental Economics and Management*, vol. 10, pp. 371–82.

Ottinger, R. L., N. A. Robinson, S. E. Babb, D. R. Wooley, D. R. Hodas, S. C. Buchanan, P. L. Chernick, E. Caverhill, J. A. Meltzer, A. Kripnick,

W. Harrington and S. Radin (1990) *Environmental Externality Costs from Electric Utility Operations* (N.Y. State Energy Research and Development Authority and the U.S. Department of Energy).

Oum, T. H., W. G. Waters II and J.–S. Yong (1992) 'Concepts of Price Elasticities of Transport Demand and Recent Empirical Eestimates', *Journal of Transport Economics and Policy*, vol. 24, no. 2, pp. 139–54.

Overseas Development Administration (ODA) (1988) *Appraisal of Projects in Developing Countries, A Guide for Economists*, 3rd ed (London: HMSO).

Owasina, F. A. O. (1981) *The Traffic Scene in Nigeria – An African Example*, paper presented at WHO/OECD/World Bank Conference on Road Traffic Accidents in Developing Countries, Mexico City.

Pasha, H. A., A. Ghaus and S. Malik (1989) 'The Economic Cost of Power Outages in the Industrial Sector of Pakistan', *Energy Economics*, vol. 11, no. 4, pp. 301–18.

Patrudu, M. (1992) *Vocational Training Courses – An Assessment Study* (India: Municipal Council of Visakhapatnam).

Pearce, D. W. (ed.) (1978) *The Valuation of Social Cost* (London: Allen & Unwin).

Pearce, D. W. (1983) *Cost–Benefit Analysis*, 2nd edn (London: Macmillan).

Pearce, D. W. (1990) *An Economic Approach to Saving the Tropical Forests*, LEEC Paper no. 90–06, IEED/UCL (London: London Environmental Economics Centre).

Pearce, D. W. and A. Markandya (1989) *Environmental Policy Benefits: Monetary Valuation* (Paris: OECD).

Penning-Rowsell, E. (1992) 'The Devil and the Deep Blue Sea?', in A. Coker and C. Richards (eds), *Valuing the Environment, Economic Approaches to Environmental Evaluation* (London: Belhaven Press).

Polinsky, A. M. and S. Shavell (1976) 'Amenities and Property Values in a Model of an Urban Area', *Journal of Public Economics*, vol. 5, pp. 119–29.

Prasada Rao, D. L. and Rajesh Patnaik (1992) *Anthropological Studies – Case Studies of Selected Families*, evaluation study of the Visakhapatnam Slum Improvement Project (Visakhapatnam, India: Institute of Development and Planning Studies).

Quinet, E. (1990) *The Social Costs of Land Transport*, OECD Monograph, no. 32 (Paris: OECD).

Randall, A. and J. R. Stoll (1980) 'Consumer's Surplus in Commodity Space', *American Economic Review*, vol. 24, pp. 217–23.

Randall, A. (1991) 'Total and Nonuse Values', in J. B. Braden and C. D. Kolstad (eds), *Measuring the Demand for Environmental Quality* (Amsterdam: North-Holland).

Resource Assessment Commission (1991) *Commentaries on the Resource Assessment Commission's Contingent Valuation Survey of the Kakdau Conservation Zone* (Canberra: RAC).

Rice, D. P., E. J. MacKenzie and Associates (1989) *Cost of Injury in the United States: A Report to Congress* (Institute for Health and Aging, University of California and Injury Prevention Centre and Johns Hopkins University, Centres for Disease Control, Atlanta).

Roselle, M. and T. Katelman (1990) *Tropical Hardwoods: A Report on the US Role in the International Tropical Hardwood Trade and the Non-Timber Alternatives* (San Francisco: Rainforest Action Network).

Rowe, R. D., R. C. d'Arge and D. S. Brookshire (1980) 'An Experiment on the Economic Value of Visibility', *Journal of Environmental Economics and Management*, vol. 7, pp. 1–19.

Ruitenbeek, J. (1989) *Social Cost–Benefit Analysis of the Korup Project, Cameroon* (London: World Wide Fund for Nature).

Ryan, J. C. (1992) 'Conserving Biological Diversity', in L. Browen *et al.* (eds) *State of the World 1992*, a Worldwatch Institute report on the progress towards a sustainable society (London: Earthscan).

Samples, K., J. Dixon and M. Gowen (1986) *The Validity of the Contingent Valuation Method for Estimating Non-Use Components of Preservation Values for Unique National Resources*, paper presented to American Agricultural Economics Association, Nevada.

Sarveswara Rao, B. and G. Ramachandrudu (1992a) *Report on the Household Survey*, evaluation study of the Visakhapatnam Slum Improvement Project (Visakhapatnam, India: Institute of Development and Planning Studies).

Information Disclosure and Endangered Species Valuation, *Land Economics*, vol. 62, pp. 306–12.

Sarveswara Rao, B. and G. Ramachandrudu (1992b) *Report on Moved-out and Moved-in Households*, evaluation study of the Visakhapatnam Slum Improvement Project (Visakhapatnam, India: Institute of Development and Planning Studies).

Schankerman, M. and A. Pakes (1986) 'Estimates of the Value of Patent Rights in European Countries During the Post-1950 Period', *Economic Journal*, vol. 96, pp. 1052–76.

Schelling, T. C. (1992) 'Some Economics of Greenhouse Warming', *American Economic Review*, vol. 82, pp. 1–14.

Schilberg, G. M., J. A. Nahigan and W. B. Marcus (1989) *Valuing Reductions in Air Emissions and Incorportation into Electric Resource Planning: Theoretical and Quantitative Aspects*, JBS Energy Inc. for the Independent Energy Producers, GEC Dockett 88-ER-8, California.

Schmalansee, R. (1972) 'Option Demand and Consumer's Surplus: Valuing Price Changes under Uncertainty', *American Economic Review*, vol. 62, pp. 813–24.

Schultze, W. D., R. D. D'Arge and D. S. Brookshire (1981) 'Valuing Environmental Commodities: Some Recent Experiments', *Land Economics*, vol. LVIII, pp. 151–72.

Scott, M. (1977) 'The Test Rate of Discount and Changes in Base Level Income in the United Kingdom', *Economic Journal*, vol. 87, no. 346.

Sedjo, R. (1989) 'Forests to Offset the Greenhouse Effect', *Journal of Forestry*, vol. 87, pp. 12–4.

Sen A. K. (1972) 'Shadow Prices and Markets: Feasibility Constraints: Foreign Exchange and Shadow Wages', *Economic Journal*, vol. 82, pp. 486–501.

Shin, E., R. Gregory, M. Hufschmidt, Yok-Shin Lee, J. E. Nickum and C. Umetsu (1992) *Economic Valuation of the Urban Environment: with Emphasis on Asian and Non-Productivity Approaches* (Washington, DC: Urban Development Division, World Bank).

Smith, V. K. (1992) 'On Separating Defensible Benefit Transfers from Smoke and Mirrors', *Water Resources Research*, vol. 28, no. 3, pp. 695–700.

Smith, V. K. (1993) 'Non-Market Valuation of Environmental Resources: An Interpretive Appraisal', *Land Economics*, vol. 69, no. 1, pp. 1–26.

Smith, V. K. and Y. Karou (1987) 'The Hedonic Travel Cost Model: A View from the Trenches', *Land Economics*, vol. 63, pp. 179–92.

Solow, R. M. (1993) 'Sustainability: An Economist's Perspective', in R. Dorfman and N. S. Dorfman (eds), *Economics of the Environment* (New York: W. W. Norton & Company) pp. 179–87.

Southgate, D. (1991) *Tropical Deforestation and Agricultural Development in Latin America*, Paper DP 91–01 (London: London Environmental Economics Centre and International Institute for Environment and Development).

Squire, L. and H. G. van der Tak (1989) *Economic Analysis of Projects*, 7th edn (Baltimore, Md: Johns Hopkins University Press).

Starkie, D. and D. Johnson (1975) *The Economic Value of Peace and Quiet* (London: Saxon House).

Stern, N. (1977) 'The Marginal Valuation of Income', in M. Artis and R. Nobay (eds), *Studies in Modern Income Analysis* (Oxford: Blackwell).

Strand, J. (1985) *The Value of Catalytic Converter Requirement for Nowegeian Automobiles: A Contingent Valuation Study*, mimeo (Oslo: Department of Economics, University of Oslo).

Swarajyalakshmi, B., B. Sarveswara Rao, B. Narayana Raju and G. Ramachandrudu (1992) *Report on Changes in Health Status, 1988–91*, evaluation study of the Visakhapatnam Slum Improvement Project (Visakhapatnam, India: Institute of Development and Planning Studies).

Taber, A. (1993) *The New York State Wildlife Conservation Society Bolivia Program*, personal communication.

Technical Research Centre of Finland, ESPOO (1986) *The Environmental Impacts of Production and Use of Energy*, Part IV, Phase iii, United Nations Environment Program, Nairobi.

Thiele, G. (1990) *A Literature Review of the Santa Cruz Colonisation Zone*, Working Document no. 78 (Santa Cruz, Bolivia: CIAT/BTAM).

Thiele, G. (1992) *The Displacement of Peasant Settlers in the Amazon: the Case of Santa Cruz Bolivia*, mimeo (Santa Cruz, Bolivia: BTAM).

Tietenberg, T. (1992) *Environmental and National Resource Economics (New York: Harper Collins).*

Uhl, C., D. C. Nepstad, Cardosa de Silva and J. M. Vicra (1991) 'Restauracao da Floesta em Pastagens Degradadas', *Ciencia Hoje*, vol. 13, no. 76, pp. 22–31 (Brazil).

UK Treasury (1991) *Economic Appraisal in Central Government, A Technical Guide for Government Departments* (London: HMSO) .

United Nations (1989) Department of International and Social Affairs, *Urban Transport Development with Particular Reference to Developing Countries* (New York: UN).

US National Research Council (1986) Population Growth and Economic Development: Policy Questions (Washington DC: National Academy Press).

Van Pelt, M. J. P. (1991) 'Sustainability-Oriented Appraisal of Agricultural Projects', Conference on Sustainable Agricultural Development, University of Bradford.

Walsh, R. G., D. M. Johnson, and J. R. McKean (1992) 'Benefit Transfer of Outdoor Recreation Demand Studies, 1968–1988', *Water Resources Research*, vol. 28, no. 3.

Ward, W. A., B. J. Deren and H. D'Silva (1991) *The Economics of Project Analysis, A Practitioner's Guide*, (Washington, DC: Economic Development Institute, World Bank).

Water Research Centre and Coopers and Lybrand Associates (1989) *Review of Investment Appraisal Techniques in the Water Industry* (Swindon: Water Research Centre).

Water Research Centre and Flood Hazard Research Centre (1989) *Investment Appraisal for Sewage Schemes: The Assessment of Social Costs*, project report (Swindon: Water Research Centre).

Watkins, L. H. (1991) *Air Pollution from Road Vehicles, State of the Art Review 1* (London: HMSO).

Watson Hawksley (1992) *Wuxi Sewerage Master Plan, Grand Canal Pollution Control*, Southern Jiangsu Environmental Protection Project, Sino-British Feasibility Study, draft final report, prepared for World Bank, Washington DC.

Watson, W. and J. Jaksch (1982) 'Air Pollution: Household Soiling and Consumer Welfare Losses', *Journal of Environmental Economics and Management*, vol. 9, pp. 248–62.

Webb, M. and D. W. Pearce (1985) *Economic Benefits and Power Supply*, Energy Department, paper no. 25 (Washington, DC: World Bank Energy Department).

Whittington, D., J. Briscoe, X. Mu and W. Baram (1990) 'Estimating the Willingness to Pay for Water Services in Developing Countries: A Case Study of the Use of Contingent Valuation Surveys in Southern Haiti', *Economic Development and Cultural Change*, vol. 38, pp. 293–311.

Whittington, D., D. T. Lauria, and Xinming Mu (1991) 'A Study of Water Vending and Willingness to Pay for Water in Onitsha, Nigeria', *World Development*, vol. 19, pp. 179–98.

Wilbur Smith (1976) *Lagos Metropolitan Area Transportation Study*, prepared for Ministry of Works and Housing, Nigeria.

Willig, R. D. (1976) 'Consumer's Surplus without Apology', *American Economic Review*, vol. 66, 587–97.

Willis, K. G. and G. D. Garrod (1991) 'Landscape Values: A Contingent Valuation Approach and Case Study of the Yorkshire Dales National Park', *Countryside Change Working Paper 21* (Countryside Change Unit, University of Newcastle upon Tyne).

Willis, K. G. (1991) 'The Recreational Value of the Forestry Commission Estate in Great Britain: A Clawson-Knetsch Travel Cost Analysis', *Scottish Journal of Political Economy*, vol. 38, pp. 58–75.

Wilson, E. O. and F. M. Peters (eds) (1988) *Biodiversity* (Washington, DC: National Academy Press).

Winpenny, J. T. (1991) *Values for the Environment: A Guide to Economic Appraisal* (London: HMSO).

World Bank (1986) *Urban Transport – A World Bank Policy Study* (Washington DC: World Bank).

World Bank (1991) *Bangladesh Environment Strategy Review*, report no. 95512-BD (Washington, DC: World Bank).

World Bank (1991) *Environment Assessment Sourcebook, Volume 1, Policies, Procedures and Cross-Sectoral Issues*, World Bank technical paper 139 Washington, DC: Environment Department, World Bank).

World Bank (1991) *Environmental Assessment Sourcebook, Volume II, Sectoral Guidelines*, World Bank technical paper no. 140 (Washington, DC: Environment Department, World Bank).

World Bank (1991) *Environmental Assessment Sourcebook, Volume III Guidelines for Environmental Assessment of Energy and Industry Projects*, World Bank technical paper no. 154 (Washington, DC: Environment Department, World Bank).

World Bank, Africa Region (1991) *The Population, Agriculture and Environment Nexus in Sub-Saharan Africa* (Washington, DC: World Bank).

World Bank (1992) *World Development Report 1992, Development and the Environment* (Oxford University Press).

World Commission on Environment and Development (WCED) (1987) *Energy 2000: A Global Strategy for Sustainable Development*, London and Atlantic Highlands (NJ: Zed Books)

World Resources Institute with the United Nations Environment Programme and the United Nations Development Programme (1994), *World Resources* (New York: Oxford Universiy Press).

Yakasi, A. H. (1992) *Measurement of Traffic Noise in Yaba Area*, MSc. thesis, University of Lagos, Lagos.

Young, A. and A. S. C. Wright (1980) 'Rest Period Requirements of Tropical and Subtropical Soils Under Annual Crops', in *Report on the Second FAO/UNPA Expert Consultation on Land Resources for the Future* (Rome: FAO).

Index